PENGUIN
DIPLOMACY

Brian Roberts

Polar explorer, treaty maker and conservationist

June Roberts and Steve Heavens

Brian Roberts, Oslo, 1975

Mereo Books

Mereo Books 2nd Floor, 6-8 Dyer Street,
Cirencester, Gloucestershire, GL7 2PF

An imprint of Memoirs Book Ltd. www.mereobooks.com

Penguin Diplomacy: 978-1-86151-963-4

First published in Great Britain in 2020
by Mereo Books, an imprint of Memoirs Books Ltd.

The address for Memoirs Books Ltd. can be
found at www.mereobooks.com

Book cover and interior design - Ray Lipscombe

Typeset in 11/14pt Sabon
by Wiltshire Associates Ltd. Printed and bound in Great Britain

I think that in perspective and when the truth is told, the Antarctic Treaty will be seen as the crowning achievement of Brian's life... Those of us who have spent much of our lives in Antarctica owe everything to the survival of the Treaty through wars cold and wars hot.

Charles Swithinbank

CONTENTS

PREFACE

Brian Birley Roberts (1912-1978) was acknowledged amongst the polar community to be Britain's foremost expert on the Antarctic, and he had been heavily involved in the Antarctic Treaty. But he was a 'behind the scenes' man who shied away from the limelight and, despite the growing widespread interest in the polar regions, to the outside world he was almost unknown.

So who was Brian Roberts?

To June Roberts, one of the authors of this book, Brian was an awesome and unfathomable uncle. It was impossible to relate him in any way to normal life, or to figure out how one man could have such energy levels and knowledge as to be able to have two different full-time jobs at once, one at the Scott Polar Research Institute in Cambridge and another at the Foreign Office in London, in addition to international conferences all over the globe where he was embroiled in endless political negotiations. Yet Uncle Brian was always warm, kind, helpful and encouraging, and he was especially supportive to his struggling niece through university and job-hunting times.

A weekend visit to Cambridge to stay with Uncle Brian in his flat overlooking Coe Fen was always a special occasion. June would sleep in his tiny study on an old army camp bed squashed tightly in between two long rows of filing cabinets, surrounded by bookshelves brimming with polar books, journals, maps and his collection of Indian Ocean corals: a treasure trove which made it hard to turn off the light to go to sleep.

Brian and his brother Denis always got on well, except for one major argument. Denis, who was an architect, tried to convince Brian of the virtues of the Universal Decimal Classification system for libraries, on which he had done much pioneering work. Brian was characteristically stubborn and wouldn't buy it at all, but after a long period of late-night debates Denis finally won Brian over. Having been converted, Brian was then unstoppable in launching UDC for the SPRI library, and on Denis' birthday three days before his death, Brian presented him with two hefty volumes of the UDC catalogue for polar libraries, newly published. Sadly Brian himself died just one year later. The untimely loss of someone who has been a formative influence on one's life leaves behind a sense of having been cheated. There were so many questions that June would have liked to ask Brian – as indeed would Steve, who was in Cambridge during the decade 1969-78 but who never knew him.

Steve's introduction to Brian Roberts was unavoidably posthumous. It took the form of a large cupboard bequeathed to June - an 18th century Welsh *deuddarn* that Brian had used as his drinks cabinet. It is still in our kitchen today, complete with a photograph of him, pipe in mouth, contentedly at the wheel of an old fishing boat (from which he explored uninhabited islands off the west coast of Scotland), and so we can say cheers to Brian every time we have a drink.

A sense of frustration was the trigger for writing this book. So little was known about Brian Roberts, and what had been published was not always accurate. We started off by interviewing surviving contemporaries of Brian – a matter of some urgency, most of them being in their 80s or 90s – and they agreed that Brian's legacy was so far-reaching that his achievements deserved better recognition. No biography of Brian had been published. In 1995 *Polar Pundit* appeared: a collection of interesting memories and anecdotes by his former colleagues and friends, but containing little on his personal life and still less about his political work. Unearthing the details of his life would take us on many visits to archives in Cambridge and London and on several voyages to the Arctic and the Antarctic. It was fortunate for us that Brian was a prodigious diary writer, almost all his output being neatly typed and preserved in bound volumes in the SPRI archives in Cambridge. These diaries were not written for our benefit: they were for Brian himself, as he often complained about his poor memory and needing to remind himself of the exciting events in his life. He remained single throughout life and for him diary writing was also a means of letting off steam. Taught photography by his father in his teens, Brian was also a lifelong prolific photographer.

There were however some big gaps in the records of Brian's life. One of the big questions confronting us was over the origins of the Antarctic Treaty, about which there has been no consensus among political historians. To what extent was Brian involved, and how? Now for the first time the story of his role in one of the most momentous events in Antarctic history can be told. At the Foreign Office the sort of question that Brian was tasked with answering was: does anyone 'own' the Antarctic, and if so who? There was no clear system of governance for the continent, and disputes were emerging between some nations (including Britain), claiming that it was 'their' territory. To Brian this outdated nationalistic attitude was futile, and the only way to manage the continent and prevent conflict was to achieve some form of international agreement. By lobbying hard he eventually persuaded a reluctant Whitehall that this was the only way forward. And so was born the Antarctic Treaty, signed in Washington in 1959 and coming into force in 1961. Since then no wars have been fought over the Antarctic, and the Treaty has survived – and flourished – for 60 years, making it one of the most successful international agreements ever.

In addition to preventing territorial conflict the Treaty had other important implications. Human behaviour towards wildlife in the Antarctic has often been barbaric, with the wholesale slaughter of whales and seals in the 19th and 20th centuries to exploit their oil, skin and bone products for lighting, explosives and even the fashion industry. The slaughter was so destructive that some whale and seal species nearly became extinct, and it was only by means of strict conservation rules that the seals, penguins and seabirds of the rich Antarctic coastal waters could enjoy some protection from human depredation. Brian would spend the rest of his life negotiating at Antarctic Treaty conferences to achieve agreement on such measures. In his position as Britain's foremost authority on the Antarctic, Brian was the key person responsible for ensuring that the Treaty worked and for enabling wildlife conservation. Obtaining international agreement in the face of competing national interests was a formidable achievement. The world needs more people like Brian with the vision, drive, patience and expertise to address today's global problems.

This overview of Roberts' life cannot claim to be an exhaustive analysis of the political, legal and scientific pies he had his fingers in. Any new information will be published at www.brianroberts.co.uk. For any shortcomings or errors the authors naturally take full responsibility.

June Roberts
Steve Heavens

PROLOGUE

SURVIVING AN ANTARCTIC
BLIZZARD WITH NO TENT

Alone in the icy wilderness, four scientists had been dropped by helicopter onto a remote unexplored area of the Antarctic coast. In their pristine white surroundings of low relief, the air was still and they were enjoying glorious sunshine. They were planning to make a survey, and had been provided with a survival kit of two tents, sleeping bags, food rations and a primus stove.

Hardly had the helicopter disappeared from view to return to the US Navy's icebreaker *USS Glacier* 45 miles away when a few gusts of wind whipped up. Soon there was havoc with the kit and an exhausting chase was needed to round up the cooking pots. Another sudden gust snapped off two ice-axe heads holding down a canvas windshield for the party's theodolite. The windshield promptly smacked one man in the face, stunning him. It was time to abandon any thoughts of surveying and put up a shelter. But now there was only one tent. All that remained of the second tent were a few charred fragments; made of nylon, it had caught fire on being used as a shield for a tea brew on an unattended primus stove. The one tent would have to do for the four of them. But the tent poles were nowhere to be found.

Three of the team were young Americans participating in an extensive US programme of Antarctic exploration, Operation Deep Freeze. All were short on training and experience in Antarctic conditions. By now the wind was so fierce that erecting a tent would have been out of the question. What should they do? They turned to the much older fourth man and asked him to take command. Brian Roberts was a 48-year-old veteran of the polar regions, who was present as the official UK observer to the expedition.

Under Roberts' direction, the men made their way downwind to find a suitable site to build a rock shelter. Suitable rocks had to be collected to form the walls – the bigger and heavier the better. The men were knocked down by increasingly powerful gusts of wind and for much of the time crawled on their hands and knees. At last the walls were constructed. A roof was fashioned from the windshield, weighted down with heavy rocks. The narrow entrance was sealed with tent cloth. Internally the shelter measured 4 ft by 6 ft, with 3 ft of headroom. After six hours the exhausted men crawled inside and lit the stove. It gave out miserably little heat, taking an hour to melt enough snow for some tepid cups of tea. Nearly all their food rations had a high water content and were frozen, so they needed heating. But their spirits were high and they all managed a meal of sorts. Roberts, the last, was grateful for a tin of frozen fruit cake.

Rock shelter, after a sketch by Larry Lepley, 1961

Outside, the blizzard raged with a wind speed of well over 100 mph. The men were now facing the prospect of being holed up for several days. After the three Americans had arranged themselves inside in their sleeping bags, there was no room to move, and there was no room for Roberts. He had to climb into his sleeping bag outside and put his head and shoulders inside the entrance, wrapping the tent cloth around his body. Lying on a slope, he was constantly slithering away from the entrance. But he was the only one to be wearing suitable clothing, right down to his mukluk boots, which kept his feet warm and dry. In the cramped conditions inside, the Americans could not get inside their sleeping bags fully clothed, as zips jammed when they tried to do them up.

Whilst no one was particularly comfortable, Roberts was confident that they would now survive the blizzard, which might last for a few days at most.

After a few hours of intermittent sleep, Roberts decided that the shelter needed modifying. The temperature was dropping and it was only a matter of time before the wind would drift fine snow through all the cracks between the rocks and cover everything inside.

They worked all morning in the searing wind to build an annexe to shelter the fourth man, roofed over with sledge and survey poles, covered with tent cloth and fastened down with rocks and rope lashings. All nooks and crannies in the rock walls were plugged with whatever could be found, from small stones to survey flags and even red bunting. The stove could now be coaxed into more efficient action, and it provided the men with hot cups of tea, washed down with some biscuits, sugar and milk powder.

Wriggling into their sleeping bags, they now all managed, with an immense effort, to get zipped right up. Outside the temperature was around -10°C, but after their exertions the men felt warm. Roberts now took up an inside position, swapping with one of the Americans, Jim Peeler, who had suffered from claustrophobia when he had been up against the innermost shelter wall. But as they settled down, fine snow began to sift over them, finding its way in through every chink in the walls.

Roberts was alert. If nothing was done straight away they would soon be entombed by snow. To plug the walls a snowball party was orchestrated, collecting the snow which was settling around them and lobbing balls of it to the man nearest the wall. In the annexe Peeler had much the hardest job of sealing the entrance, which he did with a jerry can and their sleeping bag hoods, cementing them into position with snowballs. It was important for Peeler to be able to get out, should the roof collapse and trap the rest of them under the accumulated weight of rocks and snow.

Everyone's gloves and sleeping bags were now sodden, but so long as they stayed inside they could keep warm. It was now no longer possible to light the stove and melt water or thaw food, but they kept themselves cheerful with the few remaining biscuits and cigarettes. The smoke became thick and somehow comforting, but it was impossible to relieve aching joints and cramped muscles. They whiled away the time exchanging life histories, comparing restaurants and recipes, and singing – without much success, as none of them could remember the words of any song in common. After two days and nights of incarceration, all sense of time was lost. They could not tell whether it was 10 am or 10 pm.

The following night the wind began to ease up. They were all so cramped and uncomfortable that Roberts proposed to try to erect the tent. Packed tightly in their confined space, it took them nearly an hour to struggle out. But the wind was still powerful and probably too strong for the tent to stay fast, even if they could get it erected. Larry Lepley was the only one with any strength left; the others were so weak that they kept getting knocked down by gusts. Peeler had got very wet and his windproofs were beginning to freeze solid. All their gloves were frozen like boards, and Roberts knew that they could neither continue to wear them nor work with bare hands.

Roberts was about to tell them to crawl back into the shelter and abandon the idea of putting up the tent when they heard the sound of helicopter engines. Moments later one appeared out of the clouds, flying straight towards them. All attempts at landing resulted in slithering away on the icy slopes and having to lift off again quickly, but with persistence and skill the pilot eventually succeeded in landing. Shortly after, a second helicopter arrived and landed successfully. It was a euphoric moment for the rescued foursome as they bundled themselves inside and were airlifted back to the ship. On board a heroes' welcome awaited them: dry clothes, a hearty meal, and for Roberts his special favourite of a bottle of gin and a jug of fresh orange juice, followed by much-needed sleep.

The party's survival owed much to Roberts' recollection of the life-saving rock shelter sketched by Edward Wilson on Scott's last expedition in 1911, contained amongst the collection of drawings and paintings held at the Scott Polar Research Institute in Cambridge. Wilson had gone with Apsley Cherry-Garrard and 'Birdie' Bowers to collect emperor penguin eggs at Cape Crozier in the depths of the Antarctic winter, when their tent blew away and they experienced unimaginable hardships.

In the heat of the rescue all equipment and personal possessions had been abandoned. Two days later, when the weather had improved, Lepley returned to the site with the helicopters to retrieve whatever could be found, but Roberts was devastated to lose his Leica camera and kitbag. The inevitable flurry of interest in the international press – which would celebrate Brian Roberts as the hero to whom the party owed its survival – was to him of little importance and just a source of irritation. He was never one to seek the limelight.

PART 1

THE EXPLORER

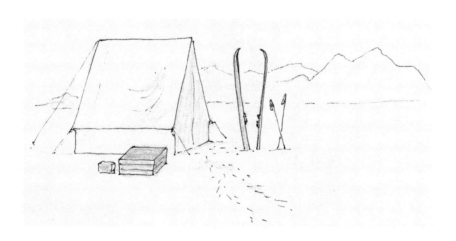

1

FAMILY BACKGROUND AND CHILDHOOD

Post funera virtus (recognition after death)
Roberts family motto

In the malaria-ridden swamps of Bengal, India, Poulter Benjamin Roberts worked as a civil engineer, advising on swamp drainage and the construction of river embankments, canals and railways. This area of the Ganges delta is one of the wettest places on Earth and the work was arduous and unpleasant. Succumbing several times to malaria and dysentery, he recovered each time, but his body became weakened until, with a poor diet lacking in fresh food, he died in 1889 at the age of 48.

Poulter Benjamin left a widow Theresa, herself in poor health, and four children under the age of twelve. With no income, she left India for England with her children. The second oldest, Charles, then aged ten, was placed in the care of an aunt who belonged to the Plymouth Brethren, a strict religious sect that strongly disapproved of technological innovation. The Sabbath was devoted to Bible readings and Charles was not allowed to make any noise – least of all banging nails into wood whilst constructing something. He got around this by pushing them in silently. The repressive evangelical ethos was torture for such a creative and ambitious boy, with only sixpence a week pocket money, which did not go far. Whilst at school Charles developed a passion for astronomy, day-dreaming during classroom lessons about what Mars and the moon must look like through a telescope. Being unusually resourceful, he built his own telescope: a 6 ft long wooden Newtonian reflecting telescope with a 4 in mirror, which won him first prize in a school competition.

One day Charles suddenly woke up to the realisation that his ambition to become a doctor would never come about unless he got a scholarship, as there was no family money to pay for his studies. By dint of hard work he achieved it and went on to train at St Thomas's Hospital. Once qualified, he entered the Indian Medical Service in early 1907 and was stationed in Meerut. He was not destined to stay in India for long. Within the same year whilst out in India, he met and married Madeline Julia Birley. The ceremony took place in Bombay Cathedral; the bride was given away by her brother Maurice, who worked in the Indian civil service. Madeline was a splendid catch for a man sorely without means, coming from a family of wealthy mill-owning Lancashire industrialists. She was attractive, but at 35 years old (six years senior to Charles) was considered to be on the shelf. There was no time to waste if they were to have a family, and happily within a few months Madeline was expecting their first child.

Madeline returned to England in early 1908. Charles, needing to complete his two years of service, followed some months later. They settled in Woking, Surrey, where Charles acquired a medical practice. At the time Woking was a small town undergoing rapid expansion. It was one of the earliest 'commuter' towns, acquiring its railway station in 1838 on the line between London and Southampton, which enabled Charles to commute to London if he wanted. At first the Roberts rented a house next to the Basingstoke Canal where Joy was born. Later they moved to a substantial sub-Arts and Crafts style house with a huge garden in a newly-developed leafy suburb not far from the middle of town. Bishopgarth (*Plate 1.7*) was to become the Roberts family home for 30 years, providing space for a family of four children, as well as accommodation for a few live-in servants.

With the birth of Joy in 1908, a nanny was engaged who was to remain with the family for the early years of all the children. In 1910 Denis arrived, followed one year later by Patrick. In March 1912, the year that Captain Scott and his companions famously met their deaths returning from the South Pole, Charles and Madeline completed their family with the birth of Brian on 23 October.

In his medical work Charles was a pioneer user of the X-ray machine. An extension was built on to Bishopgarth to accommodate a lead-lined X-ray room for his patients, some of whom came to him from Woking's Victoria Hospital. Charles was also appointed to the post of Senior Radiologist at St Bartholomew's Hospital in London.

EARLY CHILDHOOD

At Bishopgarth, Charles threw himself energetically into a new hobby: gardening. Influenced by a new wave of garden writers, Gertrude Jekyll, William Robinson and Reginald Farrer, he landscaped the gardens, creating an extensive alpine rockery using massive limestone blocks. Many lovely trees were planted, including a grey Atlantic cedar and numerous Japanese maples and bamboos. A magnificent 11 ft high limestone dovecote was commissioned as a focal garden feature and carved by a stonemason. It is still there today (*Plate 1.8*), along with the Atlantic cedar and some of the Japanese maples. Charles constructed a large pond with a little rustic bridge over it, steps and paths leading to a small round summer house with a thatched roof. Everywhere the planting was natural and informal. It was a child's paradise in which to discover the natural world (*Plate 1.9*).

Once the garden was laid out, Charles began to contemplate wider horizons. Owning a motor car would open up a whole new world of adventure and exploration. Motor cars were growing in popularity, but were still largely the preserve of the wealthy who could afford a chauffeur. Charles had limited means; he was also mechanically minded and manuals were available to help with maintenance. He relished the challenge of becoming an owner-driver. Doctors were commonly car owners, but Charles did not need a car to visit patients; for an X-ray they either came to him or he saw them at the local hospital. No, he wanted a motor car to explore the world with his family. With the aid of Madeline's inheritance he was able in 1911 to purchase a long-wheelbase Crossley tourer, spacious enough to accommodate the family, nanny and nurse.

So at the age of ten months Brian had his first whiff of sea air when the family travelled to Torquay for their summer holiday in August 1913. The Great Western Railway (GWR) was promoting Torquay as only a five-hour journey from Paddington and was the most comfortable way for Madeline, nanny, nurse and the children to travel. On the road

Charles would have had quite an adventurous drive. Petrol pumps had not yet come into being, and he needed to travel with several cans of 'motor spirit' as it was then called. Since many roads were as yet unmetalled, punctures were a common hazard and carrying at least one spare tyre was obligatory. The national speed limit being 20 mph, the 170-mile journey was quite an undertaking.

Once in Torquay Charles derived great pride and pleasure in taking his family out on excursions, exploring quiet places away from the bustling resort. In the family photograph (*Plate 1.10*) Brian, the smallest occupant, is sitting on nanny's lap. Despite Torquay's mild climate, even in August everyone is dressed warmly with their hats tied down. The car's retractable hood was raised only in bad weather and the front windscreen gave but minimal protection.

OUTBREAK OF WAR

In 1914 the Roberts' happy family life was sharply disrupted when Europe was plunged into the Great War.

Charles joined the Royal Army Medical Corps and waited to hear where he was to be posted. He was attached to the 29th Stationary Hospital, and together with the other doctors, nurses and equipment he travelled by steamer across the English Channel in December 1914. They were destined for Nevers, a pretty town some 160 miles south-east of Paris with extensive rail connections for the transport of wounded soldiers from the Front. During the war the British army developed a finely-tuned system of casualty evacuation via a series of medical treatment posts from the battlefield back to the well-equipped static hospital some distance away. The Hôpital Anglaise was the furthest port of call from the Western Front, and the one where the most severely injured soldiers were taken. Away from the town centre was a huge complex of railway sidings, depots and repair yards, where a railway company administrative building was converted into the hospital. Third-class railway carriages, converted by the Red Cross to carry four beds, could draw up next to the building to offload the wounded. Next to the operating theatre Charles had an X-ray room with equipment that was invaluable for locating bits of metal embedded in the body. Most of the patients were French soldiers with shrapnel and bullet wounds requiring limb amputation (*Plate 1.11*). Many arrived with gangrene.

In late March 1915 a new team of nurses arrived at the Hôpital Anglaise. Amongst them was Princess Louise Battenberg, a great grand-daughter of Queen Victoria.[1] With her caring personality she was a wonderful nurse, turning her hand to any task and doing her share of the difficult job of night duty in the wards. Charles was responsible for her welfare, and having his camera with him (against the rules), he took a number of photographs of the Princess (*Plate 1.12*). She was delighted with them, saying that they were the only good ones ever done of her and asking him for many more copies as she was always being asked for them.

In May 1915 Charles returned to England to enjoy a brief period of family life and his beloved garden over the summer and autumn. The war was now developing on the Eastern Front, as the Allied Powers planned to come to the aid of Serbia, which was facing a combined attack from Germany, Austria-Hungary and Bulgaria. The first Allied forces arrived in Salonika in the late autumn of 1915 but were too late to prevent the invasion of Serbia. However a relatively stable Macedonian Front was established until almost the end of the war, when Serbia was liberated as Bulgaria capitulated. It was to Salonika that Charles was sent with the 29th Hospital in December 1915, shortly after the first troops had arrived in the region.

The Eastern Front, distant from the well-documented horrors of the Western Front, is the most forgotten in the history of the Great War, as so little has been written about it.[2] There the problems were quite different. The greatest threat to the soldiers was not being shot at or shelled; it was Europe's last malarial hot spot, in a region of rugged and inhospitable terrain where the only means of transport was the horse. Due to seasonal climatic extremes and poor sanitary conditions, dysentery was endemic amongst the troops during the summer, and frostbite was rife during the bitterly cold winter. A poor diet of endless bread and marmalade did not help. This war came to be known as the 'doctors' war', since far more soldiers were invalided out through malaria than from bullet or shell wounds. Many of the Red Cross nurses sent out there found life so ghastly, or succumbed so badly to malaria, that they did not stay long.

After three weeks at sea Charles arrived with the 29th Hospital unit at Salonika, where they pitched up in floorless tents just outside the city. The winter began with continuous rain followed by bitter cold and snow, making life difficult right from the start. Charles wrote home to his children from his sodden tent, describing the need to dig ditches to keep the water out, along with tales of mice living in his kitbag and eating his tobacco and biscuits. "I have got a bit of a German bomb for you.... a nasty German in an aeroplane about a mile up in the air dropped it behind my tent, but he didn't hurt anybody." The Red Cross symbol, clearly visible on the ground, offered little protection from air attacks on nearby military targets.[3] It was not until six months after their arrival that Charles' hospital unit finally acquired a proper kitchen, operated by a Voluntary Aid Detachment of cooks.

Drawing by Charles from his letter to Denis

At home in Woking the children were badly missing their father, and Brian wanted to go to visit him. At the age of five he dictated a letter to Nanny, telling his father about the garden's neglected state in his absence. But a more serious issue had arisen: Madeline had developed breast cancer. At the time surgery for this condition was primitive, requiring a radical mastectomy. Madeline was stoical and knew that she was lucky to have the family support of her brother Maurice and his wife Jean living next door. They were childless and would be around to help Madeline's children if she were to be left seriously debilitated or did not survive.

While she was recovering in hospital, Brian looked out of the nursery window and dictated another letter to Nanny, this time for his Mummy. He describes the spring blossom on the fruit trees, forget-me-nots and primroses, butterflies, planting potatoes, and rockery flowers all coming out. "Norman has made my pigeon house, all except the door been put on." Since Brian's older brothers were now both at the nearby preparatory school he had lost his playmates as well as both his parents. However the aviary gave him a diversion and scope for his growing interest in birds. Fortunately Madeline's operation was successful and she was soon back home with her children.

The war was coming to an end, but demobilisation was frustratingly slow and Charles was not home until early 1919. On his return he took up a post in the X-ray department at St Bartholomew's Hospital, as well as other medical positions locally in Woking. After all the horrors he had experienced, Charles was longing to resume normal life again with his growing family. His children were now three years older than when he had last seen them, ranging in age from the 10-year-old Joy to the six-year-old Brian, all of whom were quite ready for some adventurous travel in the motor car.

CORNWALL

The picturesque fishing town of Looe in south-east Cornwall has a mild climate and safe bathing beaches, and a coastline peppered with rocky inlets that can be explored by boat. In the early 20th century it was an up-and-coming holiday destination served by a branch line from the GWR train service from London to Penzance. There was even a motor garage, quite a rarity at the time. West and East Looe had evolved as separate communities linked by a bridge. On the west side of the river stood the prominent Old Bridge House, which the Roberts family rented for the month of August 1919. It was large enough to accommodate three domestic servants (nanny, cook and a maid), who travelled by train with the luggage while the family motored down together.

From the safety of the veranda the children had a good view of the constant comings and goings of Looe's fishing fleet. Under their noses boats tied up to dry their nets on the quayside (*Plate 1.13*), a frequent operation needed to prevent the cotton rotting. The fishing industry was experiencing a boom. Most of the boats and the fishermen had been away during the war and the fish stocks had had time to recover. The main summer fishing was for pilchards, which were landed on the East Looe quayside. Tourists could hire a small boat with a boatman, the fishermen thereby earning a little extra money. The Roberts took the opportunity to explore the rocky coves around the harbour mouth and go out to the nearby island. Being shown the art of rod fishing for mackerel from the boat was an irresistible activity for Charles and the boys, and provided a good number of meals for the household. Madeline's dressmaker had made swimming costumes for the four children and the three servants, and the children could gain confidence with swimming practice around the boat. The tidal rhythms in Looe's busy harbour made a strong visual impression on the young Brian. At low tide the moored boats were all exposed to the keel and the seaweed-covered mudflats became a feasting ground for seabirds. On the incoming tide the children leaned over the harbour wall to catch crabs with line and bait. At high tide the boats were all buoyant as the fishing fleet prepared to go out to sea again.

Looe captivated the family, and they returned for their summer holiday for two more years. During these early holidays the three boys were able to develop their confidence with boats and the sea. On one of the long car journeys to Cornwall Joy, occupied with her knitting, began squabbling with the boys. Of the three boys Brian was the only one who stood up to his older sister when she became bossy: "Joy, if you don't shut up, I'll throw your knitting out of the window." All went quiet on the back seat. Minutes later the squabbling began again, at which point Brian snatched up Joy's knitting and tossed it out of the window. It was never retrieved.

2

ADVENTUROUS ALPINE MOTORING

Soon after Brian had turned eleven, his father Charles took delivery of a new car: a 3-litre Bentley tourer. With his passion for the natural world, he was determined to share the experience of travel and exploration with his own family. In the early 1920s it was uncommon enough to take a motor car abroad, let alone with one's wife and four children in tow. The Crossley had served the family well, but it was now the great decade of innovation for the motor car, when speed and power mattered. The races at Le Mans and at Brooklands could make or break the reputation and sales of a car. A Bentley had come fourth at Le Mans in 1923 and first in 1924. Charles was now the owner of a car possessing the two key attributes needed for negotiating the mountain passes of continental Europe – power and reliability. He once again opted for a long wheelbase version to give room for the four children in the back. Madeline, now already 51 and suffering with arthritis in her legs, would not be able to walk far and needed a degree of comfort. The Bentley cost more than any other car on the market except for a Rolls Royce and was way above what Charles could have afforded. Uncle Maurice, who held much of his sister Madeline's family money in trust, recognised her needs and would have provided the capital.

Until the 1930s most British guidebooks on continental Europe were written for the rail traveller, with additional information about horse-drawn carriages and motor diligences where they were available, such as over a number of mountain passes. But one man had as early as 1910 been singing the praises of the automobile as a means to explore Europe. With more than seven books on the subject to his name, Charles L Freeston gave many an early motor car owner the courage not only to drive into Europe but to enjoy the thrill of driving over mountain passes and places that the railway did not reach.

Freeston was a founder member of the Royal Automobile Club (RAC), but after the Great War he wrote for the Automobile Association (AA). He covered in detail every conceivable aspect of the motorist's concerns, from the need for self-confidence in one's own vehicle to an understanding of what is a mountain pass (there being no real examples in Britain, he assumes that the reader has all sorts of preconceptions based on misinformation). Unlike British roads with their variable widths, surfaces and gradients, and erratic windings, the Alpine passes of Europe did not simply evolve from ancient trackways but were designed and built by proficient engineers, many during the 19th century in the days of carriages and horse-drawn traffic. A carefully measured gradient was essential to enable horses to pull a vehicle uphill, as well as one that could be safely negotiated downhill with the primitive braking system of a carriage. Even in the days long before roads were paved, mountain passes were of a good width and reasonable surface quality, well able to take the motor car. Freeston's encouragement to the reader is nevertheless tempered with sensible warnings:

"The science of touring in any country, but pre-eminently in Alpine regions, is to know as much as may be in advance where practical data are concerned, and to leave as little as possible to chance in that respect; the scenery will provide the elements of novelty and surprise, to say nothing of any adventures that may be encountered by the way. Happy-go-lucky methods never pay in touring, and, when mountains have to be crossed, are even dangerous; the man who thoroughly enjoys himself awheel is the one who masters his available facts beforehand, and, so far from this policy interfering with his freedom of action, it enlarges it to the greatest possible degree. He it is who knows at any given stage whether he may safely make this or that diversion from his original plan, or enjoy a longer halt than he had intended at some particularly tempting spot. In no sense is he hidebound by his itinerary; the whole object of his foreknowledge is to secure the fullest measure of elasticity whenever and wherever opportunity will permit."[1]

In the days long before power steering, tackling hairpin bends demanded considerable physical stamina from the driver of a long wheelbase car. Freeston devotes a whole chapter to this topic.

THE PYRENEES

To embark on a continental tour, membership of the AA was essential: they provided all the essential car papers, route maps and helpful advice on accommodation. For his first venture Brian's father opted for the Pyrenees, the rugged mountains that create a natural boundary between France and Spain. More accessible than the Alps, and generally lower (reaching only 10,000 ft in the central Haute region), they would enable him to gain experience of driving on mountain passes before tackling the Alps. As well as the promise of spectacular views and the occasional snow-capped peaks, the region was teeming with romantic castles and fortifications, Romanesque churches (some fortified), dense forests, canyons and gorges with caves and, for the compulsive rock gardener, a stunning alpine flora.

The Pyrenees were traditionally frequented in summer by the French and Spanish, most of whom were pilgrims walking to Lourdes or taking the waters in one of the many spas. The British tended to go there in the winter: not to the mountains but to fashionable seaside resorts such as Biarritz or the Riviera, with their equable climate. The majority of visitors used the extensive rail network. In the 1920s the Pyrenees saw few cars, most road traffic still being donkeys and mules carrying people and goods. Although carriage road surfaces were generally good, they were unpaved and dusty in the drier parts, particularly on the Spanish side.

After much preparation the Roberts set off in early August 1924 on a month-long tour. Clothing was packed in a motor trunk with six drawers (one for each member of the family) strapped to the back of the car. Collared shirts, ties, mackintoshes and tweed jackets all went in. The concept of leisure clothes had yet to be invented. The children were given broad-brimmed hats to keep the sun off. The boys (*Plate 2.1*) had woollen shorts and long woollen socks. Madeline could use her command of French to replenish the family picnic basket with local breads and cheeses at every opportunity. A spare wheel and three spare tyres were attached to the outside of the car, a necessity as tyres were far from reliable.

From Woking a drive took them to Southampton for the overnight crossing on the passenger steamship SS *Hantonia* to Le Havre. The car was lifted by crane onto the ship, a precarious operation (*Plate 2.2*). Ferries designed to take cars did not appear until 1928, when up to 15 cars could be winched and craned into the hold of a passenger ship.[2]

The route south through France took them along the scenic Loire valley. For the British motorist French roads were a pleasant contrast to those at home. There were no speed limits or speed traps, and the many wide, long straight stretches between towns made for exhilarating driving. By the time they approached the Atlantic coast at Bayonne the children were wilting in the August heat, so they stopped to cool off, bathing fully clothed in the River Adour, and immersing their heads in a stone drinking-water trough. Motoring westward along the coast road they crossed into Spain and at San Sebastián headed inland to the ancient Basque town of Pamplona (*Plate 2.3*). Crossing back into France they took the Roncesvalles Pass. What this pass lacked in spectacle it made up for in historic drama, as Madeline was able to enliven the journey with a story from 8th century France. After Charlemagne's army had destroyed the city walls of the Basque capital Pamplona, the victorious army returned through the pass. Bringing up the rear were Charlemagne's knight Roland and his men, who were ambushed and massacred by the Basques. It was Charlemagne's only defeat and Roland was elevated to hero status. The story is told in the earliest surviving French medieval epic poem, the *Chanson de Roland*.

Continuing eastwards through the French foothills, they made a detour across the only two inland passes then existing across the Pyrenees. With the pleasant climate in the mountains they could travel with the hood down and enjoy picnics by the roadside. Alpine flowers were everywhere. Along the Col du Somport the flora was exceptional, with a riot of Pyrenean purple iris carpeting the Pic du Midi d'Osseau.

To continue they had to drive through Lourdes. In August at the height of the pilgrim season the town was choked with people and vehicles. As they left the town, the narrow road was still swarming with pilgrims on foot and sightseers in horse-drawn carriages or the occasional car, all heading in the same direction. Now in the heart of the Hautes Pyrenées, a few miles ahead lay the head of the valley and the celebrated Cirque de Gavarnie.

Beyond the village of Gèdre the valley narrowed into a gorge. The road entered a dramatic landscape of giant boulders – larger than houses – strewn everywhere, through which the early carriageway builders had struggled to create a route (*Plate 2.4*). Was this apocalyptic landscape really created by the forces of weathering and erosion in a glaciated mountain area, or by something more powerful? Appropriately named 'Le Chaos de Comély' it was actually formed as a result of an earthquake in 580 AD that caused the mountain of Comély partially to collapse into the valley. The French naturalist who made the connection was Pierre Bernard Palassou (1745-1830), a pioneer of geological studies in the Pyrenees. Sadly, little of this evocative landscape remains today, as the inevitable need for road-widening has resulted in the loss of much of the dramatic character of this valley floor.

On approaching the village of Gavarnie, an impressively high rock wall comes in to view, capped by snowy peaks cutting off the end of the valley. Leaving the car at the village, with its bustling throng of tourists, cars, carriages, guides and mule drivers, the Roberts set off on the path alongside a gushing stream up the last bit of the valley towards their goal. After an hour's walking, the spectacle of this immense natural rock amphitheatre, with its vertically-walled terraces trapping snow and ice even in late summer, towered in front of them. The active process of summer ice thaw was evident from the myriad narrow waterfalls everywhere, one quite spectacular in its sheer length of drop (at close to 1,400 ft nearly the tallest in Europe). From below the wall they could no longer see the snowy peaks high above forming a natural boundary between France and Spain. There was a unanimous demand from the children to climb on to the snow. With their father they scrambled across the lower scree slopes of moraine to clamber onto the nearest bit of hard residual ice. Directly under their feet lay a vast cavern, and from its mouth gushed the icy meltwater stream, the source of the river torrent they had just followed up the valley. While his father was distracted by the particularly fine alpine flora for which this spot was renowned, Brian was absorbing his first lesson in glacial geography that didn't come out of a textbook.

Continuing eastwards, they drove over the Col du Tourmalet. At 6,940 ft the highest of all the French Pyrenean passes, it was already part of the Tour de France in 1910 and today is used heavily by cyclists as a testing ground.

The Pyrenees are peppered with caves. Near Niaux the family stopped to visit one known since at least the early 1600s but which owing to a recent discovery held a special appeal. In their warmest clothing and each given a carbide miner's lamp to hold, Charles and the children followed a guide into the cold and dark, making their way along narrow low-roofed passages in and out of big caverns full of stalagmites and stalactites. After stumbling along miles of wet and slippery cave floor they ended up in a cavern deep inside to view a wall covered with prehistoric paintings of bison, horse and ibex. The finest prehistoric European cave art then known was at Altemira near Santander on the north coast of Spain, and it was 16 years before the Lascaux paintings would come to light. But it was at Niaux that Brian's interest in anthropology was born.

CARCASSONNE

Leaving the Pyrenees, the family headed north for the ancient fortified city of Carcassonne. For the boys it was not possible to see too many castles, and this was one quite beyond their imagination: a hilltop city surrounded by massive fortification walls bristling with towers and turrets. Commanding a strategic location on the ancient trade routes between the Atlantic and the Mediterranean, its history extended back to the Neolithic period. It was occupied in turn by Romans, Visigoths and Saracens. During medieval times warfare between the French and Aragon Spanish saw the city become an unassailable fortress, wrapped in two miles of double-walled ramparts. They remained the most formidable fortifications in Europe until the 18th century, when they were abandoned. On Napoleon's arrival the city was demilitarized and the walls began to crumble away. Much of the stone was robbed for the building of houses in the lower town beneath, which grew and flourished. By the 1840s quite a number of the rampart's 53 towers barely stood proud of the walls, but proposals by the French government to demolish it altogether were greeted with horror by the locals. Finally it was agreed that it should be restored as a national heritage. This was a novel idea for its time and the work would take more than half a century, beginning in 1853. The architect commissioned for the project was Eugène Emmanuel Viollet-le-Duc. With no precedent for such an undertaking the concept of preservation, as opposed to restoration (which removes and destroys), was hotly debated on both sides of the Channel – in Victorian England by John Ruskin and other founding members of the Victorian Society. Much criticism was levelled at Viollet-le-Duc, who removed all the habitation of different periods which had grown up attached to the walls, and over-restored the walls and towers with a northern flavour of sharply pointed slate roofs (traditionally in the south a pitched terracotta roof was the norm, and some of the towers may never have been roofed at all). But this was the mid-19th century, and in Victorian Britain architects who saved its crumbling medieval churches from ruin were accused of similar travesties. John Betjeman had these words to say on the subject:

The church's Restoration
In eighteen-eighty-three
Has left for contemplation
Not what there used to be.

Carcassonne

For the Roberts there was much to discover, exploring the huge ramparts with magnificent views of the Pyrenees – and inside the citadel there was a medieval castle reached by bridge over a moat, a cathedral, and the inner city itself: a rabbit warren of narrow medieval streets. Every generation enjoys a Disneyworld, and here was a real medieval one.

Another pleasant stop on the long drive north was Rocamadour, a medieval village which clings crazily to the near vertical sides of a canyon cliff in the western Dordogne. Climbing up many flights of steep steps, the visiting pilgrim would have a choice of eight churches to enter, and for the Roberts a castle at the top with splendid views. (See over)

Rocamadour

INTO THE ALPS

The following year, with his experience of negotiating the Bentley over mountain passes, Charles felt confident enough to tackle the Alps. Taking the ferry from Dover to Calais, the family motored through the lowlands of northern France around the Somme. It was only six years since the end of the Great War. The devastation of towns, cathedrals and the countryside was still all too evident, although by now the roads were largely repaired and food and petrol had become more readily available.

Crossing into Switzerland at Geneva, they drove along the valleys of the Bernese Alps. At Interlaken they went over the Grimsel Pass, at 7,100 ft one of the highest in Switzerland and with a view from the summit of the lower part of the great Rhône Glacier. Well documented by the Swiss since the 1890s, the glacier's retreat from the valley floor was mapped by markers placed at intervals. Towards the top of the even higher Furka Pass (7,976 ft), the road hairpins up right next to the glacier (*Plates 2.5, 2.6*). This had long been a tourist attraction as the nearest that a road gets to a glacier in the Alps. Since the 1890s the owners of the nearby Hotel Belvedere had been digging out an ice tunnel 100 yards long into the glacier and charging visitors an entrance fee. Glaciers have a habit of sliding downhill, and the tunnel needed to be re-cut at the beginning of every summer season. Brian and Denis were enraptured by the walk inside the ice tunnel (*Plate 2.7*), as was Denis' daughter June 35 years later, sparking off her lifelong interest in glaciers. Since then accelerated climate change has caused the glacier to recede so far from the road that the ice tunnel exists no more, and the Hotel Belvedere closed down in 2015.

The family continued down the Upper Rhône valley to Brig, crossing into Italy via the Simplon Pass and descending to the hot and dusty roads of the Lombardy plains. Needing a break, but not at the fashionable resorts edging the lakes Maggiore and Lugano, they pushed on to the less populous side of Lake Como at Lecco with its beautiful mountain backdrop. Then on through Milan to the ancient Lombard capital of Pavia, which – with its architectural gems and picturesque covered medieval bridge spanning the wide river Ticino – captivated Denis and sowed the seed for his lifelong passion of Italian Renaissance architecture. In the oppressive August heat, they made for the Riviera coast and motored westwards along the coast as far as Cannes, where the return journey began northwards through France via more castles, chateaux and churches, including Autun with its vast Roman fortifications.

THE MASTER OF THE ROLLS

Back at home Charles was not happy with the Bentley. Most likely his concerns were over the brakes, which may have proved inadequate for coping with Alpine passes. The car had been purchased in late 1923 shortly before Bentley made the change from two-wheel to four-wheel braking. During the winter it was decided to replace the Bentley with a Rolls Royce, the only car then on the road considered to be reliable enough. Uncle Maurice once again dug into the Birley family funds.

With the new Rolls, Charles intended to be both driver and mechanic. This would be a challenge: at the time Rolls Royce owners normally employed both a chauffeur and a mechanic. So on a hot July day in 1926 he attended an intensive training session for chauffeurs at Salmonds of Newport Pagnell.[3] He admitted afterwards to Joy: "I came away feeling I had rather butted above my humble sphere in life in buying a Rolls, it wants such a lot of attention. Every Tuesday and Friday one gets filthy up to the elbows in grease and oil... It is not a car for an owner driver unless he has a trained man. I am going to send Sayer [the gardener/odd job man] to the class while we are away, but unfortunately he shows very little evidence of any mechanical instincts..."[4] He went on to enthuse that "it is a lovely car to drive, but the gear lever has a catch which holds it in each position and till one gets used to releasing the catch, one gets messed up with the gear changing".

At the time, coachwork was bespoke on all makes of chassis. Charles opted for Salmonds' newly patented Tickford winding hood, raised and lowered by turning a cranked winding handle. A unique feature was made to Charles's own specification: the signalling device fitted to the driver's window. The car was ready just in time for the annual summer holiday. In addition to all the holiday planning a whole new set of paperwork was needed for the Rolls in order to take it abroad. Charles lamented to Joy, "I seem to have attempted to bite off a lot more than I can chew in plotting out this blinking tour. Thousands of papers and documents have already been filled in".[5]

Once again the family took the Dover to Calais passenger steamer, motoring through France, Belgium, Germany and Austria and crossing into Italy over the Brenner Pass. They arrived in the Dolomites, a range of sharply rugged mountains that separates southern Austria from Italy. Here they stayed a few days at a hotel on a secluded lake, the Lago di Braies, where the children built a raft and happily paddled around on it for hours. The beauty of the lake's deep green-blue colour, fringed with dark pine trees and tightly enclosed by mountains, would draw them back in the future.

Now that he had the driving experience and extra confidence with the Rolls, there was one Alpine pass in the Dolomites that Charles was unable to resist. At 9,030 ft the Stelvio Pass in the high Ortler mountains was then the highest mountain road in the Alps and a remarkable feat of early 19th century engineering (*Plate 2.8*). Charles Freeston could not sing its praises highly enough. Dominated by superb views of the Ortler (12,800 ft), the highest peak in Tyrol, "the Stelvio is the unquestioned king among mountain carriage-roads... while the Madatsch glacier, which almost adjoins the road, is one of the most brilliantly beautiful in the Alps".[6] The Madatsch glacier was just one of several glacier tongues descending into the steep-sided valley from the high snowfields. As Brian always clamoured for more glaciers, it had to be on their itinerary.

A LAND BELOW SEA LEVEL

The summer of 1927 saw a new passenger ferry in operation from Harwich to Flushing, and the family took the opportunity to explore the Netherlands. Arriving in the country's oldest city of Dordrecht, they took a large rowing boat out on the wide Oude Maas river amongst the many windmills. Motoring northwards they crossed Rotterdam, then a beautiful historic city before it was bombed in the Second World War. A 50 ft high windmill (*Plate 2.9*) incredibly survived the devastating bombing raid of 1940 (since the miller had the presence of mind to turn the sails during the raid and successfully fanned the flames away), only for it to burn down in 1954.

The family drove through the old towns of Den Haag and Haarlem to Amsterdam. Living in a country with more water than land, half the land lying below sea level, the Dutch had long been masters of water management. At the time the Zuiderzee was a huge shallow inlet open to the North Sea, which over the centuries had experienced regular storm incursions. After a massive storm surge in 1916, when many lives were lost and houses destroyed, action was finally taken to improve flood protection. By 1927 the huge project to dam the Zuiderzee was under way and only five years later a dyke 20 miles long would connect North Holland with Friesland. Thirty years later the seawater would be replaced by freshwater from the rivers that fed into it and the next phase could begin: land reclamation and creation of the polders. The enclosed freshwater lake was renamed Ijssel Meer. But in creating the dam and cutting off the sea, all the fishing communities all around the Zuiderzee were doomed.

The Roberts spent a day on a boat excursion to visit Marken. Out in the Zuiderzee, the island of Marken had been growing as an attraction for tourists and ethnographers as a relic of disappearing Dutch culture. Its isolation had enabled traditional costumes and a lost way of life to survive. Whilst all around the fishing industry was dying, the people of Marken were finding a novel source of income from tourism. Their timber houses were built on wooden stilts with storage space underneath, or clustered on little man-made hills (a survival from earlier times) to provide protection from tidal incursions. Families lived in one upper floor room, kept immaculate with rows of Delft china around the walls and curtained box beds. Men, women and children all wore colourful costumes and clogs.

Latemar, Dolomites

The journey continued through Germany into Austria, arriving in Salzburg and touring around the Salzkammergut lakes before driving west to Innsbruck. Heading back over the Brenner Pass into the

Dolomites, the family returned to the Lago di Braies, their favoured spot of the previous summer. Again the children had fun messing around on their raft on the lake, also spending a long day climbing in the surrounding mountains. In later years Brian and Denis would both return several times to the Lago di Braies.[7]

The family headed south along the Fadalto Pass into the Veneto towards Venice. Brian left the renaissance architectural splendour to Denis and instead found some bird life. The only record of their visit here is a photograph of Brian in the Piazza San Marco feeding the pigeons, an activity now banned because of the damage the birds cause to the buildings.

After Venice the family headed north again into the Dolomites, where from Cortina d'Ampezzo they took the Dolomitenstrasse, a scenic east-west tourist route through the heart of the Dolomites that had only recently been completed. Along its mountain passes they enjoyed some of the most superb scenery to be found in the Dolomites. At its western end they lingered at the top of the Stelvio Pass, taking in its magnificent glaciers. Here, climbing a little mountain peak then known as the Dreisprachenspitze, (so called as it formed the boundary between Austria, Switzerland and Italy until 1919), an exhilarated Brian photographed the Madatsch glacier with the high Ortler icefield above it. Immediately behind where he stood on the mountain top was the burnt-out ruin of a large hotel (*Plate 2.10*). During the Great War this region of the Alps had been the scene of incredible high altitude fighting between the Austrians and the Italians. Mountains had been blown up and tunnels dug by hand through the hard dolomite rock and even through the Ortler icefield itself. The severe winters and frequent avalanches claimed far more lives than did the fighting. Following its annexation by Italy at the end of the war in 1919 the region would still be subject to political turmoil until near the end of the 20th century. The stark landmark remained until the 1960s when the Italians renamed the mountain Cima Garibaldi and pulled down the hotel ruins, building next to it a *rifugio* for hikers. There have been other major changes. A ski resort village appeared in the 1970s, and as a result of accelerated climate change the Madatsch glacier has now completely disappeared.

3

SEABIRDS AND SMALL ISLANDS AROUND THE BRITISH ISLES

As Brian's interest in ornithology grew, he wanted to photograph birds and their nests. Having outgrown his small folding roll film camera, he wrote to his father from Uppingham School in the Spring term of 1928 to ask for a better camera. Charles wrote back proposing a deal. Brian could have a new camera in advance of his forthcoming 16th birthday when he came home for the holidays, but it must not interfere with his school work. Arriving home from Uppingham for the summer, Brian was to find a magnificent second-hand Dallmeyer 'New Naturalist' quarter-plate camera with several lenses waiting for him. His father warned that he would at first find the camera heavy, bulky and clumsy until he got used to it. Brian immediately threw himself into photographing anything that moved, from birds to fish in a tank. Even members of his family, as a last resort.

After four years of continental touring, it was time to explore the British Isles. A motor tour around Scotland was the plan. Taking the A1 Great North Road they reached the Borders, taking a diversion to Hadrian's Wall. At this time, the Wall had yet to receive serious attention from the archaeological world. Up until the mid-18th century it had been used as building material for field walls, farms and churches, much of it going into the foundations of the east-west military road created after the 1745 rebellion. Of the many forts (as yet unexcavated) along the Wall's length, Housesteads was then the only one worth a visit, combining a spectacular location with a well-preserved stretch of the Wall to see.

At the time one of Madeline's cousins was finishing his classics degree and would be embarking on his first excavation at the fort of Birdoswald. Archaeologist Eric Birley would pursue a distinguished career as one of the foremost scholars of the Roman army in Britain, resolving the problems then current in dating the Wall. In 1929 he was able to purchase the Roman fort of Vindolanda at Chesterholm; excavations there would give future generations a rich insight into daily life on the Northern Frontier.[1] But all that lay in the future.

THE FARNE ISLANDS

One of the frustrations for a budding ornithologist was that the school holiday period of August was hopeless for seeing nesting birds. Brian was now jubilant at the prospect of going out with his new camera to small islands which would still abound with seabirds and their young. He devoured everything he could find on ornithology, including one of the Kearton brothers' books pioneering the art of nature photography (Richard Kearton, *With Nature and a Camera*, 1897) which described the best places to see seabirds around the British Isles. The remarkable photographs taken by Cherry Kearton whetted Brian's appetite for what he hoped would be the highlight of his holiday.

The Farne Islands are a group of rocky islands lying off the east coast of Northumberland. Composed of hard igneous dolerite, they are the most easterly manifestation of the Great Whin Sill, a volcanic magma that pushed into the surrounding sedimentary rocks in the Carboniferous period. Exposed since the last ice age, it stretches as an imposing ridge from High Force in the north Pennines eastwards to the Farnes, and provided the Romans with a natural barrier on which to build parts of Hadrian's Wall. At the fishing village of Seahouses the family arranged with a fisherman to be taken by boat around some of the islands. Many are awkward to land on if there is any swell, and in all but calm conditions a small boat carries the risk of crashing against the rocks. There are around 28 islands in all, some low-lying and becoming completely covered by the tide. Billy Shiel's boat trips out to the islands began just after the Great War.[2] Having hauled his lobster and crab pots early in the morning, Billy would row any keen ornithologists out to the islands in his coble, the distinctive Northumbrian fishing boat with its flat bottom and high bow.

Blessed with good weather, the family were rowed out to the Outer Farnes. They were able to land on a number of islands which today are either out of bounds because of nesting birds, or too difficult to land on with larger modern craft. Until the early 1920s the islands received two kinds of visitor, the naturalist and the day tripper. Unfortunately the latter was no bird lover and would think nothing of destroying eggs or young, either accidentally or intentionally. Protective measures were taken in 1923, restricting access during the nesting season to only three of the islands and limiting the time allowed on Staple Island to 15 minutes. A public appeal by the Farne Islands Association raised funds to buy the islands (then privately owned) and to hand them over to National Trust management in 1924.[3] Renowned for the immense diversity of migrating birds which stop off in spring and autumn, the islands also teem with breeding seabirds throughout the summer. In August when the Roberts visited, the young were already well grown.

The Farne Islands have been well served with lighthouses. The surrounding seabed is a mass graveyard of shipwrecks, a telling sign of the hazardous nature of the islands for sea traffic. Considering the challenges for Brian to take photographs with his new heavy camera whilst bobbing up and down in a boat, his results were remarkably successful. They rowed around some of the smaller islands: Harcar, with a cormorant colony, and the North and South Wamses. Landing on the Brownsman, Brian had his first encounter with puffins. Here, as on Staple Island, there is enough depth of soil covering on the rocks to support a population of rabbits and puffins 'timesharing' burrows. That year, 1928, it had been exceptionally wet in mid-June and many of the nesting holes had been flooded, completely burying the eggs in mud.[4] Since puffins invest everything in laying a single egg, many of the birds had laid again and unusually there were still considerable numbers of puffins around with their youngsters, a stroke of luck for the young ornithologist.

Out on the Pinnacles, a magnificent group of sea stacks, guillemots were crammed onto every inch of space along the top, whilst nesting

The Pinnacles, Staple Island

kittiwakes occupied all the ledges in the gullies. Brian spotted a razorbill and its egg. There were very few pairs about, the birds having almost died out there in the late 19th century. The black, almost reptilian, cormorants fascinated him, with their huge nests full of half-grown young. Historically cormorants have not had a good time here. Until the 1950s and even later they were considered vermin by the local fishermen because of the large amount of fish they consume, and in spite of official protection the eggs were routinely destroyed by unofficial landing parties. Not surprisingly the birds endeavoured to select nesting

Cormorants on the Megstone

sites which were the most inaccessible to humans; on the Farnes those were the smaller, flat-topped islands North Wamses, Little Harcar and the isolated Megstone, their safest ancient abode. Landing on Megstone enabled Brian to study them at close quarters and even audaciously to provide a fish meal for a nest of hungry youngsters.

Rowing around the seabird city, Brian's interest was aroused by the bobbing heads of one or two grey seals in the sea, quite a rare sight at this time and a first for him. In the past the grey seal has struggled to survive against man's depredations. The Farnes were then their only breeding site on the east coast, presenting an easy target for hunters when the mothers came ashore in the autumn to give birth to their pups on land. Hunted indiscriminately across their north Atlantic range to produce lamp oil and make sealskin boots, they were slaughtered all around the coasts. Numbers plummeted in the late 19th century as the trade turned into an unregulated export business. Were it not for the invention of cheap rubber boots for fishermen and a more efficient lighting fluid (paraffin), seals might well not be seen at all today around British coasts. They were close to extirpation, and only with government regulation introduced in 1932 did the species turn a corner towards recovery.[5] Claiming that seals reduce fish stocks and damage farmed salmon stocks, the Scottish fishing industry was then, and is still today, responsible for much of the killing. Recovery has been slow, but today the Farne Islands have a grey seal population of some 6,000.

THE BASS ROCK

Just over a mile out in the mouth of the Firth of Forth lies a massive volcanic rock with near vertical 350 ft high cliffs, home for a long time to the world's largest colony of northern gannets. The Bass Rock gives the bird its scientific name *Sula bassanus*. While the rest of the Roberts were happily scrambling around the ruins of Tantallion Castle, Brian wistfully observed the rock through his camera's telephoto lens. Having read about the Kearton brothers' visits he would have given the world to get out to it by boat. Covering much of the top was a grassy green patch, which has since been replaced by a white capping of guano as the gannet gained protection and its population multiplied. Over the centuries eggs and young birds were collected in huge numbers, not just to feed the lighthouse keepers and other human inhabitants of the rock, but harvested as a highly profitable business for its laird owner. In spite of their fishy taste the young birds, almost the size of a goose, were considered a delicacy by the Scots.

From Edinburgh the Roberts made a long loop around the Firth of Forth via Stirling (there was no road bridge at Queensferry until 1964) and headed north through the Cairngorms. Breaking the journey at Perth, Brian dived into the local Natural History Museum to look at the Gallery of Stuffed Birds. One exhibit caught his eye in a glass case crammed full of bits of birds and their skulls. Dwarfing its neighbours, a toucan and a cormorant head, was a huge skull with a massive tubenose bill which Brian photographed. The label just said 'Albatross'.

On the road again, the highland scenery became more rugged as they motored alongside the railway to Inverness across the Grampian moors. At the time most visitors to the Highlands came by rail and/or passenger steamer. The sportsman travelled by train, to be collected by chauffeured car from the station and transported to a lochside hotel with its own fishing rights. Guidebooks only considered it necessary to inform the reader of the best salmon fishing lochs and the nearest golf course. Such was the poor state of the roads that well into the 1950s the independent motorist seldom toured Scotland and was recommended not to attempt more than 50 miles a day. The Roberts in their Rolls Royce – three young men in tweed jackets, flannel wool trousers and tweed flat caps – would have blended nicely into the landscape. But the lack of native trees and wildlife did not escape their notice. For the landowners of Scotland's huge estates the business has always been maintaining deer forest, grouse moor and salmon fishing. Birds of prey were – and still are – exterminated by gamekeepers to protect grouse moors, and other native birds were bagged by sportsmen and their eggs by collectors. Protection measures would be slow to arrive in Scotland. From the Viking period down to the 20th century vast tracts of Scotland's ancient Caledonian forest have been cleared: burned to flush out wolves (as well as native people), sold to be felled for industrial fuel, and after the 1745 uprising cut down to improve sheep pasture. Until recently Scotland's forests were considered an entirely expendable economic commodity.

Motoring through a bleak landscape of interminable moorland and bog, the family reached Lairg. Here the road northwards divides and the motorist was recommended by an early 20th century guidebook to take the left fork via Laxford Bridge as the better road. The route runs alongside the 17-mile long Loch Shin, most of it described in the same guide as "little better than a huge ditch".[6] Charles, by now accustomed to Scottish roads, took the right fork via Altnaharra to Loch Eriboll. The guidebook also warns that after the ferry crossing "there is a steep rise of 3 miles and an exceedingly precipitous descent to Eriboll over a bad and loose surface; the road takes a great zigzag to lessen the gradient, but even this is dangerous to negotiate".[7] Along this 20-mile stretch of rough narrow single-track road skirting the flanks of Ben More, they encountered the massively thick round walls of Dun Dornaigil, one of

Dun Dornaigil

the best preserved brochs in northern Scotland. It could not be missed even in a thick Scottish mist. Reaching Eriboll on the north coast they now enjoyed a stunning stretch of rocky coastline, motoring westwards to Durness with its striking white limestone cliffs, to savour the bracing Atlantic winds and beautiful sandy beaches.

From Durness the road turns south. Taking the more tortuous coast road where possible, they were rewarded with spectacular scenery. Along this stretch of north-west Scotland a number of ferries operated across the sea lochs. The Kylesku ferry at this time was a basic motorized wooden boat, with ramps able to take cattle or a car.[8] (*Plate 3.1*)

The family continued south and then diverted west to Loch Maree. After so much barren landscape it was a relief to revel in some ancient Caledonian pine forest, staying awhile on one of Scotland's loveliest lochs, which 23 years later would become part of Scotland's first National Nature Reserve. Gracing the shores of the loch were tall junipers and even a few oak trees, hundreds of which had been felled in the 17th century as fuel for the local iron industry. Dozens of tree-covered little islands invited exploration, and the boys worked off their pent-up energy indulging in the traditional family pastime of raft-building. There was no shortage of wood. It lay everywhere, and with the finding of some empty oil drums the rafts could be given good buoyancy. Even for the tough Roberts boys the water was cold, with their tweed jackets pressed into service worn over swimming trunks.

In the days before affordable cars the best way to see the landscape of western Scotland was by steamer, linked by rail from Glasgow. One of the most popular routes was advertised in 1928 as 'The Grandest One Day Tour in the British Isles'. Leaving their car behind at Oban, the Roberts took the day trip around the islands of Mull and Staffa, the latter already a famous attraction with its caves and spectacular basalt columnar jointing. In good weather it was possible to land by rowing boat and walk deep inside Fingal's Cave. The steamer left at 8 am and on board one could enjoy 'Breakfast, Dinner and Plain Tea' for an inclusive price of 27 shillings and sixpence, returning to Oban at 6 pm.

Continuing southward, the boys enjoyed one last bit of rocky coast before heading home. Ten miles south-west of Oban, Clachan Sound separates the island of Seil from the mainland, spanned at its narrowest point by the elegant humpback Clachan Bridge. North of the bridge the narrow channel of tidal seawater is bordered by steep rugged cliffs. Today covered in vegetation and trees, the jagged rocks were then bare.

Oban, engraving c.1880

Staffa, postcard c.1900

Brian headed up to the cliff-top for a sea view, spotting a golden eagle's eyrie some way down on a cliff ledge. The nest was empty, but it was September and any young would have long since flown. Close to the coast, but with a sheltered aspect, the nest site should have been safe, but along with other birds of prey golden eagles were tolerated neither by the managers of the grouse moors nor by sheep farmers, and they were relentlessly shot, trapped or poisoned. Risking his neck on the unstable vertical cliff face, Brian climbed a few yards down, determined to photograph it. He could only speculate as to whether its owners had been successful in raising a chick there or not.

Clachan Bridge

CANOEING DOWN THE WYE

In October 1928 Brian turned 16 (*Plate 3.2*) and was now keen to plan his own holiday adventure. He wrote to his father from school, hoping that in the forthcoming Easter holidays he could hire a boat with Pat, and perhaps Denis too, to go off by themselves to explore the coastline somewhere. After years of holidaying as a happy, self-contained family unit ('clan Roberts' as his father put it) Brian, though the youngest, was the one who most sought his independence, giving his parents a few sleepless nights before Charles gave his considered reply that going out to sea was not sensible unless they engaged the services of a professional boatman, and even then it would be fraught with risks.[9] It would be much safer to stay in a harbour somewhere. After much discussion an alternative plan evolved: to make a canoe trip down the River Wye "because it is the most beautiful river in the South of the British Isles, and because it offers over 100 miles of really interesting navigation including plenty of rapids".[10]

The party of four consisted of Brian, Pat, their cousin Anthony Paddison (two years older than Brian and now at Rugby) and another Rugby boy, Johnson. They would take two canoes. Brian was in his element organising the trip, consulting numerous guide books and river navigation handbooks. "Ward Lock & Co's guide book to the Wye valley was not very encouraging, and nor were other people. Nearly everyone seemed to think the Wye a really dangerous river and many people thought it very unwise for us to be allowed to go, but this only made us want to go all the more."[11] Advice from the guidebook told them to allow a fortnight for the 104-mile passage from Hay-on-Wye to Chepstow. Brian thought it should be possible in four to five days.

The trip was made possible by the existence of a railway line running alongside the Wye for much of the way between Glasbury (near Hay) and Chepstow. Today the railway is gone, leaving just a handful of disused railway bridges across the lower Wye as a memory of the gloriously scenic line. Driving by car to their starting point at Glasbury, they would hire two canoes from a boatman at Ross-on-Wye, asking him to send them up there by train. At the end of the river trip, Pat would return by train from Chepstow to collect the car from Glasbury and the canoes would be returned to Ross by train.

On 16 April Brian, Pat and Anthony left Woking at first light in the family's small Clyno car and drove to Glasbury, where they met Johnson who had arrived by train. All went according to plan. The two 15 ft long canoes were waiting on the station "and we got them down to the river by putting one end on the hood of the Clyno and holding onto the other end while walking behind".

At noon they were off, in good weather. From the outset there were plenty of rapids, some needing to be checked out before being attempted, but in most cases the boys could take their chances, leaping out into the cold water if necessary to manoeuvre the canoe. But rocks were another hazard, sticking up everywhere the first few miles, especially around Hay. Brian and Pat crashed their canoe headlong into a rock at speed and had to leap out either side into the chilly, fast flowing water up to their knees. An unfortunate consequence was that one of the floor planks cracked, and from there until Hereford they had to bail out every hour. To keep their possessions dry they packed the bottom of the boat with branches and laid their stuff on top. By evening they were at Whitney, having made only ten miles, and making Chepstow in four days was starting to look over-optimistic. The Boat Inn at Whitney could provide only one double bed for the four of them, but managed to find two more beds at a cottage nearby for Brian and Pat. Everyone was in good spirits and enjoying the fun, and the weather was sunny, though there was a cold wind.

The next morning was fine again, but in the strong, cold wind the river was quite rough. They attempted unsuccessfully to set up a sail. Farther downstream at Monnington they reached the most notorious stretch of the Wye. Here the river divides around an island: on one side there is a narrow and deep channel with a 3 ft fall over a steep stony ledge, and on the other a long incline which generally leads to a good deal of keel-scraping. The water was lower that year than anyone could ever remember, and the wider channel was bone dry. Brian recorded what happened next.

Monnington Fall

"Rounding a bend, we saw the island in front and heard the roar of the fall and rapids below. We landed on the island by wading and after a thorough examination decided to shoot the fall on the left [the narrow channel], but first we carried all the gear across the right channel and down the bank to a place below the rapids where we could pick it up again, and had lunch on the island. The primus comes in very useful. It is excellent to have hot soup for meals when we are wet and cold. Somehow everything cooked on that stove seems to get flavoured with paraffin, but it is delicious all the same.

"First Anthony and Johnson shot it while Pat and I watched and I took a photo, which unfortunately doesn't show in the least how bad the fall was.

"The fall is a drop of about 2½ feet. This seems nothing till you actually come to shoot a fall that height and then it becomes quite formidable. In avoiding the rocks on either side (there was only a gap of about a yard wide to steer for) they struck something underneath – I'm not sure what as they must have been going at least 20 miles an hour – and just managed to keep upright although the canoe was half filled with water.

"Then Pat and I did the same, missing all the rocks, and shot it beautifully, but we were so excited at this that we crashed into a tree overhanging the rapid just below the fall. However, we only shipped about two gallons of water and arrived at the other end of the island just in time to see the other two wading nearly up to their waists and pulling their waterlogged canoe after them.

"A Welsh terrier has followed us down the bank all the way from Whitney and won't leave us, so we have temporarily adopted him and will return him on our way back to fetch the car at Glasbury. We call him Montmorency Rufus after *Three Men in a Boat*. M. Rufus gave us plenty of entertainment since he enjoyed both being chased by cows and chasing sheep along the banks, which he would then follow by swimming out to one of the canoes to be lifted in, whereupon he'd shake himself, drenching everything." [12]

By the end of their second day the boys were becoming adept at shooting the rapids, bar the odd mishap such as getting caught up in a tree or going down backwards. Having made a respectable 25 miles that day, they arrived at Hereford in the evening, where they celebrated "out of all proportion to the rest of the trip, we have got a magnificent room with two double beds, in Mr Jordan's house overlooking the river by the bridge". Dick Jordan was Hereford's boat builder, whose boats could be rented on the river bank opposite the Cathedral by the old medieval bridge.

"In the morning we got Mr Jordan to mend our boat with a bit of copper and got started down the river at about 10 o'clock. After more rapids we had lunch on a little island and I cooked sausages and fried bread. The thing which reminds me most of that island is the thought of a very long dead sheep which Rufus spent most of his time rolling in."

This was their third day and they managed 28 miles, getting to Ross-on-Wye by the evening. They again stayed in a hotel overlooking the river and went to the cinema after dinner. "We wrote our names in the visitors' book and also Rufus as he was one of the party. The bill was sent in to Mr Montmorency Rufus, and the proprietors never knew which of us it was."

The next day they aimed to complete their journey and arrive at Chepstow in time to drive home by car. The rapids were becoming less hazardous as the river reached its lower course, but other challenges were in store. At Symonds Yat, a spectacular U-shaped bend in the river, they got out and climbed up to the top of a cliff by the river bank and "were so hot when we got down that we all bathed in the river in spite of its icy coldness". They then set off, aiming 20 miles downstream to their destination for the night, an inn at Monmouth.

> "And here began our troubles. We went to a Cinema after dinner and Anthony left in the middle feeling rotten. We got back to the Inn afterwards to find him being violently sick, and then ditto for Johnson during the night. Pat and I remained quite alright. However they seemed more or less better in the morning so we decided to carry on.
> "Shortly below Monmouth came a possible explanation – a sewer emptying into the river, and we had been drinking the river water as at every cottage we asked for water, they told us they used the Wye water. We never knew whether it was that or the chops we had at the Inn at Monmouth – they were rancid.
> "Anyway the other two recovered almost completely, and just as we started I began to feel sick – very sick. We carried on, drifting with the current most of the way, while Pat steered, and determined to get to Chepstow. Again a succession of rapids and luckily a strong current nearly all the way. At Bigsweir Pat got out to take the Wye Valley Railway to return to Glasbury, get the car, and meet us at Chepstow in the evening. We went on and got to Tintern at about midday – taking it in turns to steer the single canoe."

From just above Tintern the river becomes tidal, and conditions change considerably.

> "It is necessary to leave Tintern at high water, or before, as soon as the flood tide slackens, because at low water the falls are very bad indeed and the channels through them are continually changing. Also the banks on either side are 20 or 30 feet of semi-liquid mud on a steep incline and landing is quite impossible. In fact, the result of a mishap would be pretty serious.
> "We went down to have a look at the first weir and decided at once to wait till about 4.30 pm when the tide would have risen enough. We wasted time lying on a bank above the ruins of the Abbey – the others having lunch of

apples and some of the greenest cider I ever saw. By the time the tide was high enough to start I was feeling much better, and we got on quite fast for about a mile but then we found the canoe with two in was always having to wait for the other one. Finally we tried all three getting in one canoe and towing the other, with the result that it acted like a rudder and we just went in a zig-zag course from bank to bank. The strong tidal current upstream soon got so troublesome that we decided to wait for it to change and we moored to some reeds in the mud on the left bank.

"After about half an hour we went on again with a coat set up as a sail, but the wind only came in puffs and we went very slowly over the last 6 miles to Chepstow – arriving just before 8 o'clock. The landing here was something quite new. The river water in all the tidal part of the Wye is very muddy indeed and at Chepstow it is quite as thick as pea-soup. On arrival at the slipway we found an incline of about 15 feet covered all over with about four inches of liquid mud and we had to lift the canoes up through this, getting everything filthy.

"But we had done the 103 miles as we had wanted – only taking four days instead of the fortnight the guide said was necessary. We sent the canoes back to Ross by train, and Pat arrived with the car just as it was beginning to get dark. We didn't want to waste any time having dinner so we bought a large packet of fish and chips and started home thinking we would sleep somewhere on the way. However we soon decided to go on driving all night as Pat was beginning to feel rotten, and we had to stop periodically for him to get out and be sick. Anthony and I took it in turns to drive and it was jolly cold work. First we went to Malvern and dropped Johnson at about 2 o'clock, and then finally reached Woking at about 6.30 am and got in at the scullery window. And so ended this very enjoyable little trip."

Brian rounded off this first diary account of his with a financial statement: a detailed breakdown of their expenditure, including the canoe rental at 7 shillings each per day, accommodation, food, cinema, landing fees and tips for boatmen etc. and a dog collar at 9 pence, presumably needed for Montmorency Rufus.

BIRD RINGING ON THE ISLES OF SCILLY

In the late 1920s the bible for the serious ornithologist was H F Witherby's *Practical Handbook of British Birds*, published in three volumes between 1920 and 1924. Brian somehow laid his hands on a copy, and spent his pocket money on a subscription to *British Birds*, a magazine published monthly by Witherby. With his particular interest in seabirds he was aware of the growth of bird ringing, which would begin to provide a better understanding of migration and of individual birds' movements. Brian persuaded his father to organise a summer holiday on the Isles of Scilly and camp on the uninhabited island of Annet, known as Bird Island since it had the richest concentration of bird life on the Scillies.

From Witherby's *Practical Handbook* it was clear that, whilst all species were fully described from dead specimens and measured to the last feather, there were two whose breeding habits were almost unknown. Both were small members of the tubenose family which includes albatross and fulmar: the Manx shearwater and the European storm petrel, both of which were believed to breed on the more inaccessible rocky islands of the British Isles.[13] Why were these birds not better understood? As well as choosing breeding sites as far removed as possible from human disturbance, their breeding activity is entirely nocturnal. In the days before infrared camera technology, the study of any nocturnal species such as owls (or even a mammal like the badger) was challenging. Over the next decade studies began that would not only transform our knowledge of the nesting habits of these two seabird species but unlock some of the secrets of seabird navigation. Brian was going to play a part in this movement, but his work would be in Antarctica with a different species of storm petrel. The same year that Brian was browbeating his family into an uncomfortable camping expedition to search for these elusive birds, the young naturalist Ronald Lockley was starting his pioneering studies of the Manx shearwater on the island of Skokholm, off the Pembrokeshire coast. Lockley had a considerable advantage over Brian in that he was actually living on Skokholm and could spend many more hours in nocturnal discomfort studying the shearwater and its smaller cousin the storm petrel. Lockley's formative work would set him on a path to become one of Britain's outstanding naturalists and conservationists of the 20th century.

Essential to these studies was the need to ring the birds under study. In Britain Witherby had started a bird ringing scheme in 1909 through *British Birds,* in which the results were published.[14] This was a great incentive to its readership to participate. The first year of Witherby's scheme (1909) produced 2,171 ringed birds. By 1929 the number had risen to 25,243. At the time Witherby made the rings himself and the ringer paid 1½ pence each for them. Unfortunately the aluminium rings needed replacing every year or two as they wore out or were lost, especially when used for seabirds. It was not until 1958 that corrosion-resistant Monel (nickel-copper) alloys became available.

I'll ring you in the morning!

On 12 August 1929, Charles, Denis, Pat and Brian drove to Penzance to board the passenger steamer RMV *Scillonian* to St Mary's, the largest island of the Scillies. An experienced boatman was needed not only to sail them to Annet but also to row them around some of the smaller uninhabited islands and rocky islets, with local knowledge to negotiate currents, tides and submerged rocks, and to find the best landing spots. Securing the services of Nance and his two-masted dinghy *Rover* with a small rowing boat in tow, they sailed over to Annet. Supplies of fresh water were landed with them in large stoneware flagons, along with their primus stove, food, sleeping bags, cameras and bird ringing equipment.

The Isles of Scilly are a low-lying group of granite islands out in the Atlantic Ocean some 28 miles south-west of the western tip of Cornwall.

They abound in history, mystery and shipwrecks with terrible loss of life. The five largest islands are inhabited by humans; there are around 200 which are not, varying in size from several acres and covered with vegetation, to clusters of rocks and islets. Annet is just over half a mile long. Apart from several rocky granite protrusions known as carns which provide the only shelter, it is low-lying and washed over periodically by storms, its shores ringed by great boulder beaches. In the lee of a carn the Roberts pitched their tents. Not too far off for Brian to fumble his way in the dark was an area of squidgy tussocks of thrift where the Manx shearwaters had their nesting burrows. The storm petrels on the other hand were elusive, hiding under the huge boulders of the storm beach and they would take a lot of finding.

It would be another year before Brian began his lifelong habit of diary keeping, and there is no written account of Annet other than his submissions to *British Birds*. Fortunately his photographs survive and he was often the first to leap out of the boat with his camera to scramble up a rocky islet and capture a picture of the party making a hazardous-looking landing. There were plenty of those on Hanjague, Castle Bryher, Mincarlo and Illiswilgig (*Plate 3.3*). The first two are little more than steep-faced rocky islets and the boys could not resist climbing to the tops of them, no doubt to the indignation of the seabird residents.

Hanjague

Helped by Denis, Pat and their father, Brian ringed 100 Manx shearwaters plus a further 70 seabirds, including greater black-backed gulls, shags and cormorants (*Plate 3.4*). Many, if not all, would have been fledglings. Brian did not get much sleep that holiday and almost certainly the rest of the family didn't either. The shearwaters come ashore only in total darkness, to visit their nesting burrows and swap parental duties or to bring food for the nestling. During those hours the air is filled with a cacophony of huge numbers of crying birds overlaid by their eerie raucous cooing calls. The sounds are so strange and unlike other seabirds that even Ronald Lockley admitted that they defied description. Their nocturnal comings and goings avoid the worst of their predators, in particular the black-backed gulls. When Brian spent his nights observing the shearwater's awkward shuffling locomotion on land he could see why they were hopelessly vulnerable in daytime: "They seemed quite incapable of rising straight into the air but flapped along the ground on their fully-extended wings, increasing their speed until they reached the water's edge, at which point they seemed to gain sufficient impetus to leave the ground.... As far as could be seen all returning birds flew straight to their burrows."[15] But how do you study the egg incubation period and fledgling development of a bird that lays its single egg far down beyond human reach inside their burrow, hatching and feeding their chick in such a dark and inaccessible place? Lockley devised a means, and Brian – who was not able to observe any below-ground nocturnal breeding activity on this occasion – would employ the same method later in the Antarctic.

Neither Charles, nor Pat, nor Denis had any inclination for camp cooking. Brian on the other hand was happy to notch up another essential skill for an explorer. Getting up first to brew everyone a cup of tea and then knocking up four mugfuls of porridge slurry for breakfast was simple enough with the primus stove (*Plate 3.5*). But photographs of the family with long faces rationing a tin of digestive biscuits suggest inadequate provisioning for the evening meal. There were cans of ham, corned beef and even Libby's cooked lunch tongue, but they had forgotten to buy potatoes, and with four days of camping they were all ravenous from the sea air and their exertions.

The following April they were all back again on Annet. Hilary (who had recently begun to work for Charles as his medical secretary) and her friend were with them. With the two girls in charge of catering there were now proper hot meals and lunches from the picnic basket. On this second visit Brian brought his big wooden camera tripod in order to get some close-up bird photographs, especially of shearwaters and storm petrels (*Plate 3.6*). They explored some of the smaller islands with the girls, adding a few new ones including Rosevear and Rosevean. This time there was no more bird ringing, but as it was now spring Brian could for the first time observe seabirds in the early stages of breeding.

IRELAND, SUMMER 1930

The summer holiday for 1930 was to be a tour of southern Ireland, with a visit to the Irish branch of the Roberts family at Carrigaline in County Cork. Brian of course had his own plans to work into the timetable. He also kept a diary.[16]

Spending a first day and night in Dublin following an overnight crossing, Brian was able to do some homework on the islands on his wish-list. The family then set off across the country for Clifden and Connemara on the west coast, a distance of some 280 miles. To Brian the wild and desolate Connemara scenery seemed to be nothing but peat bogs and lakes, but he was also struck by the poverty and the desperate way of life of its people. In 1930 the population of Ireland was just under 3 million, the majority living in the countryside in small county towns and villages. For the rural poor in many parts of Ireland, but especially the west and its Atlantic coastal islands, life was on the edge. The infertile land had to be constantly nourished with seaweed to enable them to grow their one staple crop, potatoes. By Western standards, rural Ireland was trailing miserably. Electricity was only just starting to arrive in the late 1920s; Carrigaline was not connected until 1937, and even by 1943 only half the Irish population were connected. Following the Great Famine in the mid-19th century many survivors had emigrated to America, and there was still a constant trickle of people leaving for a better life. Years with a bad harvest due to excessive rain still occurred and starvation was never far away. The recently-established independent Irish Government that followed the Irish Civil War at the beginning of the 1920s had failed to tackle this huge issue.

SKELLIG ROCKS

From Galway the Roberts headed south to Kerry and around the Dingle Peninsula, via Killarney onto the Iveragh Peninsula and out to Valentia Island. Brian, now focused on what he hoped would be the high point of the holiday, was full of *angst* as he contemplated the slender chances of getting out to the place of his dreams: the Skellig Rocks. These two extraordinary islands, eight miles out from the Kerry coast, rise almost vertically from the ocean into jagged, craggy pinnacles, Skellig Michael to 715 ft and Little Skellig to 445 ft (*Plate 3.7*). Almost – but not quite – inaccessible to humans, they teem with breeding seabirds. George Bernard Shaw, following a visit in 1910, described his experience in a letter to a friend.

> "The most fantastic and impossible rock in the world: Skellig Michael… where in south west gales the spray knocks stones out of the lighthouse keeper's house… the Skelligs are pinnacled, crocketed, spired, arched, caverned, minaretted; and these gothic extravagances are not curiosities of the islands: they are the islands: there is nothing else. The rest of the cathedral may be under the sea for all I know… An incredible, impossible, mad place… I tell you the thing does not belong to any world that you and I have lived and worked in: it is part of our dream world."

Skellig Michael in fact has a long history of human habitation. Between the 6th and 8th centuries a small community of monks lived in beehive cells perched high up amongst the crags near the top.

Seen on a sunny day these magical islands are awesome enough, but when partly shrouded in mist they acquire a mystical eeriness. Today tourists can get there by a 45 minute trip in a covered diesel motorboat, but in 1930 the only means was an open boat: either hiring a fisherman or hitching a lift on the Irish Lighthouse Board's relief boat which once a fortnight took supplies to the lighthouse keepers. Brian had done his homework, but ultimately all plans are dictated by the weather. The Kerry rain lived up to its reputation, continuing relentlessly for five days while Brian stared gloomily out of his hotel window. On the fifth day the rain was accompanied by a north-westerly gale. By the sixth day Brian was crawling up the wall. He would need all his powers of persuasion to get the two reluctant hired fishermen to take them out.

At last Charles and the three boys were able to board the open boat, the two fearful oarsmen rowing hard for 3½ hours in rough, choppy seas – several times wanting to turn back – until Little Skellig was reached. As they approached, everywhere around became dense with flying birds. This was the breeding home to 9,000 pairs of the northern gannet (today the population has increased to 35,000 pairs, one of the world's largest colonies). But landing was impossible. In historic times the colony was raided annually to harvest the large, goose-sized young birds which would fetch a good price, as they did at the Bass Rock, but other than these raiding parties few people have ever managed to land on Little Skellig.

Two more miles of hard rowing brought them to Skellig Michael. In such choppy conditions the boatmen were fearful of attempting to land, but with the help of the lighthouse keepers and some rope they succeeded in landing at the main slipway, in the shelter of a cavern on the north side. From there the party took the winding narrow path clinging to the vertical cliff face up to the lighthouse (*Plate 3.8*). From there it was still up and up: over 600 steps with a sheer drop to the Atlantic Ocean on one side, to the second peak with the monastery and the monks' beehive cells. Coming back down they were invited in by the lighthouse keepers for tea before starting back to the mainland. Brian was suddenly struck with the terrible thought that after such a short time he would have to leave this island that he had wanted to visit for so long. He begged his family to leave him behind and the lighthouse keepers to let him stay.

"The others left, and soon I had the thrill of seeing them disappear into the thickening mist, and to remain with the men on the rock until the following Monday (it was then Friday) when the commissioners relief boat was expected to come over with provisions. There were seven men on the island – four lightkeepers and three workmen who were repairing some damage done by a great storm during the winter. All were extraordinarily nice, and from them I learnt an enormous amount about lighthouses and shipwrecks...

"The first thing to do was to decide where I should sleep. There was no spare bed and finally it was decided that I should sleep in the same one as the Principal Keeper. I besought to be allowed to sleep on the floor, but it was no good... The bed was only about 3 feet wide and I passed a sleepless night wedged tight between the wall and my well-meaning host."

The second night he slept on the floor and was much more comfortable. Not having anticipated a stay on the rock, Brian had only the clothes he was wearing, plus his camera and a supply of film. He spent the first day climbing and enjoying the rich birdlife, accompanied by shrieking gulls reminding him that he was an intruder. Thousands of gannets were nesting on a neighbouring rock stack, while fulmars, shearwaters, puffins, a pair of peregrine falcons and a family of young ravens were the real owners of the rock.

On the Sunday Brian was up early, helping with jobs. Everyone then tucked into a mid-morning breakfast of bread and butter (both nearly two weeks old by then), washed down with tea. Afterwards he was off with the men to climb to the tiny drystone chapel, perched high up the cliff amongst the other early monastery buildings. It was almost pitch dark inside, with only just room for five of them. "Frank read the service in Gaelic and a raven came and sat croaking just above our heads on the roof, creating a far deeper impression than any cathedral service could ever have done."

> "[Every day] we had lunch and dinner combined at about 3 o'clock and at first I found it very hard to eat practically the whole day's food supply all at one go. Especially as we had the same every day. At the beginning of the week a huge mass of 'hoosh' is made, and each day it is heated up for lunch. Hoosh consists of bully beef, dried peas and potato, but there is nothing like cliff climbing to give a really good appetite and we washed it down with rainwater collected on the roof."

After mid-afternoon lunch the man on the first night watch went to bed. At around 5 pm it was time to seek out some of the other members of the island community. There were three goats, which provided fresh milk every day. Someone had the scary job of driving them along the narrow ledges hundreds of feet above the sea down to the little rock platform outside the lighthouse to be milked. In bad weather the goats often could not be found at all, and being obstinate by nature, as Brian found, they usually took a long time to milk, "but this was the most delicious luxury on the island and was always worth the trouble".

> "At about 8 o'clock the lantern would be lit and the huge 3 ton lens set in revolution. The night was divided into 3 watches, 8-12, 12-4 & 4-8 and on the third night I was allowed to be solely responsible for the 8-12 watch. The job was very easy and consisted of winding up the weight mechanism every half hour and seeing that the oil jet did

not choke. It was a wonderful feeling to sit inside the lens as it revolved, and on other nights I used to sit inside this with one of the keepers and talk…There is hardly anywhere in the world where one of the men had not been so there is heaps to talk about…We had a wireless set and so could hear what was happening on the mainland although the Skellig is the only Irish lighthouse which has no communication with the shore.

"Monday 25 August. The relief boat was due today, but a great storm came on during the night with very rough seas, which was closely followed by a thick fog. The relief boat hasn't been able to come so I am still here."

By now they had finished the stale remains of their bread supply, and in the afternoon Brian had a lesson in bread-making, His first efforts were on his own admission "a heavy mass of brown dough tasting very strongly of soda". But he was notching up another skill that he would find invaluable in the Antarctic.

"Tuesday 26 August. Fog signal going solidly for 48 hours now without a break… at first the explosions (which are audible 25 miles away) made me jump every time but after a bit I got used to it and was able to sleep quite easily."

Brian was allowed to take some of the 4-hour watches, working at the fog signal. "Our signal consisted of three explosions every ten minutes. Each charge is 2 oz of tonite with a fulminate of mercury detonator, and all these have to be carried along a narrow little cliff path to a small wooden hut about three hundred feet up the cliff face some distance from the lighthouse. During a fog each man has eight hours on watch instead of only four, and four hours in the signal house gives anyone a splitting headache." Brian observed that another job of the lighthouse keepers was the keeping of detailed records on the weather conditions, known privately amongst themselves as 'the book o' lies' for its accuracy.

The next day the fog lifted, but there was still no relief boat. "Even the tobacco has run out – this is apparently worse than the food [running out] and Christie is smoking tea leaves which smell beastly."

Finally, after 52 hours of storm and fog, the relief boat arrived on the Thursday morning. A busy morning was spent lugging empty provision boxes down to the slipway. The lighthouse keepers had not been ashore for three months and were looking forward especially to some fresh food. But there was also great anxiety: the boat was displaying a flag, which normally signalled the presence of an inspector. Brian's impromptu stay on the island was strictly against the rules, and there could be big trouble. There was huge relief all round when it was discovered that no inspector was on board.

After three hours of rolling on the choppy sea Brian was back at Valentia Island. By this time the family had moved on. He travelled on a goods train to Killarney, where they had been anxiously waiting for him for four days. Travelling south from Kerry into County Cork, they explored one last rugged peninsula, Mizen Head, before turning eastwards towards Cork. To the south-east of the city lay the enclave of the Irish branch of the Roberts family.

THE IRISH ROBERTS

The next few days were spent meeting up with Irish cousins and visiting several of the old Georgian houses built for the Roberts family. Mount Rivers, in the small town of Carrigaline, was by country house standards small, but it was well-proportioned with large airy rooms. The house had been acquired in 1784 by William Roberts, whose oldest son Michael then lived there, marrying Frances Farmer in 1826 to have eleven children. One of them – Poulter Benjamin – was Brian's grandfather.

Mount Rivers, c.1915

At Mount Rivers they met Hodder Walworth Blacker Roberts and his family. A first cousin of Charles and the same age, he had begun a business venture a couple of years earlier, putting back into use the recently closed down family-owned flax mill next to the river and the nearby sea harbour. The enterprise was founded on his hunch that the local clay might be good for making pottery – there being already a brickworks close by – and this prompted him to dig some up, make a pot and fire it in the Aga stove. The results looking promising, he took a sample of the clay to Stoke-on-Trent, hoping to gain interest. But no support was forthcoming, and he was about to leave for home feeling dejected when he came across a young newly-trained potter, Louis Keeling, who came from a long line of Staffordshire potters. Keeling successfully made and fired a teapot from the red earthenware and decided to move to Ireland with his family to help Hodder found the Carrigaline Pottery in 1928.

At the time of the visit there were just six employees under Keeling's guidance. Over the next few decades the Carrigaline Pottery would become the main local source of employment, with up to 250 employees, producing several highly successful ranges from beautiful green and blue glazed art pottery to practical everyday ware and decorated souvenir wares for tourists. One of the factory stamp logos marking the  1930s pottery is curious, as it depicts the outline of Skellig Michael rock. Skellig Michael is in County Kerry, not County Cork. Whether this was due to Brian's influence can only be guessed.

Of the nearby Georgian residences with Roberts family connections, the grandest was Britfieldstown, an elegant 9-bay stone house rebuilt in the 1730s by Randal Roberts. It looked across a 200-acre estate towards Roberts Cove, facing the Atlantic Ocean between Cork and Kinsale. The last family member to live there, Sir Walter Roberts, fled to France heavily in debt and died bankrupt in 1828. Ownership of the house and estate passed through two other families, increasingly becoming a liability. Derelict by the 1950s it was finally demolished in 1984.

A gathering of the clans was organised with eighteen Roberts of all generations enjoying a day sea bathing at Kinsale, where the visitors were intrigued to find not only a Roberts Cove but also a Roberts Head.

THE LADY OF THE SALTEES

A week into September, the days were becoming shorter as Charles' family motored eastwards to County Wexford. There was one item on Brian's itinerary: the granite Saltee Islands, Great and Little, lying three miles off the coast. Farmed by humans in the past, they were now the preserve of wildlife. Great Saltee had been leased since 1904 by the Pierce family, owners of an iron foundry in Wexford. Occasionally they would come out to the island for sport, mainly rabbit shooting, but the annual rent of £70 had become a burden and the recently-widowed Mrs Pierce had been endeavouring to sell. Not even the Royal Society for the Protection of Birds was willing to pay such a high rent, and it was finally sold for £5 to a Dublin sporting syndicate, who never even bothered to visit it.

In Wexford the Roberts called on Mrs Pierce (*Plate 3.9*), "an enormously fat woman, who invited herself to come with us, and nothing would shake her off – a terrible nuisance as she talked solidly the whole time, much of the time repeating herself & spoilt the whole atmosphere of the islands". After a 40-minute boat journey out from Kilmore Quay to Great Saltee the family, picnic provisions and Mrs Pierce were disgorged (the latter with difficulty) onto the beach. Brian headed off with Denis and Pat to the opposite side of the island and to the Makestone Rock, an impressive sea stack. There were at least 40 species of bird known to nest on the island, but this late in the season there was little hope of seeing much. Brian's enquiries had revealed the possible beginnings of a new gannet colony, since two pairs had nested here the previous year. It was the one bird he had hoped might just still be around with a well-grown nestling, but disappointingly, there was no sign of any. There was a huge number of rabbits, and rats were spotted on the beach, ruling out the survival of any ground-nesting birds.

Rowing over to the Makestone Rock, Brian gazed wistfully at the liberal quantities of white guano covering the rock, imagining the wonderful sight in June and July when it would have been teeming with guillemots, cormorants and kittiwakes. Suddenly in front of them a huge bull seal slithered down the rocks into the sea. Close behind another adult followed. Caves were everywhere, and it was the breeding season: Brian was rewarded at last. Looking into the mouth of a cave they soon spotted a young pup. It also saw them and quickly slipped into the sea and away. By manoeuvring the boat around the caves they could watch numerous adults swimming around and lying on the rocks.

At lunch Mrs Pierce still did not stop talking. In the afternoon the three boys escaped once more in the boat until it was time to return for tea. Mrs Pierce yet again "radiated misery" amongst them with her nonstop chatter. On getting her into the dinghy to return to the mainland it sank so low in the water under her weight that they could not push off from the beach. Back on dry land she insisted on joining the Roberts family for dinner, at which Brian inadvisedly enthused about coming back to the Saltees on his own. When Mrs Pierce promptly proposed that she intended to 'mother' him on his return, Brian was left squirming (he never returned). It was time to leave Ireland.

ALONE AT LAST

Twice on previous holidays to Cornwall and the Scillies, the family had broken the long drive down from Woking and stayed at Mullion Cove on the west side of the Lizard peninsula. The rugged coastal scenery here is magnificent, but Brian had his eye on a small uninhabited island a quarter mile out from the coast (*Plate 3.10*). On both the earlier occasions they had managed to get out to the island by boat for an all too brief visit. Now, in April 1931, Brian had persuaded his long-suffering family to book in at the Mullion Cove Hotel for a whole week so that he could camp alone on the island.

But as usual the weather had a different agenda. Four days of rough seas and storms intervened before Brian's plan could be put into action. Finally Charles and Denis went out in the boat with Brian to help put up the tent, returning to leave the young explorer alone with the birds. It was 11 April; this early in the year there were no eggs, but there was plenty of courtship and mating to watch. Brian's explorer's kit consisted of tent, groundsheet and sleeping bag, primus stove and billycan, candles and a box of matches. His food supply was a 14lb sack of potatoes, 1lb of butter, a tin of condensed milk, tea and a bag of apples. That evening he dissected a herring gull which had died that morning. It was egg-bound and Brian wondered how many birds must die like that. Exploring the island he observed eleven bird species, including a pair of razorbills who arrived to inspect some nest ledges and then departed, and a pair of ravens already nesting. He went to bed exhausted but contented.

After waking early next morning to find a thick sea mist obliterating the view, he snuggled back into his sleeping bag until mid-morning, revelling in the freedom to choose his mealtimes. Breakfast was followed immediately by lunch. He packed everything up except the tent. By then the sun had burned through the mist and it was time for some more exploring. To be an explorer one really needed to include some depot laying, for which there was not much scope on such a small island, but he managed to find a small cairn and left the billycan, three candles and matches under it. "If someone else doesn't take them they should be all right for years as the billycan is watertight," he wrote. Was he hoping to return? He was utterly in his element. "There is a very nice little ledge of rock on the western side of the island. It is about three feet wide and five feet long – overhanging above and below and about 30 feet above the sea. It is hard to climb to but a splendid place to lie and write my diary. I should think anyone could search the island for a whole day and not find me there."[17]

A little later one of the ravens darted out from the precipitous cliff face below, revealing its nest with four eggs. Brian's presence was obviously unwelcome and they "flew away to the mainland after croaking about for a bit". Through his binoculars he then watched a dramatic air battle over Gull Rock (a promontory on the mainland) between the ravens, a pair of nesting cormorants ducking their swoops, and then some herring gulls that turned on the ravens. The excitement came to an end when the boat came to fetch him at tea-time.

In his diary, Brian's post-expedition report declares that "with ⅓ lb of butter, 5 potatoes of about 3 inches diameter make a very good meal".

4

A NORDIC INTRODUCTION
TO THE ARCTIC

Once again Brian was about to exploit his father's adventurous spirit and kind heart. Norway was probably the last country Charles would have wished to take the car to, but Brian had by now resolved to become a polar explorer and he was yearning to visit the largest ice cap in mainland Europe: Jostedalsbreen.

Six weeks before departure Charles was still struggling to sort the itinerary, in spite of all the help from the Automobile Association (AA). Lamenting his lack of a good map, he wrote to Denis:

> "The car has to be put either on a train or a ferry at frequent intervals, and there are certain roads which are so narrow that there is one-way traffic at prescribed times, so it seems we shall have plenty of variety. I gave them [the AA in Norway] the dimensions and weight of the Rolls and they say that the car can be taken along these routes, but everyone who has been to Norway advises against a big car, because of the narrow roads and corners...The car by the way is just 3 millimetres too wide to be legally allowed into the country at all, but the Norwegian A A think there will be no trouble about this and will see us through if there is."[1]

Was Charles relishing the prospect? With a busy professional life at the age of 53 he probably wished for a more relaxing holiday. But his budding polar explorer son would soon be going places the Rolls would not be able to take him. The car provided reliability and comfort for Madeline, as well as the one thing – freedom of the road – that the family had become accustomed to. And as a veteran driver of the Stelvio Pass – that ultimate motorist's goal in the Alps – he was up for a new challenge. Since Norway was by reputation *the* place for salmon fishing, Charles would swap his camera for some fishing tackle. Brian was grateful for the use of his father's excellent roll-film camera, instead of the heavy Dallmeyer glass plate camera, to take up into the mountains.

In the late 19th century the first tourists began to discover Norway, arriving by passenger ships mainly from Britain and America. They could enjoy a package that included a cruise of the fjords, taking in some of the finest mountain scenery in Europe. Independent travellers were a rarity, other than the occasional mountaineer. This was hardly surprising in a country with a harsh climate, two-thirds covered by forest and mountains, and more than half the land above 2,000 ft in altitude: a vast plateau known as the *fjeld*. The southernmost point of Norway lies at the same latitude as Aberdeen, the country extending as a coastal ribbon far north of the Arctic Circle to latitude 71°N. Winters are harsh and many roads impassable due to snow until well into June. In 1930 the population of Norway was 2.8 million. Human settlement was largely rural, thinly scattered in the valleys where there was enough soil to support mixed farming and forestry, and along the coast where fishing was the main occupation. Towns were few and small, scattered mostly along the coast and the fjords. Many communities were isolated but for the lifeline provided by an extensive network of coastal and fjord ferries. Travel overland was still the cart and horse especially around the fjords, where high steep-sided mountains plunge into the deep waters, presenting huge challenges to road construction in the days before mechanization.

In the south-east lowlands the railway network was gradually spreading out from Oslo. The Rauma branch line off the Oslo to Trondheim main line had been opened in 1924, leading up the magnificent Romsdal valley from Dombås to Åndalsnes, connecting to the fjord steamers at its northern end. A thin trickle of summer motorists began to arrive in the late 1920s and some of the fjord ferries would clear a space on their foredecks to make room for a car or two (a decade later, the drive-on car ferry arrived along with new roads and bridges, making travel much easier). Norway's roads were narrower than in England, mostly 10-13 ft wide, although many only 8 ft with passing places, and not suited to large cars. Upland roads had crash barriers of tall marker stones set into the edge of the road at frequent intervals. Gradients were often steeper than Alpine passes, and seasonal rock falls were commonplace. This was not going to be a holiday for the faint-hearted.

The family drove to Newcastle to put the car on board the one direct passenger steamship to Oslo. Soon after their arrival Brian headed off by himself to soak up everything polar that Oslo had to offer. He was armed with letters of introduction from Cambridge (where he had been interviewed by Frank Debenham, director of the Scott Polar Research Institute). He first sought out Professor Olav Holtedahl, a distinguished geologist working at the Geological Museum. After an hour's discourse on the stratigraphy of Spitsbergen, the professor thoughtfully rang his wife in order to invite Brian for lunch and supper at home with his family. This was to be a complete culture shock for the 18-year-old public schoolboy. Brian had never been in a private home abroad before, let alone been encouraged to eat jam and sausage off the same plate together. The *smörgåsbord* – a mix of lots of sweet and savoury dishes all served together – was so confusing. Were you supposed to eat them in a particular order? His hosts derived much amusement from his confusion. They all spoke English, which Brian greatly appreciated, and he was deeply impressed by the simplicity of Norwegian home life; it was a breath of fresh air compared to the pretentiousness of middle-class England.

Between meeting Norway's polar great and good, Brian crammed in some of Oslo's museums. The Norwegian explorers of the heroic age were barely cold in their graves: Fridtjof Nansen and Otto Sverdrup had died only the previous year, Amundsen three years before. At the time polar relics were scattered around the city, only coming together under one roof when the Fram Museum opened in 1936. Where else would you find a museum devoted to the history of skiing? Norway is the birthplace of the ski, as is evident from 4,000-year-old rock paintings at Alta in the far north. It was an expedition in itself for an enthusiast to find the out-of-town *skimuseet* at Holmenkollen where some of Nansen's and Amundsen's polar relics were housed. This hilly district of Oslo has always been revered as the home of the National

Ski Jumping Championships, which had begun in the late 19th century. The Holtedahls took Brian to the museum, housed in an old wooden building close to the ski jump.

ROMSDAL VALLEY

While Brian was having his polar fix in Oslo, the rest of the family motored up along the Gudbrandsdal valley. At Dombås they forked left into the head of the Romsdal valley. Motoring alongside an endless ribbon of lake from which gushed the Rauma river, they arrived at Hotel Mölmen at Lesjaskog, a cluster of farmsteads sitting in a tranquil landscape of low forested hills. Here they were a short walk away from one of Norway's best salmon rivers, a 17th century wooden church with a delightful painted and carved interior, and the local railway station.

On leaving Oslo Brian travelled by train towards Trondheim, taking the branch line at Dombås into the Romsdal valley. At Lesjaskog he was reunited with his family. After exchanging news, Brian's attention was drawn to a curiosity next to the hotel. Amongst the collection of more substantial farm buildings sat a little log-built hut raised off the ground on stone piers, its turfed roof sporting a huge, elegant wooden bell tower with a tall and slender spire almost competing with the one on nearby Lesjaskog church. Yet this was neither a church nor even a chapel, although it was certainly a building with status. In the days before refrigeration, as far back as Viking times, the *stabbur* was the building in which all the precious food produced by a farm was stored to see them through the long winter, like dried and salted meats, butter and cheese, grain and root crops. Brian had caught sight of these turf-roofed huts on the valley slopes from his train window. Many were more imposing and some even two-storey, but none had such a fancy bell tower. Only found on larger farms, the bell was rung to summon farm workers to meals and rest. The *stabbur* possessed only one small door and no windows, and the farmer's wife, who was sole key-keeper, ensured that it was kept firmly locked all the time. Raising the building on stilts kept vermin out, and the turf roof helped to keep the temperature stable. Well cared for, this little building is still standing today (*Plate 4.1*).

Soon the family was off northwards down the Romsdal valley, motoring in constant company with the railway and the Rauma river. This dramatic glacier-gouged valley had already become popular with tourists since the arrival of the railway a few years previously, with the most dramatic scenery and highest mountain peaks at its northern end. Here the Romsdalshorn rises to a 5,000 ft high domed peak, whilst opposite across the valley stands the Trollveggen, a vertical rock wall rising 3,600 ft from the valley floor to sharply jagged peaks which look like trolls or witches' hats. Brian, Denis and their father climbed nearly 2,000 ft up a side valley for a better view of the tallest vertical rock face in Europe. They waited in vain for parting of the clouds that enveloped the jagged peaks, but the Trolltinder were not going to reveal their full glory. There was some compensation at the bottom of the valley, where a large residual patch of ice revealed an icy grotto for the family to explore (*Plate 4.2*).

The summer of 1931 was proving to be exceptionally cool in Norway. For the family there would not be many *al fresco* picnics, but in the spectacular setting they managed a chilly one on the banks of the gurgling Rauma river. At the end of the valley at Åndalsnes they headed west for the coastal port of Ålesund. There was then no continuous road link, but a new car ferry service had begun operating on Romsdalsfjord between Norvik and Våga.

Norangsdalen

Putting your car on a ferry on the Norwegian fjords at the beginning of the 1930s was a precarious business. There were as yet few cars in Norway and the ferry companies resorted to various devices to accommodate them. Some vessels had their own crane hoist to lift the car onto the foredeck, others had a wooden ramp (*Plate 4.3*). A particular problem was the six-foot difference between high and low tide in the fjords, so boats without a crane had to schedule their timetables to align deck with dock. Ferries struggled to cope with the increasing road traffic. By the middle of the decade a widespread programme of road-building was underway and by the end of the decade the drive-on ro-ro ferry had arrived: a bit of imported Danish technology. On some occasions Charles had to drive on to the deck via a ramp while the vessel was broadside to the quay, and the tide needed to be just right. With such a large heavy car his heart must have been in his mouth.

On arriving at the busy industrial port of Ålesund the family made their way to the Dairy Pier where, surrounded by milk churns and butter barrels, they boarded the DS *Eira,* a local ferry built in 1896. The car was winched on board to sit broadside across the foredeck with not much room to spare (*Plate 4.4*). On arrival at Øye on Storfjord, the tide was a little low and the boat was listing towards the pier as Charles drove off the ferry to explore yet another rugged valley (*Plate 4.5*). Norangsdalen was reputed to be one of the narrowest valleys in Norway, 'discovered' in the 1880s by the aristocracy. Cruise ships would anchor at Øye, disgorging their wealthy passengers to stay locally at the smart Union Hotel and to be driven up the valley in a horse-drawn carriage to admire some of Norway's most wild and romantic scenery. A few miles up the valley lies Lyngstøylvatnet, a small lake with a secret hidden in its waters. In a valley particularly prone to rock falls and avalanches, a huge landslide had engulfed this area some 23 years earlier, fallen rock material damming the river and creating the lake. Engulfed by the rising waters was a *seter*, a cluster of several small farm dwellings used by families in the summer months whilst their livestock grazed on the upland pastures. In late May, when the incident happened, the farming families had not yet migrated up to the summer pastures with their livestock and fortunately no one was killed. The remains of the farm houses, stone walls and the old road through the valley can still be seen today in the clear waters of the lake. Farther up, the valley becomes gorge-like with barely enough room for the road and both sides rising to nearly 1,000 ft. Constantly choked with boulders and scree, it must have been a back-breaking job before the mechanical age to keep such a road passable.

GLACIERS AT LAST

Gradually the family's itinerary took them southwards, and they were now heading for the northern side of Jostedalsbreen, which lies between two of Norway's longest and deepest fjords, Nordfjord and Sognefjord. This vast flat-topped ice cap covering some 200 square miles has numerous glacial tongues spilling into the surrounding valleys. Although it started to become an attraction for mountaineers and tourists in the 19th century, local people had been crossing the ice cap for hundreds of years to travel between the eastern valleys and western fjords. It was even used as a drover's route until 1923. Calves purchased in the north-west region were driven across the ice field at its narrowest part to markets in the eastern lowland valleys. Along the way the cows would fatten up on the richer upland pastures as they travelled over the summer months.

On the northern flanks of the ice cap, Briksdal was one of the more accessible glaciers (*Plate 4.6*). From the settlement at Olden on Nordfjord the journey to the glacier took about four hours, involving a mixture of pony and trap, walking and steamer ferry along the seven miles of ribbon lake to the southern end of the valley (the continuous road to the far end of the lake was not built until the 1950s). From the boat there were magnificent views of other glaciers and waterfalls cascading into the lake.

The journey from the lake's end to the bottom of the glacier following the glacial river took the family a further two hours, walking alongside Madeline, who was enthroned on a pony and trap. They had breathtaking views of glaciers tumbling down from the ice cap, including Melkevolls. As yet there was no sign of the Briksdal glacier. Half an hour later the road ended at a hostelry, where Madeline probably decided to let the others continue without her. The route now left the Melkevolls valley and from here they climbed up a path which twisted steeply through birch and alder woodland. There was a sense of something huge looming ahead, although they could not yet see it properly. Soon the wall of ice glimpsed through the dense scrub thicket was dwarfing the trees and towering in front of them. Leaving the trees, a final scramble across the loose moraine brought them to the front of the glacier. It was an awesome sight, a 30 to 40 ft high wall of ice, much of it a beautiful blue colour. They stood in front of the most active part of the glacier front, where the meltwater stream emerged from underneath the glacier via a huge cavern. Frequent cracking sounds in the ice could be heard. (*Plate 4.7*)

It was a dangerous spot. Only a day or two after they stood there, the glacial river outlet and cavern collapsed, taking a great bite out of the glacier's snout.[2] (*Plate 4.8*) After a couple of years of inactivity, Briksdal glacier was embarking on a remarkable 20-year retreat, and by 1951 it had receded half a mile, exposing for the first time its previously-hidden glacial lake. But glaciers are rarely still for long, and Briksdal then grew back half as far again, covering over its lake by 1997.[3] Since then global warming has gathered pace and a further retreat is underway, taking the snout a long way back above the lake.

Brian longed to climb on the glacier, but this would have been foolhardy without crampons, ropes and a local guide. In 1874 an English mountaineer, William Slingsby, was one of the first to come to the Jostedals ice cap, returning many times and giving birth to the sport of mountaineering in Norway. One of his many daring feats was to climb down Kjenndals glacier, a very steep and twisty glacier in the next valley; it has never been attempted since. He described it as "the most awful glacier work I have ever done". The serious challenge of ascending the steep and heavily crevassed Briksdal glacier had been overcome in 1895 by Kristian Bing, a Norwegian mountaineer who had made the journey to the top with a local guide, Rasmus Rasmussen Åbrekke, in nine hours.

Quite a few decades later another Englishman turned up and decided to go in the opposite direction: down the glacier from the top. In 1970 Ranulph Fiennes was landed on the ice cap above Briksdal glacier by seaplane along with a team of scientists, surveyors and military men. He had decided that this was a suitable testing ground for his planned Transglobe Expedition. "A camp was set up [on the ice cap]... and at the end of the week the party set off to sledge 40 km down Jostedalsbreen and a connecting glacier Briksdalsbreen to sea level," *Polar Record* reported. "The four days produced most of the discomforts and dangers associated with travel in hostile conditions – including the loss of both sledges, and all equipment not being back-packed at the time, when the journey was but half completed. The final stage to a village on the shores of Oldenfjord, was made by a small boat, an experience, apparently, of memorable discomfort."[4]

Brian and Denis stayed on in Briksdal, finding basic accommodation while Charles, Madeline and Joy returned to Olden. With the weather holding well the brothers were able to do a long day's climb up Kattanakken. There was a well-marked path with a stiff climb to the top, needing hands to scramble the steep and exposed last part, the 'cat's neck', to the peak at 4,760 ft. The panorama from the top was spectacular – the whole length of the Olden valley, with its many waterfalls cascading down from the ice cap, and the glaciers Briksdal, Melkevolls and Tjota. (*Plate 4.9*)

On the second day they walked a little way back down the Olden valley to explore a neighbouring glacier immediately to the north of

Briksdal. Looking benign enough today, having retreated so much in recent years, Brenndals glacier was not a good place to live beneath in the past. Like its neighbours, the top half of the glacier is extremely steep, and in the late 17th and early 18th century, during the 'Little Ice Age' the glacier advanced considerably into Olden valley, some three miles in 50 years. In the early 18th century it sent a great burst of water – a *jökulhlaup* – tearing down its steep valley, destroying Åbrekke farm's pastureland. A few years later a second one destroyed another nearby farm's pastures and farm buildings at Tungøyane. Finally in 1743 an avalanche of ice, rocks, water and debris swept away Tungøyane farm altogether – buildings, people and livestock.

Brian wanted to be climbing on the ice. But even before modern health and safety guidelines, the Norwegians already had rules in place for anyone intent on climbing on a glacier: do not attempt it without employing a mountain guide, with ropes and crampons. Were Brian and Denis sensible enough to follow the rules? Surviving photographs of the two young men venturing onto Brenndals glacier rather suggest otherwise.[5]

The following day Brian and Denis rejoined the family. They motored eastwards from Stryn, skirting the northern flanks of the Jostedalsbreen ice cap through Hjelle towards Grotli. The rare occurrence of meeting another vehicle – in this case a truck – caused some consternation when Charles had to swerve into a ditch. They continued on the long, high level road to Grotli, turning sharply back in a westerly direction to head for Djupvasshytta. Still on a high-level plateau at 3,400 ft, they arrived at a hotel by the edge of a chilly glacial lake. Nearby was a *lavvo*, the summer tent of a nomadic family of Såmi reindeer herders.

ENCOUNTER WITH THE SÅMI

Today the Såmi (formerly known as Lapps) are recognised as one of the indigenous peoples of Europe who have suffered generations of persecution in the name of so-called progress and civilisation. Not all Såmi were fully nomadic reindeer herders. Some were coastal or forest dwellers, but the truly nomadic were those who followed their reindeer herds through the seasons of the year to the different pastures favoured by the animals. Their wealth was counted in reindeer, the animals providing a lifestyle which was largely self-sustaining (*Plate 4.10*).

But spreading across Norway, Sweden, Finland and the Russian Kola Peninsula, and speaking their own languages – as many as nine different ones – which were incomprehensible to outsiders, their nomadic ways did not fit comfortably into a world of political boundaries. Their brightly-coloured costumes developed regional styles, and even with different languages they could recognise where their fellow herders came from by their hat style, for example. At least half of the Såmi inhabit Norway, and from the latter part of the 19th century onwards the Norwegian government pursued a controversial programme to 'civilise' them by creating laws intended to deny them basic rights to their beliefs, language, land and culture.

Brian met a herding couple who had recently become victims of the Norwegian government's efforts to wipe out Såmi culture, at its worst during the period 1900 to 1940. Postcard photographs of the same couple smiling and happy with their four young children only two years previously contrast starkly with the careworn faces photographed by Brian (*Plate 4.11*). So what had happened to their children? The 'norwegianisation' programme included the removal of all children from their parents and placing them in boarding schools, to ensure they would learn to speak Norwegian only and forget their native Såmi language. Inevitably this resulted in their parents losing the ability to teach their children the reindeer herding way of life, a process learned only by being part of it.

Given Charles's love of driving scary mountain passes, it would have been surprising if they had not popped down the mountain pass to Geiranger Fjord to enjoy one of Norway's most breathtaking scenic drives. At the bottom, nestling on the edge of the fjord, the little community of Geiranger got in gear for the annual summer invasion of tourists that poured off the cruise ships docking at the end of Norway's most famous fjord. There was a seasonal living to be made here running excursions by *stolkjaerre* (pony and trap) up the steeply-winding road, which was open only between June and end of September. This pass was a remarkable feat of engineering for the late 19th century, with its numerous hairpins at one point looping back right underneath itself at a place known as *Knuden* (the knot). As the crow flies the pass is only three miles long, but the road distance is 11 miles. Once somebody in the community had seen a motor car, it wasn't long before a number of the pony-trap owners borrowed and scraped their money together, pooling their resources to buy the first motor car in Geiranger in around 1920. Inevitably the pony and trap was gradually usurped as more cars were acquired throughout the 1920s and 1930s. A steep, winding single-track road was not the ideal location for such traffic chaos, probably the first case of road congestion in Norway (*Plate 4.12*). Not even Oslo with its wide boulevards had more than a handful of cars at this time. By early September when the Roberts were touring, the last cruise ships of the season had departed and the road would have been much quieter.

JOTUNHEIM MOUNTAINS

While the parents and Joy stayed at Lom, Brian and Denis spent a few days together climbing in the Jotunheim mountains. They decided to climb Galdhøpiggen, Scandinavia's highest mountain at 8,100 ft. After a long hike along the Bøverdal valley on the north side of the mountain they climbed the path to Juvasshytta, a mountain hut some 3,000 ft below the summit, where they could stay cheaply for a few nights. Low cloud and the occasional snowstorm accompanied their three-hour ascent. At the summit hut, according to a contemporary Baedeker's Guide, coffee and champagne were available![6]

In an uncharacteristically cavalier account of this excursion that Brian wrote for the Cambridge Mountaineering Club a year later he claimed that the climb was a doddle. But part of the ascent involved crossing Styggebreen, a glacier some 1¼ miles wide, with many hidden crevasses. With the unusually cool summer of 1931 and lingering heavier snow conditions they should unquestionably have been roped together and had a guide to cross it. Surviving photographs show heavy snow cover at the summit, and no evidence of ropes or a guide – or coffee or champagne for that matter.[7]

Back down at Juvvashytta, the attractive idea of hiring a reindeer, sledge and driver for a less strenuous way of exploring the snowfield proved irresistible. (*Plate 4.13*)

South west of the Jotunheim mountains on an arm of the southern side of Sognefjord lies the picturesque small town of Laerdalsøyri, with its streets of well-preserved 18th and 19th century houses. This was to be the last leg before returning to Oslo. The town had a strategic position for east-west trade on the innermost end of Norway's longest fjord, even though it was 85 miles from the sea. Ships landing at Laerdalsøyri traded dried fish and salt from the west coast with goods such as tar and animal skins brought overland along a route from the eastern lowlands and Sweden which was generally snow-free throughout the year.

In its upper reaches the Laerdal valley is a spectacularly narrow gorge. Almost inconceivably a road had been constructed along this valley, partly alongside and partly above the raging torrent which hurtled along in the deep ravine below, its overhanging sides rising several thousand feet. An American traveller John Stoddard, who toured Norway at the beginning of the 20th century, was overawed by the experience of being driven by pony and trap through the gorge: "The space, however, between these mountain sides is barely wide enough for the river, which writhes and struggles with obstructing boulders, lashing itself to creamy foam, and filling the chasm with a deafening roar. Yet, above the river, a roadway has been hewn out of the mountain-side itself, which is lined with parapets of boulders. When marking out the route the engineers were often lowered over the precipice by ropes."[8]

Along the gorge Charles snatched some relaxing moments fishing on the Laerdal, Norway's finest salmon river. Meanwhile the boys got up to mischief a little farther upstream, finding a shaky wire-rope suspension bridge across the torrents flowing in the gorge below (*Plate 4.14*), which Brian dared Denis to cross. Above the wire bridge on both sides of the river can be seen the massive stone footings of an earlier bridge or road. This was the most important ancient route across the mountains from west to east for at least a thousand years, and several sections of old roads survive in places.[9]

At the top of the gorge the family reached the settlement of Borgund with its magnificent medieval stave church (*Plate 4.15*), the finest preserved in Norway. At one time there were at least a thousand of them. Today Norway has just 28, which have survived only because they were too remote and the parishes too poor to rebuild them. Dating from around 1180, Borgund presents an extraordinary sight with its overhanging roof layers of pointed shingles and dragon finials so reminiscent of the head of a Viking longship, all coated with black tar to preserve the timbers. In a building style unique to Norway, it is constructed with vertically-set timbers inserted into horizontal bearers, which in turn rested on a stone plinth, raising the timbers well above the ground.

After Borgund they turned southwards along the Hemsedal valley and drove the long way back to Oslo, the landscape gradually softening into lowlands.

UNFINISHED BUSINESS IN OSLO

Back in Oslo, Brian was able to get an interview with Professor Adolf Hoel, the distinguished geologist and founding director of the Norsk Polarinstitutt, who had only just returned from his latest Greenland expedition. He was intrigued by a swinging trapeze bar hanging from the ceiling in Hoel's office, Hoel explained that he used it to keep fit for exploration work. Alongside Nansen and Amundsen, Hoel was one of the most influential figures in Norwegian polar exploration at the time. His 10-year programme of scientific research and mapping on Svalbard had enabled Norway to claim sovereignty under the 1920 Svalbard Treaty. Busily engaged on writing up his Greenland expedition, he introduced Brian to some of his colleagues in the cartography department, where huge scale maps of Spitsbergen and the Jotunheim mountains had been created by the latest stereophotogrammetric survey methods. Brian was shown the stereophotogrammetric camera and other surveying equipment used in this latest Greenland expedition. Hoel gave Brian a letter for the Harbour Master at Sarpsborg asking him to arrange for Brian to see Nansen's famous ship the *Fram* in her nearby temporary moorings. She was not yet restored and not open to the public.

For the rest of the day Brian took the train out to Lysaker to visit Fritjof Nansen's house. Designed by Nansen himself, his family home of 30 years was not at all Norwegian in style but severely neo-Roman. One of Nansen's two sons showed Brian round, including the little attic room which was Nansen's study, left untidy just as he had kept it, even with the ash from his last pipe. Above his study Nansen had a viewing turret – and what a view. The gardens ran down in front of the house to the fjord. It was a rare day of glorious sunshine.

Brian was mesmerised as he looked down the Oslo fjord far into the distance with its myriad of little islands in the sparkling water. He was deep in contemplation of Norway's greatest polar explorer. From leading a team which made the first crossing of Greenland on skis in 1888, Nansen became internationally famous with his expedition of 1893-96 in his specially built ship the *Fram*, designed to be frozen into the Arctic ice and to drift across the North Pole, testing his theory of ocean currents. Defying the experts who claimed such a ship could not be built, he succeeded in getting farther north than anyone previously. His three-year voyage was full of hardship and he returned to great acclaim. Nansen's formidable mind was constantly active in science and polar issues, though his later life he devoted to diplomacy and humanitarian work for which he was awarded the Nobel Peace Prize in 1922.

On his last full day in Norway, Brian took the train to Sarpsborg, 50 miles south-east of Oslo. Presenting Hoel's letter to the Harbour Master he was given red carpet treatment, taken by speed boat down the river Glamen to where the *Fram* was temporarily anchored with a corrugated iron roof over her. A barge was then floated out to the ship, so that they could board her from a ladder. After Nansen the *Fram* had been used in the Arctic and Antarctic several times, the last time by Amundsen in 1910-12 in his expedition to reach the South Pole. Since returning, she had been left to decay and by now was almost a wreck. Moves were being taken to restore her, and she would finally come to her last resting place in the Fram Museum in 1935.

Brian's last diary entry for Oslo reads: "Our boat left Oslo at midday. I don't think I wasted a moment of my time [here] and already long to return."

5

NECESSARY EVILS:
SCHOOL AND UNIVERSITY

The curriculum had little relevant to life. Latin and Greek featured
strongly, being a requirement for university entrance and I think, for the
Colonial Service. One could hardly be expected to govern the natives of
Africa and India without some knowledge of Thucydides and Virgil.

Old Uppinghamian

From a very early age Brian knew clearly what interested him and
what did not. At the age of seven he followed his older brothers to
Allen House Preparatory School in Woking, but found the discipline of
the classroom tedious and the subjects boring. Much of his time was
spent daydreaming and gazing out of the window. Nor did Brian have
any enthusiasm for competitive sports ("He will do much better when
he takes the game more seriously." Which he never did). There was just
one activity at which, like his older brother Pat, he excelled: swimming.
He also won a prize for his garden plot.

But generally he struggled. His mother, ever kind and patient with
her children, provided constant support and encouragement, studying
all the books that Brian was supposed to be reading himself, so that she
could help him with his homework. But despite her help Brian found
the *Boy's Own Paper* far more interesting. At the age of nine he read
a serial entitled "In the Realm of the Arctic Poppy", the adventures of
a boy who joins an expedition to the Arctic under its leader Captain

Wally to seek the sacred poppy known to be tended by prehistoric ice-men. The youthful Brian, who wriggled out of reading tedious school books, was captivated, and declared that he was going to become a polar explorer.

From his summer term school report, it is evident that one unfortunate side-effect of Brian's Damascus moment was a significant downturn in his already mediocre schoolwork.

History: *Doesn't take much interest.*

Written work: *Untidy. Essays rather weak. Copy: very poor.*

Poetry: *Poor.*

Grammar: *Could do much better.*

General knowledge: *Very poor.*

Latin: *Careless work.*

French: *Inconsistent work.*

Arithmetic: *He is not fond of work. Could do very much better.*

Old Testament: *Must learn the value of attention. His work has not been satisfactory.*

New Testament: *His marks are very low.*

Cricket: *No idea at present, I think, really.*

Swimming: *Excellent.*

General remarks: *No real care with his written work. He is last in his form by a large margin.*

Brian's mind was far away. But the swathes of criticism stung him – to say nothing of his parents – and during the following years he showed a gradual if erratic improvement. At the end of 1926 he left Allen House, probably with no regrets.

ENTRY TO UPPINGHAM

Brian's older brother Denis had been admitted to Rugby School. Brian, who was probably not considered sufficiently academic for Rugby, was accepted for Uppingham School at the age of 14. Rugby and Uppingham were residential public schools with fees well beyond their father's modest means. Uncle Maurice, who lived next door to Bishopgarth and had no children of his own, probably footed the bill for the three boys' school fees and would have had a say in the choice of schools. Maurice Birley had a strong interest in education; from 1911 to 1914 he had been warden of Toynbee Hall in Spitalfields, a centre dedicated to social reform in London's East End.

At Uppingham Brian was admitted to Fircroft House. Like Uppingham's town houses, Fircroft was a maze of Victorian corridors, but in contrast to them it was a hill house on the outskirts of town, set amid playing fields and with a pleasantly rustic quality reinforced by the boys' toilets being situated in outbuildings across the yard from the main building, the cubicles having no doors on them. On the boys' arrival a bell was rung to announce tea – a welcome repast of sausages and mashed potato – which was taken in the hall, the boys seated on long wooden benches.

Afterwards Brian was summoned to follow a more senior boy along a long corridor to be given a large pile of papers known as 'fag notes', which he had to learn by heart within the first two weeks in order to pass his 'fag exam'. They contained detailed information such as the history of the school, the names of the Uppingham Houses, the names of housemasters and house captains, timetables, areas that were out of bounds, and school and house rules: the pockets of boys' trousers had to be kept stitched up, and talking was not allowed in the corridors or after lights out. Uppingham was a 'public' school in the traditional English mould, with its own fagging system (a form of unofficial schoolboy hierarchy). All new boys were fags, who were at the beck and call of the school prefects, known at Uppingham as 'pollies'.[1] To summon them a polly only had to shout 'Fag!' at the top of his voice, and the last fag to arrive was the one that had to do the duties demanded. Such duties included collecting hot water for washing and shaving, cleaning razors, polishing buttons on Combined Cadet Force uniforms, making the bed, and running endless errands. There was also a scale of punishments, usually meaning cold baths or cross-country running, or both. To understand this bizarre regime from the perspective of a century later, one has to remember that British schools of the early 20th century were not exam factories but were aimed at developing leadership quality and 'character' – suitable material for the officer class and for administration of the Empire.

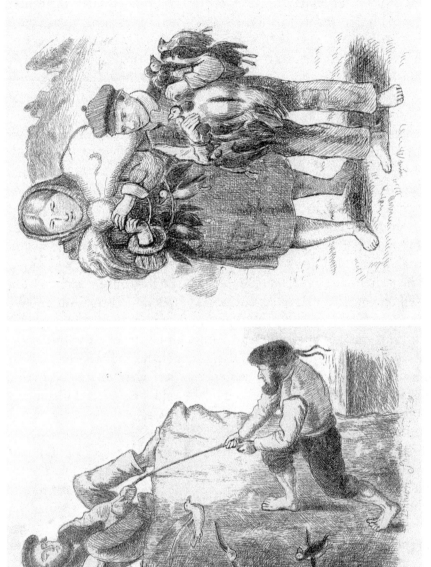

Bird collecting on St Kilda. From J Sands[2]

ARMCHAIR TRAVEL TO ST KILDA

Anyone with a passion for small islands can hardly fail to be gripped by the story of St Kilda, 40 miles out in the Atlantic from the Outer Hebrides. Brian had read Richard and Cherry Kearton's book *With Nature and a Camera* (1897), half of which was devoted to an account of their several months' stay on St Kilda in the 1890s, studying the St Kildans' way of life and how they trapped the puffins and fulmars on which they subsisted. By now Brian had acquired a few books on St Kilda and was bursting to give his very first talk about it.

In charge of Brian's dormitory in Fircroft was Peter Falk, two years senior to Brian. On being begged by a friend to let Brian give a talk after lights out, Falk decided to bend the house rules and gave his permission. He was amazed by Brian's fluency and total command of the topic, sufficient to answer in detail every question that was put to him.[3] So much did he underestimate Brian that he was astonished not only to meet him at Cambridge two years later, but also that he would be joining an expedition to Iceland with Brian as leader.

Much later in life when he reflected back on his unusual career, Brian himself commented that at school he had "failed to distinguish himself in any field except idleness". But his Uppingham school reports reveal a boy who was far from indolent. Although he struggled with certain subjects such as mathematics and languages, he did well enough in geography, science and essay writing. Teachers were impressed by his application and determination, even if he found the subject difficult and the results were undistinguished. To the public school these were good 'character' attributes.

From quite early on Brian had been presuming that after Uppingham he would be going up to Cambridge. Unfortunately academic ability could not be dismissed as an irrelevance. His father Charles dished out a salutary warning that whatever Brian's aspirations might be, unless he did better in his schoolwork he would not be heading for Cambridge. And right up until the end of his schooldays Brian's prospects remained uncertain.

FIRST GLIMPSE OF THE POLAR INSTITUTE

The story of Brian's first encounter with the Scott Polar Research Institute (SPRI) in Cambridge is eminently consistent with his lifelong propensity for breaking into impenetrable fortresses – such as the Foreign Office – via the back door. At the time the embryonic institute had only recently moved out from an attic in the Department of Earth Sciences' Sedgwick Building into Lensfield House, a small two-storey house on the edge of a field of meadow grass on the south side of Lensfield Road. The pastiche-Georgian style building that accommodates the present-day institute was built in 1934.

One day in 1929 Brian visited Lensfield House. It was a Sunday afternoon and the building was closed. Undeterred, he entered through an unsecured window at the back of the house, spent a couple of hours contentedly studying the museum collection, and departed having left a 'thank you' note on the table. Stimulated by reading Herbert Ponting's book *The Great White South*, an account of Scott's last *Terra Nova* expedition first published in 1921, his interest in the Antarctic was now becoming a serious matter and he wrote to Ponting for advice. Back came the reply:

> "Dear Mr Roberts:
>
> "I fully sympathise with your wish to be an explorer, for it is a wonderful thing to add something, however little, to the sum of knowledge.
> "Now, you cannot possibly do better than see my friend and former comrade of the Scott Expedition, Mr Frank Debenham, MA, who is the Director of the SPRI at Cambridge, who you will find full of interest for anyone who has a genuine desire to become an explorer...
>
> "Very truly yours, H G Ponting"[4]

Brian followed Ponting's advice, and his polar career was born.

TO CAMBRIDGE – OR NOT?

During the summer of 1930 Brian was entered for the Littlego examination. 'Littlego' was an Oxbridge entrance examination that was often taken by prospective students whose school exam results were judged to be of insufficient academic quality for the universities, either because of the examinations (which were not standardised at the time), or the student's performance, or both. The exam was not exactly overstretching, but it nonetheless contained Brian's bogey subjects, Latin, ancient Greek and Mathematics. Despite this he performed well in it. With his increased confidence (*Plate 5.1*) he applied to study for the Natural Sciences Tripos at Emmanuel College, Cambridge, where his older brother Denis was already studying Architecture. On 2 November he also wrote to Debenham:

> "Dear Mr Debenham,
>
> "I should feel very grateful if you would be kind enough to see me and advise me as to my future. I am 18, and am at present at Uppingham School. I expect to go to Emmanuel College next October.
> "I want to be an explorer or at any rate to take some part in exploring... I hope to be able at Cambridge to fit myself to become of use in some definite way to the members of an expedition so that I could have a chance to join them..."[5]

Brian's letter was music to Debenham's ears and he immediately offered Brian an interview. Debenham also contacted Arthur Hinks, the all-powerful secretary of the Royal Geographical Society, introducing Brian and asking for him to be allowed into the RGS library during vacations. In December Brian went to Cambridge for his university entrance examination in Cambridge and grabbed the opportunity for an interview with Debenham. Brian wanted to take biology as a major subject, but Debenham's advice was that polar work needed surveyors more than it needed biologists, and surveyors needed trigonometry. There was to be no way round that.

There also remained doubts over Brian's academic ability in general. Matters came to a head at the end of 1930, as Brian approached his final school year. He was proposing now to read geography, but a place at Cambridge was conditional on passing an exam in trigonometry, which would satisfy the college over Brian's abilities in surveying and mapping, as required by the Geographical Tripos. This echoed Debenham's own advice and it precipitated something of a crisis. Mathematics was the one subject in which Brian had consistently failed to distinguish himself at Uppingham. A spate of letters between Brian's father and the Uppingham headmaster discussed Brian's need for additional tutoring, and he was allowed to join a small Army and Engineering class to focus on trigonometry.[6]

The year 1931 started propitiously for Brian. He was promoted to the position of 'polly' (school prefect), settled down to his mathematics studies and passed the all-important trigonometry examination. After some anxious weeks of waiting, he was greatly relieved to receive a letter of acceptance for admission to Emmanuel College in October that year to read geography.

Having found an additional use for his father's X-ray machine, Brian presented his collection of bird and fish X-ray photographs for the July Natural Science Exhibition in his final term at Uppingham. The birds were a dead chicken and an Aylesbury duck, presumably destined for the dinner table at home. He was rewarded with some school prize money and bought another book on St Kilda.

UP TO CAMBRIDGE

In October 1931 Brian followed his brother Denis's footsteps and went up to Emmanuel College. Straight away he joined the Cambridge Bird Club, presided over by David Lack, who was then in his third year. Lack had spent his first day in Cambridge – and many more days besides – at the local sewage farm, which for him was a far more educational experience than sitting through lectures. The extensive muddy settling tanks were a first-rate place for observing birds, especially migrating

Emmanuel College, sketch by Denis Roberts

waders. On one occasion Lack fell from a rotting boardwalk into a sludge tank and had to walk back to his college, after being refused entry onto a bus in his malodorous state.[7]

Lack pioneered new ways of studying birds, by observing their behaviour and ecology rather than dissecting dead specimens, which was then the norm. His classic early study *The Life of the Robin* (1943) paved the way for later studies of the finches collected by Charles Darwin on the Galapagos Islands, demonstrating that differences in beak size and shape were due to adaptation to different food sources.[8] He became a long-standing director of the Edward Grey Institute, Oxford and would be recognised as the father of evolutionary ecology. Brian later recalled that at Cambridge he learnt far more by arguing with colleagues than by sitting through lectures, and Lack was clearly a formative influence on him.

For a polar explorer aerial survey had great potential, and Brian was keen to learn to fly. He made several attempts to join the Cambridge University Air Squadron, but to no avail: his eyesight was not good enough. Elected to membership of the RGS early in 1932, he began planning an expedition to cross the Vatnajökull ice cap in Iceland during the summer vacation. The preparations dominated his first undergraduate year. The second year was occupied with another Arctic expedition, to east Greenland. Brian often commented that he had found schoolwork uninspiring, doing poorly in exams as a result. It was at Cambridge, so he claimed, that he "caught fire".[9] But his academic progress remained undistinguished and the many lectures he attended at Cambridge largely washed over him. Almost every day during term-time he would hold a coffee party in his rooms, poring over maps of the world and making ambitious plans for exploration – or camp in the field next to the polar institute on Lensfield Road (*Plate 5.2*).

During his third year the inevitable Finals examinations loomed. In the end Brian achieved a Class II(1) degree, "better than anticipated" according to his tutors. But he was not to be deterred from being sucked into extra-curricular activities: presidency of the Cambridge Bird Club, helping to publish a magazine *The Wayfarer* and David Lack's first book *The Birds of Cambridgeshire*, involvement in the university Anthropological Club, and lecturing on the Arctic. And, looking for any excuse to avoid swotting for exams, he started in November 1933 to plan yet another Arctic expedition: this time to Baffin Island in north-east Canada. But life was to take a new turn. Immersed in his plans at the polar institute, he was accosted one day by a 6'4" tall, broad-shouldered giant looking down at him. It was the Australian explorer John Rymill. "Brian, how d'you feel about going to the Antarctic?"

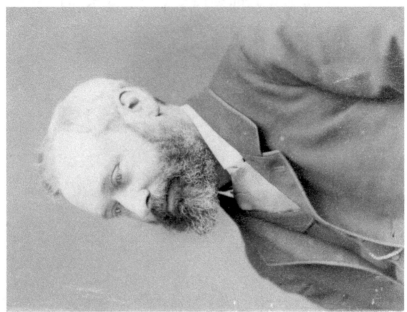

Plate 1.1 Poulter Benjamin Roberts

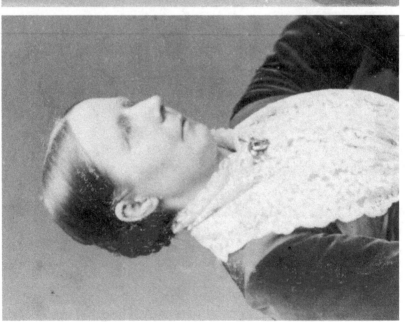

Plate 1.2 Theresa Alice de Palma

Plate 1.3 Charles Roberts as a young boy

Plate 1.4 Madeline Birley as a young girl

Plate 1.5 Madeline Birley on her
wedding day

Plate 1.6 Charles Roberts in
military dress uniform

Plate 1.7 Bishopgarth

Plate 1.8 Dovecote, Bishopgarth garden,
with one of the authors

Plate 1.9 Brian (aged 3) by the pond

Plate 1.10 Brian's first holiday, Torquay 1913. The Roberts family in a Crossley tourer

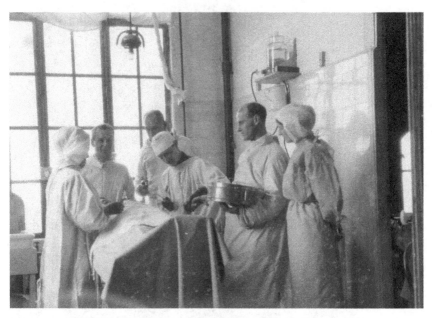

Plate 1.11 Charles (second from left) as anaesthetist operating
on soldier, Nevers 1915

Plate 1.12 Princess Louise Mountbatten and Lady Paget with Red Cross train

Plate 1.13 Looe Harbour, Bridge House above right. Fishing boat and drying nets

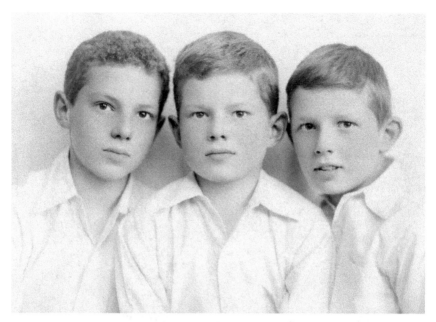

Plate 2.1 The Roberts boys, from left Denis, Pat and Brian (aged 11)

Plate 2.2 Car craned onto *SS Hantonia*

Plate 2.3 Pamplona

Plate 2.4 Chaos de Comély (early 20th century)

Plate 2.5 Rhone Glacier and Furka Pass

Plate 2.6 A walk above the Rhone glacier

Plate 2.7 Inside Rhone glacier ice tunnel

Plate 2.8 Stelvio Pass (early 20th century)

Plate 2.9 Rotterdam Oostplein (early 20th century)

Plate 2.10 The Dreisprachenspitze (1920s)

Plate 3.1 Roberts family taking Kylesku ferry, 1928

Plate 3.2 Brian aged 16

Plate 3.3 Denis jumping off Hanjague into boat

Plate 3.5 Brian cooking breakfast on Annet

Plate 3.4 Brian ringing a juvenile greater black-backed gull

Plate 3.6 Brian with his new Dallmeyer camera

Plate 3.7 The Skelligs: lighthouse (white speck) just visible on Skellig Michael

Plate 3.8 Skellig Michael, Roberts family on path up to the lighthouse

Plate 3.9 Mrs Pierce

Plate 3.10 Mullion Island

Plate 4.1 Stabbur, Mölmen farm, Romsdal valley

Plate 4.2 Inside ice cave, Romsdal valley

Plate 4.3 Driving onto Vågstrand ferry

Plate 4.4 Ålesund dairy pier, DS *Eira* preparing to depart

Plate 4.5 Ferry disembarking at Øye

Plate 4.6 Briksdal glacier, 1931

Plate 4.7 Roberts family at the glacier snout

Plate 4.8 Briksdal glacier from Kattenakken, after collapse of snout

Plate 4.9 Oldenvand from Kattenakken

Plate 4.10 Brian with Såmi herder and reindeer

Plate 4.11 Såmi couple with their laavu

Plate 4.12 Traffic jam on climb
from Geiranger

Plate 4.14 Laerdal gorge, with wire bridge, Denis halfway across

Plate 4.13 Galdhøppigen, Denis on sledge

Plate 4.15 Borgund stave church (1890s lantern slide)

Plate 5.1 Brian aged 17

Plate 5.2 Iceland party on Lensfield meadow 1932,
from left Falk, Roberts, Beckett and Lewis

Plate 6.1 Three of the Cambridge party on Vatnajökull ice cap, Roberts in the centre

Plate 6.4 Vatnajökull revisited

Plate 6.2 Falk on edge of Hveragil gorge

Plate 6.3 String of pack horses crossing wide river

Plate 7.1 The road to Þingvellier

Plate 7.2 Roberts being lowered over cliff top to a gannet colony

Plate 7.3 Emmanuel Glacier

Plate 7.4 *Pourquoi Pas?* in the ice

Plate 8.1 Roberts at the wheel of *Penola*

Plate 8.2 Watercolours of gentoo penguins (*Pygoscelis papua*) by Lisle Ryder

[a] newly-hatched chick
[b] first down
[c] second down
[d] adult ♂

Plate 8.3 Fox Moth aeroplane being loaded with provisions

Plate 8.4 Wilson's petrel gliding over storm waves

Plate 8.5 Wilson's petrel appearing to 'walk on the water' as it searches for food

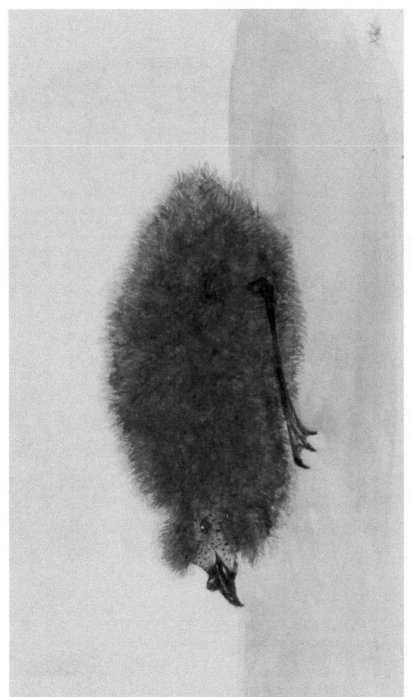

Plate 8.6 Watercolour by Lisle Ryder of Wilson's petrel chick

Plate 8.7 BGLE northern base hut and rope bridge across Stella Creek

Plate 8.8 A less stylish performance on the rope bridge

Plate 8.9 The huge chinstrap penguin rookery at Baily Head, Deception Island

Plate 8.10 Chinstrap penguin with two chicks

[a]

[b]

[c]

Plate 8.11 Chinstrap penguins painted by Lisle Ryder

Plate 8.11 Watercolours of chinstrap penguins (*Pygoscelis antarctica*)
by Lisle Ryder (2)

[a] newly-hatched chick
[b] about two weeks old
[c] chick in second down
[d] yearling ♂
[e] adult

Plate 8.12 An exchange of views between Roberts and a
bull elephant seal, South Georgia

Plate 8.13 Creche of king penguins in late winter,
Bay of Isles, South Georgia

Plate 8.14 A pair of southern fulmars, Clarence Island

Plate 8.15 Magellanic penguin painted by Lisle Ryder

6

THROUGH SLUSH
AND LAVA DESERT

During the 1920s and 1930s Oxford and Cambridge developed a 'cult of the Arctic' whereby groups of young men, including undergraduates, would spend the summer vacation in previously unexplored parts of the Arctic, in particular Spitsbergen, Greenland and Iceland. Iceland had intrigued Brian since his mid-teens and in his first year as an undergraduate he was encouraged by the Scott Polar Institute's director Frank Debenham to lead an expedition there. Little scientific work had been carried out on Europe's largest ice cap Vatnajökull, as it was such challenging terrain to cross.

Iceland, an island some 230 miles wide, just touching the Arctic Circle, is constantly assailed by earthquakes, volcanic eruptions and *jökulhlaups* (the rapid melting of huge amounts of sub-glacial ice due to volcanic eruption below the surface). In the 1960s plate tectonics became the accepted model for the outer crust of the earth, the plates of which are constantly moving. It was founded on the earlier work of the German meteorologist Alfred Wegener, who in 1912 had proposed the concept of continental drift and the idea that all the continents were once joined together into one single landmass named Pangaea. One of the plate boundaries, known as the Mid-Atlantic Ridge, runs up the middle of the Atlantic Ocean. Iceland is situated where this submarine ridge has come to the surface, cutting through the middle of the island. Accordingly the island is made up of geologically young volcanic rocks – the oldest Tertiary, 20 million years old – and many areas are covered with *hraun* (lava fields). The largest single area of *hraun* is the dry desert in the centre of Iceland, to the north of the Vatnajökull ice cap.

To travel anywhere along the southern plains of Iceland necessitates crossing many wide braided outwash rivers which descend from the ice caps. Today modern engineered bridges carry a ring road across this area, but in the 1930s the only means of transport for travellers was on horseback. Vatnajökull had been crossed a handful of times, but was little studied and its north-east corner was not even mapped.

Reading up all that he could find on Vatnajökull, Roberts came across an account by the Danish geologist and military man J P Koch, who had crossed the ice cap in June 1912 from north to south and back again using 14 Icelandic horses, in order to test their suitability for exploring the Greenland ice cap. The problem of having horse transport on ice, as Scott had found in the Antarctic, was that you have to carry a lot of fodder for them. In Koch's small party was the 30-year-old Alfred Wegener. The detailed description of their Icelandic journey intrigued Roberts. The Icelandic horses had performed well on all kinds of difficult terrain, crossing endless wide rivers created by the ice cap meltwater and traversing the undulating and unstable lava deserts of the hinterland. In this lifeless dry desert region they had also travelled through an extraordinary oasis called Hvannalindir, with bird life and lush vegetation.

Only two summers before Roberts was planning his Iceland expedition, Wegener had used a new method of measuring the thickness of the Greenland ice cap by means of explosives and a seismograph (a device used to record earthquakes). This suggested the possibility of using the same method to measure the thickness of the Vatnajökull ice cap.

Roberts' team of five was chosen for its multidisciplinary interests. It included Cambridge men J Angus Beckett (surveyor), Peter Falk (botanist), Launcelot Fleming (geologist) and Brian's supervisor W Vaughan Lewis (seismologist and surveyor). In addition there was F W Anderson from Southampton University (geologist and zoologist, and at 27 years the oldest). None of them had any previous Arctic experience, and Brian was not only their leader but at 19 the youngest member of the expedition. The main objectives of the expedition were the use of seismic sounding to determine the thickness of the ice cap, and ecological surveying, both in the lava desert north of the ice cap and along the southern coastal belt. By January 1932 Brian had acquired good organisational skills and received essential advice from Debenham on mounting an expedition. In between his studies he had just six months to prepare for it.

Since no seismograph was available in Britain, the Cambridge Scientific Instrument Company was approached to make one. At a cost of £306 it was to be by far the most expensive item. The Royal Society and the RGS each contributed £150 towards the cost. The second greatest expense was the hire of horses and their guides, anticipated at around £100. Equipment included two three-man ridge tents (each with its own cooking equipment, so there would be two cooks) and two 11 ft Nansen-type sledges fitted with steel runners. Brian's father put together a comprehensive medical kit and wrote for him a first aid book intended to cover most eventualities in the field. Some provisions were donated, such as Bovril pemmican and a case of Cadbury's chocolate. The food rations, consisting of biscuits, pemmican, butter, chocolate and sugar, were based on the experiences of the latest expeditions of the time, but today they seem grim and lacking in nourishment for a party which was not expecting the chance to hunt, shoot or fish.[1] To drink they would have cocoa twice a day, and Horlicks' malted milk tablets on special occasions. They found that although the rations were adequate, pemmican – a meat extract rich in albumen, meat fibre and animal fat – had its shortcomings, as Fleming later recalled: "You take it like a soup. A plate full after pitching camp gives you the impression you've had a five-course dinner; the great thing is to go to sleep before you discover you haven't... It is chiefly conveyed as liquid and the result is that one's inside is astonishingly empty."[2]

On 22 June the party departed from Hull with free passage on board the steam trawler *Lord Balfour of Burleigh*. Twenty-two crates of equipment and provisions, including 100lb of gelignite and a detonator, were stowed in the central fish hold. The rest, including the two sledges and six pairs of skis, was loaded on deck. A free passage meant no accommodation, so all six men had to share the skipper's tiny chartroom and his bunk: two lying on bench seats, two in the bunk and two rolling around on the floor. Predictably rough weather and the smell from the fish liver barrels on deck overwhelmed them with seasickness, all except for Roberts who wrote that "at breakfast today, I was the sole survivor of the expedition trying to keep its reputation up and my food down".[3]

On arrival at Höfn on Iceland's south coast, the party was met by Þorbergur Þorleifsson, an English-speaking Icelander who looked after all their needs and would be their guide up to the edge of Vatnajökull, where another guide Skarphjeðinn Gíslason would take over and make the ascent to the ice cap with them. Þorbergur collected a train of 28 pack horses which were to follow behind the main party, and they all set off westwards on horseback along the south coastal plain for about 30 miles to Staðardalur. Along the wide area of glacial outwash gravels an endless number of rivers had to be crossed, and they found themselves crossing more water than land. The rivers were three to four feet deep, and the horses always seemed to swim at a level at which the water flowed directly into their riders' thigh-length wellies. After each river crossing a boot-emptying stop was necessary. But the horses "were simply magnificent, galloping hard regardless of the surface, and fording the swift flowing streams in the most confident manner".[4]

The awkward ascent up to the ice cap took them 10 hours, zigzagging up steep scree slopes with the cumbersome equipment, including the heavy 300lb seismograph and explosives. At the edge of the ice cap the guides and horses left the party to continue alone (*Plate 6.1*). As Fleming described, they were expecting something of the character of a polar expedition, but conditions did not quite turn out that way:

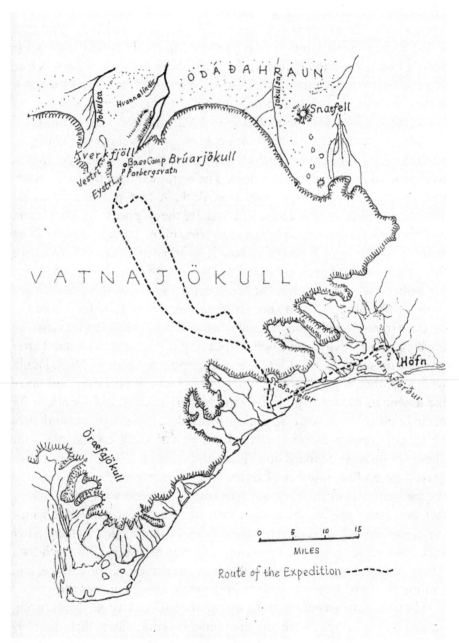

Vatnajökull expedition route 1932

"We had sledges, man-hauling harnesses, cold weather clothing and food; and we were visiting little known territory. But we had not thought of polar exploration in terms of rain. Torrential rain started the evening we pitched camp and lasted five days, soaking all our equipment, and by the time the rain stopped the snow surface all round our tents had dropped a couple of feet."[5]

In the midst of this soggy start Roberts, Lewis and Anderson tried to get the seismograph up and running, only to find that when switched on it made a horrid grinding noise, and despite many attempts they were unable to operate it. They had laboriously transported the heavy precision instrument and explosives safely up onto the ice and now they were faced with abandoning them. It was a bitter disappointment to everyone, most of all to Roberts. Disconsolately they left the equipment carefully packed up to collect on their return.

CAMP DRIBLET

On 1 July they set off across the ice cap, each sledge with 700lb of food and equipment hauled by three men. The temperature was well above freezing and the snow surface soft, which with the upward slope made manhauling arduous. The first day they covered barely two miles. Fortunately they could avoid the crevassed area, but then a thick fog descended on them, lasting ten days. Torrential rain accompanied the first five days, streams of water running through the tents to which they were confined. So much thawing was going on that the ground surface around their tents fell by some two feet and the tents collapsed. Sleeping bags were wet and cold, and leaving the tent meant a certain drenching. Fleming found one means of avoiding wet clothes, which was to go out stark naked save his boots. He returned none the worse for the experience.

Checking equipment, Roberts opened one of the packing cases to discover that it was full of water. It was the only case which the rain had warped and made leaky, and it contained everyone's camera equipment. The sodden cameras were solemnly handed out to their owners. After hours of work the two cine cameras were revived, but Roberts' films of the ascent onto the ice cap were all ruined.

After 100 hours of continuous rain the weather finally improved enough for the party to leave 'Camp Driblet', as it was christened, but sledging on the soggy snow surface was impossible. They tried sledging at night, but the temperature was not much lower and there was still a lot of fog and rain. Manhauling in oilskins and sou'westers was decidedly uncomfortable, and trying to dry out sodden clothes was hopeless.

Sledge hauling across the ice cap, Kverkfjöll in the distance

One day the cloud lifted for a few hours and they could at last see the surrounding landscape of peaks as well as a long mountainous ridge some miles away. But even as they neared the northern edge of the ice – apparent from the increase in volcanic dust – conditions were no better and everywhere there were pools of slush. A surface layer of volcanic grit meant that obtaining drinking water was now impossible unless they dug deep into the snow. Even if the surface was frozen, beneath it was up to two feet of semi-frozen slush, so that every step broke through the crust and sank them up to their knees. It was not long before one sledge got completely stuck and wouldn't budge, even with all six of them pushing and pulling. The only solution was to remove all its load of cases and transport them on the second sledge to a place where the ice was stronger – a job taking many hours through the night.

Spirits were revived by a glorious sunset which melted into sunrise, giving them nearly four hours of fiery light. And best of all, they could at last distinguish the volcanic cones of Askja and Snaefell, with their first sight of the lava desert beyond the ice cap to the north. They were heading for an unmapped part of the northern edge of the ice cap known as Brúarjökull, where they pitched a base camp on 14 July. There was plenty for them all to do here. Lewis and Beckett began surveying the area, since existing maps were inaccurate. They discovered an ice-dammed lake, naming it Þorbergsvatyn after their first Icelandic guide. They were on the edge of Ódáðahraun, Iceland's biggest black sand lava desert, which is almost completely devoid of life.

HVANNALINDIR: A GREEN OASIS

Some 20 miles north of the camp lay an area of lush vegetation along the banks of the river Lindir: the oasis of Hvannalindir, named after the plant *Angelica archangelica* (*Hvonna* in Icelandic) which grows profusely along its banks. Being the first to do any scientific recording there, the two biologists Roberts and Falk set off towards Hvannalindir with high hopes, a tent and rations for ten days, while the others stayed behind and mapped. Each carrying a load of 60lb, progress over the awkward terrain of lava scree was painfully slow. Roberts was almost bent double by his load and, pouring with sweat, quite unable to enjoy the splendour and desolation of his surroundings. Struggling to find a route through the drizzly mist in the mountains, they found themselves in a deep gorge, the river torrent some 300 ft below (*Plate 6.2*). The mist obscured what might have been a spectacular view down into the bottom. It looked hopeful as a possible way out to the lowlands, until they reached a massive waterfall where they had to climb the steep bank and walk along at high level with no certainty of a way through. They luckily found a means to cross the gorge on a natural snow bridge, some 20 ft thick. It was becoming obvious to Roberts as he struggled to keep up with his taller and longer-legged companion that he was much less fit than Falk. The one source of protein in their diet came from the pemmican, which made Roberts feel sick. His inability to consume his full ration was now taking its toll and he felt humiliated. What made it so much worse was that none of the others had this problem. According to Falk:

"It was extremely desolate country with a very occasional plant of *Arabis* or an unhealthy sea pink. As we descended, we left the mist behind and in its place we saw a landscape of monotonous black with an occasional view to the east of the dirty surface of Vatnajökull; a view that would have been depressing, if we had not been excited at the idea of passing through country which no one had explored before. Progress was slow at this stage as our loads prevented us from taking a full stride and each step sank an inch into the ground. Consequently, we planned to rest for ten minutes in every half hour and lunch came as a welcome relief when we found a block of relic ice dripping steadily on to the otherwise waterless surface of the desert. Lunch was particularly pleasant as our chocolate ration had been doubled and our biscuit ration reduced from two and a half to two a day to decrease the bulk of our load. After lunch our minds were chiefly occupied with the thought of the next meal, as our loads forced us to look down at our boots most of the time and we could not spare the breath to talk much."[6]

They were also frequently thirsty, needing to find a river as scooping up the moraine-covered ice resulted in a mouthful of lava sand.

Hvannalindir

A WILD GOOSE CHASE

Two days of walking, accompanied by the ubiquitous rain and fog, brought them late on the second evening to another oasis, a magical place to enjoy after their exertions. They were beside a small lake about three quarters of a mile long, the water bubbling up in springs. Surrounding the lake was lovely soft green moss and here they pitched their tent, especially grateful as they had forgotten the groundsheet. After the relentless dry lava desert, the buzzing insects, ducks quacking and dwarf willow vegetation gave them some joy. Next morning was spent collecting: Roberts insects, Falk plants. Then they were off once more across the *hraun*. Not far away, where the water flowed under the lava and bubbled up in a fresh oasis, they stopped by another lake. Here they found themselves in the company of a pair of whooper swans, several species of duck and a purple sandpiper. Roberts' thoughts drifted away from scientific recording and towards his poor stomach, and he made several attempts at shooting one of the swans but failed.

It was only another few miles to Hvannalindir. For the last mile or so the springs came together to form a stream which they followed, its banks a profusion of flowering angelica, willowherb, dwarf willow and moss. Having reached their destination Roberts' spirits were at least momentarily revived. Since they were staying put for a couple of days, he decided to carry out an experiment, eating a huge quantity of pemmican for lunch. This was not a success and he was laid out for the entire afternoon.

In addition to interpreting the glacial landscape features in their volcanic context, Roberts' mind was much occupied with birds; their number and diversity were a pleasant surprise. He recorded 11 different species and yet the one which he most expected to find breeding – the pink-footed goose – seemed to be absent, except for droppings and feathers. Farther north at Grafalond, where they had once been breeding, their eggs had been collected for a number of years by Icelandic farmers who took every last egg they could find. The birds had no doubt moved away to other breeding sites less accessible to human predation and this should have been one of them. It was 19 July and Roberts wished they could have been there earlier in the breeding season to settle the matter.

Since this area was poorly mapped, they more than once found themselves climbing a peak with no name, gaining a view of the great Óðáðahraun desert. Previous visitors to this area had struggled to do it justice with their descriptions: "The most gloomy and awe-inspiring

place in Europe."[7] To which Roberts added his: "The landscape was a picture of wildness and desolation. A confusion of numberless small peaks more or less the same height: some regular cones, others broad, some tooth-like, like stumps and pillars, and others like rocky castles... here and there a group of projecting rocks which resembled the ruins of a small town."[8] Walking along the top of a ridge, Kverkfjallarani, Falk found a particularly interesting flora: small colonies of alpines, including *Veronica alpina* and the intensely vivid blue *Veronica fruticans*, providing a good deal of pleasure in an otherwise desolate place.

There was one thing that Roberts wished to do before they left. Soil samples and a magnificent bluebottle (captured with great difficulty) had been added to their extensive collection of plants and insects. He now wanted to improve their diet. Armed with a revolver and great optimism, he waited by the river for an Icelandic ptarmigan to appear. "In about an hour and a half one appeared on a lump of lava about ten yards off across the river. I fired, and by a miracle the bullet hit it in the tail so that it could only fly in circles ending up in the river." On dashing in after it, a battle ensued from which he emerged wet but triumphant. The last lunch had been of pemmican, but now Roberts had something better to look forward to.

So in high spirits they left Hvannalindir late in the afternoon to return to the base camp. As well as each having eaten 5lb of food there, they had lightened their packs by leaving depots along the way, and progress was so rapid that they were back at the first oasis by early the next morning. Stopping at the lake where the whooper swans had been, they found no sign of them. With an aluminium cooking pot Roberts caught an Arctic char, which though too small to eat was a remarkable find. How had it got there, in a stream which disappeared into the ground a hundred yards from its source?

THE GATES OF HELL

One carrying a bird and the other a fish, Roberts and Falk arrived back at the first oasis, still a mass of colour and alive with the noise of ducks and insects. As they dined on pemmican with an extra ration of chocolate, Roberts thought he could see a swan on the far side of the lake. After dinner they crept stealthily round the lake, to find that there were two. One flew off immediately, but the other ignored them. Roberts fired his gun a few times, missing the bird, which seemed quite unconcerned. Finally with the twelfth shot he got it through its neck and it collapsed instantly into the water. It was Falk's turn to get wet, and he swam over to check that the bird really was dead. He then towed it to shore and in the dusk they carried their heavy trophy back together, laying it out between them in the tent so that no wandering Arctic fox could steal it whilst they slept. Next morning, with the stomach contents of both the swan and the ptarmigan carefully preserved for later analysis, they prepared the ptarmigan for lunch. The swan would make a magnificent feast for the whole party, while the ptarmigan was perfect for two. So they boiled it and spread butter over it, savouring every mouthful.

The two men set off for the Gates of Hell and the source of the river Kreppá, only for the inevitable rain and thick blanket of fog to descend upon them. This time they followed the Kreppá up to the edge of Brúarjökull, It would have been an easy journey but for the extra item: the swan was slung awkwardly on a tent pole between them.

> "The Kreppá was a remarkable sight. A wide and extremely swift flowing flood of dirty yellow water roared down a rapid where we reached the river bank, and great icebergs floated past in the fog."

They wondered how on earth a previous explorer, Þoroddsen, had ever succeeded in crossing at this place.

> "We followed up the banks in the pouring rain until we came to some falls about half a mile below the glacier. Here we sucked some lumps of ice for a drink as the river water itself is saturated with fine silt and quite undrinkable. Then we cut across a low ridge to the ice margin where the Kreppá flows along it just north of the Gates of Hell. The view here must be magnificent in clear weather. During a rift in the clouds we saw that the narrow gorge through the Gates rises in sheer cliffs to the very summits on both sides."[9]

A little farther on they discovered the source of the Kreppá. Finding a suitable place to camp was not easy. They settled on an old lake bed away from the river, sleeping on boulders as there was no vegetation. "During the night our close proximity to Hell was made evident... a tremendous roar woke us up at about midnight as a huge piece of the glacier cliff nearly 100 yards long calved off into the river, and we leapt out of the tent expecting the water to be deflected over us." However all was well and in the morning they could see a considerable diversion of the river below them. The Kreppá (meaning perilous or dangerous) was not given its name without good reason, and it was fortunate that they had not camped lower down.

From there it was not far to rejoin the others, with much relief finding everyone well and making progress with geology and surveying. A few discoveries had been made: unusual basaltic pillow lavas extruded in a former lake basin, and hot springs with surrounding vegetation nearby. But right now there was an urgent job to be done.

> "Andy, Angus and I went down to the stream with the swan to prepare it for the feast. Even with large knives and geological hammers we found this no easy matter. It must have been nearly two hours before we climbed up to the tents again bearing four pots of flesh and bone. Nothing was wasted. Even its neck was relished. That meal was worth all the labour of carrying him up from the desert. The cooking took 1¾ hours and the eating was spread out over an even longer period. The broth produced also made an excellent change from the everlasting pemmican."[10]

The feast was washed down with 'Vin de Vatna 1931-32'. With pleasantly full stomachs they all slept well that night.

There was plenty to talk about, with only one day left before the planned sledge journey home. But Vatnajökull had not finished with them yet. Drenching rain and a thick blanket of fog descended, confining them to their tents. Next morning's breakfast was more swan, as was supper. Nothing was wasted, the bones making excellent stock. It had rained and snowed hard all night, and they could not start for home. Under the moraine where their tents were pitched was a core of ice which began to ooze through the groundsheets everywhere, forming large puddles and requiring essential irrigation work during the night.

The following day, 26 July, the weather was still foul, and the tedium was getting on their nerves. A sewing party was held to repair various clothes and ski skins. Beckett repaired Falk's and Roberts' boots, which had been damaged by their excursion into the lava desert. Fierce geological arguments raged all day, and an air of grumpiness pervaded the camp. By now they had enjoyed the last stock from the swan's bones; the final meal was to gnaw the bones at breakfast the following morning.

At last the weather turned fine. After five days of confinement they jubilantly scrambled up the nearest hill to leave a record of the party's visit, deposited in a Horlicks tin and covered by a cairn. Then came the laborious task of packing up the tents and the gear. Sledges, skis, kitbags, tents and heavy wooden cases all had to be carried across the first half mile of soggy thaw pools before they could get going properly. But with lower temperatures and the weather holding, rapid progress was made back across the ice. Assessing their food rations, it was found that although nearly a month's supply of pemmican and butter remained, there was only enough cocoa and sugar for 12 days. Spirits fluctuated with the proximity of the next meal and the weather. Pulling sledges resulted in real hunger. Ironically they were now all becoming tired of the diet, except for Roberts, who felt his responsibilities acutely as leader as well as the need to keep a positive attitude. Everyone wanted to be getting home and off the ice cap; they were tired of the capricious weather, and watered-down cocoa did not help. For two days the sun blazed down on them, creating a further discomfort to sledge-pulling. On the third day, 31 July, a bitingly cold wind whipped up and the weather was starting to look stormy, but the sight of the sea some six miles away raised their spirits.

A TREACHEROUS DESCENT

As they began their descent from the ice cap, crevasses started to appear and they had to be especially vigilant. There was real danger ahead. One sledge team, far ahead of the other, suddenly encountered a huge crevasse in front of them and they only narrowly averted disaster by doing a quick U-turn. Anderson unharnessed himself to go ahead and reconnoitre.

Suddenly, to everyone's astonishment, a lone figure was seen approaching with a horse. It was Skarphjeðinn Gislásón, the guide who had brought them up onto the high ice. Starting off downhill, the second party lost control of their sledge and careered along helplessly behind it, landing in a heap of entangled sledge harness and skis, to their complete and utter humiliation. This did not even raise a smile from the stolid Skarphjeðinn, who solemnly raised his hat to each of them in turn, saying "welcome" and gravely shaking hands with them as they lay in the snow. They had no idea how he had come to make such a long journey up onto the ice cap in the threatening weather. He indicated that he had seen them from afar and had come to help them down. To describe this as exceptionally fortunate for the grateful and incredulous Englishmen would be an understatement. That he should have been there at all was a complete mystery, as they had left an indication that they would come down ten days later west of Öraefajökull, some 50 to 60 miles away. To reach the edge of the ice he had a journey of several miles to the foot of the valley, and then a steep climb of over 3,000 ft. It seemed most implausible that he had come up on such a remote chance of meeting them.

They now needed only to follow the horse tracks in the snow. At the bottom of the ice cap they were confronted by hard ice and a myriad crevasses. Even getting the sure-footed horse to cross some of the smaller ones was quite a task. Some crevasses had rifts over 20 ft across, and close to their first camp they could see how much the marginal ice area had changed in the five weeks they had been away. Their first camp remains were now perched on a narrow platform between two enormous chasms. What had previously been gentle slopes of soft snow was now hard ice broken up by dozens of enormous crevasses. It was clear that they could never have returned the same way that they had come up on the horses.

Skarphjeðinn gave them some sobering news: while the Cambridge party were at 'Camp Driblet', a German expedition which had set off to Kverkfjöll on the ice cap had never made it because of the raging storm,

Descent from the ice cap

and on their return their tent had been torn to shreds and blown away. They had then had a 12-hour forced march to reach the ice margin in terrible weather with no food. One of them was now seriously ill and was staying at a local farmhouse. With so much to talk about, it was frustrating to have a language barrier between them and the Icelander.

The wind was rising. Pitching their tents on a stony moraine, it was clear that they had only just got down in time. After sharing a meal together Skarphjeðinn left, promising to return with three pack horses in the morning. When on earth would he get any sleep? This man of extraordinary endurance and kindness left the camp late at night, riding down the mountain with a 7lb tin of pemmican under his arm.

Next morning was foggy and it was sleeting, and they doubted that Skarphjeðinn would appear. But he did so, at the agreed time and with five horses. He had brought fresh milk and butter, and a little phrasebook. They conversed in the eccentric language that only phrasebooks seem to know. The horses were duly loaded with provisions for the next base camp in the Staðardalur valley below. Well laden, they were less happy descending the steep scree slopes, and frequent stops were necessary.

After a six-hour descent they reached the foot of the mountain, relishing both the sight and smell of rich green plant life around them. The tents were set up. All were feeling wet and cold, so Roberts and Skarphjeðinn rode off to investigate a nearby farm where they might be able to get food. They were in luck, and moreover an English speaker at the farm was able to hear their stories and interpret for Skarphjeðinn.

So how had Skarphjeðinn come to find them? According to Roberts:

> "He had dreamed we were up on the ice margin, and being a believer in dreams he had come up to see if he could help us. This seems to be a genuine case of a true dream which the Icelanders often follow. He had only been twice before onto Vatnajökull: when he came up with us, and when he prospected the route before this – so the possibility of a chance meeting is most unlikely. I am sure no one would go up that mountain without a very strong faith in his dream. We also learned that the rivers are now in a dangerous condition due to the increased melting in the recent hot weather. A man was drowned a week ago along the route we shall have to follow back to Hornafjörður, and another was only saved by holding on to his horse's tail as it swam".[11]

What sort of return journey would they be in for? For now, they were tucking in to a feast of fried cod, potatoes, butter sauce, smoked lamb, black bread and milk. They were generously given some potatoes (a scarce commodity) to take back to their camp for breakfast. Six happy men returned to their tents with exceedingly full bellies. The next morning, 2 August, they were all up early in warm sunshine, joyfully frying up the potatoes in butter and savouring the wonderful change of diet. They then dispersed to work locally in their different fields of botany, glacial geography and insects while Beckett and Roberts set off on horseback for the marshes and sea coast in search of birds. The horses were not at all frightened by the noise of a gun, but the click of a camera completely spooked them. After a profitable day's work the men returned to the same farm for supper, where their hostess had invited them back for an even greater feast of mutton, potatoes, turnips and rhubarb followed by coffee. Skarphjeðinn had arrived, and produced a fishing net which he helped them set up across the river back at their camp to catch trout. Just in case they didn't catch any, he presented them with some dabs for their breakfast.

Next morning brought yet another wonderful breakfast of fish and turnips. Then Roberts and Beckett prepared to go up to the ice cap to fetch down the rest of the gear from their first camp. Skarphjeðinn arrived at 9 am with nine horses. Riding all the way they reached the top in an impressive 2½ hours. There was dense fog but they could follow the tracks left from their first descent. Skarphjeðinn was delighted, saying that no one had ever been up before in a fog. He declared that the route would now be known for all time as Kambryggjuvegur ('Cambridge Way'). With the boxes roped up, Skarphjeðinn announced that it was time for his breakfast. When Roberts and Beckett produced their lunch of chocolate and biscuit, Skarphjeðinn invited them to share his breakfast of milk, butter, black bread and a whole leg of smoked mutton. It was sleeting hard and bitterly cold, and Skarphjeðinn also produced a warming tipple of something vodka-like which hit the spot. Amongst the things left behind on the ice were the sledges, drums of wire and a lot of pemmican. All were presented by the Englishmen to their guide who was delighted, especially with the wire: an expensive item in Iceland, and he was an electrician. They descended in 4½ hours and were mighty glad to arrive back at camp, with enormous gratitude to their wonderful guide.

As no trout had been caught in the nets the previous night, breakfast on 4 August was grim: nothing but pemmican and biscuit. They had two days left to finish their work here, meeting several people at the farm over the evening meal to discuss their findings and to hear news of the world. Later that same evening Þorbergur, their guide across the outwash plains, arrived bringing fresh horses for their journey to the coast and a huge bundle of letters for all of them. They retired for the night in their camp dreaming of the next morning's promised breakfast of trout, whimbrel and fried potatoes.

WATER EVERYWHERE

The horses Þorbergur had brought were, he announced, the finest in the whole of Iceland. The south-east coast was reputed for its animals of great stamina and speed. Roberts had barely mounted his when it was off like a rocket, and nothing he could do would stop it. It jumped every obstacle including a stone wall until it reached a gate which, to Roberts' relief, it could not get over. His was not the only horse with its own agenda. Falk's had made off in the opposite direction and was halfway up a mountain with its rider before changing its mind and rejoining the rest of the party.

They crossed several deep rivers before reaching their next farm for the night. Over the evening meal they discussed the various new place names they were proposing with Þorbergur. Skarphjeðinn joined them the next day along with a local farmer to make the dangerous crossing of the rivers on the journey between Smyrlabjorg and Höfn (*Plate 6.3*). It was here that two days previously two Icelanders had been swept off their horses' backs and one had drowned. The rivers being so dangerous when in full flood, it was the custom of the local farmer at each stopping place to accompany travellers across the river near their farm and guide them across the deep channels. Water was everywhere. The first river they crossed came above their knees as they sat in their saddles, while the baggage on the pack horses became waterlogged within minutes. Forewarned of this they carried their photographic equipment and films in rucksacks on their backs. After the slow river crossing there was an enjoyable fast gallop across the level outwash plain, described by Angus Beckett:

"A grand ride brought us to the banks of the Hólmsá, the swiftest and most dangerous river on our journey. We halted for a considerable time to enable the pack ponies to catch up and the guides to test the bed of the torrent for quicksands.

"When all was ready for the crossing, we kicked our stirrups free in case of accidents, and advanced in single file. The river was about 250 yards wide and consisted of alternate shoals, quicksands and moderately deep channels with the water rushing down in an eddying flood.

"We proceeded diagonally up stream, so that the ponies would not expose their flanks to the torrent and be swept away. Following the banks of shingle as far as possible, we seemed to make fair progress up stream, but very little across. An exciting incident occurred when we were about two-thirds of the way over. A local farmer was heading the procession and leading a spare pony; Thorbergur came second. The spare pony suddenly took fright and turned round, holding up the whole cavalcade. Our ponies became excited and turned broadside on to the stream, which luckily for us was only just up to their bellies at this point. Thorbergur and the other guide acted extremely quickly and we got our ponies going again just in time. Stiff oilskin coats and trousers and rubber thigh boots would not give one much chance if deposited in a swirling glacial stream."[12]

Their destination that night was Hólmur, almost an oasis in the desert: a green patch in the midst of miles of gravel wastes and rushing waters. The farm looked prosperous by Icelandic standards and a sheep had been killed in honour of their arrival. They did full justice to the meal, after which they were sad to say goodbye to their wonderful guide Skarphjeðinn, who left to return with the other local farmer who had accompanied them from Smyrlabjorg. The table cleared, it was the moment for some musical entertainment. One of Þorbergur's guides sang, accompanied by Anderson on the harmonium. Then it was time to reciprocate, and Lewis accompanied a sing-song of all the British tunes the expedition team could think of, including rounds such as *London's Burning* and *Three Blind Mice* which were especially enjoyed by Þorbergur.[13] A successful day was rounded off with an inter-tent game of football in the meadow, using a ball made from a kitbag rolled up in a tent bag tied up with string. After only a few minutes it fell apart, to the relief of the players, who could barely stagger back to their tents after their huge meal.

The following day, 7 August, Roberts began with coffee and skinning a few birds before setting off. As he remarked: "Skinning is extremely hard when we are moving on every day, and as the boxes are submerged in the rivers it is a difficult job to make up good skins." That day would present them with more excitement in river crossing. At Hornafjarðarfljót the water was so deep the horses had to swim whilst the men sat on their backs:

> "When a route had been selected, Thorbergur gave us full instructions about managing a pony when swimming. The stirrups are lifted up and crossed over the animal's back and the reins allowed to hang loose, the rider clings hold of the unfortunate beast's mane and endeavours to remain in the saddle. Some ponies swim high, others low, and when riding a low swimmer the water reaches one's waist.
>
> "Thorbergur led the procession and we all followed in a line, the Hólmur farmer bringing up the rear. On we went with the water rapidly becoming deeper, until the ponies were forced to swim. Thorbergur's animal lurched in the most alarming fashion upon getting out of its depth, and only a magnificent display of horsemanship prevented the beast from getting rid of its rider.
>
> "It is a curious experience, riding a swimming pony, for after an initial sideways lurch down go their 'bows' and then their 'stern' in a most unsteady galloping motion."[14]

Safely all across, the next task was to empty out rubber boots and oilskin trousers, which had collected several gallons of water. They still had to make the long crossing of a shallow fjord, which meant travelling in single file because of the danger of quicksand, but there were also some enjoyable wet gallops. By now the horses realised they were nearly home and galloped for all they were worth. On arrival at Hólar, the tents were pitched in a field close to Þorbergur's family home. His father Þorleifur Jonsson was vice-president of the Alþingi (Iceland's parliament) and gave the party a warm welcome, ensuring they were well provided for with meals and comfort.

The following day was a black day. A telegram arrived from Hull with the news that there would be no trawler available to pick them up at Höfn, as the fishing grounds had altered. Fishing off the Icelandic coast had been poor and the trawlers had all moved to Norway and Bear Island. The choice was now either to ride along the coast to Reykjavik, some 250 miles, or to charter a small motor boat to take them to Vestmannaeyjar (the Westman Islands) where they could pick up the mail steamer for England. But there was another blow, in the form of a hefty bill for the horse transport. In addition to the considerable extra help needed from local farmers enlisted to help the party cross the swollen rivers, there were heavy unforeseen grazing charges for the horses at the farms. In view of their debts, the more attractive idea of riding to Reykjavik had to be ruled out as too expensive. The second option of obtaining a boat would cost only half as much, and that way they could take all their gear.

The gloom was lifted a little by the kindness and generosity of their host Þorleifur. He charged them only a pittance for his open-ended hospitality, providing support and stimulating discussions together with his son Þorbergur, who also made only a modest charge for all his invaluable help. A cheerful moment also came from the radio, when a news programme reported on the Vatnajökull ice cap expedition by the Cambridge party. Þorbergur and Þorleifur had notified the Reykjavik radio station, and despite language difficulties the men enjoyed hearing about themselves, especially when they picked up the news that at Kverkfjöll they had discovered *eina kongulo og tvaer flugur* ('one spider and two flies'). Somehow the word 'species' had been omitted.

They remained as guests for a few more days, giving them the opportunity for more scientific work along the coast. On 14 August the party was ready to leave, with all the cases packed up and taken in an old lorry down to Höfn. They were given a resounding send-off, not only by Þorleifur, Þorbergur and family but by the entire population of Höfn who had turned out to wave them off.

PERIL AT SEA

For the first few hours of their boat journey there was glorious sunshine and a calm sea, and they could enjoy the views of the mountains and glaciers descending from Vatnajökull. But it was spoilt by the severe vibration and deafening noise of an unsilenced oil engine. They were on the same vessel which had met the trawler on their arrival: a small fishing boat about 30 ft long with a wheelhouse and tiny forecastle. The deck was almost entirely taken up by oil barrels and an unseaworthy dinghy. The crew of four consisted of a skipper, mate and two deckhands, one elderly and the other a youngish boy. Only the mate, who seemed to be the most competent, had ever been along the coast to Vestmannaeyjar. All desperately hoped that the good weather would stay with them on the 200-mile voyage westwards along the coast, as there was not a single port or shelter a boat could make for if caught in one of the frequent storms.

As Roberts recalled: "Towards evening the wind freshened and an ominous looking bank of black clouds on the horizon drew rapidly nearer. A storm at sea is always unpleasant, but particularly so when one is in a leaking, rotten boat with a totally incompetent crew. It was very cold and we tried ineffectually to sleep in turns in the stern with waves constantly breaking over us... sea-sickness made things even more unpleasant but I was luckier than most. Angus and I have been least ill, and at one stage managed to consume a leg of mutton between us – no one else wanted any."[15]

The skipper had been relying on the log and views of the coast for navigation. He was deprived of both. The compass had jammed and they had no proper chart. Driving rain through the night obscured the coast, which they knew to be too close for comfort. The elderly deckhand and the young boy hid in the forecastle: Anderson and Fleming lay in the wheelhouse. Fleming "passed through those two stages of seasickness – first of fearing that you are going to die and then of fearing that you won't".[16] The other four lay on deck, continually drenched by waves breaking over the side. As the night wore on the storm increased in force. At one point a huge wave crashed over the boat, with water pouring into the hold, through the wheelhouse and into the engine room. The four in the open were washed across the deck and only by sheer luck were caught by the small rail at the stern, preventing them from disappearing overboard. Frozen stiff by the wet and cold Lewis and Falk managed to get into the forecastle, while Beckett and Roberts clung to the wheelhouse for dear life. In spite of the dangers, they both admired the beauty of the storm as "glittering phosphorescent cataracts of water swept across the deck sparkling like thousands of tiny jewels".

As dawn approached, the storm was at its worst. Fifty-foot waves tossed the boat drunkenly up and down. The boom broke loose and swung violently from side to side, threatening to reduce the wheelhouse to matchwood. The dangerous task of securing the boom was achieved by the mate, while the skipper sat with his head in his hands in the forecastle. A few hours later through the fog they suddenly saw a rocky headland all too close by and realised how perilously near to the coast they had been driven. Only providence had brought them safely at last through the mist to Heimaey, the main island of Vestmannaeyjar.

On the quay a large crowd was gathering to watch the bedraggled men disembark along with their sodden gear from the hold. Roberts made straight for the British vice-consul, who immediately gave the men hospitality in his offices. Six wretched, wet and filthy men tramped across his thick carpets with enormous gratitude. They washed, their clothes were dried, and coffee and cakes arrived (Iceland being virtually teetotal, coffee had become the national drink). Accommodation was arranged locally and their passages booked to England. The following day the local barber had six new clients, as did the local bath-house. This imposing building had one bath – the only one in Vestmannaeyjar – but none of the party was brave enough to enter, owing to rumours that they would be set upon by a woman and forcibly washed. Finally Fleming volunteered to explain to the young lady in charge that all they wanted was a bath and no additional attention. He returned clean and triumphant, paving the way for the others. Later on in the evening they walked through the town, meeting the vice-consul once again. He was unable to recognise them when they greeted him; and, much amused by the transformation, he invited them back to his house for coffee and cakes.

The next day was their last before leaving for England. Roberts badly wanted to make a census of the gannet colonies, which had not been adequately assessed. The Westman group consists of about 15 islands and at least 20 islets, with maps then showing much confusion over their names. A boat was chartered, this time a large motor boat with a highly competent crew. Roberts went out with Beckett, expecting to find a single gannet colony which was previously known about. In the event they found four, none of which was easy to reach. It was judged too rough to land anywhere, so they had to do the count sailing around close under the cliffs: a task they did separately and then compared results, which agreed closely. They arrived back late in the evening by moonlight, to find the others had enjoyed a day on *terra firma* and gone off to investigate the Helgafell volcano.[17] With still much preparation needed for their final departure, Roberts' last night was a brief two hours' sleep.

Early next morning they boarded the passenger steamer SS *Godafoss*, enjoying five meals a day and the luxury of big cabins with clean white sheets in their bunks. Three days later they arrived back at Hull, having been away for nine weeks. They had added ten new names to the official maps of Iceland, and discovered three new invertebrate species: one spider and two flies.

POSTSCRIPT: RETURN TO VATNAJÖKULL

In 2019 an expedition team of three young graduates (*Plate 6.4*) traversed the Vatnajökull ice cap.[18] Avoiding the summer melt[19] and the crevasses that the Cambridge men had experienced, they went in April. Here is a summary of the expedition by its leader Oliver Vince:

"The idea of retracing the footsteps of the 1932 Cambridge Expedition to the Vatnajökull Icecap began to form when we discovered the published account of their expedition in the Bodleian Library in Oxford. The diary *Iceland Adventure* was written by the team's surveyor John Angus Beckett and published in 1934.

"Beyond the obvious appeal of adventure, their expedition was of particular interest to us owing to its strong scientific focus. Conducting diligent scientific surveys in such hostile terrain requires a meticulously equipped basecamp and a well-fed and rested team: all things that greatly increase the overall safety margin of any expedition. The young ages and lack of prior polar experience of the 1932 team also appealed to us. Simply put, if they could do it, there was a good chance that we could too.

"Like the 1932 team, we spent a lot of time training, researching the area and contacting Icelanders who might be willing to assist us. When we arrived in Iceland (by aeroplane, not fishing trawler), we were amazed that by chance the guide that took us from Höfn on the south coast onto the icecap was the grandson of their 1932 guide, Skarphjedinn. Our guide did, however use a superjeep to transport us, rather than a fleet of ponies.

"During our first few days on the icecap we spent two days tent-bound due to a series of heavy rainstorms - an almost exact mirror of the 1932 team's 'Camp Driblet'. We did, however, have the benefit of fully waterproof tents and weather forecasts!

"We read the 1932 expedition diary as we moved across the icecap, sharing many of the experiences that they describe. At first, trepidation at what lay ahead, then the gruelling experience of dragging more than your bodyweight for many hours in whiteout conditions, and then, eventually, a sense of relief and delight from a safe crossing of the ice.

"The 1932 team pitched their scientific base camp in the shadow of the Kverkfjöll volcano, where the Vatnajökull Icecap meets the vast volcanic desert to the north. Identification of the exact location of their base camp was made easier by its proximity to a distinctly shaped volcanic dome that was recognisable from their photographs. On the summit of this dome, aptly named 'Dome 1', we found their cairn, built an astonishing 87 years before. After some rummaging, inside this cairn we discovered a sealed tin containing a handwritten wax paper note detailing the names, expedition roles and Cambridge colleges of the 1932 team. We preserved the decomposing note in a container and reburied it inside the cairn.

"In a tribute to the scientific surveys conducted by the 1932 team, we conducted a survey of the invisible microbial life living in a geothermal gorge close to their base camp, in addition to aerial drone surveys. The microbial study required fully off-grid DNA sequencing in our tent and was the first time this has been done in a polar environment. The drone surveys generated highly detailed 3D maps of their basecamp. More on this work can be found on our website.

"Now that we have returned, we look back at our time on the ice cap with the fondness that arises from the simplicity of time spent in nature, and also a sense of gratitude that the Vatnajökull allowed us to experience its majesty and return safely. Having repeated the 1932 team's journey with modern equipment, we remain in awe of what they achieved."

7

HITCHING A LIFT WITH CHARCOT TO MUSK-OX LAND

> Without Dr Charcot's aid we could never have reached Hurry Inlet. Not only did he give us our passage, but he did everything possible to help us in our programme of work and at the same time offered us every kindness while we were on board. It was a great honour to travel on so celebrated a ship as *Pourquoi Pas?*
>
> Brian Roberts

Roberts' four-week expedition to East Greenland in the summer vacation of 1933 was on a smaller scale than the previous summer's to Vatnajökull. He now had just two companions, the Cambridge zoologists Colin Bertram and David Lack. In 1932 Lack and Bertram had carried out an ecological survey of Bear Island in the Barents Sea, and now they wished to work on a continental area of the Arctic with a potentially richer fauna. Roberts also wanted to follow up his work already started the previous year in Iceland on the feeding habits of birds.

As organiser, the main challenge for Roberts was how to get to east Greenland for a month on a shoestring budget. Grants were forthcoming from the Royal Geographical Society and the Cambridge colleges. But they would still need a lift. Roberts wrote off a number of hopeful letters. Back came a warm affirmative reply from the French polar explorer Jean-Baptiste Charcot, opening a door for Roberts in the form of a treasured friendship with this distinguished 'gentleman explorer' who was so generous and kind to anyone he considered worth helping, especially students.

Charcot was a veteran of the Antarctic, having explored the west coast of Graham Land with his ship the *Français* in 1904-06 and then with the *Pourquoi Pas?* in 1908-10. Charcot discovered and named many of the features and islands of the Antarctic Peninsula. Since 1925 he had turned his attention to the Arctic, in particular visiting Scoresbysund nearly every year and assisting the Danish explorer Ejnar Mikkelsen to establish a colony there for Greenlanders. In 1929 he was appointed

to set up a French scientific base at Scoresbysund for the International Polar Year. Setting a shining example of international cooperation, he regularly gave passage to scientists from England, France, Germany and Denmark.

Charcot kindly offered to take the three Cambridge students to Scoresbysund, with full hospitality on board, and drop them off at Hurry Inlet near the mouth of the huge fjord system, an area known to have the richest vegetation in east Greenland. They would join the *Pourquoi Pas?* on 18 July when she would be taking on coal and water at Akureyri on the north coast of Iceland.

MOTORING ACROSS LAVA DESERT

On 4 July the three men sailed from Hull in SS *Dettifoss*, arriving at Reykjavik four days later. Their baggage of camping gear, provisions and zoological equipment was transported by ship around the coast to Akureyri. They also had a large item, an old 16 ft dinghy fitted with a lugsail, for getting about independently in Hurry Inlet. With two weeks to spare before the planned rendezvous with Charcot in Akureyri, they decided to charter a car for five days – a stout Chrysler with an Icelandic driver – to make the journey across the rugged interior of Iceland to Akureyri, visiting waterfalls, hot springs and geysers en route. The first day they drove to Þingvellir, the historic site of the Viking Parliament, situated in a massive rift valley. "The road from Laugarvatn to Þingvellir baffles description for its badness. Again and again we felt the car ought to fall to pieces. We carry a spade and a spare spring and use chains, which are essential."[1] (*Plate 7.1*)

Two days into their journey: "...the car is slowly falling to pieces. As we go along, all the various gadgets fall off and have to be collected and put in a box... in places the road disappears into wide, shallow rivers and is hard to find again on the other side. We are rather worried about our driver. He has had a terribly hard time and looks worn out".[2] Having crossed the barren dry desert they arrived at the famous lake of Mývatn (Fly Lake), where they paid off their exhausted driver and sent him home to Reykjavik. They were now able to enjoy the region's ornithology:

"Well has Mývatn earned its name...so many midges that they are like a thick fog and rise up in great black columns above all the dells and hollows; sometimes to a height of 10 m. or more. We landed [from a boat], expecting to be bitten to shreds, but they do not bite and only land all over one and fill up every fold or cranny, including the eyes and ears. This is a magnificent place for birds. We have already seen 14 species of duck here, a record which I do not think could be beaten anywhere else in Europe. The numbers are incomputable – the farmers here collect the eggs in thousands. The one we are staying with has already taken 12,000 this year and by law four eggs must be left in every nest."[3]

The next day they set off on horses with a guide to visit Dettifoss, the most powerful waterfall in Europe. It forms a double drop in a deep and narrow gorge of the Jökulsá á Fjöllum, a river flowing northwards from Vatnajökull across the central lava desert Ódáðahraun, familiar to Roberts from his previous year's expedition. Taking in some sulphur hot springs and bubbling hot mud pools on their return to Mývatn, it was a long day with 15 hours in the saddle and they arrived back wearily at 1:30 am. The next day a local ornithologist showed them a rarity: two young gyrfalcons, which he had caught.

Arriving at Akureyri and needing to get acquainted with their dinghy – now christened *Phalarope* – before the rendezvous with Charcot, they took her out for some sailing practice. On 18 July *Pourquoi Pas?* arrived as scheduled, anchoring in the fjord. She was a beautiful sight, a three-masted barque with white painted belly, much impressing the three young Englishmen.[4] As the ship entered the harbour, the unmistakable figure of Charcot himself stood on deck and waved to them, which he followed with a warm welcome on board and a tour of the ship, introducing his scientists and crew to them.

SEABIRD SURVEY OF GRIMSEY

News arrived that the ice was still thick at the entrance to Scoresbysund. They would have to wait until conditions improved, which might be at least a week. At Charcot's suggestion and with his help, they occupied the time with an ornithological trip to the little island of Grimsey, some 30 miles off the north Icelandic coast. A difficult place to get to, it required two boat journeys starting from Akureyri, the second of which – a six-hour voyage by rowing boat – saw them arrive late the following night. Charcot had told them to find the local pastor, Matthias Eggertsson, who lived next door to the church, through the middle of which, according to Roberts' map, ran the Arctic Circle. Everyone was in bed, but after much banging on the door they were admitted, fed and given a place to sleep.

On the tiny island three miles long by a mile wide there were then 130 inhabitants, who lived primarily from fishing and bird snaring. Roberts noted that "the success of the islanders is strangely different from that of the St Kildans in Britain, and although the birds used to be kept in check to some extent, very few are now taken for food. The people here eat adult guillemots and puffins and young fulmar petrels, gannets and kittiwakes in small numbers and take the eggs of arctic terns, guillemots, kittiwakes and eider ducks. By law four eggs must be left in each nest of the last of these".[5] Roberts was surprised how few ornithologists had visited Grimsey, considering how easily his party had managed it. They set about making a thorough survey of the bird life. Starting with the only colony of little auks, they found just five pairs. All the eggs had been systematically taken by one Icelandic dealer who sold to collectors on the international market. Egg collecting was much in vogue, especially for rarer birds. The same dealer had recently sold an egg for £1 (about £60 in today's money) to the Duchess of Bedford when she visited Grimsey.

That afternoon the Cambridge men procured the services of Eirikur Bjornsson, a very strong Icelander, who lowered them each in turn over the cliff by rope to see the gannet colony on a narrow ledge some 200 ft down. (*Plate 7.2*) On their descent they all got squirted with foul-smelling oil by young fulmar petrels – the birds' form of self-defence. After a nest count they were hauled back up the cliff by Eirikur, who effortlessly walked back inland with the rope over his shoulder. On returning to the clifftop Roberts was dismayed to find that a cow – of which there were only three on Grimsey – had managed to find and eat the leather strap of his binoculars.

Returning by boat to the mainland and on to Akureyri, the three men embarked on *Pourquoi Pas?* and on 25 July she sailed for Greenland's east coast.

ABOARD THE *POURQUOI PAS?*

Purpose-built in 1908 for Charcot's second Antarctic Expedition, *Pourquoi Pas?* was 131 ft long and equipped with both sails and a steam engine, as well as equipment for oceanographic work, three laboratories, a wireless and a photographic darkroom. Towards the end of the Great War the ship became a training vessel for the French navy. Charcot presented her to the Ministère de la Marine on the understanding that he could command her for three months every summer and they would keep her in good condition and pay the expenses of the crew. This was a perfect arrangement enabling Charcot to avoid having to pay for her costly maintenance. 1933 was the fourth successive year that Charcot would be working in Scoresbysund, the main object of the voyage being to bring home the French Polar Year party. Under Charcot were the ship's captain, four scientists, an artist and a crew of 28. The three Cambridge men were given hammocks to sleep in and offered the full use of a laboratory whilst on board.

Shortly after departure Roberts unexpectedly found himself being invited alongside Charcot and his officers to dine as a guest on a large French cruise ship, SS *Colombie*, which had arrived in the vicinity with several hundred passengers, all of whom were hungry for a chance to meet their national polar hero. Cruise ship dress code for dinner was formal evening dress, for which Roberts – who would be representing not only Cambridge but his country – was ill prepared. While Charcot and his men were impeccably dressed in dark suits, Roberts was faced with a struggle to smarten up: "The best we could raise between the three of us was not very smart: a tweed jacket with a vast darn in one elbow and a pair of none-too-clean flannel trousers with a patch in the left knee. Fortunately Colin had a white shirt which helped a great deal."[6]

The *Pourquoi Pas?* party boarded *Colombie* to much applause, and were invited to a 10-course dinner. This was a somewhat grim experience for Roberts, with everyone except himself in evening dress and conversing in French. During one of the many long speeches feting Charcot, Roberts' second elbow ripped open. At this point he gave up trying to conceal his inadequate dress. Amidst much signing of autograph albums there was at least plenty of champagne flowing. Roberts was actually not alone in longing to get back to the *Pourquoi Pas?* Charcot himself disliked these occasions intensely.

The following morning they awoke to find *Pourquoi Pas?* entering pack ice, with numerous hooded seals hauled out on the floes and two right whales close by, blowing hard. The best viewing spot was the crow's nest or the end of the bowsprit for watching the bows crashing through the ice, but astride the bowsprit you had to hold on tight, which was tiring.

The French reputation for *gastronomie* was in no way compromised by Charcot just because he was at sea. The Cambridge men enjoyed wine with every meal, and for any opportunity to celebrate – there was no shortage of those – champagne was brought out.

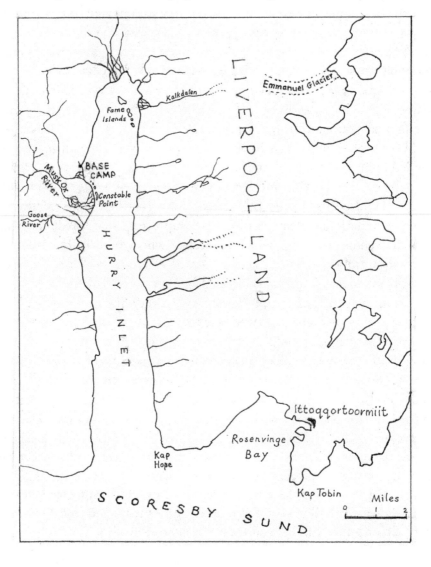

Journeying through the pack ice became slow as a thick fog enveloped them, and it was decided to halt for a while to get some exercise on the ice. Sixteen hours later when the fog lifted they were confronted with an almost unbroken sheet of ice. The only option was to retrace their course and approach Greenland farther north. This was more successful, and Greenland was sighted as they left the pack ice some 40 miles from the coast. Late on 28 July *Pourquoi Pas?* cast anchor at Ittoqqortoomiit in Rosenvinge Bay. This recently-established colony had been planned by the Danish government to prevent the dwindling isolated settlements of the east coast from being lost altogether to migration, as living conditions were so much more favourable on Greenland's west coast. The colony was founded by Ejnar Mikkelsen, who brought settlers from several locations including Angmagssalik farther down the east coast, creating a trading station for the Greenlanders and providing modern prefabricated houses for them to live in. They had a local governor and were given money for traded goods such as skins. It was hoped that these indigenous people, used to a life of kayak fishing and hunting on the ice, would continue their traditional ways. But given the number of visits by European expeditions, their desire for European foodstuffs and clothing would inevitably grow. The party was soon to witness some of the worst effects of this outside influence.

ALONE IN SCORESBYSUND

Arriving in Rosenvinge Bay, *Pourquoi Pas?* was greeted by members of the Polar Year party who came out to the ship. After their 12 months of isolation there was much news to be exchanged. After the French naval icebreaker *Pollux* had arrived from Akureyri with the Cambridge party's dinghy *Phalarope*, Charcot left Rosenvinge Bay to sail round into Hurry Inlet. The following day, 3 August, the Cambridge men loaded up all their gear in *Phalarope* and were towed ashore, before *Pourquoi Pas?* sailed away.

They had been landed at Constable Point, an extensive area of river delta which liberally deposited its loose sands into Hurry Inlet. It could hardly have been less suitable for a base camp, but since a strong gale was blowing they had little choice but to make the best of the situation. *Phalarope* had to be hauled up with tremendous effort onto the beach, as she dragged her anchor in the soft sand when they tried to moor her in the water. The nearest fresh water supply was a quarter of a mile

away, a tiny trickle of a stream a hundred yards from the sea. Here a gully provided a better spot to pitch tents, although it was rocky and sand blew into everything. Once camp was set up, they were off exploring. There were large numbers of geese around, though not many other birds. They had a sudden fright when a musk ox appeared over the brow of a hill just in front of them, but fortunately it had the same views about them and galloped away.

The next day they explored westwards up the river valley, which they named Musk-Ox River (it was later changed to Gaase Elv, Goose River). The limestone supported the rich vegetation that they had been hoping for. Valleys were carpeted with numerous Arctic species of heather, willow, dwarf birch and bilberry, as well as clumps of purple saxifrage, moss campion and white mountain avens higher up. Around their camp was a profusion of yellow Arctic poppies. Nearby vivid patches of pink willow herb covered the banks of the streams, and sheets of white cotton grass danced in the breeze on the marshy areas of Constable Point.

ENCOUNTER WITH A MUSK OX

While Lack was making a formidable insect collection, Bertram was doing the same with freshwater fauna, visiting every pond and stream. Roberts divided his time between ornithology and making a detailed compass survey of the area. Musk oxen were around them in considerable numbers, but taking photographs of the wary animals without any vegetation cover was nigh on impossible. Returning to their camp they suddenly found they were only 50 yards away from a bull, partially hidden as he was standing in a depression in the ground.

Ousted from the herd after being deposed by a new leader, old bulls become bad-tempered and aggressive. Retreat was too late. As the bull began to advance, pawing the ground and lowering its head, there was only one thing for it – to get out the rifle and fire. The first shot checked the animal momentarily. As it advanced again a second shot was fired. Because of its very heavy and thick skull a musk ox is one of the hardest animals to kill, and it took 16 shots to do it. Roberts and Bertram were both shocked by their own actions, but in the circumstances a quick decision was needed.

Another herd was feeding only about a mile from their camp. The experience was a warning not to go out without rifles, but now they had an inexhaustible supply of meat, and pemmican could be taken off the menu. The meat, cut into chunks, was all buried in a hole in a nearby snow bank. At dinner they were joined by a number of uninvited guests – ravens and Arctic foxes – who were happy to pick over the carcase.

Musk ox

Charcot had dropped four bottles of wine into *Phalarope*, and for the next few days they feasted like Frenchmen.

In the evenings, returning to camp after a long day, they would get a big fire going from the plentiful supply of driftwood logs around them, watching the ice floes drifting past in the fjord and writing up their notes into the early hours of the morning. After a few days they had covered most of the country in reach from base camp. It was time to venture out in *Phalarope*, but without much sailing experience between them navigating the constantly-moving pack ice was tricky. *Phalarope* was not entirely seaworthy and needed constant bailing out. The water was cold and in the event of a mishap there would have been no chance of a rescue. At the head of Hurry Inlet was a group of small islands, the largest of which had sheltered harbours to provide their next refuge. After camping overnight they continued sailing east across to Liverpool Land where they found good anchorage for *Phalarope*. They set off up Kalkdal (Limestone Valley) and after a long climb made it up onto the ice cap, hoping to reach a *nunatak*,[7] with the object of investigating its fauna. Roberts described the experience:

> "Distances here are most difficult to judge. It was midnight before we got to the top. Unfortunately we had no skis, and as we walked, roped and in single file, across the soft snow, the leader would constantly fall through into crevasses and have to be pulled out by the others.
> "The view from the summit was magnificent. The ice-cap is here only about five miles wide and runs down on either side in two great glaciers – one eastwards into the Greenland Sea, which we have named Emmanuel Glacier, and the other westwards to Kalkdal. Our view extended on the one side right out over the sea, thick with heavy pack ice, and on the other to the mountains fringing the inland ice sheet nearly 200 miles away to the west. North and south extended unmapped Liverpool Land."[8] (*Plate 7.3*)

As they set off down again, the sun rose over the sea and they arrived back at camp at 7 am, very tired. They had made the very first crossing of the Liverpool Land ice cap.

After catching up on sleep they awoke mid-afternoon that day to find Hurry Inlet full of heavy pack ice. Nevertheless they set off in *Phalarope* to cross the inlet back again, making for the north-west end to set up camp. Navigating between thick ice floes was hazardous, as the ice shifted about with the wind. Four days later, on 13 August, they were off again to Liverpool Land. For Bertram and Lack the abundance of insects, fish and plankton here was much more satisfying than on the western side of the inlet. They tried to vary their diet with a supper of boiled *Lepidurus arcticus* from a nearby lake. This small freshwater crustacean with a large carapace, looking much like some living Palaeozoic trilobite, was not a tasty meal. It had the flavour of warm mud.

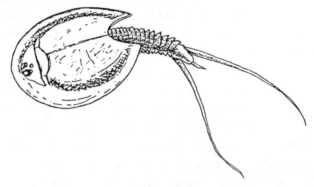

Lepidurus arcticus

The next morning a good breeze carried them back under sail to their first base camp. A galling discovery awaited them: their entire cache of musk ox meat had been taken by foxes. On burying over 100lb of meat deep in the snow, covered by a cairn of rocks, they had not calculated on the weather turning hot and melting all the snow. It was not much comfort to be back on a diet of pemmican, but fortunately they were soon due to be collected by the *Pourquoi Pas?* Their final efforts to finish experiments and insect recording were constantly thwarted by a herd of musk oxen which insisted on feeding around the camp.

BACK ON BOARD WITH CHARCOT

On 17 August, spotting *Pourquoi Pas?* near the entrance to their inlet, they hurriedly packed up in readiness. But suddenly the weather took a turn for the worse, with strong winds and a choppy sea, making communication with Charcot impossible. *Pourquoi Pas?* was forced to move away from them down the inlet to find safer anchorage for the night. The short summer was over and the first snow of the season had fallen on the mountains. The next morning Charcot returned, sending a boat ashore to collect the three men. Conditions were still rough and they had to wade up to their waists to get their gear on board. They then went to fetch *Phalarope*, having moored her in a shallow lagoon nearby, only to find her floating serenely on what was now a completely enclosed inland lake, beyond reach after the winds had sealed up the lagoon entrance with ice during the night. With much regret *Phalarope* had to be abandoned.

On board *Pourquoi Pas?* Charcot had his own news to relate. Ice conditions were so bad that he had been unable to do his planned work and instead had been largely confined to Rosenvinge Bay. Even there the ship was beset by ice and one day the pressure was sufficient to lift the ship out of the water. (*Plate 7.4*)

With the Englishmen now on board, *Pourquoi Pas?* made for Rosenvinge Bay to finish packing up the French Polar Year station. As it turned out, the station had already been visited by the crew of the icebreaker *Pollux*, which had left with the shore party two days earlier. In an inebriated state they had trashed the place, leaving chaos and confusion with rubbish and food strewn everywhere.

The following day, 19 August, manoeuvring out of Scoresbysund was slow and difficult due to thick ice everywhere. Once out in the ocean there were innumerable icebergs, but staying close to the coast they sailed southwards safely to Kap Dalton for some fossil collecting. They arrived late in the evening and the French geologists hoped to go ashore to collect fossils by torchlight. But landing in a small boat on this inhospitable stretch of coast was only possible if the sea was dead calm. With patience they finally succeeded, enabling them to collect a lot of Tertiary fossils. The presence of five polar bears in the bay, including a mother with her two cubs, created quite a distraction for everyone, especially as the first party consisting of Lack and the two geologists had no rifle protection. For safety Charcot sent Roberts and Bertram ashore in a second boat with a rifle.

This part of the Greenland coast is deeply indented with fjords, from which mountains and glaciers rise steeply up to the inland ice. It had first been sighted exactly 100 years earlier by the French naval Lieutenant Jules de Blosseville, who after returning to Iceland to report his discovery set off back to investigate further and was never seen again. It is a notoriously difficult coast to access. Champagne was opened to drink Blosseville's health. Despite a potentially treacherous landing Charcot, not one to miss an opportunity for international celebration, suggested a photograph ashore with the flags of France, Denmark and England – as he said, "Pourquoi pas?" Rowing through newly-formed thin ice, they managed a successful landing at 5 am. No sooner were they back on board than a thick fog descended and the ship was forced to anchor in D'Aunay Fjord, away from the danger of icebergs. By the evening sea ice was forming again and it was looking as though they might even have to overwinter there. Thankfully the fog lifted a day later, allowing them to put to sea again and enjoy the spectacular scenery along the coastline of King Christian 1X Land, indented with fjords from which precipitous black basalt mountains rise straight up from the sea. Having passed innumerable glaciers spilling down from the ice cap, they sailed eastwards for Iceland across an ice-free Denmark Strait.

Only 38 hours after leaving the Greenland coast, they arrived at Reykjavik. After a few days there *Pourquoi Pas?* set sail homeward to Brest. Charcot dropped his three hitch-hiking Englishmen ashore at Tobermory on the island of Mull. Sailing with this kind polar gentleman had been an unforgettable experience for them. Eight new place names (including Emmanuel Glacier) had been added to the Danish map of East Greenland, and the area west of Hurry Inlet – previously a blank on the map – surveyed. And Roberts and Lack had made the first ever seabird survey of Grimsey Island.

8

THREE YEARS IN THE ANTARCTIC: THE BRITISH GRAHAM LAND EXPEDITION

No major British expedition had been to the Antarctic since Shackleton's days in 1917. The Americans were now in competition: in 1928 they funded a pioneering Antarctic flight by the Australian Hubert Wilkins 600 miles south from Deception Island. The following year the US naval officer Richard Byrd had flown to the South Pole and now the millionaire Lincoln Ellsworth was planning to fly across the continent. In Britain, owing to the prevailing depressed economic climate, the charismatic young explorer Gino Watkins planned an Antarctic expedition in 1931 but was unable to raise funds. The previous year he had led the British Arctic Air Route Expedition (BAARE) to East Greenland, and when Pan-American Airways offered him more funding to investigate flying possibilities he returned there in 1932, only to die soon after arriving whilst out seal hunting alone in his kayak. Someone would need to step in as leader for the remainder of the expedition. It was the solidly dependable Australian big man John Rymill, who had come to England in 1923 keen to learn navigation and surveying skills and obtain a pilot's licence. Rymill now set his sights on the Antarctic.

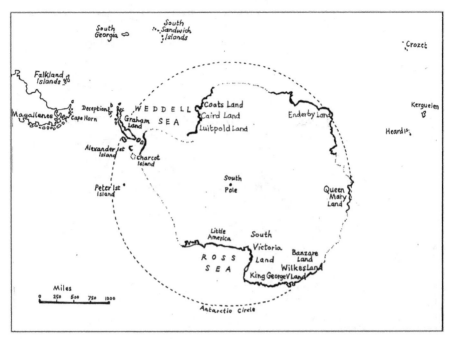

The Antarctic as known in 1934

MAKING PLANS

Upon returning from Greenland to Cambridge in 1933, Rymill began to plan his Antarctic expedition, with advice from fellow Australian Frank Debenham and also from the French explorer Jean-Baptiste Charcot, whom he visited in St Malo together with two recruits. The venture was to be called the British Graham Land Expedition (BGLE). Graham Land, the name given by the British to the 'tail' of Antarctica that stretches towards South America, was thought in 1930 to be an archipelago of islands. Backed up by aerial photographs Wilkins had reported that the region was broken up by at least three east-west channels, the largest of which he named Stefansson Strait. Rymill's plan was to work down the west side of Graham Land, using Stefansson Strait to break across eastwards by dog sledging and explore the coast behind the Weddell Sea. The western side of Graham Land was accessible down to 65°S latitude, but farther south had been little explored, heavy pack ice making it difficult to reach the coast by ship. In 1904-06 Charcot's *Français* expedition had reached Adelaide Island and in 1908-10 on the *Pourquoi Pas* he had made it to Marguerite Bay, naming features

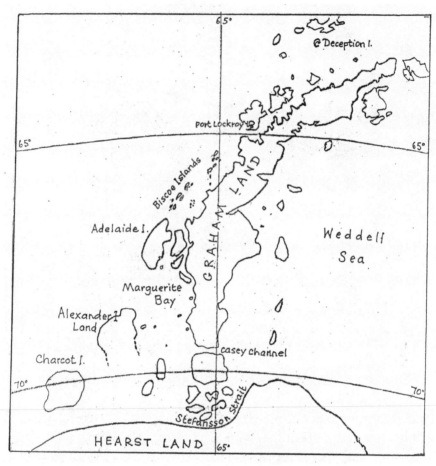

Graham Land as known in 1934

on the way. Now that aerial survey had become feasible, Rymill had hit a good moment to gain support. Official backing came from the Royal Geographical Society and a £1,000 grant was forthcoming in early 1934, kick-starting the daunting task of raising funds in the midst of an economic depression and the absence of any UK Treasury grant funding. The plans then gained support from the Colonial Office and with a cheque from them for £10,000 Rymill began recruiting his team (Annex II).

First on board were two of Rymill's trusted companions from BAARE. Wilfred Hampton, with a Cambridge degree in aeronautical engineering and experience of flying and repairing Gipsy Moths, was to be Rymill's second-in-command. Quintin Riley would multitask as meteorologist, commissariat officer and boatman for the shore party. Next on board was Roberts, whom Rymill initially wanted as a surveyor but who, backed up by Debenham, convinced Rymill that scientific work should form an important part of the programme. As a result two companions from Roberts' previous Arctic expeditions were invited to join: the newly ordained Launcelot Fleming with his dual role as geologist and chaplain, and biologist Colin Bertram. Rymill invited two more of his companions from BAARE: Alfred Stephenson, as chief surveyor and meteorologist, and Surgeon-Cdr 'Doc' E W Bingham, a doctor with the Royal Navy and a veteran of Watkins' expedition, who would take responsibility for the sledge dogs. Jim Moore was recruited as second engineer and surveyor, and I F Meiklejohn from the Royal Corps of Signals as wireless operator. Nearly all had Arctic experience.

To keep costs down, Rymill's plan was for the ship to be crewed by the expedition members themselves under the command of Lt R E D ('Red') Ryder, seconded from the Royal Navy, with another paid naval officer Lt-Cdr H Millett as chief engineer. The rest of the ship's party were J H Martin, first mate (who had served under Sir Douglas Mawson in the Antarctic), second mate Captain Lisle Ryder of the Norfolk Regiment (Red's older brother), and sailor Norman Gurney who had previous experience in polar seas.

The single greatest expense was the ship. After much searching Rymill found an old Breton 3-masted topsail schooner, built in 1908 and designed for cod fishing on the Newfoundland Grand Banks. Characteristically heavy and lumbering, she had a good carrying capacity of 200 tons and was capable of crossing the Atlantic both ways with a fair wind but performing poorly against it. She was refurbished in 1931 into a luxury yacht fitted with new masts and two Junkers 50 hp diesel engines for an American who subsequently discovered that his new wife hated the sea. Rymill was able to purchase the ship for an all-in cost of £2,680 and have her refitted for BGLE for an extra £5,179.61. Rotten timbers were replaced, and she was given 16 new berths and ice-strengthened with greenheart sheathing up to midships. Her bow was reshaped from the usual curve to a straight sloping stem, enabling her to ride up on the ice on impact and split it with her weight. She was also strengthened and protected by horizontal steel bands extending some 15 ft on either side, as well as being stiffened on the inside to withstand shock. All these necessary alterations would however limit her capabilities as a sailing ship. Two new bronze propellers were fitted. The single square topsail at the fore was fitted with roller reefing (working like a roller blind, but operated with chains and tackles) and the main sail and mizzen fitted with roller booms.[1] Her registered length was 106 ft and her beam 24 ft, and she was rechristened *Penola* after Rymill's family farm in South Australia.[2]

The next most expensive item on Rymill's shopping list was the aeroplane. A small single-engined De Havilland Fox Moth of wooden construction would work equally well as a seaplane and as a ski-plane. Hampton's experience over 18 months in Greenland with an aeroplane of wood rather than metal construction persuaded him to stick with wood, for which even major repairs could be carried out far more easily. Since they would be away for two winters a base hut was needed. A large prefabricated wooden hut with two storeys was designed for them in Denmark, upstairs to be sleeping quarters and the whole integral with an aircraft hangar. There were 1,500 parts, all numbered and colour-coded.

As the plan was to travel chiefly by dog sledge once their base was established, 64 dogs were bought in Greenland. Unfortunately on the way south they developed distemper and all but 15 died. A new lot of 34 dogs had to be hurriedly bought in Labrador. Several Nansen-type sledges and a motor tractor donated by Fleming's father completed the BGLE's transport needs.

On their shoestring budget, many supplies needed for survival over three years were obtained at discount or by goodwill gesture for free. Roberts needed to buy equipment for his intended biological work, and in Woking an appeal was launched on his behalf by Sir Arthur Bagshawe (a family friend, knighted for his work in tropical medicine), which brought in £287. Brian's uncle Kenneth Birley contributed £200 plus an additional £90 from his family, topped up by £50 for "an extra fur coat or something for your personal use or comfort. This is for you and not for the expedition".[3]

To make the most of the austral summer, Rymill hoped to be ready to sail at the beginning of September. Hampton and Stephenson had left two months earlier by cargo boat bound for the Falkland Islands with the Greenland dogs, aeroplane, timber for the hut and most of the stores. With the disaster of losing most of the Greenland dogs to distemper, Bingham had to stay behind to wait for the new consignment of Labrador dogs, which had not yet arrived.

On 10 September 1934 *Penola* finally sailed from London's St Katherine Dock. Covered in streamers and with sirens hooting, she was cheered off by a large crowd. Her deck was a farmyard and Roberts had been appointed 'farmer' to look after all the livestock. There were several crates of hens, two half-grown pigs and two Greenland huskies (veterans of Watkins' last expedition), plus two cats, Peter and William. The dogs and pigs had the run of the deck, but after inspecting each other the dogs kept well away from their grunting neighbours. The cats, after being trodden on, learned to keep out of the way. Settling down to their new surroundings and routines, the men were grateful for some calm weather over the first few days. It didn't last. Once out in the Atlantic Ocean the gales arrived and nearly all the new crew were seasick, leaving only Martin and Lisle Ryder available to shorten the sails. Roberts built the pigs a sty to sleep in; as pigs grow quickly he soon had to build them another larger one. The hens were all eaten in the first two weeks, except for one which escaped and was lost overboard.

The first of *Penola*'s shortcomings emerged when they tried to tack. Even with engines running she failed to turn, and heavy damage was caused to the sails. On crossing the Bay of Biscay, fierce squalls resulted in floods of water through the ventilator. Roberts' bunk was drenched. With seawater pouring into the wireless cabin an unscheduled stop was needed in Madeira on 24 September for replacement parts.

It took some weeks for the amateur crew to learn how to handle the sails. On landing at Montevideo after 62 gruelling days at sea, Roberts

Penola

lamented to his parents: "We have not had an easy time of it, and all my ideas on the 'Romance of Sail' have now gone. Colin and I both felt it quite strongly on *Pourquoi Pas?* when the only work to do was our own and we had the night to sleep."[4] Deck work on *Penola* was never-ending: manning the sails, tarring the decks to make them more watertight, overhauling and altering the rigging, blacking down all the rigging with a preserving mixture of Stockholm Tar and raw oil with bare hands, sewing torn sails, painting woodwork, oiling spars and much more. It brought home to everyone the huge amount of upkeep this type of boat requires. For the Cambridge men it was back to school discipline under Martin, who, used to giving orders to men with neither brains nor enthusiasm for work, used methods based on instilling fear. He expected them to learn 80 different ropes in the first three weeks during pitch dark night watches, which no one managed. They were then kept on deck out of watch hours until they achieved it. To begin with the watches were four hours on and four hours off, which meant working a 12-hour day and never getting more than three hours' sleep at a time. Later on this was altered to six-hour watches, more onerous but at least more conducive to achieving a decent period of sleep. Imposing naval discipline on the university-educated bunch of amateur crew members often resulted in friction. Roberts enjoyed being at the wheel (*Plate 8.1*), but wearing wet spectacles in the rain he suffered from eye strain during the long periods of extreme concentration needed to follow a compass bearing, made worse by not allowing himself to be distracted even if an interesting bird came along. As they sailed farther south the birds began to interest all on board, and with good rapport between scientists and non-scientists everyone contributed to recording observations.

THE FALKLANDS

Landfall at Port Stanley on 28 November was the most welcome of any made during the three-year voyage. "Never so much, either before or afterwards, had most of us longed so much for dry land and sleep," Roberts wrote.[5] Bingham, who had arrived a week earlier, now had a plentiful supply of healthy huskies. But there was considerable work ahead to sort out some of *Penola*'s problems, most seriously concerning her engines. The engine beds (installed before Rymill bought *Penola*), being made of unseasoned wood, had warped and split badly during the voyage through the tropics, causing the engines to shift out of alignment.

Also docked in Port Stanley was RRS *Discovery II*, a hydrographic and marine biological survey vessel operating in the Southern Ocean and Antarctic waters. She had been commissioned by the Colonial Office's Discovery Committee since the 1920s to assess and monitor the economically exploitable resources of these waters (primarily whales). *Discovery II* would transport the aeroplane, hut, boat, stores and dogs south with Hampton and Bingham while the others were occupied with the essential work on *Penola* of taking down the topmasts, altering rigging, re-stowing the hold and tarring the decks. As a result of this liaison, Able Seaman Verner ('Duncan') Carse migrated from *Discovery II* to join *Penola*.

After a week of ship work Roberts, exasperated by his proximity to the wildlife paradise which lay out of reach around him, used some of his personal funds earmarked 'for scientific purposes only' to hire three men to take his, Fleming's and Bertram's places while they took a week off for scientific work. Fleming sped off inland geologising on horseback, whilst Roberts and Bertram were dropped off by motor boat to camp for a week on nearby Kidney Island, some seven miles from Stanley. This small island, ¾ mile long and ½ mile across, was thickly covered with tussock grass and teeming with wildlife. In spite of pouring rain much of the time, the two men's spirits were undampened. Magellanic penguins were scuttling to and fro under the thick clumps of tussock, whilst the flatter areas were home to a huge colony of rockhopper penguins covering several acres. For Roberts the nesting season in full swing was a golden opportunity to observe penguin behaviour for the first time. At the time behavioural and life cycle studies of these birds had hardly begun.[6]

> "You have to see a Penguin colony to believe it. Before your eyes all the little affairs of human family life are mimicked and exaggerated to an absurdity. Love affairs – a feeble wife giving way to the advances of another gentleman while her husband is away. Bad, bold bachelors spreading discord wherever they wander through the colony, and husbands trying to look innocent while they steal nest material from the pair next door."[7]

Roberts and Bertram spent their week making skins, photographing and note taking whilst dodging ferocious-looking sea lions which

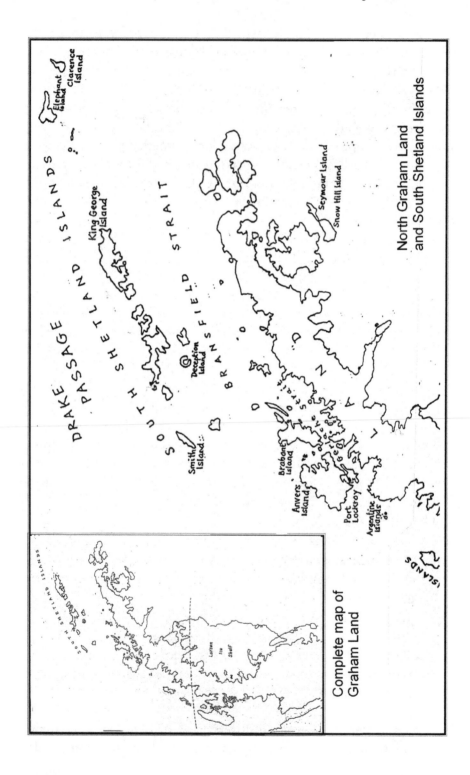

North Graham Land
and South Shetland Islands

Complete map of
Graham Land

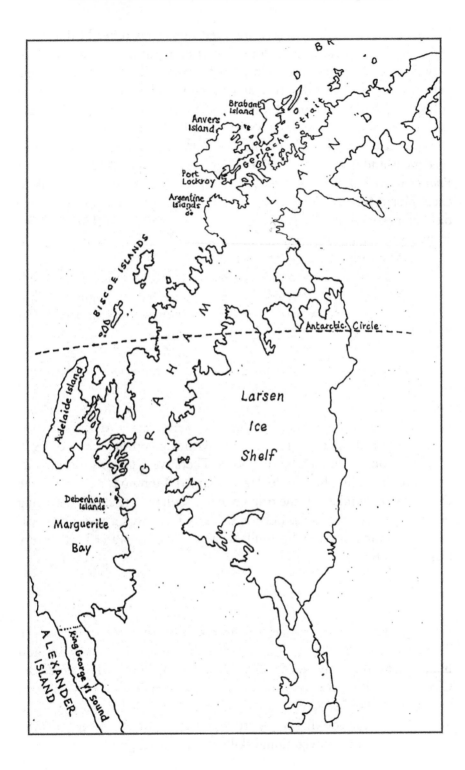

lurked in the tussock. Roberts observed numerous other bird species, including an imperial shag colony, a nesting night heron, cape petrels, grey-backed storm petrels, kelp geese, steamer ducks and scavenging vultures. On their last day two tussock cutters came over to the island collecting pony fodder and Roberts was able to send two penguins back with them to Stanley for Lisle Ryder to paint. (*Plate 8.2*)

Back on board *Penola* on 12 December, they sorted and packed specimens and it was then back to ship work. Various delays prevented *Penola* from sailing until New Year's Eve, when she departed only to encounter a full south-westerly gale, forcing her to anchor again one day later after only six miles. At midnight Roberts suffered griping stomach pains, putting him out of action for 24 hours without food. It was the first ominous sign of something more serious.

Things were not looking good for *Penola*. Her warped engine beds had been weakened by the stormy seas and caused the engines to shift out of alignment. She would be in no condition to work in pack ice or heavy seas until properly repaired, but staying in the Falklands would mean missing the chance of getting to Graham Land that season. So they decided to sail south with the engines disconnected and carry out repairs later. As Rymill reflected, if the early sealers and whalers could make it to the Antarctic without steam power, why couldn't they?[8] But *Penola* was forced to return to Stanley, where a ton of cement was taken on board for the repairs, along with a plentiful supply of fresh food generously donated by the locals. There were now three new cats on board, including Lumsdale (later renamed 'Lummo'), a gift from the Dean of Port Stanley. Of the original cats, William had died after being bitten by one of the dogs, but for Roberts Peter was a treasure, a cat with a soothing nature who fulfilled the role of hot water bottle every night in his bunk.

TO THE ANTARCTIC AT LAST

From the Falklands they faced a 900-mile journey ahead across the Southern Ocean under sail alone to rendezvous with Hampton and Bingham at the only known harbour Port Lockroy, discovered by Charcot in 1904. In near windless conditions their journey was slow, the 'Roaring Forties' never roared and the ship rolled dreadfully up to 40°, which made cooking on board "a good test of character". Owing to Ryder's excellent navigational skills *Penola* made good progress even through patches of fog. The grandeur of the scenery lifted everyone's spirits, seeing for the first time tabular icebergs and the steeply rising snow-covered peaks of Smith Island, the westernmost of the South Shetland Islands. From the crow's nest (near the top of the mainmast), Roberts watched the rich bird life and the fin whales blowing around the ship, reflecting on all the years he had longed for this day, their first sight of land in the Antarctic. "How infinitely small and insignificant all human efforts become in these surroundings."[9]

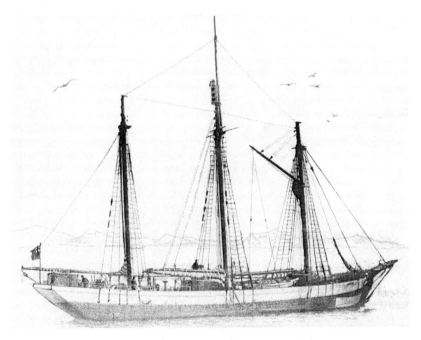

Under a leaden sky they passed through Gerlache Strait and the spectacular narrow Neumayer Channel, with precipitous mountains rising almost sheer on either side to 6,000 ft. Reaching Port Lockroy on 21 January the party met up with Hampton and Bingham, who were camped nearby with aeroplane, dogs and stores. They now needed to look farther south for a suitable safe winter site to erect the base hut, with good anchorage for *Penola*.

SETTING UP A WINTERING BASE

A week later, on 26 January, the Fox Moth (*Plate 8.3*) was ready for her first reconnaissance flight piloted by Hampton, accompanied by Rymill and Red Ryder. Working down the mainland coast, they found it to be an almost continuous fringe of glaciers terminating in ice cliffs along the shore, but 40 miles south of Port Lockroy they spotted a group of low-lying rocky islands only five miles out from the coast. Visited and named by Charcot, the Argentine Islands offered shelter from winds, currents and heavy ice, with good anchorage in a narrow creek for their crippled ship.[10]

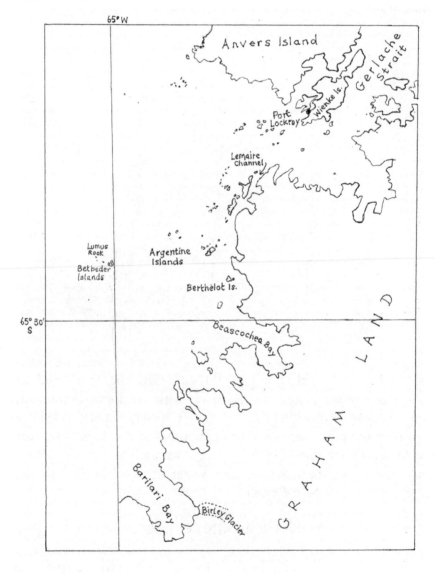

Graham Land coast

Discovery II had brought down 65 tons of gear, including extra fuel salvaged from the recently abandoned whaling station at Deception Island. *Penola* would need two journeys to move everything to the planned new base. A level spot to erect the hut was found on Winter Island, only 300 yards from a sheltered cove for wintering *Penola*. The task of moving everything down from Port Lockroy was underway. Riley and Roberts went down with camping gear in the motor dinghy *Stella* to be ready to receive the aeroplane and tow her on floats into Stella Creek. They arrived at Galindez Island and were in bed by 6 pm, sleeping through until 10 am and glad to be away from the ship: "As we lay in our bags we thought of the others, loading rotten seal meat, and hoped the ship might be delayed a little."[11] Their first job the next day was to lay in a meat supply. This entailed killing seals, something Roberts disliked intensely: "It is a hateful business killing them when they blink their great eyes at you and roll over on their backs utterly unaware of danger, but we have got to lay in a good meat supply."[12] That evening they ate shag for dinner.

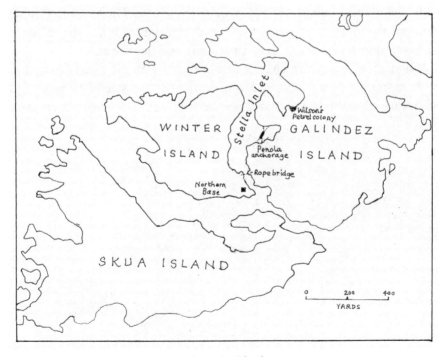

Argentine Islands

Two days later Roberts had his first Antarctic flight, covering some 70 miles. Much stimulated by the experience, he began to see the potential of low-altitude flying for plotting the positions of penguin and shag colonies and moss patches. Exploring their new surroundings out in a dory, Roberts found a fine patch on Galindez Island where a breeding colony of Wilson's storm petrels (*Plates 8.4, 8.5*) had made their nest burrows in the soft peaty moss. While waiting for *Penola* to return he numbered and marked their nests, just as the first chicks were hatching. Lisle Ryder was commissioned to produce watercolour paintings of the chicks at various stages of development.(*Plate 8.6*) On 14 February *Penola* was finally berthed in her winter quarters, where a long list of repair work awaited her.

After another few days of landing stores and fuel, building of the base hut commenced. By early March the superstructure was complete and the party could start to move in. The living quarters comprised two large rooms, with a porch in front. Downstairs consisted of a kitchen with Aga cooker, which also provided the main source of heating, plus dining room and workshop with a corner partitioned off for Meiklejohn's wireless office. A ladder and open hatch in the ceiling led to the living room and sleeping quarters above. The hut had double walls insulated with asbestos-reinforced aluminium foil. Integral with the living quarters was the aircraft hangar and dogs' hut.

It was an exhilarating change of atmosphere to get away from ship work in rough conditions under orders, and the scientists now had the luxury of empty berth space on the ship where they could create a

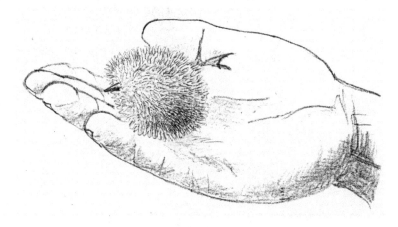

Day old Wilson's petrel chick

darkroom and biological laboratory. Fleming consecrated the new lab and Roberts celebrated by shaving off the patchy and uncomfortable beard that he had grown since Christmas. A combined housewarming party and 30th birthday celebration for Rymill was held, with good food and alcohol putting everyone in high spirits, including the normally unexcitable Martin, who fell headlong down the hatchway.

COOKING AND EATING

Everyone took their turn by rota to do a week's cooking, rising well before the others and planning and providing the meals on the Aga cooker. For the cook it was an intensive period, with no time to do anything else. A 5lb loaf of bread had to be baked every day, along with either scones, biscuits or a cake for tea. Water had to be fetched as ice and melted. Evening dinner was normally seal meat, which needed thawing and cutting up. Dried vegetables and powdered potatoes had to be reconstituted. Pudding options were created from stores of jam, blancmange powder, custard powder, jelly, rice, cocoa and powdered egg. Rations were not over-generous and the cook needed imagination and skill in creating variety for the week. On *Penola* the cook was on duty usually from 5 am until 10:30 pm, with just one hour off in the afternoon, and he had to do all the washing up. Rough weather could then present challenges for the simplest of jobs like baking and bread making, but at least the cook was dry and warm and could be guaranteed 7½ hours sleep at a stretch. Christmas and birthdays were special occasions, and a tin of condensed milk was allowed to the birthday boy to indulge himself. Donations to the expedition by family and friends ensured a good supply of beer, wines and spirits.

Owing to the expedition's shoestring budget, living off the land was essential. When the opportunity arose, penguins and their eggs were a welcome addition to the diet. The eggs, twice the size of a hen's egg, were considered tasty, although on cooking the albumen does not turn white and solidify but remains rather like jellyfish. Gentoo and rockhopper penguins will lay several times if their eggs are stolen. It was possible in principle to collect them sustainably, but this was rarely adhered to. Successive robbing of eggs would result in a progressively smaller egg size, down to half that of the first one laid. The Falkland Islanders made annual egg-collecting trips to a number of the islands, returning with boatloads full. As many as 13,000 rockhopper eggs were gathered in one visit to Cochon Island in 1915, Rollo Beck observed.[13] Roberts was told by a tussock cutter that in 1930 he had collected more than 11,000 eggs over nine days on Kidney Island. When Roberts was on Kidney Island in 1936 almost 5,000 eggs had already been taken at the beginning of the season. He also observed that when they found a

Egg collecting on Kidney Island, after a photograph by Rollo Beck 1915

suitable stone to incubate, they would not lay again.[14] The eggs would keep for up to nine months packed in layers of sand in casks.

Overall 558 seals were killed for both human and dog consumption. Seal meat was normally eaten twice a day, except on sledge journeys when they had to eat pemmican. The slaughter provided Bertram with study material for his doctoral thesis on seals, with measurements of skulls and examination of gut parasites. The potential problem of scurvy, especially in the last year of the expedition when the shore party was on long sledging trips, was overcome by taking a daily tablespoonful of Califorange concentrated orange juice.

THE APPROACH OF WINTER

Dog sledging was to be the essential means of travel from the base. Several of the expedition members had already gained sledging experience in Greenland, Labrador and north-west Canada. The sledges were designed by Hampton and Rymill to cope with the variable conditions they could expect, including sea ice. BGLE was to be the most dog-orientated expedition ever made. Bingham had the major task of breeding and training of puppies, more than half of which were born during the expedition. All the members of the shore party learned the art of dog driving, each having their own team of 10 dogs.

Roberts and Bertram decided to visit the Berthelot Islands, a few miles south of the Argentine Islands, where an extensive area of vegetation had been spotted from the plane. On 18 March, with camping gear and biological paraphernalia, they were dropped off in the motor boat *Stella* on the most northerly of the islands, which they named Green Island on account of its four acres of moss.[15] A busy few days were spent collecting plant and lichen samples, while they caught and cooked their dinner from the nearby shag colony.

But winter was already on its way. Snow suddenly put a stop to their fieldwork, laying a thick white blanket over the moss patch and confining the scientists to their tent. Returning by boat to the base, they could see penguins in their thousands assembling to depart from their breeding grounds for the winter. It was also the time for the engineers Millett and Moore to tackle the unpleasant task of making a solid repair of the engine beds. Spending several weeks crawling in the dank chilly engine room they secured the warped timbers with a maze of wires and iron, ready for cementing. Martin, Gurney and Carse had the task of digging sand and gravel from beneath the ice covering the beaches to mix with the cement. Some 12 tons of concrete were then poured into the iron skeleton, locking the timbers to the hull as one solid piece and giving the engine beds no further chance of movement.[16]

On 1 April there was a resurgence of Roberts' griping stomach pains, but he once again recovered after a day resting in a warm bed. All hands were directed to a sealing operation out west to lay in a meat store for the winter, housed in an ice cave near the base. They returned to find the creek full of brash ice. The air temperature had plummeted, but it was not yet safe to walk across the ice and the ship's party was unable to get across the creek to Fleming's early morning Sunday service on Easter Day in the aircraft hangar. Those in the hut fared better and continued the Easter celebrations with Benedictine liqueur presented to them by Port Stanley's Dean Lumsdale for consumption on church festivals.

THE ROPE BRIDGE

The ice being in an unstable condition, Roberts and Bertram decided to construct a rope bridge across the narrowest part of Stella Creek, so that it would be possible to cross from the hut and to walk the remaining 300 yards to the ship in soft snow – in theory. The bridge, spanning 25 yards, had two ropes running from a scaffolding tripod near the hut to the ice cliff at the other. (*Plate 8.7*) With some skill it was possible to walk the lower rope, taking the weight with one's arms on the upper rope. An alternative option provided was a bosun's chair on a pulley. Roberts made eight successful crossings on foot with ease. Bertram also achieved a crossing – albeit less elegantly – with the ship's party watching dubiously. (*Plate 8.8*) Eventually Lisle Ryder got into the bosun's chair and negotiated the bridge successfully to the middle. At this point the ropes slackened, gently lowering him up to his armpits into the freezing water below. After wading through pancake ice to the shore he was speedily warmed up with dry clothes and a shot of whisky. From then on there was even less enthusiasm for walking between base hut and ship.

Since nearly all the chicks had now flown, Roberts' first-year record of his Wilson's petrel colony was nearly complete. On 4 April with a feeling of satisfaction he rowed out to the moss patch, only to find that two of the dogs had swum across the channel and eaten two of his last three chicks, the ones from which the most interesting results were expected. The only sympathy he received was from Stephenson, who had also recently suffered a similar experience when the dogs tore down and ate two of his most important survey flags.

Midwinter Day, 21 June 1935, was celebrated according to Antarctic tradition. A Christmas tree was decorated, presents were distributed and for a short time the winter blues were lifted. Wine and beer flowed freely, and a dance was held on the upstairs floor. But according to Roberts, "John [Rymill] lost all his customary reserve and tact after a few drinks and said a few things he really meant... In essence he confirmed all our worst fears that science means absolutely nothing to him". Roberts was left feeling disillusioned and at a low ebb.

THE OPERATION

On 6 July, the next time that Roberts was on cook duty, he was laid low once again by stomach pains. This time the symptoms were more severe and he rapidly became delirious. It was becoming clear that Roberts had full-blown appendicitis.[17] 'Doc' Bingham, realising that he might have to operate, made preparations.

> "With the operation imminent, the kitchen table in the Base was scrubbed, as were all those to be involved, and all the other preparations were made. These included Brian receiving pre-op sedation out of a brandy bottle, which Doc (Bingham) shared with him while thumbing through his surgery manual.
>
> "However, concern mounted amongst the others when Doc was heard to mutter, 'I don't remember that' and 'I don't think this is right'. They soon realised that he had done very little major surgery since leaving medical school, having served predominantly on small ships (destroyers, etc.) where such cases could always be transferred to a larger one with proper facilities and specialist surgeons. As the brandy bottle emptied, the others realised they would have to take matters into their own hands, and proceeded to sterilise their few instruments and scrub down the kitchen table.
>
> "John, as leader, assumed the role of surgeon. As he said afterwards, he had castrated plenty of calves and spayed a few heifers as well as gutting plenty of sheep. Having

checked Doc's manual, he thought it should all be pretty straightforward.

"Fortunately Doc remained sober enough to explain merrily that, as Brian's temperature rose, the infected appendix would eventually go either way. The cyst could either burst into the intestine, and all would be well. Or it could go the other way, into the peritoneal cavity, when it would be fatal unless they operated immediately."[18]

This whimsical account by Rymill differs somewhat from Bingham's, for whom the whole episode was a nightmare.[19] During the day of preparation Ryder and Rymill were instructed in how to assist Bingham. Everyone was talking in whispers while disinfecting, scrubbing and sterilising every pie dish and pudding basin available. Roberts' condition continued to worsen. At midnight Bingham alerted everyone and prepared to operate. But to his immense relief Roberts' temperature started to fall and he could delay operating, albeit remaining on high alert. Over the next two days two-hour watches were kept by Bingham and Fleming, taking Roberts' pulse and temperature every hour until it had dropped sufficiently for everyone to breathe out, no one more than Bingham himself.[20]

Meanwhile three sledge parties left the base for reconnaissance missions, leaving only four men behind. The hut was warm and peaceful, and Roberts' condition continued to improve. He felt homesick: "What wouldn't I give for a few hours in the garden at Bishopgarth." Sitting upstairs reading by the fire all day he recuperated, listening to classical music records on the expedition's gramophone player. Three weeks later he ventured outside and was soon back at work, the only problem for him now being the continuous icing up of his spectacles in the midwinter cold. But although there was general relief at the operation being called off, it left a worrying situation concerning a possible resurgence of the appendicitis. Roberts was acutely aware that expedition plans would be messed up, particularly during the next winter when Bingham would be off sledging in Matha Bay and would not be available to operate at short notice. There was another issue: the BGLE party was not alone in the Antarctic. In addition to the presence of *Discovery II*, the American aviator Lincoln Ellsworth was not far away, waiting on Snow Hill Island to make a trans-Antarctic flight. Roberts was utterly miserable, sensing that he might be sent home with Ellsworth.

GLOOM

On 6 August Roberts' worst fears were confirmed when, after prodding the taciturn Rymill, he found out that in everybody's interests he was to be sent home. Ellsworth had agreed to take Roberts back to South America, but Rymill was trying to make alternative arrangements with *Discovery II*, which was scheduled for a voyage round the Antarctic continent. Either way Hampton would fly Roberts the 200 miles to Deception Island, to be collected at the end of the year. Roberts was desolate.

> "There is little that I can say. My feelings will not bear writing. All the pleasure of life seems to have been swallowed up in a moment… at least Colin can continue some of the work I have begun, and there is much to be done for the expedition in England when I get back. 'Penola' will get home about 1½ years later. This afternoon I climbed the hill behind the base. The same old scene looked infinitely different. I wanted only to be alone for a time."[21]

One week later Roberts held a sale of some of his gear, raising £15, which might at least enable him to stay in the Falkland Islands for a while. He was cheered a little when Hampton flew him and Rymill southwards to Cape Evensen to view from the air the remarkable topography of the Graham Land coast. Preparations were underway for sledging south to lay depots, but were repeatedly delayed by worsening weather and ice conditions, frustrating Rymill's hopes of getting far south that year. He had to be content with a local ground survey, an essential task since the only existing map (Charcot's) was quite inaccurate. But for Roberts even the darkest clouds had a silver lining, in that he would now get some sledging. While the survey party continued along the coast Roberts and Bertram remained at Beascochea Bay for some biology and glaciology. It was early September, pleasant to sit in the late winter sun relaxing against the sledge, drinking cocoa from a thermos flask.

PROLONGED CONFINEMENT TO BASE

By October 1935 strong wind and warmer water had rapidly dissipated the blinding whiteness of the winter scenery, but owing to poor ice conditions and foul weather the party remained confined to the base. From loudspeakers powered by an electric generator, the BBC news was being received from London nearly every night. War had been declared between Italy and Abyssinia, generating heated arguments about the League of Nations. Roberts' 23rd birthday was celebrated with sherry, sausages, new potatoes and tinned strawberries, followed by whisky. Four days later it was Riley's birthday on which Rymill, after a few drinks, expressed criticisms of the ship's party that Roberts considered unfair. Rymill's frustrations are understandable considering the expedition's chronic delays and financial problems, being holed up for a year too far north and with no prospects for any exploratory sledging southwards until the following year. There was a real danger that BGLE might be forced to return home with no significant discoveries or surveys of uncharted territory. In contrast the biologists had already spent the long year in the Argentine Islands profitably, with an impressive haul of specimens and observations.

By 8 November it was warm, with a feeling of spring in the air and an end in sight to the confinement to base. Roberts was delighted to hear that his sister Joy was now engaged to be married. He was still more elated to learn that he would gain several months of precious expedition time, since *Discovery II* would be visiting Deception Island in April 1936 and he would not have to return north earlier with Ellsworth. In the event Ellsworth got lost, losing radio contact after flying at 13,000 ft over a plateau at latitude 76°S, having covered some 800 miles in 7½ hours. *Discovery II*, having wasted a lot of time searching for him, decided not to visit Deception Island at all. BGLE was now faced with no supportive transport in prospect.

This was a crisis, but it was also an opportunity. A completely new expedition plan was now proposed: *Penola* would head north to Deception Island around 1 January 1936 to collect mail, coal and wood for a new southern base hut, go south to Marguerite Bay to drop the shore party at a base site suitable for southern sledging expeditions, and return north to Port Stanley for a winter refit. The ship's officers were keen on the plan. Roberts was ecstatic. He would now be able to have his appendix out in Stanley and remain with the expedition for the duration without needing to go home early. Rymill gave the new plan his approval.

It was now the beginning of the breeding season and Roberts could focus on his ornithological work on the islands, collecting information on the breeding habits and incubation periods of different species. On 24 November he was especially cheered when the first Wilson's petrels began to arrive. He was able to observe their courtship, measuring temperatures to time their arrival and departure, noting a pair that he had marked the previous year returning to the same burrow. It was wonderful to discover that after their tremendous migration flight up into the north Atlantic – 9,000 miles each way – they returned each year to the same burrow and the same mate.

DECEPTION ISLAND

By New Year 1936, after a week of sawing the ice and laying cinders to free *Penola* from where she had lain icebound for the past nine months, the anchors were up and the ship was towed out of the creek. With a crew of eight including Roberts, *Penola* sailed northwards in calm seas to Deception Island. After nearly a year confined to base it felt good to be at sea again, despite the routine of six-hour watches.

Deception Island is an active volcano whose centre forms a caldera flooded by the sea. The whaling station there had been abandoned, trashed and looted, and it was now deserted and decaying. But BGLE had been given authorisation to make use of the materials, and for the members of an impoverished Antarctic expedition it was treasure trove. Arriving inside the shelter of the caldera at Port Foster, they were greeted with a maze of deserted rusty boiler sheds, loose corrugated iron clanging in the wind, a morass of rotting whale debris and a whalebone-strewn beach. But there was ample timber to provide for a new southern base hut, sheet metal to roof it, and as much coal as they could carry. "Even a few pounds of ancient, but still edible, bacon and a giant can of marmalade were not to be despised."[22] For the biologists there were laboratory supplies available from the derelict hospital storeroom. For several days everyone was involved in salvaging timber from the collapsing weatherboarded huts. Most eagerly awaited by everyone was the mail – written almost a year ago, and left some months earlier by Ellsworth prior to his unsuccessful flight.

After several days of humping timber, Roberts and Bertram were given an afternoon off to visit one of the largest colonies of chinstrap (previously known as ringed) penguins in the world. Climbing the volcanic slag up and over a steep mountain ridge on the east coast of Deception Island, they were pitched into the blanket of fog that

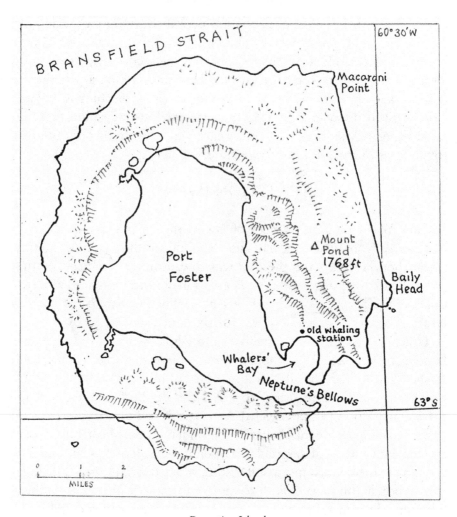

Deception Island

invariably envelops the top and had to navigate their way down by smell. Descending below the fog they were greeted by the dramatic sight of 15 acres of chinstrap rookery, stretching out as far as the eye could see along and behind the cliffs around Baily Head (*Plate 8.9*). Roberts made a conservative estimate of 145,000 birds, at roughly one nest per square yard. Unknown to him at the time, this represented a significant recovery from previous years when the whalers had been taking huge numbers of their eggs, this species being less resilient to constant egg robbing than rockhoppers and gentoos. According to R C Murphy "the timbre of many of the Ringed penguins' notes is... peculiarly ear-splitting... nor is the noisiness all bluster, for the Ringed penguin has the universal reputation of being the boldest, most pugnacious, and most agile member of its genus if not, indeed, of the whole penguin tribe. The relative reactions of the three species of *Pygoscelis*, when brought face-to-face with man, might be broadly characterised as follows: the Johnny [gentoo] penguin turns tail; the Adelie stands his ground; the Ringed penguin charges".[23]

After a few more days helping to load *Penola*, Roberts returned to the colony. This time he ventured right into the middle of it, but soon wished he hadn't. Chinstraps, as he now learned, not only favour the highest cliff tops to breed, but as the smallest of the brushtail penguins they are, as Murphy had observed, the feistiest and noisiest. With young families to guard (*Plate 8.10*), the angry birds attacked his knees from all sides with their sharp beaks as he struggled to beat a hasty and undignified retreat, whilst plugging his ears with cotton wool against the ear-splitting din.

Lisle Ryder produced for Roberts a series of watercolour paintings showing different stages of development of the chinstrap penguins, the first ever to be made of chicks of this species. (*Plate 8.11*)

SETTING UP THE SOUTHERN BASE

On 23 January 1936 *Penola* headed back south from Deception Island under a strong south-westerly wind, heavily laden with stores, timber and coal from the whaling station. The ship rolled badly and made heavy weather against the strong current, wind and sleet. Deck work was unpleasant and several of the party were feeling distinctly unwell. Back at the Argentine Islands she was gutted of her interior fittings in order to create enough space to accommodate timber, coal and stores, plus more than 80 dogs chained in rows on top of the deck cargo, before sailing on 16 February to search for a southern base site. Now extremely heavily laden, the ship rolled 45° each way in a heavy swell. The ship's crew had to improvise sleeping quarters anywhere they could find a few dry inches of space. One casualty of this tough journey was Roberts' cat Peter, who died soon afterwards as a result of his lengthy confinement on deck.

On reaching the Léonie Islands in the northern part of Marguerite Bay, wireless operator Meiklejohn sent a message to Stephenson and Hampton, who had remained at the old base with the aeroplane. They boarded up the hut, painting on it a 'To Let' sign and flew south to join the ship. Next day the plane was off to look for a new base site on the eastern side of Marguerite Bay.

Having taken 12 hours to cross Marguerite Bay in the heavy pack ice, *Penola* finally dropped anchor close to a raised beach at 68°S. A suitable spot for the base was found on a group of small, low rocky islands, which would become known as the Debenham Islands. On 11 March, following several hard days of unloading, Roberts was compensated with an aerial view of the surrounding country. The south of Marguerite Bay was full of fast sea ice with no cracks or leads, stretching right out towards Alexander Land. *Penola* could get no farther south, so it was time for her to leave the southern base party of nine men and return northwards.

Roberts had now become a member of the ship's party, having exchanged places with Bertram, who was to join the shore party's sledging teams. With only seven men to crew, *Penola* set off for the Falkland Islands, a journey of some 1,250 miles. Gale force winds made for unpleasant ship work in the cold and wet, but with favourable winds they made good progress under sail alone and reached the Falkland Islands on 24 March.

Despite the generous hospitality of their hosts in Port Stanley – and that of the Governor, who kept them supplied with fresh vegetables from his garden – the *Penola* crew found the town's parochial social life tiresome. "There are few people here with whom I can feel at home," lamented Roberts. "In this place it seems that snobbishness and class distinctions are about as marked as anywhere in the world."[24] With ordinary people they could feel at home, but Government House was another matter. The obligatory dressing up in the evening was particularly irksome after a day's ship work. Roberts was unable to escape the undesired attentions of the Governor's two eligible daughters, whose invitations to late-night parties could not be refused, despite his need to be up early the next morning for ship work. Likewise with Mrs Williams, who would lose no opportunity to remind her guests that her mother had been lady-in-waiting to Queen Victoria. Before anyone from *Penola* was allowed to sit down her chairs were covered with newspaper.[25]

Roberts arranged his appendectomy with the Falkland Islands doctor Rex Cheverton. Whilst awaiting surgery he was able to use the Government Naturalist's Office, which, though small and cold and smelling unpleasantly of rotting specimens, had a useful library and was a place to hide away in quiet. His mounting collection of bird skins could be properly dried and despatched by ship for the British Museum, and he planned detailed studies of the local penguins and a census of the island rookeries.

THE OPERATION: THIS TIME FOR REAL

On 26 April Roberts, entering hospital for his appendectomy, found himself to be the object of more unwanted female attention, as he related to Betty Creswick, Debenham's assistant at the Scott Polar Institute in Cambridge. Her reply was: "We laughed at your predicament, being victimized by hoards [sic] of lovely painted ladies who rallied round your bedside watching the 'polar hero' recovering from his wounds. I can't imagine anybody who would hate it more! Think, however, of the ROMANCE you are bringing into their bleak lives... no doubt by now you're quite the ladies' man: and the joy of starring tea parties! It's an awful waste – when you think how some men would have revelled in same after 18 months monastic life!"[26]

Out of hospital, Roberts convalesced at first in the company of the pompous Mrs Williams, followed by two more congenial weeks with Rex Cheverton and his wife, luxuriating in the comforts of a bed with sheets, a peat fire in his bedroom, an interesting library and a collection of Beethoven and Bach gramophone records. Meanwhile news came through on 9 June from Stromness, South Georgia that *Penola*, which was in need of a major refit, had been offered free docking and cheap skilled labour there for the winter months of August and September. She would have to leave for South Georgia on around 20 July, returning to the Falklands around 1 November. For Roberts this was unwelcome news. As a member of the ship's party, his current ornithological work on the Falklands would have to be abandoned unfinished. Moreover, following the operation he was unfit for heavy work. He was however able to hatch a plan: if he could pay someone to take his place on *Penola*'s return voyage to the Falklands, he could come back on a faster ship in mid-November. He could then finish his work in the Falklands on penguin breeding behaviour and surveying Kidney Island instead of having to spend around 30 days at sea returning on *Penola*. However the ship's captain had to await instructions from the expedition committee in England, as some funds would be needed to pay for *Penola*'s refit.

For the time being there was no news. With *Penola*'s uncertain predicament, Roberts and Lisle Ryder decided on the spur of the moment to get away from Stanley on a short break, boarding the cargo ship *Lafonia* bound for the Magellan Straits. *Lafonia*, having collected 400 sheep from the Falklands, meandered its way through the numerous channels of southern Chile until dawn broke in Seno Otway (Otway Sound) on a magnificent panorama of high snow-covered mountains. Arriving at the coal mine of Mina Elena on Seno Skyring, the two men revelled in their first sight of a forest in two years. Weather-beaten Antarctic beech lined the shore, and behind lay a huge area of temperate rainforest, almost impenetrable with its chaotic underbrush of dead trees, spongy moss and lichen coverage. During the three days that *Lafonia* was anchored up, they walked for hours savouring the smell of trees, moss and decay. On her return journey *Lafonia* called in at Magallanes (as the port of Punta Arenas was named at the time). The world's southernmost city "formed a sort of dumping ground for discontented humanity: exiles, escaped prisoners, runaway sailors, gold-diggers, guanchos, shepherds, traders". Isolated at the southern end of Chile, Magallanes had lost most of its trade on the opening of the Panama Canal in 1914. Roberts observed the effects on its population: poverty, alcoholism and vice were everywhere. Most of the residents lived in drab houses of concrete and corrugated iron. Apart from the two main streets "there is so much mud that sea boots are needed for a shopping excursion. Endless heaps of garbage and large numbers of loafers are the chief features"[27]. Nonetheless it had been a stimulating 16-day trip for Roberts and Ryder, who returned to Stanley on 6 July.

A week later news came at last from England that £500 had been raised towards the cost of *Penola*'s refit. She now had a new crew member, 17-year old Sidney Barnes, and in addition Bill Halliday, engaged as cook at £12 a month. Roberts was still unfit for heavy work and was allowed more time off for ornithology. Just before departure for South Georgia, the long-awaited mail arrived, but the essential engine spares ordered from England had still not turned up. The planned repair work in South Georgia on *Penola*'s ailing engines would not now be possible.

SOUTH GEORGIA

On 1 August *Penola* finally cast off, only for the crew to discover that Lummo the cat had inadvertently been left behind. However a wireless message reassured them that he was safe and would be reunited with them when they returned to the Falklands. This accident of fate probably contributed to his survival. Lummo would become famous as the first cat to 'overwinter' two years in the Antarctic, but perhaps this accolade of a feline 'Polar Medal' was not fully warranted.

It was midwinter, and conditions soon became unpleasant with sleet, snow and a strong wind which soon turned into gale force. The nights were long and dark, and deck work in slippery frozen slush was grim. The ropes were frozen stiff and the sails rigid like boards. During the gale, attempts to take in sails resulted in the squaresail getting badly ripped. Then *Penola* would be becalmed, followed by another gale. Progress under sail alone was painfully slow: at one point they were blown back to where they had been three days earlier. When there were no jobs to do on deck, the crew were now allowed the luxury of warming themselves by the peat stove below deck. Roberts struggled to resolve clothing problems. Keeping warm with many layers resulted in discomfort for energetic jobs like climbing the rigging or pulling ropes. Oilskins, while waterproof, became brittle in freezing conditions.

Twelve days after setting off, *Penola* arrived at the coast of South Georgia. In poor visibility it was difficult to locate Stromness Bay and they were nearly blown past it. In one of the heavy snow squalls characteristic of South Georgia that suddenly appear with hurricane force, violently lashing the sea, it was a struggle for *Penola* to anchor and a motor boat from the shore was needed to help secure her to a buoy. A catcher from Leith came to collect Roberts and Millett, speeding them round into Cumberland Bay, where they handed in *Penola*'s papers to the magistrate Mr Barlas, who invited them in to his house opposite Grytviken whaling station. Elephant seals were everywhere, on the beach and lolling around the houses. Over coffee, cakes and whisky Barlas gave Roberts an account of the history of the South Georgia whaling and sealing industries.

The Norwegians had begun whaling in 1904, establishing the shore stations at Grytviken and Husvik. Soon afterwards the Scottish company Salvesens arrived, founding the shore station at Leith Harbour. With the rapid expansion there were soon six stations on South Georgia, making it by far the most important centre for the booming industry. Each shore station was equipped to cater for several hundred men over the season: workshops for blacksmiths and carpenters, stores and a repair yard ensured that everything could be manufactured or mended on site. There were livestock to provide meat and eggs, a hospital, laundry, recreational facilities and a cinema. The principal product of the industry was whale oil, which was extracted by cooking the blubber. Industrial society had numerous uses for it, including cooking fats, cosmetics, candles, soap and lubricant. Meat and bone residues, known as 'guano', were extracted as a secondary product to be sold as animal fodder and fertilizer.

In the 1920s pelagic whaling gradually took over from the shore stations and by the 1930-31 season there were 41 factory ships operating in Antarctic waters, with 232 catchers. Able to go wherever the whales were abundant, the ships led to the closure of several of South Georgia's shore stations in 1932-33.[28] For the Antarctic as a whole the catch totalled 46,000 whales in 1937-38, the highest ever recorded. Either side of this peak around 40,000 were caught annually for 10 years. Of these, an estimated 350,000 were blue whales. Pelagic whaling led to overproduction of oil and the market eventually collapsed. As whale stocks became exhausted the industry declined and finally came to an end in the 1960s. Roberts viewed these statistics with a mixture of bafflement and repugnance. The failure to exercise any regulation to conserve stocks was an issue that would preoccupy him throughout his later diplomatic life.

One of the magistrate's functions was to ensure that the whaling companies paid their licence fees to the Falkland Islands Government, but attempts to regulate pelagic whaling were hopelessly ineffective; quotas were ignored and the licence fee could be avoided. It was to be another 50 years before the International Whaling Commission introduced a moratorium on whaling in 1986, and even that has been ignored by Norway, Iceland and Japan. Today, only 5-10% of the original great whale populations have survived.

At the time of *Penola*'s refit South Georgia's stagnant whaling industry was being partly replaced by sealing. In early September catchers would be going out on short trips to the coves and beaches around the island once the sealing season began. For Roberts this was a golden opportunity but he was gloomy about the prospects for getting any research work done. The chances of getting anyone to take his place on *Penola* for her return voyage had diminished. Furthermore it was doubtful that Ryder would let him stay on in South Georgia to observe the arrival of breeding birds and return on *Lafonia* in November.

HARD TIMES: *PENOLA'S* REFIT

In 1936 Stromness shore station was no longer actively operating, but the floating dock was still in use cooperatively between the whaling companies. With its skeletal staff of five men it had been made available for *Penola* during the harshest winter months. The refit was expected to be completed by the end of September. Discharging cargo from *Penola* took three full days of heavy work, and there were 35 tons of ballast to be removed before she could go into dry dock. Disgorging the ballast, consisting of pig iron and heavy chains coated with evil-smelling grease, was punishingly hard and filthy work. It took them four days, during which it snowed hard all and every day. Three carpenters had been found to help, one from each of the stations at Leith, Stromness and Husvik. They were all that could be spared; the extra labour originally promised by Salvesen would not materialise. All available hands were put to work scraping, recaulking, cleaning and painting the hull, removing the propeller shafts and replacing badly-worn bearings. Roberts had wisely bought a small oil stove in Stanley, as the temperature was now below freezing the whole time.

To add to his trials, Roberts was troubled by toothache and unable to eat or drink anything hot. After enduring it for three days he needed to get over to the doctor in Leith. But with a big swell coming into the bay no boats could go out, so he decided to climb over the mountain west of Stromness and down into Leith. There was quite an easy way round, he was assured; the Norwegians would often ski round in about 45 minutes. Since the first part of the route was along a steep snow slope ending in the sea, he decided not to take skis but rather climbing boots and an ice axe. Setting off along what he believed to be the ski route, he found himself cutting steps with the ice axe and started to have doubts. In two hours of hard climbing he reached the top of the ridge between the two bays, only to find a sheer precipice of 2,000 ft separating him from the snow slopes of Leith Harbour. It was not until he was descending back to sea level on the Stromness side that he found a way round, and he still needed to cut steps along the route. Four hours after leaving the ship, he was once more at the top of the ridge enjoying the wonderful view. All trace of toothache had disappeared. Looking down at *Penola* in the distance, he thought of the others scraping away at her hull. Before him a steep but perfectly smooth snow slope descended right down to Leith Harbour. It took him about two minutes to slide down to the bottom, where the Leith doctor successfully dealt with his tooth.

The gruelling work of refitting *Penola* continued relentlessly. There was no wireless news, and everyone wondered what was going on in Europe. In South Georgia they were more out of touch with the world than they had been in Graham Land. Occasionally days were good, when Roberts enjoyed working with Martin ashore in the metal shops, which he found "splendid and a pleasure to work in". There were good lathes of every type in working order, as well as plenty of scrap metal.

One day Ryder made an unexpected decision that Roberts had hardly dared hope for. Whilst he was still to spend all his time in South Georgia on ship work, he would be allowed to stay on when *Penola* left, giving him a valuable few weeks for ornithology at the beginning of the breeding season, before returning to the Falklands on *Lafonia* in late November. It would seem that Roberts had allies in England who had been pulling strings. Betty Creswick at SPRI had begged Debenham to write to Ryder to allow Roberts to "do his stuff".[29] Debenham did so and also wrote to Roberts: "First, with regard to your work at the Falklands – I sincerely hope this can be done because the scientific output of the Expedition will be very important in the end as the geographical results so far have been so meagre."[30] In a later letter he expressed deep concern at the debts that the expedition had accumulated, in view of the lack of results: "It is no good pretending that the RGS as a whole, or the public in general, are very impressed with the work so far."[31]

September arrived and there was still much to be done on the ship whilst in dry dock. Although the crew members were working harmoniously and in good humour, Roberts was "living for the day when I shall see Penola sail away over the horizon".[32] Sunday was usually the one day of respite, often largely spent sleeping, but occasionally Roberts was able to get back to his own work: "Time to go ashore and get through a few stomach analyses to see what the local birds are eating. I made a fine collection of penguin parasites today."[33]

His onboard laboratory was extremely damp, most Sundays having to be spent drying everything out. By the second week of September *Penola* was ready to come out of dry dock and she was moored back in the bay. Working hours were now stepped up to an 11½ hour day, as there followed more gruelling work reloading the ballast, coal and cable in the cold and wet.

By mid-September the last major job left was to replace the rigging. For the two Ryders and Martin it was an obsession, and the sole topic of conversation, but for the ship's crew actually working out in the punishingly cold, wet and windy conditions it was simply unpleasant. "A miserably cold day with fine rain and strong wind. I have spent most of it in a bosun's chair swinging about under the jibboom trying to set up the bobstays and feeling thoroughly dejected."[34] Roberts was not the only one who was bored out of his skull and tired of always being cold and dirty. The crew now had to work on the rigging through their weekends if the weather was good, and the feeling was that it had become more of a pointless exercise than a necessity. With no weekends to look forward to, tempers started to fray. They had only had one day off in the last month.

On 18 September Roberts received a terrible wireless message. Charcot's ship *Pourquoi Pas?* had been wrecked of the coast of Iceland and all on board except one were drowned. Thirty corpses, including that of Charcot, had been washed ashore. An exceptionally violent storm had blown the ship onto some reefs. Roberts was devastated. "Charcot was one of the finest men I ever met. Perhaps he would have liked best to die thus in harness. Even in his seventieth year it was difficult to think of him settling down to a life of retirement, but for the others it was different." Roberts had known most of those on board *Pourquoi Pas?* from his Greenland expedition in 1933, especially the seven scientists, who were of a younger generation than their leader. "All day I have been trying to get rid of pictures which keep coming into my mind: the familiar faces, and the ship which was so different from all others."[35]

By late September *Penola's* crew were beginning to see elephant seals ashore in the distance and to hear the roaring bulls, a sound with extraordinary carrying power over several hundred yards. Females were coming ashore to pup. Millett, Martin and Roberts took the opportunity of an afternoon off from rigging to go ashore and take a look. "Both this sound and the smell which pervades them is peculiarly revolting... It is possible to go right up to them and throw stones by the dozen into their widely opened mouths. No amount of stones will either make them shut their mouths or stop their disgusting belching roar."[36] The largest bulls were around 20 ft long, weighing between 3 and 5 tons and clumsy on land. It was not too difficult to dodge them. (*Plate 8.12*)

Back on board ship Roberts boiled down some rat skulls to get the meat off (in the name of science) and decided to have a taste of one. It was not so bad, he thought, apart from the strong smell. But he was unable to persuade any of the others on board to try any.

FREEDOM AT LAST

The longed-for day finally arrived when *Penola* left South Georgia on 1 October. Roberts was taken by catcher to Grytviken and was soon installed in a large armchair in front of the Barlas' fire, at last able to accept their offer of hospitality. He had a comfortable bedroom and, best of all, use of the well-equipped shore-based Discovery laboratory to work in with its good library. In spite of being unoccupied for seven years it still had heating, water and electric light, plus a splendid view of the bay. Roberts was utterly content.

A week later he joined a sealing boat, the *Diaz*, which was going out to the eastern end of the island. The crew of 19 were not all toughs as he had expected, but a cosmopolitan lot: besides Norwegians, the nationalities included Swedish, Russian, Italian, Finnish, Lithuanian and Icelandic. All were from Buenos Aires and conversed in Spanish. Roberts was no linguist and depended on the skipper and chief engineer, who spoke some English. The ship's mate, Carl Jansen, stood out from the rest. A brother of Barlas' clean and well-mannered cook, he possessed neither of those attributes. His old and filthy clothes stank of seal oil, whilst his stocky, wild appearance with long black shaggy hair and beard were further enhanced by a large scar across his nose. The rest of the crew were remarkably clean, washing and shaving regularly, "some even brushing their teeth".

Roberts observed Carl Jansen's eating habits with fascination. During meals he would fill his mouth alternately with knife and fork, both grasped firmly like daggers in his dirty hands. During the meal there were continuous gurgling noises, surplus food dribbling out of the corners of his mouth and down his neck inside his clothes. Every now and then a loud belch indicated his satisfaction.

As work started at 4:30 am, everyone turned in straight after supper, which was usually fish, sometimes Nototheniid ('anti-freeze') fish, which are exceedingly bony. Only Jansen could eat them whole, all but the tail.

In rough weather they put into Larsen Harbour off Drygalski Fjord, a narrow channel bordered by spectacular ice cliffs and mountains. Roberts went ashore to observe Weddell seals with newborn pups, here in South Georgia at the most northerly limit of their range and their only known breeding place on the island. *Diaz* then steamed off into to Cooper Bay, a sheltered spot harbouring several hundred elephant seals. It now being the mating season, the large old bulls were lying up on the beaches with their harems of cows, numbering anything up to 30 per bull. The strongest bull would be continually fighting for possession of his cows, keeping a watchful eye on potential rivals and roaring until he had finished pairing. "He then rushes blindly for his rival regardless of all obstacles. If he is in the middle of his harem he goes looping over his cows and pups, and one would expect the latter to be squashed flat, but they do not appear to suffer any harm. The fight which generally follows is impressive. Approaching close to each other, face to face, and both roaring repeatedly, the two bulls rear up as far as possible on the after part of their bodies, and fall forward with wide open mouths and inflated proboscis, trying to gash their opponent with the upper canine teeth."[37] Over three days *Diaz* had taken 230 elephant seals and the hold was now full. The sealers' methods were noted carefully by Roberts.[38] He also made his first observations of gentoo penguin courtship, but drawing conclusions from them was much harder.

Back at Grytviken, Roberts was on the lookout for any opportunity for ornithology. He got permission to join *Discovery II* on her imminent voyage to the South Orkney Islands, Elephant Island and the Falkland Islands. In the meantime he was off on another sealing trip around South Georgia, encountering foul weather most of the time but still able to visit and collect valuable information from several penguin rookeries. Reaching the Bay of Isles, he listened with delight to the trumpeting of king penguins during the night, the next day making his first acquaintance with them in the wild. (*Plate 8.13*) Landing in blizzard conditions, he endured a chilly couple of hours making penguin observations and then struggled with the crew to return to the boat, their pram (small dinghy) helplessly capsizing three times and filling with water, so that they ended up leaping into the sea and having to swim.

Roberts lost the collection of penguin eggs he had made for embryonic research, but whilst still in the Bay of Isles he had another king penguin rookery to study and photograph. In the icy water they again had problems landing in the surf, and got very wet. Roberts came close to losing both his cameras as the pram kept capsizing, the men spending long periods up to their armpits in ice-cold water. Back on the ship everyone was exceedingly wet and cold, though not grumbling; the crew were a cheery and good-humoured lot. This time Roberts managed to get back four king penguin eggs for their embryos. Farther on in another cove he found nesting sooty albatrosses. This was followed by another drenching; in consistently foul weather the boat was unable to get ashore and rested up for a day in Prince Olaf Harbour. Every muscle in Roberts' body was aching from the continuous wet and cold and he was glad of a day's rest and the chance to dry his clothes. It was also his 24th birthday, but other than opening a letter from home it was rather lonely for him; making conversation in Norwegian or Spanish was too much effort. But returning to Grytviken six days later having visited every cove in the Bay of Isles, Roberts was pleased that he had been able to map and census all the penguin rookeries and collect as many eggs as he needed to show different embryonic stages.

Barely stopping for a day to deal with his specimens, Roberts crammed in another short sealing trip, this time on the *Lillekarl* and accompanied by Dr J R Strong from *Discovery II*. The two men made a census of the king penguin colony at the Bay of Isles, one of South Georgia's largest rookeries.

It is challenging enough to make a count of any large penguin rookery, but king penguins are especially difficult. With their unique breeding cycle of 14 months,[39] at any one time in a rookery there are birds at different stages of breeding and chick development. Generally the birds breed only two out of every three years. Until the 20th century the young, in their fluffy dark brown down congregating in crèches, were even thought to be a different species.[40]

On returning to Grytviken after two days of hot weather, the station was unrecognisable. The snow had melted and the asphalt tennis court was in use. A blast of dance music came floating across the bay from a new German factory ship, *Jan Willem*, which had just arrived. A tour around the ship – Germany's first attempt at Antarctic whaling – was an eye opener to Roberts, with its air of German, efficiency, comfort and even a few luxuries. But he was repelled by the unpleasant Nazi atmosphere, excessive saluting and portraits of Hitler in every cabin. The day concluded with a game of tennis by the edge of the sea, surrounded by ice-covered mountains, in the company of three gentoo penguins masquerading as ball-boys.

CLARENCE ISLAND

Two days later Roberts was aboard *Discovery II* as she left South Georgia for the South Orkney Islands, working westwards along the edge of pack ice until they were close to Hope Bay where Nordenskjöld's ship had been crushed in the ice in 1902. Roberts hoped to collect the fossils left there by Nordenskjöld, or collect new ones from Seymour Island (well known for its fossil penguins), but the skipper was wary of the uncharted waters and no landing was made.

On 13 November *Discovery II* was dredging close to Clarence Island in the South Shetlands, where with a telescope Roberts could see an immense colony of silver-grey petrels (southern fulmar). Like its better-known neighbour Elephant Island, Clarence Island is challenging to land on. Only one previously recorded landing had been made there in 1928 by the Norwegian geologist Olaf Holtedahl, whom Roberts had met in Oslo before going up to Cambridge. The whole island is thickly covered by snow, ice and several glaciers, with a steep sided mountain ridge along its 13-mile length rising at the southern end to 6,400 ft. Landing is perilous in anything but calm weather. There are numerous submerged rocks and islets, almost no beaches, and conditions are seldom favourable. Nevertheless Roberts, marine biologist Francis Ommanney and *Discovery II*'s hydrologist George Deacon succeeded in landing on a shingle beach near Cape Bowles at the southern tip of the island, which was not very safe due to a high cliff with an ice cap behind the beach. In two hours on the island Roberts found nesting cape petrels (*Plate 8.14*) and a huge chinstrap penguin rookery. Photographing the nesting fulmars would have demanded some extreme rock climbing with a bulky camera, but for Roberts that was nothing new. He was the first ornithologist ever to have landed on the island. Not many have followed.[41]

That evening *Discovery II* headed north for the Falkland Islands. Her arrival at Port Stanley on 17 November was marked by a two-day long liquid party between the two ships' crews of *Penola* and *Discovery II*. *Penola* had taken 31 tedious days to travel back from South Georgia beating against the westerlies, charting an erratic course. Four days later Roberts was greatly cheered to receive long telegrams from Bertram and Fleming, relating the southern party's exciting new discovery that Wilkins' so-called channels were broad glaciers and that Graham Land was actually an unbroken continental landmass.[42]

On 28 November Roberts left Stanley to spend another week on Kidney Island, hoping to discover nesting sites of the sooty shearwater. The island was honeycombed with burrows of Magellanic penguins and cape petrels. Like other shearwaters, the sooty is nocturnal and Roberts needed to work at night with a torch. He was overjoyed to find some burrows and even a few birds incubating eggs, "the first found in this part of the world".[43] Roberts' passion for petrels did not make for an easy schedule. As darkness fell he would venture out with the torch to study the birds' habits, going to bed at about 3.30 am and getting up at 10 am to spend the day making a rough census of all the birds on the island. It was the only occasion during the entire expedition on which he admitted to needing courage, working at night amongst the tussock grass where the sea lions lurked. Even though they were more frightened of him than he of them, there was a great risk of getting bitten while trying to avoid stepping on one. He nonetheless delighted in the solitude of this special place, away from the pettiness of social life in Port Stanley.

Only one other thing troubled him. Spending all his time lying in the tussock and excavating penguin and petrel burrows, he was plagued by fleas and had to strip several times a day in his tent to pick them off. Nonetheless, ever the careful scientist, he collected them in a tube to take back for identification. Two of the three different species he collected turned out to be new to science and one was named after him: *Listronius robertsianus*. On 4 December he returned to Stanley with a huge collection of prepared skins, eggs, embryos, birds and parasites along with all his field notes.

In Stanley the sole topic of conversation was the abdication of King Edward VIII (who happened to be the expedition's patron). As no official details had emerged, the town was rife with rumour and scandalmongering. The next day the long-awaited spare parts for *Penola*'s engines arrived, only for Millett to discover that not a single part was the correct size. *Penola*'s remaining voyage would have to be completed under sail. Red Ryder informed Roberts that he proposed to bypass Deception Island and make straight for the Argentine Islands from the open sea. But almost the entire scientific collection of 33 cases of specimens from the first year had been left at Deception Island. After a year in such a damp climate they would need urgent attention, and after much remonstration by Roberts, Ryder reluctantly agreed to make the attempt to stop over. Roberts was now in a frenzy of packing and finishing his penguin studies. He had to hire a man to take his place on ship work for a week.

Christmas was just another working day, but at last on 29 December *Penola* was ready to sail south once more and a large crowd of friends saw her off. Rejoining the ship after her 6-month break from duty was chief (and now only) ratter, Lummo the cat. Also on board, extending the crew with an extra four pairs of hands, were Bill Halliday the cook and three Falkland Islander boys.

MUTINY ON THE *PENOLA!*

On New Year's Eve an incident took place on board which brought to a head the friction which had existed for a long time between naval and civilian expedition team members. Roberts had been assigned to the early morning watch, one for which he had a planned ornithological programme. At 11 pm he was informed that the captain wanted him transferred to the other watch for meteorological observations. Roberts was profoundly irritated, pointing out that the meteorology could be done for the purposes of the ship's log by one of the Falkland Island boys who had been taken on board. He asked to remain on the same watch, the mornings being far better for bird observations. Martin, the mate, returned saying that the captain had refused. Roberts merely wished for an explanation, since there was obviously a clash between the interests of the ship and scientific work. But the captain had nothing more to say. Roberts was to go below and join the other watch at 5 am.

Roberts decided to see the captain in person, to settle what he considered was his right to a hearing over any matter affecting the scientific work. Ryder once again refused to discuss the matter. After an angry exchange between them, Ryder shouted to Martin, "Call the watch below. Put Roberts under arrest." Roberts went below and *Penola* changed course to head back to Port Stanley.

In the morning Roberts was called by Ryder, who produced a signed document formally charging him with insubordination for disputing the mate's commands and for addressing himself as captain of the ship in an "insolent and contemptuous manner". "This offence will be entered in the log as a permanent record, and is to be signed by you...It is apparent to me that you are not prepared to accord to me the respect which is due to my position as captain. You have therefore become a menace to my authority, and it is expedient for me to discharge you ashore at Port Stanley, which I propose to do. This is not to be considered as a punishment but as a necessity to the safe navigation of the ship".[44]

Roberts denied the charges of insubordination and insolence, producing a lengthy memorandum defending his position. Since Ryder was now placed in a difficult position, Roberts (and two witnesses) agreed to sign a counter-memorandum to the effect that the captain's authority was not to be undermined. At noon the ship was put about once more and the journey continued southward. The incident had proved to be something of a south Atlantic storm in a teacup.

For the next six days *Penola*'s journey south was becalmed and progress was painfully slow. Finally the wind arrived, but in the wrong direction and they were blown rapidly back towards Port Stanley. They took shelter three miles off Beauchêne Island, the most isolated of the Falkland Islands, some 34 miles to the south. With field glasses Roberts could see the immense colony of black-browed albatross stretching along its western side which he considered likely to be the largest albatross colony in the world. For many species of bird and seal Beauchêne was one of the few havens safe from man's depredations, mostly undisturbed and with no introduced species. The Antarctic fur seal, hunted to near extinction, was swimming in some numbers around the ship. Roberts was wistful and would have given anything to be able to land. "No one capable of giving an accurate description of the island and its wildlife has ever landed there," he wrote.[45]

Penola continued towards Deception Island painfully slowly, eventually dropping anchor in Whalers' Bay. It was a moment of some trepidation for Roberts, knowing that the station had been revisited by whalers since *Penola*'s previous visit. The jetty was badly damaged and all the huts had been broken into. The door of the hut in which he had left his specimens was wide open. Roberts went up to the hut and peered inside. His worst fears were confirmed. Every box had been thrown about and many were broken open. Specimens were strewn on the floor and everything was extremely damp. He spent the whole day and night unpacking cases to dry and clean the bird skins, which were in a dreadful condition. With the limited facilities on *Penola* for drying, he had to drape them round the stove last thing at night and clear them away before the cook started work in the morning.

AWAITING THE PLEASURE OF THE WIND

On 26 January *Penola* attempted to continue its voyage to collect the shore party from the southern base. On moving out of Whalers' Bay in rain and fog the ship rolled heavily in the swell. They were in poorly-charted waters with no clear idea of their position. In the fog, with icebergs a constant hazard, it was unsafe to motor and they had to raise sail to clear them. Five days later *Penola* had still not moved, and even getting back into harbour through Neptune's Bellows was dangerous. With supplies of water and seal meat running low, advantage was taken of this unplanned return to lay in both.

At last *Penola* succeeded in leaving Deception Island, but after 80 miles a stiff south-westerly breeze sprang up, against which the engines were powerless. Eventually, after some days of frayed tempers and temperamental wind, *Penola* reached the Argentine Islands. The base hut was damp and mildewed, but otherwise in good condition. Roberts could not resist the temptation at the first available moment (which was midnight) to row round to his colony of Wilson's petrels, catching several birds that he had ringed the previous year.

Penola was now safely anchored and everyone had a day of rest. Roberts could now attend to his scientific material, especially the damp specimens from Deception Island. He was pleased with his Wilson's petrel results: out of 27 birds ringed the previous year, 21 were recovered and found to have returned to the same burrow and the same mate.

RENDEZVOUS WITH THE SOUTHERN PARTY

On 14 February *Penola* headed south past Adelaide Island via the open sea route. A radio message from the southern base reported a violent force 9 gale in Marguerite Bay. *Penola* was now to experience the foulest weather of the entire expedition. All the crew had to work continuously, struggling to raise, reef and lower frozen sails in bitterly cold biting winds and snow to maintain the ship's position. The sails and ropes were frozen solid, cutting into bare hands numb with cold (gloves having been removed to get a good grip in the rigging). Eventually *Penola* was able to penetrate Marguerite Bay under engine power and head for the Debenham Islands, where the rendezvous had been planned. She anchored only 100 yards from the base, but the storm continued and it was several more days before the ship and shore parties were reunited. To celebrate the reunion the nearby glacier obliged with a massive calving event.

The sledging party had many exciting discoveries to report. They had photographed and surveyed over a thousand miles of Graham Land's western coastline. It was the first time that Graham Land had been traversed and its east coast was surveyed 300 miles farther south than ever before. Crane Channel and Stefansson Strait did not exist. The map of Graham Land would need to be substantially redrawn: it was not split into north and south, but was actually a peninsula forming an integral part of the Antarctic continent. Alexander Land was now known to be an island of fossil-bearing sedimentary rock 250 miles long, separated from the mainland by a huge ice-filled depression, to be named George VI Sound.

After all the exchange of news and catching up on sleep, the shore party had several days of packing up and loading, hampered by yet more gales. By 11 March the ship was fully loaded, and with 20 men now on board there was not a spare inch of space. Since all the berths had been removed, sleeping arrangements were improvised: Fleming and Bertram had the forecastle and Roberts slept on his bench in the lab, whilst a dormitory for seven was created in the hold. On deck were the aeroplane (partially dismantled in her crate), the motor boat *Stella* and two dories, drums of fuel oil and eight dogs in crates. On reaching South Georgia in poor visibility they dropped anchor in King Edward Cove opposite Grytviken. The comfort of baths, clean clothes, fresh food and reading their mail gave the party a feeling of well-being.

The night of 5 April was Roberts' last on *Penola*. Following a farewell party aboard, the homebound contingent departed on the cargo ship *Coronda*, her hold full of whale oil destined for Europe. Their last view of South Georgia was of its panorama of snowy peaks slowly disappearing below the horizon.

Coronda crossed the equator in hot sun in a calm blue sea, arriving on 9 May at Las Palmas, Gran Canaria where the party transferred to RMS *Gascony* for the home run. Roberts, Bertram and Fleming took the opportunity to relish the sights and smells of a temperate climate in spring: "From 6,000 ft. there was a wonderful view… but best of all was the vegetation, with the smell of flowers and earth… tall Eucalyptus trees, banana groves and Indian corn, olives and vines, figs and conifers.

It was wonderful to see butterflies, brilliant flowers, and birds singing. How one appreciates the buzz of insects after not hearing them for so long, and in the evening frogs began to croak loudly in every pool."[46]

There was a much less pleasant atmosphere in the city of Las Palmas. The Canary Islands were under martial law, with large numbers of armed soldiers roaming around. It was a shock to return from three years in a remote and peaceful part of the world to a Europe that was at war. On 12 May, with a sense of anticlimax, the party listened on *Gascony* to the broadcast of the coronation service for King George VI. Five days later they disembarked sombrely at Liverpool docks. Roberts boarded a train alone to London and on to Woking.

After a four-month voyage north *Penola* eventually arrived at Portsmouth in August 1937. She had travelled a total of nearly 27,000 miles, of which 15,000 were under sail alone, and thanks to the cats she had remained completely free of vermin throughout. For an Antarctic expedition of just 15 members, BGLE was an outstanding success. They had returned with every member safe and sound, major geographical discoveries had been made, and for Roberts there was a cornucopia of new research material.

PART 2

THE MANDARIN

9

WARTIME

The late 1930s were anxious times. War was seemingly inevitable, valuables were hidden in secret vaults and gas masks were issued to the British people. Three weeks after returning from the Antarctic Roberts was back in Cambridge, fixing himself up with digs, a room at the Scott Polar Research Institute, and money from his college. In December 1937 he registered with the university for a PhD degree with a thesis on the biology of Antarctic birds. By then he had acquired rooms in Emmanuel College's Front Court, spending many hours with Bertram and Fleming sorting photographs from the British Graham Land Expedition and planning their scientific reports. Of the ten published reports, Roberts contributed four. He was awarded a 'minimum subsistence' grant by the Department of Scientific and Industrial Research, which recommended that he complete his PhD thesis before being considered for any war service. It was not the easiest time to be writing up research: money was tight and he was unable to use the watercolour bird paintings that Lisle Ryder had created for him during BGLE.

PENGUINS AND PETRELS

Roberts' doctoral thesis comprised two research fields, both of which were published as his contribution to the BGLE scientific reports:[1] a study of Wilson's storm petrel, and the breeding behaviour of penguins.

Of the seven species of penguin observed, he focussed mainly on the gentoo which he had found to be the most widespread in the Antarctic.

At the time few people had ever set eyes on a penguin, even in a zoo. Roberts set out to relate penguin behaviour to physiological processes initiated by environmental factors and to record their pattern of behaviour throughout the breeding season. He was the first to plot penguin rookeries in the Falkland Islands, South Georgia, the South Shetland Islands and (incompletely) in the Antarctic Peninsula. Although others had written about penguins, knowledge of their breeding behaviour was then piecemeal and accounts were often anthropomorphic and conflicting. Roberts commented that "in the case of penguins it is remarkable how their behaviour often conforms to the national characteristics of the different authors who have described them".[2]

Thomas Wyatt Bagshawe had made a remarkable year-long study of the gentoo whilst spending a year confined to a small islet in Paradise Bay on the west coast of Graham Land in 1921-22.[3] Bagshawe lent his unpublished field notes to Roberts, who in return helped him to get them published by the Zoological Society.[4] The American Robert Cushman Murphy's *Oceanic Birds of South America* was not published until 1936, by which time Roberts' own observations were more or less completed. Roberts' supervisor in Cambridge was an 'old school' physiologist F H A Marshall of Christ's College whose legacy, the treatise *The Physiology of Reproduction*, was first published in 1912.[5] This approach required the dissection of a lot of corpses in musty laboratories and by the 1930s was becoming outmoded in favour of behavioural studies of living birds, pioneered by Konrad Lorenz, Niko Tinbergen and Cambridge's home-grown David Lack. Ultimately they would have far greater influence than Marshall on Roberts' own ornithological research.

Wilson's storm petrel is a little bird hardly larger than a swallow, with impressively long legs. (*Plate 9.1*) Although common globally, until Roberts' pioneering study its breeding habits were barely known as it breeds in remote and inaccessible locations in the Antarctic. In common with other small petrels it only comes ashore nocturnally, in order to avoid its predators (gulls and skuas). During BGLE Roberts discovered a breeding colony on the Argentine Islands, just 400 yards from the base hut where he made a detailed study, keeping 23 pairs under daily observation in their burrows throughout the entire breeding season. To avoid disturbing them, a cylindrical portion of hard compacted moss was carefully cut from above the nest cavity and a numbered wooden peg driven through it to use as a handle. A thermograph recorded the comings and goings of individual pairs and every bird in the colony was marked with a small numbered aluminium ring. In this way Roberts could determine what share each sex took in incubating and rearing the young. He observed that the birds returned each spring to the same burrow and mate: an extraordinary feat, migrating up the American seaboard as far as Newfoundland and back. At 18,000 miles this is one of the longest known migrations of any bird.[6] Monitoring the growth rates of the chicks revealed their extraordinary resilience in the tough environment. (*Plate 9.2*) Towards the end of the season snow often blocked the burrow entrance, preventing a parent getting in with food. On such occasions the chicks stopped growing and had to live off their own fat reserves. One of them was buried for 20 days and survived.

It would take Roberts three years to write up the ornithological work for his thesis and the BGLE scientific reports. Early in 1940 he was awarded the Polar Medal, the Bruce Memorial Medal by the Royal Scottish Geographical Society, and finally his doctorate at Senate House, Cambridge. Now a fully-fledged polar expert, he was to become involved in specialist war work.

CLOTHING FOR THE MILITARY

James Wordie, as chairman of its management committee, was keen to promote the Scott Polar Research Institute for war work. So were the younger generation at the institute: Colin Bertram, Launcelot Fleming, Andrew Croft, John Wright and Roberts himself. But Frank Debenham, in his capacity of SPRI director, had always retained strong personal views about the institute's role and purpose as an 'open house' for polar explorers and he took exception to any involvement of SPRI and the use of its resources for military and secret purposes, particularly for non-polar work.[7] However, Debenham's stance appears to have been ambivalent. He had no objections to war work when it came to the university's geography department, through which Roberts was approached to undertake an investigation for an unnamed government department that paid in cash, on means of destroying installations in various parts of the world.[8] At the outbreak of war SPRI was closed to the public and was immediately commissioned by the Admiralty to write a confidential report on possible German U-boat bases in Arctic ports.[9] Roberts, Croft and two others were recruited to go out and search for U-boat bases on the coast of Iceland, but as they were about to depart on a trawler from Hull the operation was abandoned, being judged too risky.[10]

SPRI was inextricably tied to the war effort, whether Debenham liked it or not. On 9 May 1940 military staff visited the institute, appointing Roberts and Bertram to the War Office to prepare a Handbook for the military on clothing and equipment for cold climates. This involved them in testing prototypes of everything from snow shoes, skis and sledges to camping equipment and camouflage. Military operations could hardly be undertaken in oilskins, wellingtons and sou'westers; there was a real need for weatherproof clothing, which was still made from wool and cotton, neither of which provided good protection against water. Trials at ICI and at the British Cotton Industry Research Association Shirley Institute, Manchester resulted in the breathable waterproof cloth 'Ventile', enabling the traditional heavy army greatcoats to be replaced by Ventile anoraks.[11]

Today considered a fashion garment, the string vest (*Plate 9.3*) then had a serious role to play in the system of layered clothing worn by polar explorers and the Norwegian military. It had been invented in 1935 by Captain Henrik Brun who, experimenting with cotton fishing nets, successfully produced a wide-mesh garment to be worn next to the skin. The *brynje* vest would trap air close to the skin, providing insulation, absorbing sweat when the wearer was under physical exertion and keeping woollen layers on top dry and warm. By 1940 it was in use by skiers in Norway and Sweden. In September 1941 Roberts organised and took part in trials for the War Office with army recruits running up and down Ben Nevis to test the string vest's performance. Following a favourable assessment from the recruits, there was a rush to get the vests into production. Since no machinery existed capable of manufacturing the wide-open mesh, armies of WVS ladies were called upon to get knitting on big needles to produce the thousands of string vests needed for the troops. In 1943 Roberts introduced the string vest to North America. It was later used by troops in Egypt and Korea, and in 1953 by all the mountaineering team that conquered Everest. It is still a practical undergarment in the colder regions of Scandinavia.

THE *POLAR RECORD*

Back in 1930 Debenham had decided that SPRI should produce its own house journal, to be published twice yearly. The *Polar Record*, with Debenham as official editor, first came out in 1931 and was the first ever journal devoted exclusively to polar topics. It would become the *raison d'être* of the institute, particularly during the difficult wartime years when Roberts made great efforts to ensure that the journal continued to be published, regardless of whatever might happen to SPRI itself.

The member of staff responsible for preparing and editing material for the *Polar Record* was the director's assistant, the only person to receive any remuneration. In 1938 Dorothy Fetherstonhaugh took over this role from Betty Creswick. Dorothy's letters to Roberts reveal her need for a guiding hand in preparing each new issue and the consternation that his frequent absences from Cambridge caused her. By July 1939 the demands of the job were beginning to overwhelm her: "Dear Brian, the enclosed from Sandy [Alexander Glen]. What does A do? It arrived tonight and John and I both hate to think of it being published... Quick Brian – please help – and I suppose I had better show it to Deb soon... Why have you gone away? Oh dear!"[12]

This was followed by an implicit potential threat to Roberts' bachelorhood: "Dean Lumsdale called this afternoon from the Falklands hoping to see you and joy oh joy he had Miss Carey outside... he wouldn't show me your postmistress although I was pining to see her... he said he thought Miss C would go and see you [in Woking]. Now we know why you have gone home Brian – oh you naughty boy! Please bring her here and please can I be your wife for the day! Have a good time and Brian my boy, be good and be careful." Miss Carey, the colonial postmistress at Port Stanley, was "a formidable woman"[13] and likely to have been one of the 'painted ladies' who had visited Roberts in his Port Stanley hospital bed while he was recovering from his appendectomy in 1936 during BGLE (chapter 8). But not even the wily Dorothy could get Roberts ensnared by a member of the opposite sex.

During the bitterly cold winter of 1939-40, when the river Cam froze over and Grantchester Meadows turned into a skating rink, Dorothy's anguish over the *Polar Record* continued: "Dear Brian, I have never heard anything so frightful... I am really distressed to hear of the footgear article, but I do really think too that I can fix Deb... He simply hasn't a leg to stand on after telling you and even more perhaps Andrew 'to go ahead as much as you can, we want to make it a big splash!' I hope you are getting some good skating – tell it not to thaw until after the weekend after next. <u>Blast</u> everything! Yours aye, Dorothy".[14] The reference was to a 50-page two-part article on polar footwear that Roberts and Andrew Croft had written for publication in *Polar Record*.[15] It was arguably the most authoritative treatise ever written on the subject, but Debenham had declined to publish it, objecting to its length. The style and content of the journal would continue to cause dispute between him and Roberts during the war.

FAMILY MATTERS

During the Great War of 1914-18, Brian's surgeon father Charles had joined the Royal Army Medical Corps to operate on the severely wounded at a base hospital, firstly in France and then on the Eastern Front in Salonika, Greece (chapter 1). The prospect of another major war was utterly devastating for him. A month before his 60th birthday, while putting up the blackout on the eve of the declaration of war, he suffered a fatal heart attack.

Six months later Brian lost another family member. His brother Pat had trained at Dartmouth College to join the Royal Navy, qualifying as a Russian interpreter. By the age of 26 he had risen to first lieutenant and second-in-command on the destroyer HMS *Daring*. On 18 February 1940 the ship was escorting a convoy from Norway to Britain when she was torpedoed by a German submarine off the north-east coast of Scotland. Sinking rapidly, *Daring* took nearly all her crew with her, including Pat.

Brian's other brother Denis was pursuing a career as an architect. Being in a 'reserved occupation', he was required to remain in London throughout the war and rented a flat near Sloane Square. His nerves degenerating, he smoked heavily and was not getting much sleep. On many occasions his mother Madeline wrote to Brian expressing deep concern for Denis' state of health. London was bombed by the Luftwaffe for 57 consecutive nights from 7 September 1940. With bombs falling everywhere, travel became a nightmare for London's citizens. Brian (travelling from Cambridge) and Denis nevertheless managed regularly to get home to Woking to see their recently widowed mother. On one occasion Denis had to return to London during an air raid lasting from 9 pm until 3 am. Wimbledon station (which was on his route) was bombed and it took him all night to get back to Chelsea, arriving just in time for work in the morning. In time Denis found a solution to his problem of sleep deprivation: he could disappear every night into the Peter Jones department store and sleep soundly on a Louis XV sofa in the basement secondhand furniture department.

Joy, her husband David and their young family were living in Esher, some 10 miles from Woking. Following an uncomfortably close bombing raid the family evacuated to Bishopgarth. For the ever-stoical Madeline, this was a welcome distraction to her painful and debilitating chronic arthritis. Joy had her work cut out managing a large household with cook, maids, odd job man and day and night nurses for her ailing mother. Madeline's frequent letters to Brian detail much news of the bombing in London and eventually in Woking. "Three nights ago we had our first screaming bomb, which had not exploded. One person said they heard the thud as they were outside and it seems to have been fairly near. Our garden was searched by an air raid warden. Very soon after 9 ordinary ones were dropped at intervals of 2 or 3 seconds..."[16]

Meanwhile Denis, dodging bombs and experiencing the destruction of London all around him, had met Lilian Ulanowsky, a refugee from Vienna. She had established prior contacts in England and had escaped by a whisker from Nazi-occupied Austria in May 1938, shortly after the *Anschluss*. Her family were musicians: Lilian was a singer and viola player and her elder brother Paul, who had emigrated to the US in 1935, was a professional concert pianist and regular accompanist to the much-loved lieder singer Lotte Lehmann. In May 1941 Denis married Lilian in Knebworth, Hertfordshire. Sending Brian a sketch map of the location with his architect's precision of detail, Denis asked him to give the bride away, worrying whether Brian would turn up at all, let alone arrive on time. Brian did both. Following the wedding Denis and Lilian moved into an upper floor flat in Pelham Court on the Fulham Road, South Kensington. Sadly, Madeline did not live to witness the event. Her health had been in terminal decline and she died a month before the wedding.

Bishopgarth, the Roberts family home for 30 years, was put up for sale. Thereafter Brian often stayed at Joy's new home in Woking, on one occasion making himself popular by turning up with a brace of rabbits – much appreciated during the long period of meat rationing – which he skinned, then curing the skins so that Joy could make smart muffs for her two young daughters Jennifer and Susan to wear for Easter.

THE SPECIAL OPERATIONS AGENT

An occasional visitor to Pelham Court was Lilian's younger brother Peter, who from 1940 until 1946 gave Denis's flat in Pelham Court as his official address. But for much of the time his actual whereabouts were obscure.

During the 1930s Peter Ulanowsky had been working in a Jewish accountant's office in Vienna. At the time of the *Anschluss*, the office staff were rounded up on 31 May 1938 and imprisoned in Dachau. After surviving a year in Dachau and Buchenwald concentration camps, Peter was finally got out by his family's persistent efforts, and with a large bribe paid by Lotte Lehmann. Following a year's recuperation in London he enlisted as a private in the Pioneer Corps of the British Army, serving in France and the Middle East.

In October 1941 Peter, a native German speaker, was recruited to the Special Operations Executive (SOE), spending two years in training and waiting for the call to go out on SOE's Austrian operation codenamed Greenleaves, a small but vital part of its Mission Clowder aimed at linking up with Slovenian partisans to infiltrate Austria and stimulate an uprising against the Nazis.[17] He had to wait for Tito's agreement in October 1943 to the British despatch of Austrian agents to Slovenia; it then took another seven months of anxious waiting and five failed attempts before Peter's group was finally parachuted into Slovenia. They crossed into the southern Austrian province of Carinthia, only to find that owing to the advance of the Soviet army through Hungary, the area was heavily occupied by German troops. After still more weeks hiding in dangerous territory, disaster struck. The whole operation was betrayed by an Austrian deserter employed by MI6, and SOE's secret bunker was discovered by the Gestapo. It had contained a hoard of SOE paraphernalia, including false German documents and photographs of the agents. 'Operation Greenleaves' was promptly aborted and Peter, his career with SOE effectively over, was evacuated to Italy to serve out the war as a reserve wireless/telegraphy operator. He continued to serve in the British Army under the Allied Control Commission in the post-war occupation of Germany and Austria until 1955.

LIFE AT PELHAM COURT

By early 1944 Brian had left Cambridge to spend most of his time in London. After living in bed-and-breakfast lodgings in South Kensington, on the advice of Denis to "get a proper roof over his head", he moved into a basement flat in Pelham Court. So began a seven-year period during which the two brothers were near neighbours. During the summer of 1944 the building next door to Pelham Court received a direct hit from a V1 pilotless 'buzz' bomb, causing substantial damage to Denis and Lilian's flat. (*Plates 9.4, 9.5*) Taking refuge under their bed they survived relatively unscathed, but all their furniture was pock-marked from flying shrapnel and glass shards. Brian opened up his relatively safe basement flat to affected neighbours, providing refuge and cups of tea.

On 8 May 1945 the war in Europe was at last over. Whilst Lilian escaped from the war-torn capital to Cornwall, Denis and Brian remained in London. In a tender letter to Denis, she included the following rebuke: "I am shocked to hear Brian keeps you up till 2.30 am I shall have something to say to him."[18] What she did say to him is unrecorded, but Brian had evidently been encouraging Denis to lapse into bachelor habits in her absence.

One of the fruits of their discussions late into the night concerned the organisation of information for library cataloguing. Denis was involved in developing the Universal Decimal Classification system for architecture and civil engineering. Unusually for the gentle-mannered Denis and the forceful Brian, Denis seems to have had Brian on the back foot. He was now exhorting Brian to implement UDC in polar libraries. Brian was initially sceptical, but Denis persisted. Eventually Brian was converted to the merits of UDC, launching into it with a characteristically ferocious and unstoppable obsession. So was born the UDC for Polar Libraries which was to occupy most of Brian's life, and would cause the SPRI librarians much perspiration, not to say tears.

There was another matter that was bothering Lilian. With her brother Peter and brother-in-law Brian frequently around at Pelham Court, she and Denis had little privacy. It was still common practice in Britain to leave doors unlocked and Brian would often walk into their flat without warning. Lilian had to drop a hint that she and Denis would occasionally like to have some privacy – something that Brian, as a bachelor, saw no need for, nor indeed was used to since privacy was an uncommon luxury on shipboard and polar expeditions. Eventually Brian got the message and in early 1951 June, one of the authors of this book, was born to Denis and Lilian.

THE SCOTT POLAR INSTITUTE AT WAR

At the beginning of February 1941, the Admiralty summarily requisitioned the two upper floors of the SPRI building for its Naval Intelligence Division NID5. In Oxford and Cambridge academics were recruited to the division to write detailed geographical handbooks on various countries of strategic interest to the armed services. The 'Blue Books' project was the brainchild of a senior figure in the UK's military hierarchy, Director of Naval Intelligence Rear-Admiral John Godfrey, whom Debenham and Wordie had met to discuss the matter at a vice chancellor's dinner in Cambridge on 16 June 1939.[19] At the time Debenham had not foreseen the consequences for SPRI.

As the Cambridge NID5 section expanded, SPRI's ground floor museum was also taken over by the Admiralty, leaving just one small room for Debenham, who had neither been consulted nor invited to join NID5. Wordie was appointed director-in-charge of the Cambridge section, along with Dr Henry Clifford Darby as overall editor-in-chief. Owing to his long-standing involvement with the Discovery Committee, Wordie had been presumed by the Admiralty to be effectively in charge of SPRI. When the normally mild-mannered Debenham found out about the Admiralty takeover and that the prime mover behind it was Wordie, he was incandescent.

Roberts was the first to be appointed to the Blue Books project at Cambridge, responsible for the volumes planned to cover Iceland, Spitsbergen and Greenland. In contrast to the meticulous and ambitious Darby, Wordie adopted a laid-back approach to personnel management and allowed – even encouraged – Roberts to continue other activities as a sideline, mainly at night and outside 'official hours'. The situation was a recipe for friction. Roberts was being employed full-time on the Blue Books project, but he never seemed to regard this as a barrier to taking on other jobs if he happened to find them more interesting.

Even before the Admiralty takeover, trouble had been brewing between Debenham and Wordie. Debenham was gentle, open and straight, enjoying the collegiate atmosphere of Cambridge and disliking politics, war and confrontation. In contrast, Wordie relished the scheming and devious side of Cambridge life. He and Debenham were often consulted by government departments on polar matters, only to give conflicting advice without consulting each other. At meetings of the SPRI management committee Wordie, who was chairman, would agree to a course of action and then revoke it afterwards by telephone, without informing Debenham. Matters came to a head at an acrimonious meeting of the SPRI management committee on 28 March 1942.[20] Debenham maintained that the Institute had to respect the views of its founders and supporters. He could never bring himself to accept the presence of the Admiralty in the building and found it humiliating that SPRI had become reduced to the minimal level of activity of answering correspondence and producing the journal *Polar Record*.

In July 1942 the *Iceland Handbook* was ready for publication.[21] Work started on a new *Spitsbergen Handbook*, but Roberts was frequently becoming diverted away from the Blue Books. In addition to committees on cold weather equipment and clothing for the army, there was the *Polar Record* to produce. His loyal colleagues had left: Colin Bertram for a post in fisheries in Palestine, and Dorothy to join her husband in the Sudan. During the first few months of the war he and Dorothy had been overnight firewatchers in the SPRI building and in her tender and affectionate farewell to Roberts she recalled how they had "unbelievably spent the night together every night for two months and still remained friends".[22]

Despite the pressures on Roberts' time, Wordie encouraged him to keep the *Polar Record* alive. Although Debenham continued to be the named editor of the journal throughout the war, he seldom entered the SPRI building and the first time he saw each new issue of *Polar Record* was after it had already been proof-read (by Roberts), printed and distributed. In the later years of the war Roberts would have to travel to Cambridge to produce the journal, and having been obliged to give up his spacious rooms at Emmanuel College, he pitched up overnight wherever he could – either inside the SPRI building, in a tent on the nearby meadow, or at the home of Dorothy's successor Kathleen Benest.

Despite the need to produce *Polar Record* almost single-handed and in difficult circumstances, Roberts was far from wanting to reduce its scope. In September 1942 he sent Debenham a draft policy proposal for the journal, complaining that it was excluding all technical and economic content. He made a comprehensive list of the topics that he wanted covered: administrative, political and social issues, whaling, sealing, fisheries, furs, minerals, agriculture, human settlement, transport, buildings, game conservation, clothing, nutrition, medical problems, diseases, sciences, equipment, history, museums, libraries and polar organisations in general. He concluded pointedly: "Are we to be a research centre as well as a Scott memorial?"[23]

Debenham took one look at this formidable mission statement, sighed, shook his head and picked up his pen. "Dear Brian, as you see, we part company in the very first sentence of your memo... I'm sorry you have such a poor opinion of the Institute but we must limit our activities to our charter."[24] He explained that SPRI was established as a depository for expedition reports and similar polar information not available elsewhere. In order words, constitutionally SPRI was – despite its name – not a research institute. Debenham advised Wordie not to put Roberts' draft on the management committee's agenda.[25] He would also frequently complain about Roberts, particularly over the editing of the *Polar Record*.[26]

One outcome of Roberts' 'sideline' appointments was a proposal in November 1942 by the US government's Office of Strategic Services that he should visit the US and Canada to exchange information on polar clothing and equipment of interest to the military.[27] After some months of awaiting official approval to go, he grabbed the opportunity and flew out in August 1943.

In Washington it was hot. The air-conditioned luxuries were a stark contrast to the deprivations of wartime England, and Roberts was impressed by the openness, friendliness and hospitality of Americans and the cooperativeness and freedom they enjoyed. At the Washington Round Table Group of the Explorers' Club he met many people who would figure importantly in his later life as a diplomat. For the youthful Roberts, this hectic programme of visits to important people and places was heady stuff, but a problem was looming. His authorised six-week leave period would all too soon come to an end, as he was expected to return to England by 21 September. For the time being he continued to bask in his elevated status and soak up the convivial American hospitality. He visited Harvard, Cambridge Massachusetts and the Rothschild bird collection in New York, meeting Ernst Mayr and other distinguished ornithologists. For light entertainment he ascended the Rockefeller Centre and the Empire State Building, and watched a variety show hosted by actress Carole Landis at the vast

Radio City music hall (capacity 6,000), accompanied by jitterbug dancing with 'volunteers' from the audience including – to his horrified embarrassment – Roberts himself.

OMINOUS NEWS FROM CAMBRIDGE

On 7 October 1943 Roberts was brought down to earth with a bump. The Naval Intelligence office in Washington brought the disquieting news from Cambridge that Wordie had resigned from the Blue Books project, leaving Clifford Darby fully in charge at SPRI.[28] This was later confirmed by a telegram from Wordie:

> "LONDON, ENGLAND Bryan Roberts:
> READJUSTMENTS HERE AM CUTTING DOWN RUDMORE HANDBOOK PROBABLY DROPPED. IS THERE LIKELIHOOD YOUR TRANSFERRING TO EQUIPMENT JOB. IF SO, FURTHER STAY DESIRABLE. STRICTLY PRIVATE."[29]

"Rudmore" refers to Professor Rudmose Brown of Sheffield University who, together with Alexander Glen, Wordie and Roberts, was contributing to the Admiralty Handbook on Spitsbergen. Roberts replied to Wordie that he was planning to return to England around 18 October and that there was no obvious prospect of transferring to a different job. The next day he took a train to Ottawa to attend a conference on Cold Weather Tests. In the group photograph Roberts appears unusually gaunt and anxious, as he had good reason to be.

On 9 November, following a farewell dinner, he took a train to New York and boarded the liner *Queen Elizabeth II*, returning to England in the company of 17,000 American troops.

Roberts' forebodings were confirmed immediately on his return to Cambridge. Director of Naval Intelligence Edmund Rushbrook (who had replaced John Godfrey) informed him that, due to a reorganisation of the Cambridge Geographical Handbooks Section, his Admiralty appointment had been terminated with effect from 11 December.[30] Now it might appear that Roberts, by accepting the invitation to the US, had been infringing the terms of his employment on the Blue Books, and that is certainly the way his boss Clifford Darby would have seen it. But Roberts had been authorised by the Admiralty itself to make the visit.[31]

The US Naval Intelligence office had also given London due notification of his request for an extension,[32] but it seems that the divisions of the notoriously secretive Admiralty had not thought to inform each other, let alone Darby. Darby had clashed with Wordie many times over the Blue Books project,[33] and promptly seized the excuse to wrest control of the project away from Wordie and exert authority over the Cambridge section by appointing himself as editor-in-chief.[34]

On 9 December Roberts handed the draft *Spitsbergen Handbook* to Clifford Darby, seemingly unaware that it was Darby who had engineered his dismissal. The unfinished handbook was abandoned in January 1944 and no trace of the draft has been found. The Cambridge Blue Books programme continued at SPRI in the absence of Roberts and Wordie until it was finally wound down in 1945.

In February 1944 Roberts received a letter from Rudmose Brown, still smarting over the termination of the *Spitsbergen Handbook*. "I have been so disgusted with recent happenings that Cambridge in all its aspects has disgusted me. The perfidy of recent actions on certain people's part has been almost incredible. But I am grateful to Wordie & you who, too, have suffered & been sacrificed. I continue to improve it... even if I see no hope of publication."[35]

In the event Roberts' dismissal and Wordie's resignation were of little consequence. There was seldom any lack of interest in their potential contribution to the war effort as polar specialists. Wordie, with Roberts in tow, was soon to be given a new top-secret military mission of far greater significance, and the Blue Books were soon forgotten.

OPERATION TABARIN

Wordie had long been associated with the Colonial Office through the Discovery Committee. Its brief was to assess the economic potential of the Antarctic and sub-Antarctic and to exercise British authority over the Southern Ocean and the Falkland Islands Dependencies (FID), an area claimed by Britain that included the Antarctic peninsula (Graham Land), South Georgia, the South Shetlands, South Orkneys and other islands in the South Atlantic.

Britain was not the only nation with an interest in the region. Political agitation by Argentina and Chile had been brewing, and with the UK's preoccupation with the war in Europe, Argentina grabbed the opportunity to bolster its claims to the territories. In February 1942 the ice-strengthened naval transport vessel *Primero de Mayo* raided Deception Island, after which a statement from Argentina declared its intention to take possession of the Antarctic sector between 25°W and 68°W. Whitehall argued rancorously over what the British response should be. The Colonial Office and the Admiralty lobbied for gunboat diplomacy. The Foreign Office was worried that armed confrontation could imperil Anglo-Argentine relations, jeopardize the £400 million of British capital invested in Argentina, damage vital trade relations and put at risk the imports of meat that were vital to staving off starvation in the UK.

Following intelligence reports of another visit to the region by *Primero de Mayo*, the War Cabinet decided on 28 January 1943 to send out the armed merchant cruiser *Carnarvon Castle*[36] on a voyage to the FID that included a 'goodwill' visit to the Argentine meteorological station in the South Orkneys. But it was realised that a single visit by a ship did little to secure British territorial claims, which could be reinforced only by setting up permanent bases of occupation. The Colonial Office proposed to set up bases at Deception Island and at Signy Island in the South Orkneys, taking expert advice from SPRI and the Falkland Islands Governor on logistics and personnel.[37] By the end of April 1943 Captain J L Hayward of the Colonial Office was requesting authorisation to proceed. At a meeting of the Discovery Committee he spoke to Wordie in private.

Wordie needed to be discreet (something that was not at all difficult for him), and he advised Hayward to write to him privately at St John's College. He assured Hayward that they would be able to find "a few scientists who would be prepared to remain in the Antarctic for a year with the object of studying the habits of seals", providing a genuine scientific aim to the expedition.[38] Hayward was now confident that with Wordie's assistance the enterprise would be viable, and at an interdepartmental meeting on 21 May the 'top secret' mission to set up permanent all-year round British bases in the FID was formally approved.[39]

Within hours of the meeting, the operation was launched by the Admiralty's M (Military) division. An expedition committee was formed, co-opting Wordie, Mackintosh and Roberts and headed by John Mossop, an expert on international law. The operation was deemed to be of the utmost urgency. Expedition plans had to be drawn up within four weeks,[40] working day and night, with Roberts snatching the occasional hour of sleep at his brother Denis' flat at Pelham Court.

By 28 June 1943 Neil Mackintosh, assisted by Wordie and Roberts, had compiled a lengthy memorandum detailing the history of the FID.[41] The expedition was given its codename unofficially by Roberts "after the 'Bal Tabarin', a night club in Paris – a code name chosen by John Mossop and myself when this operation started because we had to do a lot of night work and the organisation was always so chaotic just as the club".[42] In November 1943 the codename was officially adopted: "Until such time as the need for secrecy in regard to the Expedition is no longer necessary, it will be referred to in all telegrams, Admiralty signals, and other communications under the code name OPERATION TABARIN."[43]

While Roberts was touring the US and Canada, Wordie and Mackintosh continued to serve on the Operation Tabarin committee at the Colonial Office. Foreign Office officials continued to worry over the political implications of the venture. On 9 September 1943 Victor Perowne proposed that "the time is at hand when it may be desirable to go a little more closely into the question of Antarctic claims in general. Perhaps the Foreign Office Research Department could be kind enough to undertake this".[44] By the end of October, Foreign Office legal adviser William Beckett was still more emphatic:

"We are almost certainly in dispute with the Argentine about the Falkland Islands Dependencies. It may be that we shall be in for a dispute with Chile too. Further, there may be proposals for an Antarctic Conference to parcel out the area... Now our information about all this territories [sic] is in a most inconvenient form at present... I am sure that we need one booklet which covers all the ground. As I see it, the booklet should contain everything that is relevant to the question of claims of sovereignty. The purpose of this minute is to urge that steps should be taken for this study to be undertaken."[45]

Immersed in his activities in North America, Roberts was not remotely aware of it at the time, but his whole future was being determined in Whitehall there and then. On 9 November Wordie informed Mossop that Roberts would shortly be terminating his Admiralty employment and was ideally qualified for the work of producing the booklet.[46] Mossop notified Perowne at the Foreign Office and on 29 November it was recommended that Roberts carry out the research and write the booklet.[47] A week later he received a telephone call from Arnold Toynbee asking him to turn up the following day for interview at the Old Stationery Office in Westminster. He was to be employed by the Foreign Office on an extendable three-month contract, starting on 1 February 1944. It was a watershed in Roberts' life. From the encyclopaedic knowledge he would acquire in carrying out the task, he would become Britain's pre-eminent political expert on the Antarctic.

THE FOREIGN OFFICE

Professor Arnold Toynbee had been Director of Studies at the Royal Institute of International Affairs, Chatham House. At the outbreak of war he founded the Foreign Research and Press Service, with the brief of providing foreign intelligence to the UK government. In June 1943 he became head of the newly-created Foreign Office Research Department (FORD), formed by merging the Press Service with the Foreign Office's Political Intelligence Department.[48] Toynbee had his critics, but he adroitly cultivated his connections in Whitehall and gave Roberts a free hand in prioritizing the work of what would later emerge as the Polar Regions Section of the Foreign Office.

The staff of FORD were employed only until the end of the war, when most academics returned to their universities. Roberts' situation was unique. The 'booklet' requested by the Foreign Office turned into a 200-page foolscap document, *Territorial Claims in the Antarctic*,[49] which summarised all the historical, geographical, political and legal issues concerning Antarctic sovereignty and took a lot longer than three months to research and compile. It was eventually issued in May 1945. By that time Roberts' job at FORD had expanded immensely: he was dealing with policy, planning, logistics, equipment and recruitment for Operation Tabarin, assisting the Foreign Office American Department with Antarctic political problems, and undertaking 15 years of preparation for a post-war Antarctic conference and its aftermath. Roberts would remain embroiled in Foreign Office Antarctic matters for the rest of his working life.

CAMBRIDGE AT THE END OF THE WAR

With Roberts' new posting in London, there remained the question of the work at SPRI. Far from wanting to relinquish his responsibilities in Cambridge, he circulated in November 1944 a characteristically ambitious seven-page memorandum, proposing that the institute should become an international information, research and educational service to be administered under direct government funding along the lines of national polar institutes elsewhere in the world.[50] For good measure he also proposed to establish a permanent UK research station in the Arctic. There was no mention of any involvement of Cambridge University.

The immediate response of Roberts' SPRI colleague Launcelot Fleming was: "Brian, I do hope we shall get the chance of a good talk about this. I agree with the lines of development which you would like to see... I feel very strongly that it is high time that you were made the Director. You are far the best person for the job. Will you kindly get yourself appointed?"[51] Fleming's views commanded much support from the younger members of the institute.

Wordie also supported Roberts' appointment, but only as a research director, not as institute director. In January 1945, Wordie started lobbying Hugh Robert Mill of SPRI's board of management about the situation at the institute. SPRI was due a large back-payment of rent by the Admiralty for their use of its building and Wordie proposed to use this to fund a research director.[52] Mill was also consulted independently by Debenham, whose contrasting views were predictable. Debenham made it clear that Roberts was at the centre of the controversy: "I spoke straight [to Wordie] about Brian Roberts, and he now knows that I won't have him as any kind of Assistant, and he accepts that. Incidentally I fancy he knows why too, because he himself has had a certain amount of trouble and debate with him."[53]

But Debenham suffered from emphysema and was becoming more and more ill. By April 1945 he was contemplating a year's sick leave on medical advice. Over the next few weeks Wordie sent several handwritten notes to Mill, expressing considerable alarm at the situation at SPRI and proposing to appoint Fleming as acting director of the institute.[54] Debenham, however, was still planning on remaining director himself on his return from leave. During his year of absence, spent travelling abroad, the SPRI management committee appointed Roberts as a part-time Research Fellow, effective from 1 January 1946. He was offered a half salary for work to be carried out over extended weekends while away from his part-time Foreign Office job in London. Moreover he was now an official editor of *Polar Record*. Shortly before his return to Cambridge in July 1946, Debenham tendered his resignation from the

SPRI directorship and Fleming was formally appointed director in his place. Debenham's receipt of the news that Roberts had been offered and had accepted a post at the institute was almost certainly the straw that broke the camel's back.[55]

Debenham's expressed antipathy to Roberts was not unexpected, and was of little consequence but for one regrettable incident. In July 1945, when SPRI repossessed its building from the Admiralty, Roberts' collection of classified Arctic papers was removed and destroyed, apparently under instructions from Debenham and Darby. Roberts was not consulted. He was not normally one to harbour grudges, but this scorched-earth action soured his relationship with Debenham permanently. SPRI had now lost a unique historical archive of World War II in the Arctic: the few surviving papers are those that were locked in a single filing cabinet, the key to which Roberts had ferreted away in London. Apart from the Admiralty Geographical Handbooks, no other record of SPRI's wartime activities has survived.

10

EARLY YEARS OF THE BRITISH ANTARCTIC SURVEY

The Antarctic can do frightful things to a man. Boredom and inactivity insidiously undermine morale. The utter loneliness breeds introspection. Grievances become exaggerated, irritations become obsessions and depression can rot into the soul.

Ellery Anderson, FIDS recruit[1]

THE FALKLAND ISLANDS DEPENDENCIES SURVEY

At the end of the war, Operation Tabarin acquired a new name, the Falkland Islands Dependencies Survey. What had been a secret naval operation administered by the Admiralty now became a civilian operation funded and administered jointly by the Colonial Office and the Governor of the Falkland Islands. FIDS – much later to become the prestigious British Antarctic Survey – was to have a difficult birth.

Roberts was made responsible for the annual relief ship sent to the Antarctic bases. Crates of equipment and stores had to be assembled and packed in his small office at the Foreign Office, until down the obstructed corridors echoed the booming voice of Roberts' neighbour the political historian Sir Charles Webster: "You had better bring those cartons of biscuits into my room, but you must not be surprised if I eat a lot of them."

The FIDS committee included Neil Mackintosh, James Wordie and Roberts, "three benign paladins who presided over the general planning and organisation",[2] and three Colonial Office mandarins. From the start, personnel and equipment were their biggest headaches. The situation in the field was so chaotic that Wordie was sent out on the 1946/47 relief ship to investigate. In addition to disquieting reports from Commander Ted Bingham,[3] Roberts was told by a FIDS recruit: "I am [here] for one year and one year only. I do not wish to stay under the present regime. I have seen enough of the present chaos to have no faith in the supposed support we should get... As you predicted the local arrangements in Stanley are appalling. I feel extremely sorry for Wordie, he is battling wonderfully against colossal odds... But I wish to god you had come out instead of Wordie. He is too old, and is still living on Elephant Island..."[4]

The brunt of the widespread criticism of FIDS administration was generally borne by the three benign paladins and the FIDS secretary in the Falkland Islands. But usually the source of the problems lay elsewhere. A common gripe of recruits was lack of information on the purpose of the setting up, occupation and scientific programme of British bases in the Antarctic, but then the Colonial Office management had little grasp of these either. Vivian Fuchs, who was to become director of the FIDS Scientific Bureau, confirmed that none of the Colonial Office committee members had any interest in the needs of scientific expeditions.[5] It was left to Roberts to explain to Falkland Islands meteorological officer Gordon Howkins the overall purpose of FIDS:

"An active programme of research, which can be justified on scientific grounds alone, is an essential part of the preparation of a case which can be used if necessary to demonstrate to Foreign Governments or a Tribunal that HMG is taking all reasonable steps to develop and exercise sovereignty over the area, and is not merely attempting to prevent foreign encroachments. There is no doubt that both the Chilean and Argentine Governments would like to set up meteorological stations in the Dependencies for political reasons. It is essential therefore that while we have to exclude them from doing so we must take every possible step to ensure that we do not lay ourselves open to the same charge. Whilst FIDS was political in origin, it is important to maintain it as far as possible as a normal administrative activity in which motives of research, exploration and development predominate."[6]

AERIAL SURVEY

One of Operation Tabarin's first objectives had been a survey of Wiencke Island. Situated between Anvers Island and the continental shore of the Antarctic Peninsula, it is familiar to today's Antarctic tourists as the site of the Port Lockroy post office. But the terrain was found to be so difficult for ground-based survey that aerial photography was thought to be essential.[7] In July 1945, Major Peter Mott of the Ordnance Survey Office submitted a proposal to survey the Antarctic Peninsula using long-range amphibian aircraft, ship-launched helicopters, airborne magnetometers and stereoscopic vertical photography, to be supported by ground controls. Getting the survey launched would take Roberts ten years of lobbying and would embroil him in frequent clashes over priorities for funding. It was not going to be cheap. Mott's company Hunting Aerosurveys quoted £70,000 for each of its three seasons (a total equivalent to £5 million today), over and above the cost of fuel, food and accommodation, which were to be provided by FIDS.[8]

The proposal was accordingly shelved until 1952, when an Argentine machine gun incident at Hope Bay[9] (near the northern tip of the Antarctic Peninsula) was sufficiently serious to refocus UK government minds on the Antarctic, only to be followed by another two years of interdepartmental wrangling. Roberts warned that if the air survey was not given high priority the UK would no longer be able to retain possession of its Antarctic territory: "In the long run the British claim must depend largely on a clear demonstration that we intend to make the fullest possible use of the region. For this, it is necessary to provide a sound assessment of the potential value of the area in order to formulate a long-term Antarctic policy. For such an assessment there must first be a comprehensive topographical and scientific survey, and without air survey of the kind proposed this may well be delayed for 20 years. The present political situation indicates that such a long period will not be available to us."[10]

In 1955 the Cabinet decided at last to launch the aerial survey, but Roberts' and Mott's problems were not over. Administration was now the responsibility of the Directorate of Colonial Services, in the form of Brigadier Martin Hotine, who was initially enthusiastic but who began to baulk at the cost of the operation, as though the money were coming out of his own pocket. In one of his more obtuse senior moments Hotine informed Mott bluntly that he could take only a single helicopter. When Mott protested that a reserve craft was essential for safety reasons Hotine retorted: "Go with one or not at all."[11] In December 1956, during the survey's second season, the one helicopter crashed on Tower Island.[12] When Mott requested a replacement helicopter, Hotine replied: "Do without one and continue the ground survey triangulation by astrofix from open boat landings," oblivious to the absence of landing sites along the ice-cliff coast of the Antarctic Peninsula, to say nothing of the absence of dark night sky during an Antarctic summer. Eventually a replacement helicopter did arrive, and Mott gave Roberts much credit for knocking sense into Whitehall officialdom. But constraints of funding continued to plague them, and it would be another 15 years before the maps were published.

THE ANTARCTIC: NO LONGER COOL?

Quite a few recruits to FIDS in its early years went out hoping for adventure, excitement and recognition, only to return depressed, bitter and disillusioned. When in February 1946 the original team from Operation Tabarin returned to Port Stanley, they were given the resounding traditional reception from the Falkland Islanders to returning Antarctic veterans.[13] But on their return to London's Chatham dock in March 1946 there was no welcoming party, except for Wordie, who turned up alone some hours late. Base commander Andrew Taylor reported to Roberts and was greeted with the same indifference. "I went to see Roberts about one thing and another and he diddled me around. I just seemed to be waiting on things to happen and I had been away from home by that time for more than five years."[14] Roberts, who like the rest of the British Graham Land Expedition party had returned to England ten years earlier without the need for a fanfare, was not particularly sympathetic to such complaints, being embroiled in his own personal problems. Austerity in postwar Britain was biting harder than at any time during the war. In January 1946 the rent payment on Roberts' Pelham Court apartment was increased by 33%. Having been working at the Foreign Office Research Department full time for a year on half pay he was at the end of his tether and on the point of resigning.[15] In any case his retention by the Foreign Office could by no means be taken for granted.

In April 1946, things took a turn for the better. The Treasury approved Roberts' retention by FORD,[16] made a settlement of his overdue pay and promoted him to Principal Research Officer. But there was a catch. His salary was to be £446 per annum, one half the full salary for men. His status in Whitehall was unclear, with potential implications for his later diplomatic life. Part-time employees were not established members of the civil service and not entitled to their privileges.

FIDS PROBLEM 1: MANAGEMENT

It did not take long for meetings of the interdepartmental FIDS committee to become decidedly fractious. One meeting in late 1946 recorded that "Dr Roberts insisted that either he or Mr Wordie should be allowed to go to the Dependencies with the new arrivals and stores in order that proper arrangements could be made for the selection of the stores. This was not agreeable to the Colonial Office representatives". To which Roberts pencilled in:

"These are silly minutes and in no way represent what passed at a rather heated meeting. They were written by GWH [Henlen] who has let us down badly by saying that he had taken action on many matters about which he had done nothing. I asked for this meeting to be held in order to inform the Committee of the present state of FIDS affairs this end, and did not mince my words. The Colonial Office representatives did not take my remarks kindly, as I had expected, but less than two weeks later (during which I have nagged ceaselessly), GWH had left the FIDS Committee and Wordie had been sent down to the Antarctic to help clear up the mess."[17]

Ted Bingham, the BGLE 'doctor' and now FIDS commander on board the relief ship MV *Trepassey*, received from Roberts a detailed account of FIDS committee dealings: "It has been necessary to spend a very large proportion of my time on fundamental problems upon which the continuation of FIDS ultimately depends. FIDS is now formally established... no one now ever questions its necessity. That is quite a step forward! [But] we still have a very long climb ahead... Henlen (until two weeks ago) was secretary and has been a constant thorn in my flesh [who] has nearly driven me off my head... He has now left us having got the whole organisation into a pretty good mess and I am not sorry to see the last of him."[18]

Three years later G W Henlen was awarded an OBE for his 'services to the nation'. He would not be the last of the Colonial Office mandarins to cause Roberts to blow his top.

In January 1947 the newly-appointed Governor of the Falkland Islands, 'Ginger George' Miles Clifford, reported to the Colonial Office that all was not well with FIDS: low morale, lack of initiative and the prospect of two immediate resignations. Wordie echoed Clifford's comments, but had little sympathy with the men. "I found that the party remaining here were all very restive, and the grievance habit had become a bit infectious."[19] A tough laconic survivor of Shackleton's *Endurance* expedition, Wordie responded to the men's whingeing: "Shackleton's men didn't have sheets!"[20] John Huckle, *aide-de-camp* to Clifford, confirmed the grievances of low pay, loss of mail, demobilisation problems and a general lack of communication.[21] In March 1947 Roberts interviewed a disgruntled FIDS recruit, concluding: "With so many of the men starting out in this frame of mind we must expect really major psychological troubles during the winter isolation."[22] But not all the men recruited at the time felt so aggrieved. Some went on to pursue distinguished polar careers and regarded their time with FIDS as formative and even enjoyable.[23] Roberts' view was that all the problems were avoidable in principle and were due largely to one person.

Sir Cecil James Juxon Talbot Barton was a 6'6" giant who had pursued a career in British Colonial administration of southern Africa and Fiji, much of his ample spare time being spent on the cricket pitch as a fast bowler. Roberts accused Barton of chronic obstructiveness, indecisiveness, procrastination and deliberate withholding of vital Falkland Islands despatches and telegrams.[24] He was not alone. At the end of September 1947 Bingham and Wordie were also raising numerous complaints about Barton.[25] By 17 October the issue had reached Under-Secretary Roger Makins, who proposed a solution: a new Assistant

Under-Secretary, Mr Bennett, had just been appointed with charge over the Antarctic department and he would be instructed to "take a direct personal interest in Antarctic matters and get a move on". If that did not work, "further measures" would be taken.[26]

That solved nothing. Over the next six weeks the FIDS committee continued to meet, with Barton present and Bennett absent, and still no action was being taken. The 1946/47 relief ship had still not departed. On 1 December the Foreign Office's Evelyn Shuckburgh called a meeting summoning Barton, Bennett, Roberts and representatives of the Admiralty, demanding an explanation for the delays. Shuckburgh was astounded to hear that Bennett had been on leave the whole time and had neither attended a single FIDS committee meeting nor responded to any enquiries from the Foreign Office.[27] Relations between Roberts and Barton had reached boiling point. According to Shuckburgh Roberts was in a "somewhat hysterical" state.

Being in a mood to try almost anything, Roberts went out over the Christmas holiday to buy an instruction manual on witchcraft. Back at his flat he made a wax effigy of Barton, dimmed the room lights, murmured appropriate incantations and plunged pins into the effigy. Afterwards he sat back and poured himself a drink. Although sceptical that the ritual had any real chance of a successful outcome, he was satisfied that at least it made him feel better.

To his astonishment and delight, there was an instant result. Immediately after Christmas Barton was taken off the FIDS committee, permanently.[28]

PROBLEM 2: PROVISIONING

Richard Laws, based at Signy Island during 1947-49, has described some of the problems faced by FIDS men in the field.[29] In general the food was adequate, if lacking in variety: the 4,000-7,000 calories the men consumed daily would have been regarded as luxurious in post-war Britain. There was plenty of tobacco. Alcohol was in short supply, but mainly because it got 'lost' (actually, stolen) on its way to the London docks.

Laws had much criticism of the quality of equipment provided, as did Bernard Stonehouse.[30] Clothing was also inadequate, especially in men's large sizes, and Laws was reduced to wearing his Cambridge suit trousers. Nothing was waterproof, except for heavy oilskins and sou'westers. No mukluks were available; the men had to fall back on leather-soled sealskin boots that were too small, inflexible, too cold for winter wear, hard on the feet on a stone surface and vulnerable to ripping on sharp rocks, which would result in ingress of snow and consequent frostbite. To get a grip they had to fix hobnails, resulting in even more loss of body heat. Rubber thigh boots provided for boat use leaked and there was no repair outfit. It is no wonder that many of the early recruits had a miserable time.

In the austral summer of 1948/49 the standard of clothing and equipment provided did improve. However the commonest gripe of FIDS recruits, referred to as 'winteritis' since it became exaggerated during the winter months, was the lack of information and communication for those in the field. There was no firsthand news, no information on ship movements, no mail deliveries and no advice on where and why they were being sent. They would find out eventually, usually by accident.

The most scathing and persistent critic of FIDS was actually Roberts himself. As late as 1956, on being asked to serve on an advisory committee on recruitment, he penned a lengthy indictment of the organisation, listing all the issues described by Laws and adding others for good measure: poor leadership in the field, inappropriate ratings and inadequate remuneration.[31] One scientist was apparently told in Stanley: "You get low pay because you are having a holiday at the same time." In fact low pay for British scientists was not at all confined to those working for FIDS. During the 1950s and 60s there was a tacit assumption that because scientists enjoy their work they should expect to be paid at a lower level than other professions. The outcome of this policy was predictable: a sizeable 'brain drain' from the UK to the US.[32]

PROBLEM 3: INTERNATIONAL POLITICS

In late 1946, the irascible Norwegian-American commander Finn Ronne announced his intention to take an expedition to Stonington Island in Marguerite Bay, the former US East Base established by Richard Byrd and which had been abandoned in 1941. Ronne was unaware that FIDS had meanwhile set up its own base on the same island, just 200 yards away. On being informed of this by Neil Mackintosh, Ronne's response was that the British were trespassing.

Mackintosh warned Roberts that trouble was in store. Roberts, not one to be easily intimidated, replied testily: "I have explained till

I am sick of explaining that one cannot have two expeditions with dog transport on the same tiny island."[33] He pointed out that Ronne was a troublemaker and should be kept out of the area. It was a futile gesture; there was nothing that the Foreign Office could do to stop Ronne, who was operating a private expedition that was not sponsored by the US government.

Another nuisance factor for the British was the greatly enhanced naval presence of Argentina and Chile. The Chileans turned up at Stonington Island in two ice-strengthened ships, the *Iquique* and the *Angamos*. It was the first Chilean visit to the Antarctic since the *Velcho*'s rescue of Shackleton's men from Elephant Island in 1916. Shortly thereafter Ronne's party arrived to find that the US base had been trashed. Ronne blamed the British. The British blamed the Chileans. There was an uncomfortable stand-off between the US and British parties, with Ronne instructing his men "no fraternisation". But after a while, relations became cordial and Ronne was grudgingly persuaded that the British, far from trashing the base huts, had attempted to clean them up following the Chilean visits. Ronne continued to maintain a strong personal antagonism towards the British – Roberts excepted.

There were also problems over surveying. Ronne was accused of copying and publishing FIDS maps as his own work with no acknowledgement, even for regions in which he had never flown, still less sledged. Roberts and Alfred Stephenson expressed strong criticism of American surveying methods and claims, Ronne's in particular.[34]

THE DISAPPEARANCE OF THE BRITISH BASE HUT

A curious incident from this convoluted period of Antarctic history concerns the BGLE northern base hut on the Argentine Islands. The site was subsequently occupied by the FIDS base, Wordie House, today a designated historic monument. In January 1947 the relief vessel *Trepassey* visited the Argentine Islands for the second year running, to find that the BGLE hut had vanished. All that was left was a dory tethered to a mooring.[35] Later on some of the hut timbers were found scattered over the neighbouring Skua Island.

As FIDS recruit Kevin Walton noted at the time: "Theories were put forward of tidal waves and high tides, but none of them rang true. In this time of tangled Antarctic politics it seemed to me, to quote an Irish inquest verdict, 'an act of God, under very suspicious circumstances'."[36] Thirty years later Roberts visited Wordie House, finding no trace of the original BGLE hut.[37] Like Walton, he had never swallowed the story of a tidal wave sweeping away the entire hut and hangar while leaving the dory tethered in its original position. Roberts suspected that the building had been dismantled by the Argentines, but there is no record of any Argentine visit to the Antarctic Peninsula during 1946. Historians usually refer to the hugely destructive tsunami that hit Hawaii on 1 April 1946 and the tidal wave observed the next day at Port Lockroy.[38] But there is a more plausible story that a local tidal wave, caused by a collapse of the nearby ice cliff on Galindez Island, scattered the timbers of the hut.[39] Moreover it may have been the impact of ice, rather than water, that caused the hut to disintegrate. Such tidal waves are common events in the polar regions, leaving a trail of evidence in the form of large blocks of ice which have been thrown onto the shore by the surging water.

A DUAL LIFE: LONDON AND CAMBRIDGE

From the beginning of 1946, holding down two part-time jobs, Roberts worked a seven-day week, from Tuesday to Friday at the Foreign Office in London and from Saturday to Monday at the Scott Polar institute in Cambridge. Every week he would drive to London on Monday evening and return to Cambridge on the Friday evening, continuing this schedule for 30 years until his eventual retirement from the Foreign Office.

Any excuse to escape from the relentless office routine was not to be passed up. In the summer of 1947 Brian joined his brother Denis and sister-in-law Lilian for a hiking holiday in the Swiss Alps. Taking the train up to the Jungfraujoch, they booked a guide to take them down the immense 13-mile Aletsch Glacier to Fiesch. The hikers got up at 3 am, only to be told that the walk was cancelled owing to poor weather. Two hours later it cleared and they were off. With barely time for a stop, they just made it to Fiesch by dusk. The following summer Roberts was off on another Alpine hike, along the spectacular and challenging Tour of Monte Rosa. The second highest peak in the Alps, Monte Rosa (15,200 ft) is a serious climb, needing ropes (*Plate 10.1*). At the age of 35 he was still in a good state of fitness.

ROCKALL

In late July 1947 Roberts was invited by naturalist James Fisher to join a party on an RAF Sunderland flying boat (used for slow low-flying operations) to assess seabird colonies on the Outer Hebrides and St Kilda and to visit Rockall.[40] The party of six included photographers Eric Hosking and Robert Atkinson. Roberts, positioned over the front gun-sight of the large noisy aircraft, was tasked with being a bird spotter.

The isolated granite islet of Rockall, lying in the north Atlantic some 300 miles west of the Scottish mainland and 180 miles from its nearest neighbour St Kilda, rises sheer to a height of some 60 ft. It had attracted only a few intrepid visitors, and it held an intriguing question: could any bird really succeed in raising young on this inhospitable rock? Seabird species – mostly guillemots, but also gannets, kittiwakes and fulmars – had been recorded, but since storms often result in waves that wash right over the rock (*Plate 10.2*), it is a challenge for seabirds to do anything other than rest on the top. On the flight Roberts and his fellow observers noted a complete absence of juveniles in the vicinity and they concluded that if any birds did succeed in laying an egg on Rockall, high waves would wash them off the rock before they could hatch.

Previous human visitors to Rockall had made up unlikely stories of their landings: very few had actually managed to land, as conditions were hardly ever calm enough. "More people have landed on the moon than have landed on Rockall from the sea," one MP commented.[41] One success story was that of Jean-Baptiste Charcot.[42] Whilst carrying out oceanographic work in 1921 he was asked by the French geologist Alfred Lacroix if he could gather specimens of Rockall's unique granite. Charcot engineered not one but two successful landings a few days apart, contributing much information on Rockall's geology, ornithology and algae (the only form of plant life present).

Rockall had got under Fisher's skin, and he wanted to return to land there. He did so eight years later, by which time, as the known authority on Rockall, he had amassed a considerable photographic archive. In 1955, at the height of the Cold War, a top secret British naval operation was launched in an effort to prevent the Soviets from spying on planned guided missile tests on South Uist in the Outer Hebrides. Two Royal Marines, accompanied by Fisher as a civilian scientist, were winched by helicopter from HMS *Vidal* onto Rockall. Cementing a plaque to the rock and flying a Union Jack, they claimed the islet officially for the UK.

Rockall

Fisher had another obsession: the fulmar. Until the 20th century this large seabird was almost unknown in the British Isles, other than on St Kilda, where for centuries the young birds had been taken as an invaluable food source (as they were in Iceland and the Faeroes). Superficially resembling a gull, the fulmar is actually a member of the tubenose family which includes storm petrels and albatrosses. Its range was always further north in the Arctic, until in the late 19th century it began to spread southwards spectacularly to breed around north Atlantic coasts. In 1933 the newly formed British Trust for Ornithology encouraged fulmar recording amongst its members. Records came in from all around Britain, enabling Fisher to amass material for his monograph on the species.[43] But colonies on the remoter islands of the Outer Hebrides were too inaccessible to locate, providing another pretext for the Sunderland flight, on which eight new colonies were discovered.

Two months later, at the end of September 1947, Roberts was again invited to join Fisher on a Sunderland flight, this time to identify and make a census of all the breeding sites of Atlantic grey seals and gannet colonies on the islands off Wales and Scotland, including Orkney and Shetland. The team included Max Nicholson, Ronald Lockley, Eric Hosking, Frank Fraser Darling and Robert Atkinson. They discovered new seal colonies in Orkney and Shetland and a huge unknown colony on the remote island of Gasker.[44] But farther south they were thwarted. Off the Pembrokeshire coast the grey seal tends to breed in caves rather than on open beaches and was not going to emerge specially to be counted or photographed. Distinguishing between a piece of bleached driftwood and a young seal calf was a further difficulty. Nonetheless the flight did enable the first – albeit rough – map of seal breeding distribution to be produced.

For Roberts there was a spin-off from the Sunderland flights in meeting the photographer-naturalist Robert Atkinson, who owned an aged fishing boat, *Heather*, and needed a crew. Together they were to make an annual summer exploration of remote uninhabited Scottish islands[45] that continued for ten years until the boat was declared unseaworthy. For Roberts this was the perfect relaxing antidote to the political turmoil that was about to engulf him in his two professional lives in London and Cambridge. Immersed in the wildlife – seabirds, seals and storm petrels – and climbing Burrival on North Uist to find and photograph a golden eagle's nest with two chicks and a dead rabbit in it (*Plate 10.3*), he was enjoying probably the happiest days of his life (*Plate 10.4*).

THE DISAPPEARING GERMAN NEIGHBOUR

On his appointment in 1946 to a part-time post in Cambridge, Roberts had moved into an unfurnished rented university flat, No 41 Causewayside, on the upper floor of a block of flats on Fen Causeway. Most of the occupants were temporary visiting scholars. For Roberts it became his main home for life where, surrounded by his enormous library, he could contemplate the view over the rural meadows of Coe Fen from his window. The flats were not well soundproofed. Roberts at times complained of the noise of some neighbours, and likewise they would overhear the strains of classical music gramophone records and the noise of slamming filing cabinets emerging from No 41 late at night.

In 1948 a new neighbour appeared at No 42 Causewayside. Dr Werner Kissling was an anthropologist who like Roberts had a passion for remote islands, and was particularly interested in crofting life on the islands of Eriskay and South Uist in the Outer Hebrides. One evening in 1951 Roberts knocked on Kissling's door. Getting no response, he opened the door to find the flat completely empty, all the furniture having been removed. Kissling had vanished.

Werner Kissling was born in Silesia in 1895 into a wealthy aristocratic family. Having studied international law and history in Berlin and Königsberg, he trained at the Consular School in Vienna for a diplomatic career in the Weimar Republic. Posted to London as Second Secretary in the German Embassy, he resigned in 1931 to pursue his amateur interests in ethnology, settling in Cambridge as a research student and keeper of the lantern slide collections at the Museum of Archaeology and Anthropology. Every summer until the war he would visit Eriskay and South Uist. His family had strong anti-Nazi credentials: in 1944 his elder brother Georg Conrad, an officer in the German army, took part in the 20 July plot to assassinate Hitler, committing suicide to avoid arrest and execution.

At the end of the war Kissling, aided by a scheme devised by Roberts' colleague Andrew Croft, smuggled his mother out of Germany via Austria, together with the family fortune of £2 million. On his disappearance in 1951 Kissling terminated his rent payments on Causewayside without giving notice to the university authorities. He was eventually traced to an address in Scotland,[46] where he purchased the Kings Arms Hotel in Melrose. In the summer of 1953 Roberts was on one of his voyages on Atkinson's *Heather* when he discovered Kissling at his favourite haunt in the Lochboisdale Hotel, South Harris. It was the last time Roberts and Kissling would meet. By the late 1950s Kissling's hotel business was in receivership and he had lost the entire family fortune. Until his eventual death in 1988 he lived alone in poverty, working as an anthropologist, writer and photographer for Dumfries museum. Kissling was always an enigmatic and self-effacing figure, but his sympathetic recording of the traditional life of the Western Isles and his empathy with their inhabitants remain cherished by them.[47]

SCANDINAVIANS IN ANTARCTICA

In September 1946 the Swedish geographer/glaciologist Hans Ahlmann suggested to Roberts and to Harald Sverdrup, head of the Norsk Polarinstitutt in Oslo, the exploration of a mountain range in Dronning Maud Land, the sector of Antarctica claimed by Norway. Ahlmann postulated that these ice-free rocks represented evidence of glacier retreat due to climate change.

The Norwegian-British-Swedish Expedition was to provide Roberts with his first chance for years to return to the cold desolation of the Antarctic. But there would be a price to pay: the headache of responsibility for its administration, with three organising committees in three different countries. Even within the UK the organisation of the committee and its proposed name 'Joint Polar Research Sub-Committee' was enough for Roberts to protest: "If the Committee is to be Polar rather than Antarctic, its constitution will have to be different... I am amazed at this continued failure to apply any of the elementary principles of committee procedure."[48] Another instance of sloppiness driving Roberts to apoplexy was the frequently used abbreviation NBSX, causing him to complain at considerable length that X had never stood for 'expedition' in published accounts.[49] It was just one of a long series of battles on naming and terminology that would preoccupy him for his entire life.

In November 1950 *Norsel*, a small Norwegian ocean-going tug converted into a sealer, was on its first NBSE relief voyage, with expedition administrators Roberts and Sverdrup on board as observers. They soon ran into heavy seas and a strong head wind, causing an unpleasant rolling and pitching of the small and overloaded ship. Each evening Roberts tried to encourage all on board to meet for pre-prandial drinks in the bar, only to find the men all horizontal in their bunks, trying to cope with seasickness. With his cast-iron stomach that needed filling, Roberts was often the only one present in the dining room. He relished the stormy weather and was overjoyed to see Wilson's storm petrels for the first time in 15 years.

Norsel crossed the Antarctic Convergence on Christmas Day. On the night of 30 December everyone was woken at 3 am by the sound of the ship hitting ice. During the day the floes gradually became thicker. Late that night out on deck Roberts watched a couple of emperor penguins standing on a distant ice floe. Absorbing the peace and stillness of this cold desolation brought him much contentment. The floes finally merged and the ship became locked fast in the ice. Three charges of explosives failed to move her. As the pressure closed all the gaps near the ship, ice on either side of the ship rapidly began to build up in great hummocks, causing her to list as she was 'nipped' by the ice. Finally after an ordeal of 15 hours, the ice broke up enough for *Norsel* to be squeezed out ahead into clear water, like a pip from an orange. Dense ice cover slowly gave way to open leads and by 6 January they had made it to Norsel Bay on the coast of Dronning Maud Land. From the sea nothing could be seen beyond the towering 100-foot-high ice cliff.

Roberts and several of the crew walked the two-mile route marked only by a line of stakes from the ice front to the base hut, known as 'Maudheim'. With no horizon and no feature except the stakes, they walked in a measureless whiteness. All that could be seen of the station was a forest of radio and meteorological masts, the buildings being almost completely buried with no sign of any entrance. (*Plate 10.5*)

The first one to arrive tapped on a window and called out: "Is anyone at home?" From the blinding glare outside, the visitors slithered down a steep and narrow entrance burrow into an icy black tunnel, at the end of which they found the door into the base hut. The arrival of the *Norsel* visitors produced an uncanny reaction from the seven men in the station: they were white-faced and speechless, taking a considerable time to understand that the ship had arrived. There was total apathy, nobody having the slightest desire to read mail or exchange news. Several days of heavy drifting snow had cut off the normal entrance to the base, and for most of the men inside, the poor ventilation and inability to get outside had resulted in sleeping badly.

A WRETCHED ANTARCTIC SUMMER

During the previous winter the Maudheim base party had been living a troglodyte existence and had been looking forward for several months to the summer season. But base leader John Giaever described the summer of 1950-51 as the most miserable he had ever experienced. For those in the field, September was a time of anticipation and exhilaration as the first Weasel (tracked snow vehicle) expeditions headed south inland. But for those confined to base, fatigue and listlessness set in. The men were weak, devoid of energy and at their wit's end. In turn they all went down with food poisoning. It was with some trepidation that they had awaited *Norsel*'s arrival, dreading an inspection of the base by Sverdrup. As the weather worsened, damp drifting snow started to block up all the doors, windows and ventilators. The air in the corridors was a damp, nauseating mist of steam and engine fumes. The cause of their sickness was not difficult to identify: carbon monoxide poisoning.

Gradually the atmosphere at the base became more cordial, but there was still no activity and no clear direction from Sverdrup. Roberts, attempting to suppress his irritation, passed the time by taking photographs. After three days unloading started, but no stock checking was done even when Roberts remonstrated with Sverdrup that on *Norsel*'s previous visit several cases were never unloaded and had been transported back to Norway unopened.

The following night the two Norwegian aircrew made a reconnaissance flight over a mountain range. On their return, accompanied by Sverdrup, they furtively took their photographs down to their cabin. Roberts, after begging repeatedly to see the photographs, was not popular for pointing out that they showed a range discovered by British pilots the previous year, in addition to the Kraul Mountains recorded by the Germans on the pre-war *Schwabenland* expedition.[50]

After a week of continuous blizzards another flying attempt was made, this time to the expedition's advance base 300 miles away. With no radio contact there was considerable difficulty locating the base, and they arrived back at Maudheim with an empty fuel tank. Some days later the pilot entered the base hut, slumped into a chair, downed two glasses of brandy in quick succession and lit a cigar, grumbling that that he and Sverdrup had not had a single proper discussion about the flying programme. Until then he had been teetotal and non-smoking. Further chaos was recorded by Roberts:

> "There are so many cross currents in this expedition... At times I feel it is like a madhouse. This afternoon five of us have been sitting round the table writing letters. Bjarne Lorentzen, who is now the Maudheim cook, was in the kitchen alcove... He was drunk and incapable of coordinated movement. We had to clear away the lunch for him and wash up. Then he poured a whole pot of melted butter on the floor, thinking he was pouring it into another pot, and he would keep walking in it and spreading it everywhere despite our efforts to restrain him. We settled down to write again, but suddenly the kitchen was filled with sheets of flame and black smoke. Bjarne had been trying to light the primus stove. We put out the fire and sent Bjarne to bed. Five minutes later I looked into his cubicle to see how he was getting on. His cigarette, left burning on the table, had burnt deep into the wood and was still alight. Bjarne was asleep. John Jelbart and I took more than an hour to clean up the greasy chaos which he had left in the kitchen. Both of us came to the Antarctic expecting to do some scientific work, but so far we have shovelled snow, chipped ice, cleared out rubbish and constructed a new lavatory. *C'est magnifique, mais ce n'est pas la guerre.*"[51]

The next day Sverdrup – who was sleeping on board *Norsel* – paid a visit to the base hut. On his entry everyone except Roberts disappeared rapidly into their cubicles. Once Sverdrup had left, the six of them re-emerged to consume the entire contents of two whisky bottles that Roberts provided. Sverdrup had admitted to Roberts his bitter disappointment at the failure of the flying programme. In the stormy weather during *Norsel*'s short stay the ill-equipped and inexperienced Norwegian aircrew had managed only three flights inland. Worse was to come. On 29 January the pilot misjudged a low pass and a wing tip hit the snow. The aircraft cartwheeled and was a write-off. The pilot refused to make a formal report of the accident, and his passenger continued to shiver uncontrollably from shock. Giaever advised Sverdrup and Roberts to leave for home straightaway. It was barely three weeks since *Norsel*'s arrival.

On *Norsel*'s return journey Sverdrup continued to be apathetic and negative about the expedition. "As far as I am concerned, we could just as well give the land back to the penguins," he grumbled in his diary.[52] What was Sverdrup's problem? Possibly he was unhappy with the make-up of the expedition party, in which the Norwegians were providing not only the bulk of the funding but almost all the logistics and support staff, while others from Sweden and the British Commonwealth were young polar scientists who would reap the kudos from publishing results. But the international makeup was arguably fair game. It was in essence a Norwegian expedition with support from Sweden and Britain, strengthening Norway's claim to that sector of the Antarctic by 'effective occupation', which had not been feasible during the war and which in any case could not have been funded in full by the Norwegian government.

Towards the end of *Norsel*'s return journey the ship's party received a devastating telegram from John Giaever. Four men at the Maudheim base had gone for a test drive in their Weasel snow tractor, hit a blanket of fog and plunged over the edge of an ice front. Three of them had drowned. Roberts and Sverdrup ate dinner in stunned silence.

THE AFTERMATH

The main expedition party finally returned home a year later, in February 1952. Despite its trials and tragedies, NBSE was a remarkably successful expedition. A large amount of scientific data was obtained, some of it spectacular, showing for the first time that the Antarctic ice sheet could be as deep as 1.5 miles. But national aspirations and shortage of funds continued to dog the venture. Sverdrup wanted the Canadian

Fred Roots to write up the geological results in Norway, but Roots insisted on remaining in Cambridge at the Department of Mineralogy and Petrology, lodging in Roberts' Causewayside flat during 1953-54. He had an ulterior motive for doing so. At the Scott Polar Institute a vivacious Oxford graduate, June Blomfield, had become assistant to the director Colin Bertram. A high-speed courtship ensued between her and Fred Roots, described by eyewitness Margaret Elbo as "chaotic, improbable and unreal".[53] The repeated visits of a young woman to the Causewayside flat were a complication to Roberts' ascetic life, and he felt obliged to instruct his long-serving and loyal housekeeper Mrs King to scotch any rumours, insisting that the visits were from a professional librarian. Mrs King was however a sharper observer of human nature than Roberts was.

In October 1954 the forthcoming marriage of the couple was announced, and on a severely cold Saturday in mid-January 1955 Roberts was called upon to officiate as best man at the wedding in Beccles Church, Suffolk.[54] Undeterred by the harsh East Anglian winter and the lethal icy road conditions, many from the Cambridge polar community turned up for the occasion. The newly-married couple immediately departed permanently for Canada, where Roots had secured a position with the Mackenzie Mountains Geological Survey. It marked the end of the NBSE episode. By then Roberts was already embroiled in other political complexities, in both London and Cambridge.

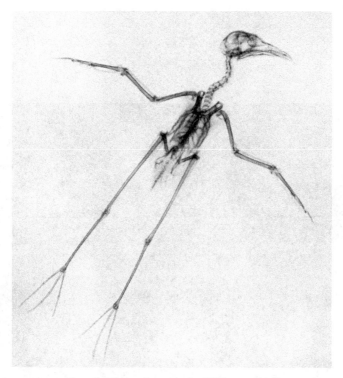

Plate 9.1 X-ray photograph of Wilsons petrel

Plate 9.2 Wilsons petrel chick

Plate 9.3 String vest, made in 1943

Plate 9.4 Bomb damage, Fulham Road.
View from Denis' flat

Plate 9.5 Bomb damage Pelham Court

Plate 10.1 Roberts climbing with friends on Theodul Pass, with Matterhorn

Plate 10.2 Large wave over Rockall, March 1943

Plate 10.3 Eyrie with two golden eagle chicks and dead rabbit

Plate 10.4 Roberts at the wheel of Heather, Shiant Islands

Plate 10.5 Maudheim base buried by snowdrift

Plate 11.1 Ena Thomas on Macquarie Island

Plate 11.2 Nesting rockhopper penguin, Macquarie Island

Plate 11.3 Nesting black-browed
albatrosses, Macquarie Island

Plate 11.4 Nesting sooty albatross,
Macquarie Island

Plate 11.5 Nesting sooty albatross, Macquarie Island

11

ANTARCTIC MAPS AND WHITEHALL RUMBLINGS

I regard the interdepartmental committee as the last refuge of a bureaucratic scoundrel. When you can't find any argument against something you don't want, you set up an interdepartmental committee to strangle it. Slowly.

Jonathan Lynn and Antony Jay, *Yes Minister*

Having been recruited to the Foreign Office as a technical expert – bypassing the normal competitive examination process – Roberts was seen by the diplomatic staff not as 'One of Us' but rather as an eccentric polar enthusiast who would "breeze in, bringing almost visible flurries of snow and ice with him", and informally known as 'Mr Antarctic'.[1] Along with administration of the Falkland Islands Dependencies Survey, Roberts was there to assist the Latin American Department, which was responsible for Antarctic matters in the Foreign Office.[2] His main contact, third secretary Margaret Anstee, recalled him vividly as "stout, enthusiastic, meticulous, strongly work-focused and rather shy with women".[3]

Early on Roberts decided that a major administrative problem with the Antarctic concerned place names. They were in a state of chaos, with many thousands of misplaced ice features and confusing names ending up in common use. Even if a geographical feature was unambiguously identified and accurately located – by no means always the case – the question of allocating and agreeing a name to a particular feature was often politically loaded and controversial. Roberts' aim was to produce a gazetteer of agreed place names for the Falkland Islands Dependencies. It would prove to be a monumental task.

Names are emotive things to many people.[4] Not so to Roberts, who regarded them as purely functional: "The primary purpose of a name is to identify a feature; not to commemorate the discoverer or some other person."[5] Many of those wanting to name features were surveyors returning from the Antarctic, but they were generally advised not to argue with Roberts about names.[6] Allen Clayton, base commander at the British Antarctic Survey's Halley station in 1971, returned from his tour of duty brimming with ideas and suggestions, only to receive from Roberts what was evidently a standard lecture explaining that the days of explorers discovering features and plonking their own favourite names on Antarctic maps were long over.[7] Place names had to be agreed internationally and approved by appointed national committees. Personal preference did not come into it.

An early example of inappropriate naming concerned Casey Channel, which had been named by aviator Hubert Wilkins in honour of his friend Richard Casey, the Australian External Affairs minister. During the British Graham Land Expedition it was discovered that Casey Channel did not actually exist. Eventually the name was deleted from the map, prompting a miffed protest from Casey to expedition leader John Rymill.[8] Rymill explained diplomatically that it was the inaccurate geography, not Casey personally, that they wished to wipe off the map. The Minister for External Affairs' self-esteem was eventually restored by naming the nearest confirmed geographical feature Casey Glacier.

One man who did get unjustly wiped off the map for a long time was Lord Wakefield, a generous sponsor of BGLE and for whom Rymill named Mount Wakefield, which he located accurately just north of 70°S.[9] On the grounds that aviator Lincoln Ellsworth had got there before Rymill, the mountain was subsequently renamed Hope, one of a set of three (Faith, Hope and Charity) reported by Ellsworth. But Ellsworth's own map[10] shows that he had failed to locate them accurately, placing them well south of 70°S. Even though subsequent surveying by BAS revealed that Hope and Wakefield were one and the same feature, the name Hope should be invalidated under place naming rules (Annex III): a name should be rejected if the accurately determined position is found to differ greatly from its earlier reported position(s).[11]

The voluminous correspondence on place naming in SPRI archives is testimony to the struggles to secure agreement on the naming of upwards of 7,000 geographical features, selected from some 50,000 proposals.[12] Roberts admitted that much of the correspondence on place names was "infinitely tedious". But he threw himself into it with extraordinary zeal. Why were place names so important? Without names one could not produce maps, and without maps one could not administer territory. It was the essential prerequisite for advancing territorial claims, the subject of his Foreign Office Handbook.[13] He was profoundly sceptical of many of the existing claims, particularly those based on inaccurate observations from the air.[14]

Roberts' first move, in May 1945, was to revive the interdepartmental Antarctic Place Names Committee, originally a sub-committee of the Polar Committee responsible to the Dominions Office. The APNC had no official sanction other than to propose names for Antarctic features on British maps. It was this small but influential power base that Roberts, as secretary of the committee, would exploit to the full in the battles to come.

A NEAR MISS: THE LADY IN ROBERTS' LIFE

Roberts' self-imposed mission was to get all Antarctic place names accepted internationally, at least in the English-speaking world. But the task soon became too large for him to cope with alone, and after much lobbying he was able in May 1947 to recruit an assistant. Joan Ena Thomas was appointed to serve on the APNC and to assist with all aspects of Antarctic place naming, which she would continue for the next 14 years until her retirement from the Foreign Office in 1961.

Ena Thomas was a Cambridge graduate who had worked on aerial photographic interpretation (PI) during the war. She had been trained by the former BGLE surveyor Alfred 'Steve' Stephenson, who organised all the PI training courses at RAF Medmenham. In 1942 Ena completed her geography degree, which had included the use of a 'Wild' stereo plotter, an optical magnifier with which a skilled operator could produce a detailed 1:25,000 map from aerial photographs taken at an altitude of 34,000 ft.[15] Along with other Oxbridge geography graduates she reported for duty in August 1942 and was immediately thrown into work on the North African landings. Ena then joined the map-making unit of the 'W' Section of photographic interpreters based at RAF Nuneham Park, a few miles from Medmenham. The work involved the preparation of up-to-date large scale maps of continental Europe for the D-Day invasion, and required intense concentration, meticulous attention to detail, and speed. One of PI's spectacular successes was in identifying and detailing the missile launch sites at Peenemünde, enabling Britain to take defensive measures against the weapons.[16]

Ena never spoke about the work at RAF Medmenham. Under the Official Secrets Act recruits were required to maintain secrecy indefinitely, and the contribution of aerial PI to the war effort was not recognised until many decades later, except for the award of an OBE to Stephenson in 1949.

In 1946 FORD, the Research Department, was exiled from the main Foreign Office building in Downing Street to become an outer colony at Cornwall House in Stamford Street near Waterloo Station, where it would remain for the next 30 years. In their upper floor map room Roberts and Ena Thomas would pore over Antarctic maps, engaging in interminable correspondence on place names with authorities in the US, Australia, New Zealand, Norway and France. For Roberts to be able, with his frequent absence from the office, to delegate the work to Ena – particularly the voluminous correspondence with the US Navy Department's Captain Harold Saunders, chairman of the US Board of Geographical Names – was a testament to her professionalism.

Ena was single, and after some years at FORD she confided to a few friends that she was in love with Brian and wanted to marry him. Brian hugely valued Ena's loyalty, sharp intellect, efficiency and warm personality, but any idea of marriage and family was way off his radar. His weekly routine remained unchanged and inflexible over 30 years, always starting work late and finishing late in the day. Thursday night was theatre night. When a business lunch was taken, it was either at Scott's (then in Piccadilly) or at Bianchi's in Frith Street, Soho, and was always the same meal: smoked eels and Wiener Schnitzel, washed down with white wine. The hallmarks of confirmed bachelorhood.

Ena's hopes of marriage with Brian would never be realised. But her other dream – of going to the Antarctic – at long last came to fruition on her retirement from FORD in 1961. Working briefly in Melbourne with Australia's Antarctic expert Phillip Law, she secured a position with the Australian National Antarctic Research Expedition (ANARE) as a cook for the ice ship *Nella Dan* on its annual relief voyages to Macquarie Island during the austral summer seasons of 1963-65 *(Plates 11.1 to 11.5)*. Returning afterwards to her Guernsey birthplace, she taught maths and geography for the rest of her working life. She continued to travel the world until prevented by terminal illness in her early 90s.

TURF WAR ON ANTARCTIC MAPS

As Roberts saw it, his most essential task at FORD was to sort out once and for all place names for maps of the Falkland Islands Dependencies. But that was not necessarily how others saw it. Securing agreement on names was problematic even within the UK; everyone insisted on having his own say in the matter. The Colonial Office, given responsibility for FIDS, had its view. The Royal Geographical Society, in the form of James Wordie, had its view. The Foreign Office, represented by Roberts, had its view. The Colonial Office was mystified, and its mandarins were becoming tetchy. Why were Roberts and Ena Thomas doing this at the Foreign Office, and why was the US involved in what was seen as an exclusively British matter?

On 11 January 1950 Roberts received a prickly enquiry from the Colonial Office: "We feel very strongly that until we receive a memorandum from you explaining (a) your position in this business, why you are called upon to do this particular piece of work, why place names in the Dependencies Sector have to be agreed, etc. and (b) what precisely the Surveyors and you would do and how long their services would be required, we shall never make any sensible progress in this matter."[17] On being accused by the Directorate of Colonial Services of causing delays in the production of maps of the South Orkney Islands, Roberts retorted: "I am not prepared to shoulder responsibility for delays when in fact I have been doing everything I could since early in 1946 to get maps of the Dependencies published as an urgent political and practical necessity."[18]

A LONG-RUNNING FEUD

John Sloman Bennett was the Colonial Office Mediterranean Department's 'Antarctic man'. Ostensibly responsible for the management of FIDS, Bennett was notable more for his absence from interdepartmental committee meetings than his presence. An Arabist and an academically outstanding expert on Middle Eastern history, languages and culture, Bennett was seen by the Colonial Office as a potential high-flyer. However his disposition to logical and perspicacious argument, sarcastic witticism and sheer rudeness rubbed his superiors up the wrong way just once too often and his career finally ground to a halt.[19] He took early retirement, ending his days quietly in Oxford researching 17th century English music for viols and contributing an article to *Grove Dictionary of Music* on the composer Richard Mico.

At Whitehall Bennett and Roberts were to become thorns in each other's flesh. In April 1950 Bennett objected that the Foreign Office had apparently been dealing with the American Embassy "without reference to the Colonial Office",[20] following this up with a more focused attack. "You will remember that Carter wrote to you on 11th January asking for a memorandum on the question of place names... I wish to distinguish: (a) what international commitments exist, if any, governing selection and approval of place names (b) what inter-departmental clearance in London, if any, is necessary and what status the Polar Committee has in this matter (c) what personal contribution you wish to make as a member of the Scientific Committee."[21]

Roberts replied irritably that he was authorised to obtain international agreement on proposed Antarctic names before they went to national committees.[22] Three months later, following a further complaint from Bennett,[23] Roberts sent him a 21-page memorandum on place names.[24] He got no reply. Robert Cecil, who had then become acting head of

Foreign Office Latin American Department, followed up by requesting Colonial Office funding to provide Roberts with an additional assistant for the place names work.[25] Predictably this did not go down too well with the Colonial Office.[26]

On 5 October 1950 the Antarctic Place Names Committee held its first interdepartmental meeting. It was not a congenial occasion. Bennett, for once putting in an appearance, accused the APNC of interfering in a Colonial Office matter.[27] Roberts complained that Bennett was being difficult and obstructive and had failed to understand the need for Anglo-American cooperation in addressing place name problems.[28] It was not just a personal feud: Roberts got solid backing from the Foreign Office.[29]

A SPY IN THE FOREIGN OFFICE

During the summer of 1950 the Foreign Office Latin and North American departments were amalgamated to form an American Department. On 1 November a new Head of American Department was appointed: Donald Maclean.

Maclean was one of the 'Cambridge Five' icons of 20th century espionage, infamous for leaking classified information from the UK and the US to Moscow. The bizarre circumstances of his appearance at the Foreign Office have been chewed over many times.[30] As Head of Chancery at the UK's Cairo embassy, he had acquired a track record of drunkenness and physical violence sufficient to warrant him being sent home to London for psychiatric treatment. His subsequent reappointment to the London office baffled many people, not least the Russians for whom he was spying. But the Foreign Office "very much wanted an employee with a penetrating mind, sound judgment and quiet industry" to return to the fold.[31]

Having left for the Antarctic on 10 November 1950 as observer on the Norwegian-British-Swedish Expedition (chapter 10), Roberts was to see little of Maclean during the latter's brief tenure as head of American Department. On his return from NBSE in February 1951 Roberts was to find the turf war on place naming between the Foreign and Colonial Offices still raging unabated. He proceeded to fan the flames by repeating his request for an extra assistant. The Colonial Office wanted all work on place names to be brought under their aegis, but far from seeking an excuse to transfer Roberts elsewhere, the Foreign

Office was determined to keep him. As Margaret Anstee commented: "It is in great part due to Dr Roberts that we have managed to maintain our legal position in the Antarctic and have convinced the Cabinet that it is imperative to step up our activity in the area rather than reduce it as the Colonial Office recommended."[32] Maclean took a different view: "I believe that the only logical and workable course is to make the Colonial Office solely responsible for work on place names. They administer the area and control UK policy... It is anomalous that the Foreign Office should pay for this work, however useful it is to us to have Dr Roberts as our adviser."[33]

At an interdepartmental meeting on Tuesday 29 May, chaired by Under-Secretary of State Francis Evans, it was proposed to transfer place naming to the FIDS Scientific Bureau at the Colonial Office, the work to be carried out by Ena Thomas, with Roberts remaining at the Foreign Office. The conflict of personalities involved was acknowledged. Mr Bennett would be "warned that the question of responsibility for the work is under discussion at a higher level... The evident difference existing between Dr Roberts and Mr Bennett has been an embarrassment to the Chairman at previous meetings".[34]

But the Foreign Office was soon to experience embarrassment on a whole new level. Needing to secure the agreement of the Head of American Department, Evans appended a footnote to his minute: "Mr Maclean: May I have your views, please? This will require reference to Chief Clerk and Mr Passant."

Francis Evans never got an answer. Over the weekend Donald Maclean had gone missing.

To the Foreign Office Maclean's sudden disappearance, with not a word to anyone, was at first regarded as strange, but not necessarily suspicious. That was not at all the view of MI5, who for some weeks had been closing in on Maclean and had just secured Foreign Secretary Herbert Morrison's authorisation to interrogate him. The last person to see Maclean at the Foreign Office was his immediate superior Roger Makins, at 5.45 pm on the evening of Friday 25 May. Maclean was leaving the building, carrying a heavy cardboard box and several parcels,[35] but not wishing to rock the boat, Makins asked no questions. He was aware of the MI5 investigation but had assumed that Maclean was under surveillance, since a watch had been placed on him ever since 23 April and his telephones were being tapped. The Foreign Office was however unaware that the MI5 watchers invariably went off duty at Victoria Station once Maclean had boarded his train home to Tatsfield, Surrey. For Makins it was "a source of surprise and minor irritation to him that he had not known the watchers did not work at weekends",[36] seemingly on the premise that enemies of the state would not work at weekends either, if they were gentlemen. Normally the MI5 watchers covered Maclean on Saturdays,[37] if not Sundays (on which it would be difficult to place a watch undetected). In any case Burgess and Maclean had left the country by midnight on the Friday.

During Roberts' annual summer holidays voyaging around the Outer Hebrides in *Heather* with Robert Atkinson, they would play the same gramophone record over and over again late into the night. It was the zither signature tune to the film *The Third Man*.

By Friday 1 June, news of the disappearance of Burgess and Maclean had broken in the press. The Foreign Office, in a state of catatonic shock, attempted to soldier on with a stiff upper lip. Returning stoically to the issue of Antarctic place names, Margaret Anstee argued that Evans' proposal to split up Roberts and Ena Thomas was unworkable,[38] and that both of them would have to be transferred to the Scientific Bureau. But E J Passant, the Foreign Office personnel officer, pointed out that Roberts and Bennett were "so opposed on policy that the situation would be impossible".[39] One week later Cecil came to the rescue with the Foreign Office's time-honoured fall-back position: do nothing. "In these circumstances Mr Passant and I recommend that the status quo should be maintained until next February, when the problem can again be considered. There is also the possibility that by then Mr Bennett may have been transferred to other work."[40]

And so this potential crisis for Roberts was averted, but his chances of getting extra assistance had evaporated. The Foreign Office had rather larger worries on its plate.

MORE ACRIMONY OVER PLACE NAMES

Another year passed before the Antarctic Place Names Committee met again. True to form, Bennett failed to appear. He subsequently complained to Roberts: "Your agenda consists of 7 papers every one of which concerns Colonial Office territory. It would I think have been natural to suppose that in those circumstances some effort would have been made to meet the convenience of the Colonial Office as regards a date… In the circumstances I fear it will not be possible for the Colonial Office to be represented, and I must reserve our position as regards any business transacted."[41].Bennett received a riposte from committee chairman Gerald Fitzmaurice, the essence of which was: "We waited half an hour for you at the meeting but you didn't show up."[42] Bennett then went into a bigger sulk, suggesting that the Colonial Office (i.e. himself) should cease to serve on the committee. Unfortunately for Roberts, Bennett's implicit resignation was not accepted.

Bennett resurfaced on 9 June with the rebuke that the Colonial Office was being sidelined procedurally by the APNC.[43] Cecil was unimpressed: "Quite apart from the specious nature of Mr Bennett's objections… it seems to me that we should pass over his insistence that meetings of the Committee can only be held at his convenience and that if he does not choose to attend, the proceedings are invalid."[44] Like his namesake from the court of Queen Elizabeth I, Robert Cecil was always lurking in the background, and he had once more become acting head of the Foreign Office American Department in Maclean's continued absence.

After another month of bickering, Roberts vented his frustrations. "What we want is freedom to get on with the job without this constant raising of irrelevant and time-wasting difficulties by Mr Bennett, who, despite rulings from higher authority, has never accepted the competence of the APNC to discuss and make recommendations on names, or that we should give any weight to American views. There are times when I feel Miss Thomas and I will never get the job finished if we have to waste so much time overcoming obstruction."[45] But eventually in January 1953, to Roberts' utter relief, Cecil's prediction came true and Bennett was off the stage.

In late 1951 a few cracks appeared in the amicable relationship that Roberts had cultivated with Harold Saunders of the US Board of Geographical Names. One concerned the proposed name for the Antarctic Peninsula, as it is called today. At the time it was referred to as Graham Land by the British, Palmer Peninsula by the US, Peninsula San Martin by the Argentines and Peninsula O'Higgins by the Chileans. Whilst there was little prospect of securing agreement with Argentina and Chile, Roberts was optimistic of some chance with the US. He was to be disappointed: Saunders wanted the whole peninsula to be named Palmer Peninsula. This created a political problem for the UK, and from his involvement in the BGLE Roberts naturally had a personal interest in the matter.[46]

Over the next two years Saunders proposed various compromises, but to no avail owing to objections from the Falkland Islands Governor Miles Clifford.[47] Saunders was not at all happy, protesting that despite all the efforts of the place name committees just one person appeared to have the final decision.[48] The rift with Saunders dismayed Roberts,[49] and it would take another ten years for the dispute to be resolved between the APNC and the US Advisory Committee on Antarctic Names. Since then the name Antarctic Peninsula has been adopted, not only by the US and the UK but also by Argentina and generally accepted internationally.

Roberts also had issues with the Americans over the name Stefansson Strait.[50] The BGLE had proved beyond all doubt that this strait reported by aviator Hubert Wilkins did not exist. An issue that should have been settled in 1937 was still being misunderstood in Washington 15 years later. But despite the difficulties, Roberts was able in February 1953 to report triumphantly that a total of 350 place names had been agreed with the Americans,[51] and to propose to Saunders a list of 200 new names. It included the names of all the members of BGLE, with one notable absentee: Roberts himself.

Roberts' aversion to the naming of Antarctic features as a form of commemorating individuals was such that he would decline any proposal to use his own name. But having himself approved the naming of features after other members of BGLE, his stance seemed to others to be *outré*. While Roberts was away from the office Ena wrote surreptitiously to Saunders on the need for a name for an ice piedmont in north-east Alexander Island.[52] She asked Saunders to leave the feature unnamed, ready to be given the name Roberts Ice Piedmont, which was in the end agreed.

By September 1955 the voluminous correspondence on place names had slowed to a trickle. Roberts was able to publish an updated *Gazetteer of the Falkland Islands Dependencies*, now including more than 2,100 names.

MUSIC IN THE ANTARCTIC

Various attempts have been made by members of polar expedition teams with musical skills to entertain the local wildlife, but the outcome is generally disappointing. The response of penguins to the sound of bagpipes is even less enthusiastic than that of humans. Even the famous posed photograph of the piper and the emperor penguin from Bruce's *Scotia* expedition reveals that a rope had to be tied to the penguin's foot to stop it scampering away.[53]

It is rather surprising then to find that Alexander Island, the vast mountainous island to the west of the Antarctic Peninsula, contains a plethora of features named after composers: Bach Ice Shelf, Beethoven Peninsula, Mozart Ice Piedmont and so on. Derek Searle of FIDS, who was the first to survey Alexander Island accurately, collaborated with Roberts on mapping and needed a large number of new names for features. Neither of them was a practising musician, but both had a passion for classical music and composers' names were suggested as a unifying theme. On Searle's 1960 map there were around 45 names.[54] By 1976 twenty more had been added. To generate names, Roberts enlisted the help of his musician sister-in-law Lilian; this is evident from the appearance of Wilbye and Vittoria, names that would have been familiar only to singers of of madrigals and motets. The omission of Vaughan Williams, composer of the theme music to the then topical film *Scott of the Antarctic*, and the Brazilian Villa-Lobos – which would help to dilute the inherent Eurocentricity of the theme – was probably due to the proscribing of double-barrelled names in the guidelines (Annex III). Wagner is present, but cut down to size in the form of a tiny ice piedmont on the western side of the outlying Rothschild Island, invisible to all except those venturing into the icebound Bellinghausen Sea.

WHAT DO EAST AND WEST MEAN IN ANTARCTICA?

Long after completion of the 1955 *Gazetteer* another place-naming controversy was to erupt, this time concerning the Scott Polar Institute. Its house journal *Polar Record* had an editorial committee consisting of editor Alan Cooke, long-serving stalwarts Terence Armstrong, Harry King, Gordon Robin, Charles Swithinbank – and Roberts, who had been involved in editing the journal ever since the 1930s. On 25 March 1975 Roberts handed in his resignation from the committee, in something of a huff.

Antarctica consists of two clearly recognisable land/ice masses separated by the Trans-Antarctic Mountains. On today's maps they are labelled East Antarctica (the larger part containing the polar ice cap) and West Antarctica (the smaller part that includes the Antarctic Peninsula). In the 1970s there was still no consensus on these names. Roberts had persuaded the APNC to recommend the names Greater and Lesser Antarctica, and the Australians and New Zealanders concurred. But the Americans favoured East and West Antarctica.

The SPRI editorial committee was divided on the matter. Things came to a head with a review paper on the radio-echo sounding of Antarctica, in which the names of the two parts of the continent appeared frequently. Cooke and Robin strongly favoured the names East and West Antarctica. The rest of the committee either favoured Greater and Lesser Antarctica or had no strong opinions either way. Roberts' view was that the choice of name was not a question of personal preference but one of conformance with an agreed policy that took wider international issues into account: "It seems to me most unfortunate that as an employee of the British Antarctic Survey and therefore bound to follow UK government decisions, Charles Swithinbank has to report his radio-echo soundings in 'Lesser Antarctica' while Gordon Robin and his associates refer to the same area as 'West Antarctica'."[55] Roberts wished to propose a compromise solution, but Cooke did not want to know, refusing to hold an editorial committee meeting to review the matter.

Roberts' resignation from the editorial board of *Polar Record* was ostensibly not over the names themselves, on which he professed no strong views. It was much more to do with *Polar Record*'s editorial policy, in which he had an obsessive interest. He accused Cooke of adopting a personal policy over place naming without consultation and in contravention of the journal's publicly stated policy.[56] Roberts told Terence Armstrong: "I must resign from the Editorial Committee if the SPRI does not feel able to compromise... I cannot any longer be associated with the SPRI editorial position. I am too exhausted and I do not any longer wish to fight this kind of issue." No doubt some members of SPRI were relieved to hear that.

Notwithstanding Roberts' apparent disinterest in the choice of names, he did have grumbles over East and West Antarctica; for example the confusion for Australians and New Zealanders. If one heads west from Australia one ends up in East Antarctica. And if one heads eastwards, one ends up in West Antarctica. It gets still more confusing within Antarctica itself. Roberts wrote: "In parts of East Antarctica, West Antarctica is east, in others west. This of course depends on whether you are in east East Antarctica or west. However, if you are in west West Antarctica, East Antarctica is west unless you want to go to west East Antarctica in which case it is east. The same holds for east West Antarctica only in the reverse except that if you want to go to west East Antarctica, you will go east. No wonder we did not know where we were!" The following year Geoffrey Hattersley-Smith, Roberts' successor on the Place Names Committee, submitted his paper containing this extract. Published in 1980, it was to be Roberts' posthumous parting shot.[57]

12

THE BATTLE OF
THE ICE SHELF

I am quite certain that Roberts has made the wrong decision and that it is due to his wish for uniformity and rigid adherence to certain shibboleths. To retain the word 'shelf-ice' now is merely a piece of pedantry. There is no doubt in my mind that the word 'barrier' is not only the original term but also the best term, and it is the one which men on the spot will always wish to use... The word 'barrier' has been used so widely by Scott and other sledge parties that to change it now for 'shelf-ice' would be ridiculous.

James Wordie[1]

Whatever terminology is adopted must (a) make a clear distinction between the line of seaward facing cliffs and the area of these ice features, (b) make a clear distinction between ice cliffs afloat (which may change their position) and ice cliffs aground at sea level (which are fixed in position), and (c) ensure that no terms adopted are liable to confusion with the term 'continental shelf'. It will certainly cause trouble later in connection with the definition of territorial waters if Mr Wordie's proposal to have the terms for both the seaward facing ice cliffs and the areas of these features synonymous and interchangeable is adopted, or if the terms of either of these can be confused with the continental shelf which lies beneath it... Sooner or later there is bound to be a dispute about territorial waters in the Antarctic. At present the confusion in terminology makes nonsense of any discussion of the subject, also of charts and sailing directions.

Brian Roberts[2]

Place naming was not the only problem with Antarctic maps; not even the terminology for ice, snow and mountain features had been agreed upon. It was only in 1966 that Roberts and his Cambridge colleagues were able to publish a monograph on the subject, giving precise terminology and definitions.[3] In 1950 there was still no agreed descriptive name for the thick floating fringe of ice that surrounds a large proportion of the Antarctic continent and forms a line of ice cliffs along its outer edge. Now and then huge tabular icebergs break off from it, floating out to sea and resulting in major alterations to the coastline. On today's maps the feature is shown as an Ice Shelf. But behind those two innocuous words lay a titanic five-year power struggle between two obstinate Cambridge individuals: one of them James Wordie, the other Brian Roberts.

SHELF ICE OR ICE BARRIER?

The largest ice feature of the continent, a huge floating plain of ice, had always been referred to by 'heroic age' explorers as the great Ross Ice Barrier. Roberts, in his position as secretary of the Antarctic Place Names Committee, wanted to establish consistent terminology for the naming of similar ice features, including those named after Larsen and Filchner. But he was to come up against fierce opposition. "The need to secure James Wordie's agreement with proposed solutions often seemed more difficult than the need to reach agreement with the Americans. The terminology of ice shelves... became at times an absurd diversion from our much more urgent political problems. But they had to be faced."[4] To Roberts, ice naming was not an issue that could be shelved.

The term 'shelf ice' was not new; it had been proposed in 1930 by the US cartographer Wolfgang Joerg. Having appropriated the term for the Larsen and Filchner ice features, Roberts proposed further to adopt the name 'Ross Shelf Ice' (words in that order) for the Ross Ice Barrier. This greatly upset Wordie, who did not like the name Ice Shelf, and still less Shelf Ice. Wordie was convinced it should remain known as the Ross Barrier, the name given to it by James Clark Ross in 1841 when it was first sighted. At that time the name seemed appropriate, because the towering white ice cliffs presented an impenetrable barrier to Ross' ships *Erebus* and *Terror*. Roberts insisted however that the term 'barrier' should refer only to the ice front facing the Ross Sea. The

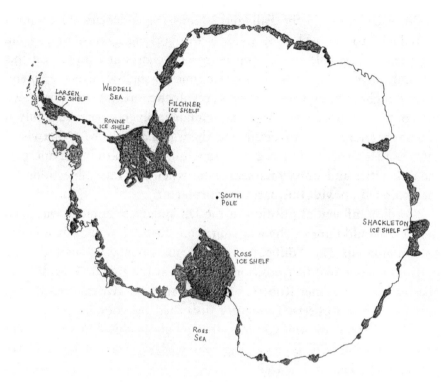

Antarctica and its ice fringes

floating ice sheet behind it was self-evidently not a 'barrier' to travel since it had been used to get to the South Pole. But Wordie was having none of it.[5]

OPENING SHOTS

In March 1948 Roberts proposed to Alun Jones of the Admiralty Hydrographic Department a list of corrections of names and terminology in the *Antarctic Pilot*, a British guide for naval vessels in the Antarctic. When Wordie got to hear of this he characteristically did not argue with Roberts in person but instead wrote to Cdr Jones, objecting particularly to the change from 'ice barrier' to 'shelf ice'.[6] After a three-month exchange of letters Roberts confronted Wordie in person, only to encounter vehement objection to the use of the term 'Shelf Ice' as a cartographic name. The following day Roberts remonstrated angrily with Wordie: "You are actively holding up work on a problem that crops up in a practical form for me almost every day... We have about

6,000 place-names in the Falkland Islands Dependencies which must be reduced to about 1,000, and we are working against time. I am not prepared or able to hold up maps and charts any longer on this account... We cannot afford to waste time on shelf-ice every weekend when I ought to be getting your views on much more important matters. In short I will discuss shelf-ice and similar problems with you only if you show more signs of discussing them constructively. Otherwise I can see no alternative but to go ahead without consulting you and face the difficulties and embarrassments later when you raise objections... I really am fed up with this particular problem."[7]

Wordie's influential position in the UK polar community was such that few would dare to challenge him, but Roberts was disinclined to be intimidated. The "difficulties and embarrassments" would arise inevitably from Wordie's position of power at the Royal Geographical Society. Two days later Roberts received a curt handwritten reply from Wordie: "Dear Roberts, I am very disturbed by your letter, which I prefer to destroy. I know you feel strongly about this, but so do other people. I am still hoping you will agree to <u>what we are preferring</u>. I have given a great deal of time to it."[8]

With this impasse, the issue was laid to rest as a sleeping dog for two years. It would reawaken, with a vengeance.

In April 1950 there seemed to be some chance of a compromise when Wordie wrote to Roberts. "You asked for my opinion on the placenames in Graham Land due shortly for consideration by the Antarctic Place Names Committee... on the whole well chosen. The particular place name to which I take exception is your choice of <u>Larsen Shelf-Ice</u>... I think it best to refer to this as the 'ice feature'. Ice shelf in that order is a geographical term."[9]

To which Roberts commented in the margin: "Ice shelf meets all our needs." For the first time he was prepared to concede 'Shelf Ice' in favour of 'Ice Shelf'. Wordie however continued to dodge the issue; he could not bring himself to let 'Ice Barrier' go. Following some support for 'shelf ice' from Canberra, Washington and Stockholm[10] Roberts wrote a year later to Wordie outlining various options over 'Shelf Ice' and 'Ice Shelf'. Wordie stalled by demanding to see the whole correspondence file stage by stage. Roberts protested at Wordie's tactics. "You are always welcome to come to my office and study the whole appalling dossier stretching back to 1949 and earlier..."[11]

DEVIOUS BUREAUCRATIC TACTICS

In October 1951 Wordie, now president of the RGS, instructed its Council to appoint a sub-committee to make recommendations about ice terminology. Two days later Roberts, smelling a rat, sent him an ultimatum:

> "It is now 24 October and you have had the various papers about 'shelf ice' since 20 June. Repeated requests for your comments... have met with no response, and I find it difficult to avoid the conclusion that your sole aim is to postpone any solution which differs from your own personal one. You have now succeeded in postponing a decision since 1948, despite the fact that the names for these features had to be omitted from the first edition of the 1:500,000 maps. Surely this is long enough? Unless we can get on with the matter now, they will also have to be omitted from the second edition... if I do not hear from you by next Wednesday, 31 October, I shall assume that I cannot expect any written comments from you and I will circulate the other papers without them."[12]

On 30 October Wordie replied, complaining that he had been kept in the dark about Roberts' proposals[13] – a claim categorically denied by Roberts. "Apart from the suggested change from 'shelf ice' to 'ice shelf' for the generic term for the <u>area</u> of these features, which everyone is now prepared to concede to you, there has been no change of principle for 3 years..."[14]

Roberts continued to seek support from the Foreign Office, explaining that territorial waters could be measured only from the seaward edge of 'shelf ice' areas, because in most cases the position of the true coastline was unknown.[15] He lamented the absence of an official stance on terminology, insisting that to secure international agreement it was essential that terminology should not be ambiguous and interchangeable. The Foreign Office agreed. Roberts then pointed out what, or rather whom, he saw as the root cause of the problem. "It is clear that he [Wordie] regards himself as the judge in this matter; not as one of the disputants. He refused to provide for the Committee a written statement... and kept repeating that he regarded the whole thing as settled by his paper in the Journal of Glaciology."[16] Roberts again complained to Wordie[17] and also to RGS secretary Larry Kirwan[18] about the 'concealed' RGS sub-committee on ice terminology. In desperation he also lobbied Gerald Seligman.[19] But Seligman was not particularly supportive of 'shelf ice'.[20] For Roberts this was a disappointing response from a fellow founder member of the British Glaciology Society, and he followed up with several tirades against Wordie: "All along, his main tactic has been to try to get binding decisions (from which retreat will be most difficult) made by the other bodies before my Committee has discussed it... I shall, of course, abide by any decision reached constitutionally, but I will fight to my last gasp against the kind of methods which James has been employing in an attempt to force a minority opinion on the majority."[21] He warned the APNC chairman Gerald Fitzmaurice to expect trouble at the next committee meeting, scheduled for 8 May 1952:

> "The attached paper from the RGS on 'shelf ice' terminology has at last arrived... It is rather a strange document. The covering letter and summary were both drafted by Mr Wordie, who is President of the RGS and who represents the RGS on the APNC. He personally steered this whole thing through the RGS Council... [he] is obviously not prepared to give way or compromise with any views opposed to his own..."[22]

Roberts' anxiety was well-founded. Before the meeting Wordie handed Fitzmaurice a note headed "Dr Roberts and the RGS decision", which included the advice: "It does not seem suitable that negotiations should now be left in Dr Roberts' hands in view of his particular prejudices..."[23] Wordie still thought that he could get his own way, if necessary by attempting to ease Roberts out of the place names committee.

THE AMERICANS AND AUSTRALIANS TIP THE SCALES

In August 1952 Roberts received unexpected support from the Commonwealth Relations Office, which recommended deleting the term 'ice barrier' from the polar vocabulary.[24] Meanwhile Wordie visited the US, soliciting support for 'ice barrier' from the Navy Department in Washington, only to find that Harold Saunders considered the whole debate to be an esoteric dispute between two strong-minded protagonists. "The fact that all of us just sat and listened during his [Wordie's] 'barrier' presentation must have given him an inkling that we were not being moved."[25]

On 3 October the US Advisory Committee on Antarctic Names met to review ice terminology. It recommended that (i) the generic term agreed upon for shelf-like ice bodies, either shelf ice or ice shelf, be consistently used for all features of this type, since to make the two exceptions suggested (Ross and Filchner Barriers) would perpetuate confusion, and (ii) further consideration be given to the selection of a term other than barrier for the seaward face of such masses (shelf cliff, shelf front, ice cliff etc.).[26]

Wordie's last-ditch attempt to gain US support for 'ice barrier' had failed. He conceded to Saunders: "If the RGS Committee agrees to the use of the word 'front' for the edge, and to the adoption of Ross Ice Shelf and Filchner Ice Shelf in preference to Barrier, the two decisions would, as I see it, remove any further difference of opinion between America and ourselves."[27] During November 1952 the newly-formed Australian Committee on Antarctic Names agreed on 'ice shelf' for all names without exception, the only dissenter being Douglas Mawson, who had been nobbled in private by Wordie.[28]

By December Roberts was beginning to smell victory,[29] and wrote to Saunders seeking his agreement to the resolution of the 'ice shelf' issue. The Australians had proposed

(a)   that, for compounding in place names, the term 'ice shelf' is to be used, and to ensure uniformity no exceptions are to be permitted;

(b)   that 'ice shelf' be also used as the generic or morphological term and that, in order to avoid confusion, the term 'shelf ice' be dropped from usage; and

(c)   that to avoid confusion the word 'Barrier' be excluded from modern usage and that the term 'Ice Front', with a date, be applied to the floating seaward-drifting cliffs of an ice shelf.[30]

During the first months of 1953 Roberts still felt the need to warn Saunders about Wordie's continuing attempts to avoid a decision,[31] but in May he was at last able to issue his APNC report promulgating the name 'ice shelf'.[32] The next day it was rubber-stamped: "Following the decision of the Polar Committee I circulated this to the APNC, understanding that is was a decision upon which we are now to act. Mr Wordie, however, said yesterday that it is not a decision, but merely an item on the agenda for our next Committee meeting. I told him that it was a decision taken by our parent committee and was circulated for information, not for further discussion. I also said that this was a decision on place names for use in official publications; he is free to do whatever he likes about it at the RGS."[33]

That was the end of the matter. Today 'ice shelf' is used throughout on all English language maps of the Antarctic. Wordie had been checkmated by Roberts, but it was a victory more for policy than for Roberts personally. New controversies were about to erupt over a trans-Antarctic expedition, the International Geophysical Year and the directorship of SPRI. In all these matters Roberts and Wordie were to clash again, and Wordie – to whom the defeat of 'ice barrier' was manifestly painful – was still armed and dangerous.

13

CRISIS AT THE POLAR INSTITUTE

Scott Polar Research Institute

Not long after he was not appointed Director at SPRI (which I personally thought was a disgrace), the Arctic Institute of North America was looking for a new director. I wrote to Brian asking him if he would take it on... How different both SPRI and the Arctic Institute would have been if he had accepted.

Graham Rowley[1]

At the end of the war the Scott Polar Research Institute was able to repossess its building from the Admiralty, although it was not officially re-opened until a lunch ceremony in March 1947 at Trinity Hall, director Launcelot Fleming's college. But just one month later a dark cloud appeared on the institute's horizon. The SPRI building still enjoyed pleasant surroundings overlooking a meadow with Lensfield

House on the far side. Under a scheme proposed by Cambridge University's buildings syndicate, the site would be bulldozed to accommodate a six-storey monolith for the Department of Chemistry, overshadowing the small SPRI building, as it does today. Fleming was not by nature an activist and, much to Roberts' irritation, would always attempt to see other people's point of view, even at the expense of his own. In any case there was little that Fleming could do; nobody was harbouring any illusions that the old meadow could somehow be preserved.

The SPRI directorship was still a part-time post. Fleming fulfilled its duties in the mornings, leaving his afternoons free for coaching the Trinity Hall eights and the evenings for visits to his rooms by his many disciples. Fleming's capacity for disorganisation was legendary. During the British Graham Land Expedition his bunk was "in a permanent state of chaos with prayer books, geological hammers and specimen rocks, sermon notes and articles for the Times and the Glasgow Herald, all mixed together".[2] By 1949 Roberts was becoming increasingly concerned by the disintegrating administration at SPRI, and from his Foreign Office room he wrote several pages to Fleming:

> "While you have been away I have been thinking about the organisation of work at the [S]PRI. I know that you will not mind my usual bluntness. We need to give more thought to general administrative problems, or I can see very little hope of concluding the current state of chronic muddle... It is essential to have some regular system for (a) circulating papers to those who ought to see them (b) deciding what action is to be taken, who is to take it and allocating priorities where necessary (c) checking that the necessary action has been taken within a reasonable time and (d) filing the papers so that they can immediately be found again when required. Not one of these items is working properly. I have tried various experiments but they all break down hopelessly, primarily, I think, because you yourself do not conform to any procedure; nor do you give any lead in a matter which is essentially one for the Director. Indeed you set an example of disorder which is the wonder and despair of your whole staff! There are far too many cases which have dragged on for months without decision.

The papers have been repeatedly brought together and put before you only to become scattered or lost again... I am grateful that I can write to you a letter like this without being sacked instantly. Yours, Brian Roberts"[3]

Fleming promptly lost Roberts' letter amongst his piles of papers and did nothing. Shortly afterwards, on 8 July 1949, he received out of the blue a letter from the office of Prime Minister Clement Attlee announcing that his name was to be put forward for the vacant Bishopric of Portsmouth. This was undoubtedly an honour for Fleming, but the timing was awkward; having just been invited to visit the Canadian Arctic, he rather hoped that the clerical appointment could be delayed at least until his return. "I am afraid that Portsmouth needs a bishop," was the uncompromising ecclesiastical response. Fleming asked Roberts to go to Canada in his place and promptly resigned as director.

The Canadian Arctic expedition, organised by Graham Rowley, was a unique opportunity for Roberts to take part in an archaeological dig. Rowley had spent much time amongst the Inuit, researching the newly-discovered paleo-eskimo Dorset culture,[4] a people who had no dogs and no bows and arrows, but who manhauled sledges and hunted mostly seal and walrus through ice-holes with harpoons. As the climate changed the Dorset people were displaced by the Thule (ancestral Inuit) people with their improved hunting capabilities, and by the 16th century the Dorset culture had died out. Over five days Rowley and Roberts excavated a mass of artefacts and carved objects from an occupational midden near Thule house ruins on Igloolik Island.[5] It was most unusual for a site to reveal occupation by both Dorset and Thule people.

A NEW DIRECTOR, BUT NO CHANGE

With Fleming's resignation the SPRI directorship was now vacant. Wordie wrote to Colin Bertram, suggesting that he apply for the post. He wrote likewise to Roberts, although by then their growing disagreements were creating doubts in Wordie's mind about Roberts' suitability. Roberts was himself equivocal: "I should like to be considered as a candidate for Directorship, but there is a complication of my other job at the Foreign Office... I am anxious to leave the Foreign Office and to work full time at the Institute... the political work has reached a stage when I must decide whether to get out or take it up as a career..."[6] Eventually, after a delay of several months, Bertram was appointed director.

Several months after his return from Canada Roberts' reiterated his dilemma in a long, anguished letter to Graham Rowley:

"When I first got back to England I found such arrears of work that at times the task of catching up, let alone going forward, seemed almost hopeless. You will remember that Launcelot had left the PRI, and until Colin was appointed quite an astonishing quantity of papers accumulated. The stacks of unanswered letters were to be measured in piles feet high, and from every quarter correspondents were pressing for their enquiries to be dealt with urgently. In the Foreign Office I also found the same kind of situation... I was immediately plunged into negotiations for a renewal of the Anglo-Argentine-Chilean naval 'holiday' agreement in the Antarctic, a job which had to be completed before the southern season opened. There were a thousand and one arrangements to be completed before getting off on the Norwegian-British-Swedish expedition to Queen Maud Land, and the usual chaos over the FIDS, both political and practical, for the Colonial Office is still as muddle-headed and obstructive as ever in its lack of understanding of the problems. Not only was Launcelot not at the PRI to help, but Terence Armstrong was abroad, and John Elbo out of action with his brain operation. I can never remember a time when so many polar things seemed to happen all at once with so few people here to do them... I have tried, but quite obviously failed, to cope, even though I have devoted my entire time to the job since I got back, except for 3 days (mostly spent in sleeping) over Christmas... At quite an early stage it became obvious that my cherished hope of getting away from the Foreign Office seems an impractical dream, so I have continued to live a double existence, rushing back and forth between London and Cambridge."[7]

Roberts recognised that Bertram's organisational ability was an improvement on Fleming's, but he bemoaned Bertram's lack of vision, direction and leadership. Another four years at SPRI left him exasperated, frustrated and disenchanted by the chronic shortage of funds and staff. In a long rambling letter to Fleming he was about to drop a bombshell:

"My dear Launcelot,

"You will remember that I have already spoken to you about my fears for the Institute, and the prevailing feeling that it cannot survive the recent lack of forward policy... I have been asked whether I would like the job of Director of the Arctic Institute in Montreal... this [would solve] the struggle with Colin to get decisions that solve problems instead of merely shelving them.

"I have tried, again and again, to explain to Colin that in my opinion the Institute cannot survive a policy of drift... I have almost given up making suggestions to Colin because so little notice is taken of them... I know he has very great difficulties, especially in finding a midway path between James [Wordie] (who can't bear to give a bold lead in anything, or even state a clear-cut view) and myself... I count myself lucky if I see him for 5 or 10 minutes a week. The root problem: finances... I say that I think we need to do so-and so: how do we finance it? Colin's attitude is almost invariably that we can't afford it, and there the matter drops."[8]

The invitation to apply for the vacant directorship of the Arctic Institute of North America had come from Graham Rowley. Not even Fred Roots, who was himself involved with AINA and who was at the time lodging in Roberts' Causewayside flat, was aware of it.[9] Roberts had his supporters within SPRI and it seemed likely that if he did leave, three of his colleagues would follow suit. In January 1954 he expressed deep concern to Bertram over the situation at SPRI, which he saw as rapidly approaching crisis point.

"My dear Colin,

"Douglas, Terence and Margaret have given me the attached memoranda for my comments. I have told them that I think the papers should go through you to the Committee of Management and that I would write a separate note, expressing my own agreement with what they have written.

"All of us are very concerned about the present situation, and would like to make certain that the Committee is fully aware of our conviction that things cannot go on in this way without a complete breakdown in the near future...

"As we see the position, we must either acquire more funds now to enable us to keep abreast of rapidly advancing events in the polar regions, or we must drastically review our whole policy. It seems to be a straight question between going forward with vigour or being left hopelessly behind the times... we do not believe that the Institute can survive as a significant organisation unless it is sustained by a vigorous forward policy...

"As you know, I have during the past year been able to see so little prospect that the Institute's administrative problems are likely to be solved that I have been seriously considering going to Canada...[10]

Roberts thought long and hard about the offer of the post at AINA, but eventually decided against it. By the end of 1954 the tangled politics resulting from the Commonwealth Trans-Antarctic Expedition and the International Geophysical Year were causing him to spend almost all his time in London, and the internal politics of Cambridge were shelved – for the time being.

THE COMMONWEALTH TRANS-ANTARCTIC EXPEDITION

By March 1953 Vivian Fuchs, director of the FIDS scientific committee, was at an advanced stage of planning a 'post-Shackleton' Trans-Antarctic Expedition, strongly supported by Miles Clifford and presented formally to a Polar Committee meeting. It was not generally well received by the Foreign Office, to whom "the effects of a trans-continental sledge ride were evanescent and any money that could be got should be spent on something of more permanent value".[11]

A rival plan to Fuchs' was being put forward by Duncan Carse, who was then in South Georgia and had asked Roberts to present his case. There was no real chance of Carse's over-ambitious plan being approved, but Roberts' concerns were more fundamental. On 2 December 1953 Wordie convened the FIDS scientific committee to review the CTAE. Roberts attempted to open up the whole question of the CTAE's motives, priority and funding, but was promptly slapped down by Wordie. For Wordie the expedition was cast in stone and the only discussion was the choice between the two candidates Fuchs and Carse.[12] The growing rift between Roberts and Wordie was to open up into a gaping crevasse.

In early 1954 Fuchs embellished his plans in an attempt to accommodate the Foreign Office's political concerns. A new starting point from Stonington Island on the Antarctic Peninsula was proposed, with aerial photography included and support from Sunderland flying boats based on Deception Island. Roberts now became more supportive of the CTAE,[13] but this apparent change of heart was only temporary; soon Fuchs reverted to his original plan of starting from Vahsel Bay on the Brunt Ice Shelf.

In March 1955 Colin Bertram, who was both SPRI director and a co-founder of the CTAE management committee, wrote to the committee's chairman Air Marshall Sir John Slessor, expressing deep concerns over competition from Argentina and the US and the absence of a British ice-strengthened ship to cope with the notorious pack ice of the Weddell Sea. "As Director of this Institute I cannot allow its name to be used to whitewash decisions which have been reached without consultation and in evident disregard of the facts."[14] Bertram objected particularly to Wordie's proposal to constitute CTAE as a limited company and declined the offer to him of a directorship of the Trans Antarctic Company."[15]

The response from Slessor's deputy rapped Bertram over the knuckles for failing to represent SPRI as a supporter of the CTAE.[16] But Bertram was not alone. Like Roberts, Kirwan of the RGS was opposed to the CTAE and insisted that the money would be better spent on a dedicated British icebreaker that would send a strong signal of intent to Argentina and Chile. But there were powerful Establishment figures stacked against them. A story circulated that Roberts was telephoned by an irate Duke of Edinburgh, who was not only contributing financially to CTAE but who himself wanted to be part of the show: "What are you doing to my expedition?" the Duke wanted to know.[17]

It was a difficult time for both Roberts and Fuchs, who greatly respected each other. Roberts' opposition to Fuchs' plans was purely political and not at all personal. In late 1955 he sent Fuchs translations of Argentine and German documents that were intended to help in navigating the Vahsel Bay area.[18]

THE INTERNATIONAL GEOPHYSICAL YEAR

A dinner party in the US in 1950 has passed into folklore as the origin of the IGY. The diners proposed to hold an International Polar Year in 1957-58, but it eventually turned into a global scientific enterprise to be renamed the International Geophysical Year.[19] The main scientific frontiers were to be the Antarctic, the upper atmosphere and outer space. It was during IGY that systematic measurements started of atmospheric gas concentrations, leading to the generation of continuous long-term data on greenhouse gas accumulation and ozone depletion. At the time nobody realized how vital those measurements would be for global climate monitoring.

UK scientists were keen to be part of IGY, but Roberts was uneasy about the huge scale of the US Antarctic programme. To him the IGY smacked of a game of one-upmanship between the US and the USSR that would result in threats to the British Antarctic to which Whitehall was seemingly oblivious.[20] Moreover, as he put it: "Argentina is being asked to make Deception Island a principal observatory for the IGY. This will suit her well as it gives a measure of international recognition to the station and would certainly make it much harder for us to throw them out."[21] Another issue was the perceived need for a dedicated ice ship. "The Royal Society has concluded that an IGY station can only be established and maintained at Vahsel Bay with an icebreaker. Mr Wordie was in a minority of one on the advisability of attempting this with any of the available ships."[22] To Roberts the difficulties of an IGY station on the Brunt Ice Shelf were formidable: the need to penetrate the Weddell Sea pack ice over several successive seasons, the risk of the need for a rescue by the Argentine icebreaker, and the short life span of a base constructed on an ice shelf.[23]

By now David Brunt, chairman of the IGY British National Committee, was becoming extremely irate about being "led up the garden path" by the widely-conflicting advice that he was receiving from SPRI. On 1 May 1955 he visited the institute, where Bertram noted Brunt's "harsh words" about the CTAE muddling the IGY position. "In his opinion even the sharing of shipping between the two ventures is undesirable.

Apart from appreciating the political repercussions that there might be if there were to arise any question of rescue by the Argentine icebreaker, he has fears that in the eyes of the world the Royal Society might be suspected of being politically motivated if an IGY party goes to Vahsel Bay."[24]

Brunt summoned Roberts for a further meeting. He had received flat refusals on icebreaker support from the US, both from American IGY officials and from the US Navy Department. Brunt, now at the end of his tether, was contemplating abandoning the Vahsel Bay station entirely, with the embarrassing consequence that there would now be no British IGY station on the Antarctic continent. At the Royal Society tempers erupted. The Foreign Office observed: "It would be the greatest pity if the Royal Society were to abandon all participation in the Antarctic plans for the IGY. The inference abroad – particularly in the US – will be that HMG prefer spending their money in strengthening their sovereignty and backing spectacular ventures across the South Pole than in genuinely useful scientific research."[25]

Eventually, in July 1955, Brunt reluctantly agreed to site the UK IGY station at Vahsel Bay, but the logistics issues would not go away. On 20 July the Foreign Office reported to the Cabinet: "Our prestige will suffer if we alone amongst the major participants in IGY have no icebreaker. We must also reckon with the possibility that countries establishing IGY stations will not dismantle them when the IGY ends, but will turn them into national bases. Everyone will then be claiming a slice of the Antarctic cake."[26]

The last two sentences express in a nutshell the political significance of IGY, which the scientists involved did not wish to admit, let alone discuss.

Roberts complained to Bertram that due to its differences of opinion SPRI was exacerbating the dispute, which had "introduced an atmosphere of suspicion and intrigue into all polar matters in the UK... As a result, the reputation of the SPRI has sunk quite rapidly to a lower ebb than I can ever remember. The Foreign Office will not I think be able to carry the grants alone, or to recommend them to the Treasury".[27] He followed up by demanding a change in the chairman of the SPRI management committee, implying that "either he goes or I go". For the second time in two years Roberts was threatening resignation from the institute. He could be guaranteed a sympathetic hearing from his friend and colleague Colin Bertram. But how could

Bertram engineer the removal of the chairman of the committee that had originally appointed him as director?

On 25 October 1955 Bertram wrote to Wordie, expressing concern over the damage being done to SPRI's reputation by the disputes between the director and chairman of SPRI and the conflicting advice being given to others.[28] Shortly afterwards he tendered his resignation to the SPRI management committee, but was asked to stay on while the future of the institute was being discussed at a high level. On 6 November Bertram agreed to remain as director on condition that a 'neutral' chairman was appointed, implying that Wordie should be replaced.[29] On being interviewed he hinted that in the event of his resignation "two senior members of his staff" would also resign.[30]

Vivian Fuchs, who was on the management committee, agreed that changes were needed at SPRI to stop the chronic bickering, but objected to the attitude that "the employed Director can dictate who is Chairman of the Committee which appoints him".[31] Nevertheless Bertram's tactic worked: at the end of 1955 Wordie was voted out as chairman. Bertram remained director for another year and resigned at the end of 1956.

LAUNCHING OF THE CTAE AND IGY EXPEDITIONS

The CTAE advance party sailed from Millwall Docks on 14 November 1955 in the 800-ton Scottish/Canadian sealer *Theron*. One week later the IGY advance party sailed from Southampton in the 540-ton Norwegian sealer MV *Tottan*. *Theron* soon became trapped in the Weddell Sea's notorious pack ice, and on 4 January 1956 the Foreign Office received a telegram from the UK Naval Attaché in Buenos Aires: "We have only Press reports on *Theron*'s situation but the [Argentine] Chief of Staff has personally this morning offered help of ice breaker *General San Martín* in the friendliest possible way, stressing that this would naturally involve no propaganda on the Argentine side." To which J S Whitehead of the American Department responded: "This move was to be expected. The fact that the offer has been made before the *Theron* has got into any really serious trouble detracts from the assurance that the offer was not made for propaganda purposes. I think we should decline the offer quickly, but pleasantly."[32]

Wordie had long maintained that staying close to the eastern shore of the Weddell Sea would provide the safest access route to the Antarctic mainland. But the CTAE party ignored his recommendation and *Theron* became trapped in the pack ice 200 miles to the west.[33] Eventually *Theron* was able to break out, but Fuchs later admitted that they were lucky to do so. The IGY party followed Wordie's advice and had a relatively quick and easy passage, but *Tottan* also got held up on its way to Vahsel Bay. On 16 January a press release issued from *Tottan* reported that *General San Martín* was nonchalantly ploughing through ice that *Tottan* had been unable to negotiate: "It is galling to see a foreign ice-breaker travelling freely like this, and extremely bad for British prestige and Antarctic claims that we could not do likewise."[34] The *Tottan* party also wanted "to place their base next to an Argentine one so as to be able to obtain fresh meat". Suspecting that the scientists in the field were mischievously winding up their bureaucratic masters, the Royal Society suppressed the press release.[35]

THE POLAR INSTITUTE AND THE UNIVERSITY

Roberts was still nursing an ambitious vision of SPRI as a national polar information centre, using his Whitehall contacts to get more financial support from the UK Treasury and from Commonwealth governments. The Treasury's grant-in-aid had increased from £1,800 in 1946 to £5,666 in 1955 (equivalent to £200,000 today). Some senior members of Cambridge University were however starting to raise uncomfortable questions about the acceptability of earmarked grants, with their political, industrial and military undertones that in their view compromised academic independence. But was SPRI part of the university, or not?

During 1956 a further increase in the institute's grant-in-aid was requested from the Treasury, which responded by proposing to terminate the direct grant and add an equivalent sum to Cambridge University's block grant via the University Grants Committee. This was to have major consequences for the institute, which would become subsumed into the university's Department of Geography. Unlike the Treasury grant, the UGC grant was not earmarked for SPRI. As the university's General Board reported in November 1956:

"The UGC made it clear that they would neither wish nor be prepared to provide an ear-marked grant for the Institute and that, if the University agreed to their proposal to assume financial responsibility for it, then it would be for the University to decide from year to year, and from quinquennium to quinquennium, the extent to which the work of the Institute should be developed or limited."[36]

The General Board admitted that it had no interest in funding the SPRI library, archive and museum, which they felt were the government's responsibility. Nor did it wish to fund the expansion of the institute then being proposed by its management committee. One consequence of the university takeover was that the existing institute staff, including the director, would in effect lose their jobs and have to re-apply for them: a classic retrenchment tactic. Bertram took this as an opportunity to resign and did so forthwith. The institute's management committee was not at all keen on the idea of the university takeover, and lobbied in vain for the grant to be routed instead via the Royal Society. For the SPRI staff, uncertainty prevailed and morale plummeted. By 1957 the institute was, in Roberts' words "almost at breaking point, and very nearly collapsed into nothing more than a mausoleum in memory of Captain Scott".[37]

CONTEMPORARY VIEWS OF BRIAN ROBERTS

With Bertram's resignation, the post of SPRI director was once again vacant. This time Roberts was extremely keen to be appointed, but he was at something of a disadvantage owing to his dubious standing with Debenham and Wordie, both of whom would use his undistinguished academic record as ammunition against him. Debenham's view was that Roberts was an assiduous collector of information but not a good researcher. "He has the reputation of being a 'difficult' colleague and that... is due to his persistence in considering his view of a problem is always right and his readiness to use rather regrettable methods to attain his end. His forceful character often wins against the judgment of his colleagues, but I would consider his outlook to be rather a narrow one."[38] In private Debenham was still more outspoken about Roberts.[39]

Larry Kirwan of the Royal Geographical Society was usually an ally of Roberts, but even his letter of reference was to some extent equivocal. He started off by pinpointing Roberts' unrivalled encyclopaedic knowledge of polar matters, energetic and capable administration, and strong reputation in the Foreign Office, the Commonwealth and the US. But then came the controversial issues: "He tends sometimes towards an excessive concentration on <u>minutiae</u>... a man of strong character and decided, sometimes somewhat rigid, opinions who has for some time been the moving spirit in the Institute but subordinate to a part-time Director, intellectually able but administratively weak. This position, not always easy for a man of energetic and sometimes impatient temperament, combined with the rather emotional atmosphere engendered by the recent clash of personalities within the Institute, has on occasions provoked him to indiscretions which in more normal circumstances he would be unlikely to indulge."[40]

Roberts' long-standing friend and colleague Launcelot Fleming also acknowledged Roberts' unique encyclopaedic knowledge and tremendous influence on the life and development of the institute, but then came to the crux of the matter: "The difficulty lies in regard to personal relations. When he is opposed to someone else's view... he can be very difficult. This is partly I think a liability to annoyance mixed with the kind of perfectionism which can make him obsessed with an issue and carry on a campaign about it out of all proportion to its importance, though he may regard it as a vital question of principle involving honesty and truth."[41] A month later Fleming started to worry that his reference might have been misinterpreted: "The personal problems have primarily come from those senior to himself and I should say have certainly been due in some measure to the fact that his own knowledge has sometimes been greater than the responsibility, and the situation would be changed if he was to be in the position of Director... I am sure the place would have great vigour and would be run most competently."[42] But Fleming had probably said too much. As a man of the cloth he was probably naïve concerning the serpentine nature of academic appointments.

Although it is not clear whether his opinions were being sought by the appointments committee, Wordie was unhesitant about expressing them. He did not think much of any of the candidates. "Importance will always be attached to the Director's views. This point is important and indicates that an entirely new man should be appointed rather than anyone in the present set up, many of whom have lost the confidence of people either here [Cambridge] or in London."[43] Roberts was no exception. "His important asset is his industry and attention to details in indexing and classification. I am not sure about his degree and I think that may have been his initial trouble. He is very persistent, almost obstinate, and over-anxious to have his own way. I know him to be deficient in the wider outlook but competent in small details." The disparaging comment about Roberts' degree seems to have been targeted at his Class II(1) in Archaeology and Anthropology. Wordie continued with a broadside attack, accusing Roberts of "activities towards preventing the IGY Committee from carrying out its programme and for a time he held up plans for the Halley Bay base. He should have understood its great national importance. This shows his weak side".[44] He concluded that Roberts should be offered one of the lesser posts at the institute.

Ironically Wordie was himself to be sidelined. By May 1957, due to the change in SPRI's constitution, a new management committee had been formed, no longer including Wordie even as an ordinary committee member. Most of the staff, even Roberts himself, were happy with the make-up of the new committee.

But there was a further consequence of SPRI's constitutional change: its management committee no longer had the authority to appoint the director. That was now the prerogative of the appointments committee of the Department of the Faculty of Geography and Geology, whose chairman and secretary Alfred Steers and Benny Farmer handled the applications. Eventually the appointment went to Gordon Robin, a geophysicist then at the Australian National University in Melbourne. Roberts was deeply disturbed. During August 1957 he held his own 'doom and gloom' SPRI staff meeting, glumly informing his supporters that the transfer of funding responsibility to the university and the appointment of Robin would mean that the institute could not continue in the way that he had always hoped. Because Robin had his own personal research agenda, Roberts believed that none of the institute's other polar interests could expect to receive support. Posts related to those interests would most likely disappear and the staff would be dismissed. In the end those fears turned out to be over-pessimistic; eye-witness accounts suggest that Robin was quite supportive of the institute's broader interests, including those in the humanities.[45]

Roberts' friends, well aware that he had been hoping for the directorship himself, wrote him letters of condolence. Kirwan tried to console Roberts that at least Robin was a good 'true research' man; Bertram and Fleming expressed similar sentiments.[46] But of more concern to Roberts than his own personal situation were the proposed constitutional changes and the insecurity of the junior staff. Roberts trusted nobody in the university hierarchy.[47] On 29 September 1957 a memorandum addressed to Steers, prepared jointly by Roberts, Terence Armstrong and librarian Harry King, stressed that SPRI could only provide its services as a polar institute if staff were retained for those purposes.[48] Roberts then showed his true colours by advising the Foreign Office that "if the University goes forward with the conversion of this national institute into a University sub-department of geophysics it can have no possible case for receiving outside grants".[49] He acidly pointed out that the SPRI building, library and archives – the primary assets of the institute – had been built up entirely from funds raised outside the university. This was not entirely a gift to the university, which would acquire the responsibility of funding and staffing. But could it be trusted with this?

In November 1957 Henry Hankey, responsible for polar matters at the Foreign Office, became aware of sinister manoeuvres in Cambridge.[50] Steers had approached the Foreign Office with a request to pay Roberts' salary in full, leaving SPRI to provide a greatly curtailed information service, most of the existing staff to be "suppressed" and publication of *Polar Record* to be suspended. When Hankey responded that such ruthless pruning of the activities of SPRI would diminish its utility to the UK government so greatly that the annual Treasury grant would no longer be justified, the proposal was quashed.

After two more years of wrangling the university made significant concessions. The SPRI librarian's post became full-time and Roberts was awarded a part-time *ad hominem* university post of Research Associate. The institute's polar information facilities, far from undergoing retrenchment, expanded considerably. Shortly afterwards approval was given to double the size of the SPRI building, which became feasible due to a huge award by the philanthropic Ford Foundation. Roberts was himself enthusiastically involved in the design and planning of the new building. Gordon Robin was proving to be an able director and the institute's international reputation as a polar research centre was greatly enhanced.[51] It was a golden age for SPRI; but throughout Robin's long tenure as director there would always be tension between him and Roberts.

14

THE FOREIGN OFFICE
AND THE BIRTH OF THE
ANTARCTIC TREATY

The true story as it emerges from the confidential documents is, in my
personal view, painfully at variance with a lot of the published versions.
In saying this, I refer, of course, only to the political and other motives
of each government. I fear it will be some years before this bit of history
can be published.

Brian Roberts, May 1978

Underlying Roberts' recruitment to the Foreign Office in 1944 was
the idea that sooner or later an international Antarctic conference
would be needed, along the lines of the one originally planned for
Bergen in 1939 but abandoned owing to the outbreak of war.[1] With the
increasing competition for Antarctic territory Australia, New Zealand,
France and Norway had all laid claims to a chunk of the continent. In
addition the UK and Argentina were squabbling over essentially the
same patch, overlapping to a large extent with a claim by Chile. Roberts'
boss Arnold Toynbee invited James Brierly of Oxford University to
visit the Foreign Office Research Department weekly to provide advice
on problems related to international law. Brierly was intrigued by the
Antarctic problem, and he and Roberts spent many hours grappling
with ideas for the political future of the continent.[2]

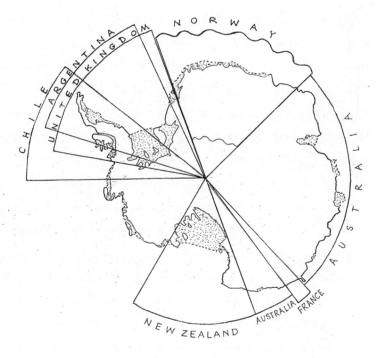

Claims to Antarctica

THE MEANING OF 'INTERNATIONALISATION'

Ever since the beginning of the 20th century there had been proposals by various groups and individuals for internationalisation of the Antarctic.[3] From WWII onwards they usually took the form of a United Nations trusteeship, but this idea was repeatedly dismissed by the UK Foreign and Colonial Offices. To them the proposal was a source of irritation with the potential for unwanted publicity that could easily derail their own efforts at achieving a confidentially negotiated multilateral agreement based on concepts explored by Roberts and Brierly. They wanted to establish an independent supranational authority for the Antarctic, constituted exclusively from those states that had a proven interest and investment in the region. This was politically sensitive, and the need for secrecy was paramount.[4]

Consequently, when in 1948 the US State Department approached the UK Embassy in Washington with a plan for international administration of the whole Antarctic continent under UN trusteeship, the response was cool, particularly when the plan got leaked to the press.[5] The

State Department then came back with an alternative proposal for a condominium in which the seven Antarctic claimant states might pool their claims in a scheme of joint sovereignty together with the US. Articles 3–5 of the US Draft Agreement provided for the creation of an Antarctic Commission with full administrative powers, one member per country. This idea would be taken up and considerably expanded by the Foreign Office in due course.

In the event the condominium proposal fared little better than the UN trusteeship idea and was not generally welcomed by the Antarctic claimant states. However Roberts felt that a condominium, despite its cumbersome nature, represented the best hope of achieving a solution to the Antarctic problem.[6] In spite of the unfavourable initial reactions he hoped that at least some of the Antarctic claimant states such as France could be progressively won over by UK leadership. So alarmed by this possibility were the Chileans, who were unequivocally hostile to the idea, that they approached the French Foreign Ministry in an attempt to make them suspicious of British motives.[7] The Chileans' distaste for a condominium was likely to have originated in their own historical experience of border disputes in the Atacama Desert.[8] In their view a condominium solved nothing and would create further problems worse than those that the treaty was intended to settle.

By November 1948 it had become clear that only the UK and New Zealand were in favour of the State Department's initiative, and it ground to a halt. The Argentine Foreign Minister Jan Artilio Bramuglia objected that he could not begin to contemplate the surrender of Argentine sovereignty rights in the absence of any proposal to hold a conference. The UK's formal positive response to the US did reveal some shift in its policy over the Antarctic – even described as a 'U-turn'[9] – but it would take many years of lobbying by Roberts for that policy to achieve any coherence.

ARGENTINE TANGO

Partly for reasons of economy and partly because they (wrongly) believed that threats to UK sovereignty in the Antarctic were diminishing, the Colonial Office proposed in 1950 to reduce the number of bases in the Falkland Islands Dependencies from seven to four, none of which would be on the mainland of Antarctica.[10] The Foreign Office viewed this intention disparagingly. Roberts complained that ever since the Colonial Office and the Falkland Islands Governor had assumed joint responsibility for FIDS it had suffered from chaotic administration, poor communications, wastage, inadequate facilities, shortage of trained staff and low morale in the field.[11] In short, the UK could not afford to economize on its presence in the Antarctic; any UK presence at all needed efficient management, more secure funding and a focused sense of purpose.

The Colonial Office's assessment had been way off the mark. Whilst the US and Chile were negotiating a renewable five-year standstill agreement devised by the Chilean Professor Julio Escudero,[12] Argentina and Britain were raising the stakes by expansion of their respective Antarctic programmes. Despite an Anglo-Argentine-Chilean tripartite naval agreement, tensions increased during 1952–53 and surfaced with potentially serious incidents at Hope Bay and Deception Island.[13] The UK government was sufficiently concerned as to set up a Ministerial Committee on Antarctica towards the end of 1954. Moreover Argentina had gained a significant edge over the UK by acquiring the icebreaker *General San Martín*, sending the vessel to the east coast of the Weddell Sea and constructing Base Belgrano, which opened early in 1955. News of this provoked an immediate reaction from Roberts.[14] He complained that the "watertight" Chinese walls between the various Whitehall offices were preventing the UK from formulating a coherent Antarctic policy in the face of increasing threats to which Whitehall was seemingly oblivious: not only from Argentina and Chile, but also potentially from the US and the USSR.[15] It was an age-old Whitehall problem; the Foreign Office's Evelyn Shuckburgh had made the same complaint five years earlier.[16]

DEADLOCK AT THE FOREIGN OFFICE

To Roberts the situation had become a matter of urgency, but the response from Morgan Man, recently appointed head of the Foreign Office American Department, was discouraging: "Pending the high level agonizing reappraisal of the UK Antarctic policy I do not think we can usefully do anything at present." Man nonetheless circulated a draft Cabinet paper that incorporated much of Roberts' own advice,[17] despite his apprehensiveness of causing interdepartmental fireworks at Cabinet level. The more combative Roberts might well have relished such a prospect. In March 1955, frustrated at the perennial impossibility of getting any proposal on UK Antarctic policy through the Foreign Office, the Colonial Office, the Commonwealth Relations Office, the Governor of the Falkland Islands, the Admiralty, the Joint Chiefs of Staff and the Cabinet, Roberts submitted three papers for consideration by the ministerial committee on Antarctica at its next meeting at the Cabinet Office. One of the proposals was for the wholesale reorganisation of FIDS, an issue that he had himself raised five years previously.[18] He pointed out that Australia, France and Norway had all set up specialist Antarctic departments to deal with its administration, research and politics under a single authority and it was time that the UK did the same. Man warned Roberts that his proposal to reorganise FIDS was 'dynamite' and that open criticism of the Colonial Office would get them nowhere.[19] None of Roberts' papers was put to the ministerial committee on Antarctica.

When an attempt was made by the UK Cabinet to resolve the dispute with Argentina and Chile over the Antarctic by offering arbitration, both countries declined. The UK responded with a unilateral application to the International Court of Justice, claiming trespass by the two adversaries. The proceedings, prepared by Humphrey Waldock of Oxford and Foreign Office legal adviser Gerald Fitzmaurice, with substantial factual input from Roberts, were filed with the Court on 4 May 1955. In August that year Argentina and Chile declined to accept the Court's ruling and the case was finally removed from the ICJ list in March 1956.[20]

Meanwhile an alternative proposal was being mooted at the highest level of government: that the UK should withdraw from the Antarctic, which was dismissed in some quarters as "worthless wastes".[21] The prospect of UK withdrawal would rear its head on several occasions over the next few years.[22] Despite this, in August 1955 the Cabinet officially approved a new five-year programme for FIDS. Forcible eviction of trespassers from the FID was being recommended by the Foreign Office legal advisers, demanded by the House of Commons and even contemplated by some Foreign Office diplomats.[23] In the words of Foreign Secretary Harold Macmillan: "I hope we may be able to get tough."[24] Prospects for a negotiated settlement seemed more remote than ever.

However, during the following month a significant political shift was created by a military coup in Argentina that resulted in the ousting of President Juan Perón. which seems to have delighted the occupants of the Argentine Antarctic bases.[25] On 24 October a Parliamentary

Question was raised, asking the Foreign Secretary to make a statement on the Antarctic dispute in the light of the new Argentine situation. The debate was deferred to 7 November, but on that day the almost full House of Commons had other things on its mind and the question was brushed aside. The Commons then settled down to a 7-hour debate on the missing Foreign Office diplomats Burgess and Maclean.[26]

Roberts also had many things on his mind, and circulated a robust strategic appraisal of the British position:

"(1) Rejection of the use of force really means that we have accepted the principle of negotiated partition; if we do not take a tough line we cannot hope to hold the whole of the Falkland Islands Dependencies.

(2) Since we cannot secure a legal settlement, and we are not prepared to use force, we should plan now for a political settlement. Every year this becomes more difficult. By 1958 our Antarctic activities will appear relatively insignificant.

(3) We should start planning our retreat at once to retain as much as possible of the Antarctic territory with the minimum loss of prestige. Whitehall, especially the Colonial Office, seems unaware of the dangers to the British claim. The Foreign Office should circulate a considered paper reviewing the whole position.

(4) We appear to be following two incompatible policies: the need to reduce our overseas commitments, and the arousing of public interest (for example via the Commonwealth Trans-Antarctic Expedition) that will result in political pressure to exert forceful action to defend our sovereignty.

(5) UK support for the International Geophysical Year has been unavoidable but is politically inconvenient, and is likely to continue to be a major embarrassment until 1959.

(6) Unless we continue to aim specifically for retention of the whole territory, or partition by negotiation, our position must continue to deteriorate rapidly.

(7) If we believe that an international Antarctic conference is unavoidable, the UK should initiate one as soon as possible, preferably by 1956.

(8)   We cannot initiate such a conference unless we are prepared to make substantial territorial concessions, which the Colonial Office has never seriously considered; it may be the only way to get Whitehall to adopt a more realistic approach.

(9)   We cannot possibly keep the US and the USSR out of the Antarctic, so we should not incur the odium of appearing to do so.

(10)   Any agreement should allow common access to Deception Island by the UK, Argentina and Chile.

(11)   Loss of our position in the Falkland Islands Dependencies will open the door to more serious trouble over the Falkland Islands themselves."[27]

This time Roberts' paper provoked heated debate amongst his colleagues in the American Department, which at least looked like some advance in his ability to influence Foreign Office policy. But once again there was a damp squib response from Morgan Man: "I agree with much of this but I do not think that the time is yet ripe for a Foreign Office paper... I do not think that it is practicable for HMG to take the initiative now in order to bring about a formal settlement."[28] In a lengthy memorandum on Antarctica the American Department arrived at some singularly anodyne conclusions: "(1) It is in the UK interest to promote a close understanding with the Americans in the Antarctic, modifying its own claims if necessary (2) But it should aim at postponing any reconsideration until the 5-year plan has made further progress (3) Meanwhile the UK should make unofficial soundings of the new Argentine Government (4) UK should refrain from forcible action against Argentina and Chile (5) The tripartite naval declaration should be renewed (6) UK should seek closer cooperation with the Americans."[29]

In other words, do nothing.

AN ANGLO-SOVIET *ENTENTE CORDIALE*

For British diplomacy the year 1956 was notable for a thawing in relations with the Soviet Union – including a goodwill visit to the UK by First Secretary Khrushchev and Soviet Premier Bulganin – and a concomitant deterioration in relations with the US, that extended to Antarctic affairs and was manifested by a growing suspicion of US intentions regarding the continent.[30]

In April 1956, concurrently with the Soviet state visit, two academicians from the Leningrad Arctic Institute visited Cambridge as guests of SPRI. Despite Terence Armstrong's ability as a fluent Russian speaker to oil the wheels, it was not an easy occasion. The Russian visitors showed little or no interest in SPRI, and attempting to entertain them for nine days with visits to London and Liverpool was onerous, not helped by unappetising meals in dingy Midland hotels en route. The contrast with the lavish Russian hospitality that Roberts and Armstrong would experience on their 10-day return visit to Leningrad and Moscow two months later was to be almost embarrassing.[31] They were plied with huge quantities of food and drink, breakfast consisting typically of four courses of caviar, fish, meats and wine. Evening meals, involving up to 24 guests and lasting over three hours, were similar except that the number of courses was closer to 30.

In Moscow Roberts got drawn into political discussions with the head of the Northern Sea Route Directorate which, being present as a representative of SPRI and not the Foreign Office, he was not strictly authorised to engage in.[32] He ascertained that the Soviet motive for Antarctic involvement was a broad directive to make a conspicuous contribution to the International Geophysical Year. Whilst they clearly intended to maintain a sizeable indefinite presence in both the Arctic and Antarctic, the Soviets seemed to be completely open to exchanges of scientific information and facilities in the polar regions. This was remarkable in the context of the Cold War, then at its zenith. Between 1955 and 1962 the US and the USSR both amassed colossal stockpiles of nuclear weapons, increasing from around 2,000 to 25,000 and sufficient to wipe out all life on the planet many times over. It would take only one incident at one of the numerous potential flashpoints around the globe – Berlin being just one of many – to bring the Armageddon clock to less than one minute to midnight. In this febrile atmosphere any talk in the West of international governance of the Antarctic uncompromisingly excluded the USSR. The Soviets had other ideas.

The final banquet on Roberts and Armstrong's exhausting visit was followed by an obligatory tour of the All-Union Agricultural Exhibition. Escaping from the huge banquets and the long lines of tractors, the two

English guests were finally escorted to the airport for their return flight via Helsinki. On the way Armstrong called in at the Finnish shipyard Värtsilä-Koncernen with a view to purchasing an icebreaker for FIDS, but the order would have to wait for official UK approval. It was eventually granted, 60 years later in 2014, when the British Antarctic Survey was authorised to order the RRS *Sir David Attenborough* from the Cammell Laird shipyard.

While confusion continued to reign in Whitehall on what the UK should do about the Antarctic. there were rumblings elsewhere. A development that was particularly unwelcome to most of the Antarctic claimant states – notably the UK, Argentina and Chile, who for once found themselves on the same side – was the request by the Indian government for an item 'The Question of Antarctica' to be placed on the agenda of the 11th Session of the UN General Assembly. It was tacitly supported by the USSR. The Foreign Office was totally against this proposal: UN trusteeship had already been dismissed in 1948, the UN was suspected of collective anti-colonialist sentiments, and its involvement would inevitably result in unwanted publicity.[33] But ironically the Indian initiative may have contributed in its own way towards the evolution of a treaty by focusing the minds of the claimant states on what might happen if they failed to achieve agreement amongst themselves.[34]

A NEW MAN AT THE HELM

At the end of August 1956 Morgan Man was redeployed to a posting in the Middle East, to be replaced as head of American Department by Henry Hankey. Hankey, a man with long interest in and experience of the Americas, had been Head of Chancery at the UK embassy in Santiago, and would later on play a major role in the Cuba missile crisis of 1961-62. During World War II he had pursued a colourful diplomatic career at the UK embassy in Madrid, entailing a good deal of chicanery against pro-Franco elements. Collaborating covertly with MI9 he transported UK escapers and evaders around Spain and into Gibraltar, concealing them in his car boot in order to cross the frontier.[35]

Hankey's arrival at the Foreign Office American desk coincided with a sea change in Antarctic policy. There was no more talk of encroachments on sovereign territory, judicial proceedings, protests to Argentina and Chile, or advocacy of forcible action. All discussion was to be on the negotiation of a political settlement. Hankey attempted to persuade

Charles Empson, his successor at the Santiago embassy, to approach the Chilean authorities informally over the Antarctic dispute.[36] But with the imminent crisis over the Suez Canal, that was to prove over-optimistic. The mood in the Foreign Office American Department was sombre. Its reputation, already sullied by its harbouring of one of the country's most notorious traitors, was at rock bottom: as indeed were Anglo-American relations, a matter that greatly perturbed Hankey.[37]

Roberts, who for years had needed for his cause a champion with a sufficiently high level of authority and commitment, seized his chance. Two Foreign Office eye-witnesses, resident clerk Richard Parsons and assistant legal advisor John Freeland, were impressed by the teamwork of Hankey and Roberts.[38] "Shortly after Donald Maclean had been head, it had been necessary to say that the American Department was really peripheral or unimportant, which of course it wasn't," commented Parsons.[39] His testimony is supported by Foreign Secretary Macmillan's statement to the House of Commons during the 7 November debate on Burgess and Maclean.[40] Parsons added: "Owing to the Maclean fiasco the American Department was deeply embarrassed. Hankey wanted to do something big, to restore the department's prestige."[41]

During the 1970s Hugh Carless, then head of the Foreign Office's Latin American department, recalled that "Hankey was a leading player in the Antarctic Treaty negotiations and much of the credit for the treaty must go to him".[42] This was recorded by Roberts himself: "1957–59. Main activity preparing for 12-nation Antarctic Conference in Washington which signed the Antarctic Treaty. The idea of this Treaty originated in the Foreign Office; not the State Department as is often claimed, and owed a great deal to Mr Hankey, who was then head of American Department."[43] And in Roberts' own curriculum vitae there appears the entry: "1959. October 12 – December 1. Visit to Washington for 12-power Antarctic Conference as member of UK Delegation to negotiate Antarctic Treaty signed on December 1. Preparations for this have been a major activity in co-operation with Henry Hankey (especially) and many others. We did in fact initiate the whole idea, despite later American claims to the contrary."[44] Roberts had wanted the Antarctic conference to be hosted in London, but he conceded that Argentina and Chile would probably refuse to attend. The US was in a far stronger position than the UK to host the conference.[45] On being proposed in 1965 for a non-stipendiary fellowship of Churchill College, Cambridge, Roberts expressed doubt that he could find the time to fulfil college duties: "The 12-nation Antarctic Treaty of 1959 was in many respects a special 'baby' of mine, and I must continue to nurture it... These problems absorb almost all my time. I cannot at present take on any more administrative responsibilities."[46]

THE CHATHAM HOUSE PARTY

The Antarctic question acquired further impetus at the end of 1956 from an eclectic discussion group set up at the Royal Institute of International Affairs, Chatham House, to examine the loss of the UK's leading position in the Antarctic in the context of IGY activities. At a first meeting, chairman Colin Bertram analysed the motives for the increasing competition by other nations over the Antarctic.[47] A second meeting at Chatham House considered ideas for international governance of the Antarctic. It was chaired by the physicist Patrick Blackett and attended by 48 people, including Ivor Vincent and Roberts as representatives of the Foreign Office and SPRI respectively.[48] Vincent was disenchanted and sceptical of the value of the exercise, mainly on account of the entrenched positions taken by certain speakers, in particular the 'World Government' lobby.[49] In contrast Roberts commented half a year later in a letter to Bertram that the meeting had played a major part in winning over the upper echelons of the Colonial and Foreign Offices to an Antarctic settlement and that "we have made big strides in the past five months".[50] Such big strides in fact, that in April 1957 Charles Empson at the Santiago Embassy protested to the Foreign Office that nobody had told him what was going on, asking how he could be expected to represent UK policy if he did not know what it was, and how was it that strategic matters had been discussed not with the Foreign Service but unofficially at Chatham House under a chairman who at one time had been considered a security risk owing to his Fabian political views?[51] In response the evolving Foreign Office policy was explained to Empson by Sammy Hood,[52] a senior official who had originally favoured complete UK withdrawal from the Antarctic until a review by the Chiefs of Staff gave that option a categorical 'no'. Hood would later on become the UK's chief negotiator at the ambassadors' meetings in Washington prior to the Antarctic conference. Ironically he had himself been investigated as a possible security risk under the Foreign Office's positive vetting procedure introduced in the wake of the Burgess and Maclean debacle.[53]

UNPRECEDENTED DYNAMISM
AT THE FOREIGN OFFICE

At the end of 1956 the UK Embassy in Buenos Aires notified Hankey that the British Naval Attaché had been approached by the Argentine Chief of Staff and by the Head of the Argentine Antarctic Institute, Rear-Admiral Rodolfo Panzarini,[54] signalling that they wanted to discuss the Anglo-Argentine dispute and were confident of reaching an agreement. The initiative was likely to have been prompted by another change in the political situation within Argentina.[55] Panzarini was perhaps best known for a rather intemperate political outburst during the 1956 IGY meeting in Paris, from which he had to be diplomatically extracted,[56] but he was popular with the British and would later develop a warm friendship with Roberts.[57]

In February 1957 Hankey requested a reappraisal by the Chiefs of Staff of the strategic value of the Antarctic to the UK. The response was that withdrawal from the Antarctic was not a remotely acceptable option. This was crucial for Roberts: had the decision gone the other way Hankey would not have been in a position to put forward UK proposals for international administration of the Antarctic.[58] In addition Whitehall was concerned about the heavy involvement of the US and the USSR in the IGY and the inability to predict what would happen at the end of it.[59] It was in this sense only that the IGY can be said to have had a causal or catalytic effect on the creation of the Antarctic Treaty.

To formulate specific proposals Hankey now needed the input of the Foreign Office legal department. Antarctic matters were reserved to head legal adviser Gerald Fitzmaurice, who asked his assistant John Freeland to draft a skeletal Antarctic treaty.[60] Fitzmaurice was impressed by this first effort and within 24 hours elaborated it into a comprehensive proposal. It provided for the establishment of a multinational administrative council for the Antarctic with its own bureaucratic and legal structures, including a police force.

Not wishing to be outsmarted by the Foreign Office, the Colonial Office's Under-Secretary Philip Rogers produced his own proposal for internationalisation of the Antarctic.[61] Rogers, who was also chairman of the ministerial committee on Antarctica, admitted that to his "imperialist sentiment" the internationalisation of British territory was not entirely agreeable, but it was less disagreeable than being "squeezed out". Despite his aversion to the idea, Rogers was keen enough to claim "equal rights of discovery or invention", as though the treaty were somehow patentable. By September 1957 a Foreign Office-Colonial Office Note had been jointly drafted by Hankey and Maurice Willis for consideration at a meeting with Commonwealth representatives.[62] Of all the options analysed, it recommended the setting up of an 'International Authority for the Antarctic without sovereignty in name'. Some contentious issues remained, one concerning the parties to be involved in the proposed international authority. The Foreign Office was now recommending that the USSR be included, not excluded. Legal advisor John Freeland explained the other main innovation in the UK draft proposal, namely the presence of a reversionary clause.[63] A condominium, as originally proposed by the State Department, is generally understood to be an indefinite pooling of sovereign rights. In contrast the UK proposal stated explicitly the retention of pre-existing claimed sovereign rights by participating states in the event of a breakdown of the treaty: arguably an uncomfortable compromise, but a necessary one if the southern hemisphere states Australia, Argentina and Chile were to be kept on board. It would end up – in a mutated form – as the celebrated Article IV of the treaty that was eventually signed in Washington.

After a long period of Antarctic hibernation, the State Department suddenly woke up to realise that London was seizing the initiative. Secretary of State John Foster Dulles, responding positively to a Foreign Office proposal for a US-UK-Australia-New Zealand quadripartite meeting, appointed former ambassador Paul Daniels to advise on Antarctic matters and represent the US.[64] There was another incident that helped to focus American minds: not an Antarctic event, but nonetheless one associated with IGY. It was the launch of Sputnik I, the world's first artificial satellite. The Soviets were leading in the space race.

On 7 October 1957 – three days after the launch of Sputnik – Daniels convened the first quadripartite meeting in Room 5104 of the Department of State in Washington. The finalised Foreign Office proposal for internationalisation of the Antarctic, dated 3 October, was circulated as a working paper.[65] During November UK legal advisers Fitzmaurice and Freeland drafted a Convention and Constitution based on the Foreign Office vision of a High Authority for the Antarctic, including a two-tier membership scheme that would prove to be controversial.[66] But it was Ambassador Daniels, already arranging further meetings in Washington, who was now in the driver's seat.

In December Daniels wrote to Dulles, proposing a treaty – then referred to as a 'statute' – to be drafted at an international conference. By this time Daniels was himself converted to favour the inclusion of the USSR.[67] However the Australian Cabinet was not only resolutely against the 'surrender' of Australian sovereignty,[68] but also opposing any internationalisation of the Antarctic if Japan and the USSR were to be included.[69] After all the efforts at persuading the US to accept Soviet participation, such an intransigent position was a setback, but it was not entirely unexpected owing to the breaking off of Soviet-Australian diplomatic relations following the 1954 defection of Vladimir Petrov and the unilateral occupation of Australian Antarctic territory by Soviet bases during IGY. This setback would by no means be the last: the wrangling would continue for more than 18 months at the 60 confidential ambassadors' meetings convened by the State Department, at which states with tangible interest in the Antarctic were represented.[70] For one thing, the UK proposal for rigorous international control by an Antarctic Commission would receive a hostile response from the southern hemisphere.[71] During this long gestation period, with voluminous diplomatic traffic between the UK embassy in Washington and Hankey at the Foreign Office, Roberts remained behind the scenes. All that was to change at the Washington Conference of October-December 1959. Roberts was about to be thrust into the forefront of international diplomacy.

15

THE HISTORIC
ANTARCTIC CONFERENCE
IN WASHINGTON

Brian used to tell me that he had conceived the idea of the Antarctic
Treaty while seated one evening in the Plaza Gomila.

Toni Martorell[1]

Did Roberts really have a 'eureka moment' and find a solution to the
Antarctic problem while relaxing over a dry Martini cocktail in a
Palma square? Quite possibly...

Roberts' first holiday in Mallorca was in September 1955. At the
time of his second, one year later, Henry Hankey had just been installed
at the Foreign Office American Department and the treaty was a hot
topic. But what Roberts meant by "the idea of the Antarctic Treaty"
was the concept of a multilateral High Authority for the Antarctic, a
seemingly innocuous proposal, but audacious enough to stimulate the
Foreign Office into dynamic activity and also to encounter considerable
resistance from other Antarctic claimant states.

Two years later, in August 1959, Roberts and Martorell first met
in Mallorca, and the Washington conference was imminent. The stage
was set for what would be either the fulfilment of Roberts' dream or a
disappointing anticlimax. With Hankey's influence Whitehall had been
won over, but it had taken nearly two years of international wrangling

and 60 secret ambassadors' meetings to agree even the terms of reference of an Antarctic conference, let alone the draft text of a treaty.[2] And signing of the treaty was far from being a foregone conclusion.

The first crisis emerged even before the conference opened. The French delegation announced that they had been instructed not to accept the clause relating to the suspension of territorial sovereignty claims. For the UK this Article IV was a cornerstone of the treaty and had been substantially agreed between the UK Foreign Office and the Quai d'Orsay (the French Foreign Ministry). Why had the French waited till the eleventh hour to dispute this? Later on during the conference the respective chief legal advisers André Gros and Gerald Fitzmaurice had to be summoned to Washington to slug it out.

THE BRITISH DELEGATION

Befitting the importance of the occasion, the UK fielded a strong team: Sir Esler Dening as head of delegation, Viscount 'Sammy' Hood and Derek Benest from the UK Embassy in Washington, Maurice Willis from the Colonial Office, and several from the Foreign Office in London: Norman Brain, Henry Hankey, Richard Parsons, John Freeland and Roberts himself.

On Thursday 8 October 1959 an advance party consisting of Dening and Parsons set out for Washington. It was an inauspicious start for both of them. While Roberts was fulsome in his praise for Dening's negotiating skills, Parsons' opinion of Dening was less charitable: "a gloomy bad-tempered bachelor", who blamed Parsons for everything that went wrong, including their failure to gain entry to a first-class departure lounge at Heathrow airport. Nor was their arrival in America congenial. Due to a forced landing Parsons and Dening became marooned together for 48 hours in Goose Bay, Labrador, described by Parsons as "a ghastly place".[3]

Parsons and Hankey were the jokers in the pack. For the UK delegation the gruelling weeks of negotiations were to be lightened by Hankey's portrait sketches of the various international delegates and by Parsons' comic verse.

A Chilean observer at the South Pole
Found himself in a dreadful hole
With the temperature well below zero

He cursed Professor Escudero
For having failed to secure him the right
To an outward as well as an inward flight.

The Chilean professor Julio Escudero had already achieved renown in Antarctic political circles for the 'Escudero plan', but Parsons was unable to take his legal hair-splitting seriously.

Willis and Freeland had, together with Hankey, contributed to the drafting of the UK's treaty proposals, but Willis' contribution to the conference was undistinguished. Bored and mystified by diplomatic tactics, and unable to stay awake during social occasions, he returned early to London, clutching his report to the Colonial Office that Roberts and Parsons had had to concoct for him.

What role did Roberts himself play? One of his main functions was to check that the drafts actually made sense. Legal adviser Freeland thought that Roberts deserved much credit for the drafting owing to his all too rare ability to explain each Article's intentions clearly and concisely.[4] There were also inevitable problems of terminology and language. The geographical extent of the treaty's zone of application could only be resolved once the term 'ice shelf' had been correctly translated. The French wanted to use the inaccurate and misleading term *banquise* (sea ice); and the Argentines and Chileans, who were still using the word *barrera*, seemed not to understand the meaning of 'ice shelf'. Roberts' battle with James Wordie over ice terminology (Chapter 12) had returned to haunt him once again.

ANTARCTIC OR ANTARCTICA?

Another terminological can of worms opened up when the drafting committee had to decide between 'Antarctica' and 'the Antarctic' in naming the treaty. Roberts explained that 'Antarctica' was restricted to the continent, admittedly ambiguous as to whether that included ice shelves and fast ice. The 'Antarctic' referred to a much larger region with a northern boundary at the Antarctic Convergence. Most heads of delegation were content with the name 'Antarctic Treaty'. Australian External Affairs Minister Casey had a different reason for preferring 'Antarctic', admitting privately to Roberts that he had difficulty pronouncing the word 'Antarctica' in his speeches.

But the US wanted the name 'Antarctica Treaty'. Conference chairman Herman Phleger thumped the table, insisting that they had been invited by US President Eisenhower to discuss 'Antarctica', not 'the Antarctic'. That, in his opinion, settled the matter. Paul Daniels, the drafting committee chairman, prevented any discussion of the geographical distinction, and adamantly insisted on the US position. He was asked by Roberts to consult the US Board of Geographical Names, but refused to do so. In the end, when the drafting committee pointed out that the text of the treaty would have to be entirely redrafted to conform to the title, there was a reluctant consensus and the 'Antarctic Treaty' entered into history.

NOTABLE – AND NOT SO NOTABLE – INTERNATIONAL DELEGATES

Of the one hundred delegates present, only four had ever visited the Antarctic, one of them Roberts himself. Most others were politicians or career diplomats. Walter Nash, Prime Minister of New Zealand, who had always favoured UN administration for the Antarctic, was expected to cause trouble during his brief attendance, and did so. 'Dick' Casey, Australian External Affairs Minister, was another short-term attendee whose early departure was a relief to the rest of his national delegation.[5] Parsons cheerfully admitted that he had a difficult relationship with Casey. At their first meeting the 6'4" Casey greeted the short-statured Parsons in a not entirely friendly voice by saying: "I remember you!" A couple of years earlier Casey had visited the UK embassy in Vientiane, Laos where Parsons was posted (possibly as a symbolic downgrading from Washington following his inadvertent trapping of Foreign Secretary Selwyn Lloyd's fingers in a car door). At the entrance to the embassy Parsons ushered Casey through a spring-loaded barrier which he then carelessly let go of, with the result that the barrier swung back and struck Casey painfully in the crotch.

The outstanding negotiator of the Soviet delegation was their second man Grigory Tunkin. During the later weeks of the conference he was to become a formidable adversary in an elaborate game of chess played out between East and West, with the southern hemisphere states as the pawns.

At the start the Argentine head of delegation, Adolfo Scilingo, was frequently obstructive, but as time went on he became rather more amenable to compromise and ended up with considerable personal credit. The Chilean head of delegation was formally Marcial Mora, but his contributions were frequently repeated by his two colleagues Julio Escudero and Enrique Gajardo. Like Cerberus, the three of them would all feel the need to make a speech, a scene that might have been seen as grotesquely comic but for their alienation of everyone else by going on at insufferable length about Chilean sovereignty.

On the evening before the official opening, the UK delegation met the Washington working group that had been preparing for the conference over the previous 18 months. The one member of the group to whom Roberts took an instant and visceral dislike was US ambassador Paul Daniels, described variously as arrogant, drunk, partial, muddle-headed and incompetent.[6] Roberts emphasised that his diary of the event was personal and not to be treated as an unbiased account,[7] but the Foreign Office was itself disparaging of the US ambassador, particularly over his perceived bias in favour of the Latin Americans.[8] Partly due to Daniels' inept chairmanship, the drafting committee became increasingly exhausted, frustrated and bad tempered. It took them three days to coordinate the texts in the four official conference languages – English, French, Spanish and Russian – for the treaty's Article IV, just 12 lines of text.

THE GRAND OPENING

On Thursday 15 October the conference opened in the auditorium of the Department of the Interior. "With gay tea-time music, bright lights and a background of potted palm trees and the flags of the 12 nations, it seemed more like prelude to a theatre than the opening of an International Conference," observed Roberts.[9] The 12 heads of delegation entered the auditorium one by one, Dening's entry accompanied by Tudor dance music. Each national delegation made opening statements, the Soviets' being noticeably brief and cordial. The Argentines and Chileans predictably emphasised their opposition to any formula involving relinquishment of their sovereignty. "Yes, we know all that and it is why we put in Article IV," Roberts muttered to himself irritably.

After some hours of nit-picking, the Rules of Procedure, expected to cause real trouble, were finally agreed. The Latin Americans made a last-ditch attempt to avoid signing a treaty by lobbying for the word 'treaty' to be omitted from the final conference document. That cut no ice with the other delegations, all of whom, with barely concealed irritation, pointed out that this was precisely what they had all come to Washington for.[10] By then thoroughly unpopular with the other delegations, the Argentines and Chileans were forced to concede. Such are the ways and means of international diplomacy.

For the UK delegation, each day started with a private meeting on tactics, followed by a morning Committee I on legal and political matters, an afternoon Committee II on scientific and administrative topics, and an evening cocktail party and dinner. It was a relentless daily routine, but at least the conference would soon be over; or so it was thought at the time.

MUSHROOM CLOUD ON THE HORIZON

It was during the first full week of negotiations that the real obstacles started to surface. Scilingo, the Argentine representative, was adamantly opposed to Article II regarding freedom of scientific investigation, on the grounds that it gave unlimited freedom to the Soviets to do what they liked in the Antarctic and was therefore impossible to defend before Argentine public opinion. Daniels had many times pointed out to the Latin Americans that the Soviets – and for that matter the US – would do whatever they wanted to in the Antarctic. To the Soviets, freedom of scientific investigation was a cornerstone of the treaty. The Argentines tried to get Dening to agree to a fudged and meaningless compromise. On being rebuffed Scilingo retorted "then there will be no Treaty".

But, little by little, progress was made. Article III on scientific cooperation was uncontroversial and was provisionally agreed. Article I on the peaceful use of Antarctica should also have been straightforward, but the US objected that an implicit ban on military manoeuvres would compromise the 'freedom of the high seas', a tiresome issue that would recur frequently.

There was another problem. Scilingo wished to add the following clause: "Nuclear tests and explosions of any type, regardless of their character and purpose, shall be prohibited." He recognised that the Soviet proposal covered nuclear weapon tests, but was now arguing that all nuclear explosions, including 'peaceful' non-military ones, should be explicitly prohibited due to radiation dangers. This was to become a thorny issue later on. To Roberts it was classic stupidity to introduce a completely new subject into a conference agenda without previous discussion and briefing. It had not been raised during any of the 60 preparatory meetings convened by Daniels. To the US delegation, the Argentine proposal to ban all nuclear explosions did not fall within the conference terms of reference as outlined in the US invitation and might "dangerously limit scientific enquiry". The ban on nuclear weapons in the Antarctic was not remotely controversial and the question of 'peaceful nuclear work' was a matter for a forthcoming Geneva conference. But the southern hemisphere states all expressed deep concerns over radioactive fallout and were not prepared to be tossed aside by the 'northerners'. Finally it was agreed that 'peaceful' nuclear tests could be covered separately and the drafting committee was able to agree Article I. But that would not be the last of the matter.

During the second week, jurisdiction proved to be a predictably tricky subject. The French raised endless legal objections: the Argentines and Chileans continued interminably to argue about their sovereignty. On the topic of observers and inspection to ensure compliance with the treaty's principles, there was to Roberts' dismay widespread and vigorous opposition to his idea of an international control commission for the Antarctic. He was already becoming over-tired, and there was little respite for him at the weekend except for a quiet Sunday afternoon at the Smithsonian Institute.

Towards the end of the second week the US hosts attempted to turn the screws on the more recalcitrant participants, with the aim of having the treaty in the bag the following week. In an attempt to curtail extraneous speech making, the Friday afternoon committee was replaced by an unminuted meeting of the heads of delegation. But the Chileans continued to make speeches, apparently addressed more to the Chilean government than to the conference. When Hankey pointed out that they were wasting everybody's time because no formal record was being kept, he was roundly reprimanded by chairman Phleger for saying so.

There was however progress when the Argentines agreed to a South African draft of Article II on freedom of scientific investigation. Some advance was even made on Article XIII, the contentious issue of accession of new parties to the treaty, and by the following Monday, 2 November, it seemed as though agreement on a treaty might be reached by the Friday. That night Roberts wrote a postcard to his brother Denis complaining about the interminable debates and his lack of sleep, but confident that "a satisfactory end is in sight – perhaps by the middle of next week". But that would turn out to be greatly over-optimistic.

MID-TERM BLUES

During the third week the conference got bogged down on an Australian-Argentine redraft of Article V dealing with non-military nuclear devices. Senator Mora made a passionate appeal to save the Chilean flowers, vegetables and children – in that order – from radioactive fall-out, and was unable or unwilling to distinguish between testing of weapons and peaceful use of nuclear energy. The Soviets were suspected of attempting to wreck the treaty by splitting the Western parties on the issue. By this time Roberts was becoming seriously fatigued and under considerable strain. Due to the oppressive heat and lack of fresh air he would wake up in the middle of the night in his stuffy hotel room, confronted by a kaleidoscopic mirage of faces, languages and contradictory draft legal clauses on accession, jurisdiction and inspection:

"I must remember that we want to dispose of 'radioactive waste' in Antarctica, not 'fissionable material' as in the present draft.... The High Contracting Parties agree that they will not for their part, either individually or collectively, assist or countenance, either directly or indirectly, any action, activity, or claim ... Any or all of the rights established in the Treaty may be exercised (I cannot for the moment remember any rights established except inspection)... The drafting of this Article has been referred to the Drafting Committee... What exactly was the point of substance left unresolved in Article V?... The Charter of the United Nations...The interests of all mankind... Thank God Mr Nash has gone. What is the best French and Spanish translation for ice shelves?... The substantial contributions to scientific knowledge resulting from international cooperation during the IGY... (surely such platitudes can only be relegated to the Preamble, the resting place of all vague aspirations?). What exactly was it that was agreed last week about the exchange of scientific observations?... No acts or activities shall constitute a basis for asserting, supporting or denying a claim... What was the third New Zealand draft to paragraph 1 of Article VIII?... and so on, without pause. There are sudden glimpses in my dreams of lobbying at Embassy cocktail parties, ice shelves being destroyed by atomic bombs, unauthorised submarines stuck under some strand crack, exchange scientists being tried by foreign courts for unspecified acts of omission, teams of exhausted inspectors arriving unannounced at the most improbable of places and demanding food and lodging. I think of Senator Mora's emotional outbursts suddenly interrupted by nose-bleeding while his co-delegates continue his speech with hardly a break in the same translator's voice, and the barely-concealed delight of the members of other delegations. These are the kind of things I shall remember when all else is forgotten."[11]

During the day Roberts lobbied Dening on the nuclear testing issue, convinced that an outright ban would be unworkable in practice and incompatible with the freedom of scientific research stipulated by

Article II. This was ironic: Roberts had always had doubts about the International Geophysical Year and yet here he was expounding one of its sacred principles. He persuaded Dening that 'peaceful' nuclear detonations might be important for experiments on the earth's magnetic field, or for determining the thickness of the earth's crust. Accordingly the following day Dening addressed the conference, aiming to point out the illogicality of the Soviet position.

In response Tunkin, the Soviet representative, reiterated his main concern that nothing should inadvertently interfere with the use of the Antarctic solely for peaceful purposes, as expressed in Article I of the treaty. To him it was realistic to allow the peaceful use of nuclear energy, but if the majority at the conference thought otherwise he was prepared to accept an outright ban. In his view, allowing certain types of nuclear detonation was a potentially disastrous fudge and he could not understand how southern hemisphere countries could possibly agree to it. It would be extremely difficult to decide in practice what was meant by the loose wording 'devices of a non-military nature'. But Roberts and Dening continued doggedly to argue the point.

The fourth week got off to a sticky start. In Buenos Aires the Argentine navy had come out against signing the treaty and Scilingo now doubted that his government would accept Article II on freedom of scientific investigation. The Soviet delegation continued to maintain its reservations on the four unresolved issues. The French delegation now had instructions that the treaty was to be between Heads of States, not Heads of Government, which caused consternation for others whose government would not authorise signature on behalf of a Head of State. It was not a good week.

BRINKMANSHIP

During the fifth week agreement was at last reached on the difficult issue of jurisdiction, but there remained deadlock on two intractable issues: accession of new parties to the treaty, and fissionable materials. Scilingo said that he could sign the treaty if it contained a prohibition on nuclear explosions except by unanimous consent. This was agreeable to all except the Soviets. Tunkin now turned up the heat, stating that his government wanted the following text included: "Nuclear explosions and disposal of radioactive material in Antarctica shall be prohibited."

All efforts to find a compromise with Tunkin only stiffened his resolve, and it seemed that nothing would shift his stance. The lunch interval produced a sheaf of compromise drafts, all of which Tunkin brushed aside. In the afternoon he produced his own redraft, containing the additional proposal: "The present Article shall cease to be in effect if all the contracting parties to this Treaty... will become parties to a general international agreement which may be concluded in the future concerning the use of nuclear energy, including nuclear explosions and disposal of radioactive material." Tunkin's address was greeted by a stunned silence, interrupted only by the symbolic ticking of a clock. It was now feared that the Soviets' next move would be to jettison all articles on nuclear matters, knowing full well that this would be unacceptable to any of the southern hemisphere countries.

By the Monday most of the UK delegation had returned home, leaving only Freeland, Parsons and Roberts from the London contingent. It was to be another day of frustration: nobody could see how either the US or the Soviet Union could give way on the nuclear issue, and to everyone present the prospects of signing the treaty seemed to be vanishing before their eyes. Roberts was utterly miserable.

The next day produced an eleventh-hour U-turn. The US delegation, although still unconvinced by the Soviet arguments, decided to accept the articles on accession of new parties and on fissionable materials, solely for the sake of securing the treaty. After all the ups and downs, the treaty was now going to be signed.

Two days later Roberts spent Thanksgiving in Arlington, to be fed an enormous meal of turkey, cranberries and pumpkin pie. It had been six exhausting weeks in Washington. Being weary and with no wish to stay for the ceremony of signature, Roberts left on Friday 27 November. Still dressed in lightweight summer clothes, he travelled alone in snowy weather to spend two days in a bitterly cold and windy New York before returning home.

RATIFICATION OF THE TREATY

The Antarctic Treaty conference was in its way a sign of the 'winds of change' from the 1950s to the 1960s. During the six-week absence from his home country Roberts saw colour television for the first time, and he returned to find that the first motorway had been opened (the

M1, including Watford Gap Service Station). Britain would never be the same again.

The conference had been difficult, fractious, tedious and immensely fatiguing, but there was the political will for it to succeed. Even so, it could easily have come to grief. Seen from today's perspective, the effort expended by the US and the UK delegations on negotiating to allow for 'peaceful nuclear explosions' in the Antarctic seems inappropriate and irrelevant. Global radioactive contamination was at the time becoming a major environmental issue and negotiations for a nuclear test ban treaty were already underway, to be agreed in Moscow four years later. It banned globally all atmospheric and underwater nuclear tests, regardless of purpose. No nuclear devices have ever been detonated in the Antarctic.

Signing of the treaty in Washington was not the end of the matter: to be legally enforceable, it had to be ratified by participating governments. There would be 18 months of anxious waiting while governments deliberated, the last three countries to ratify being Australia, Argentina and Chile. For the UK, ratification was little more than a formality and was never debated in the House of Commons.[12] The House of Lords did have something to say on the matter.[13] Lord Shackleton expressed concerns over secrecy and the unresolved problems of jurisdiction, concluding that "the Antarctic should be fully internationalised and be the first United Nations territory... I hope that the Government will take a lead." Although Roberts was reputed to have written all the speeches for the Lords debate, it is hard to imagine him agreeing with Shackleton's sentiments. But there was widespread support from their lordships, and on 31 May 1960 the UK became the first nation to ratify the treaty.

The treaty contained a formal commitment to hold follow-up annual or biennial conferences, to become known as Antarctic Treaty Consultative Meetings. Roberts, now a fully fledged international diplomat, was to be a key player at the first meeting, scheduled to take place in Canberra in 1961. The Washington Conference was not the end of a chapter in Roberts' life, but the beginning of a new one.

PART 3

THE DIPLOMAT

16

ROLLING ROUND ANTARCTICA WITH UNCLE SAM

And what is it that will make it possible for NASA to spend 20 billion dollars of *your money* to put some clown on the moon? Well, it's good old American knowhow, that's what.

Tom Lehrer

During the austral summer of 1960-61 the US sent two powerful icebreaker ships on an expedition to the Ross Dependency, with several international observers on board, including Roberts. The purpose of official observers was to ensure compliance with the principles of the newly-established Antarctic Treaty, a scheme that was not always popular with scientists, who tended to take international cooperation for granted and resented being subjected to a form of 'police inspection'.[1] In the event, Roberts' involvement would turn out to be rather more than that of an observer.

USS *Glacier* was a state-of-the-art diesel-electric powered icebreaker capable of penetrating ice up to 20 ft thick.[2] Its mission on Operation Deep Freeze was firstly to crack open a channel for supply vessels through the Ross Sea to the US McMurdo Base, and secondly to meet up with the second icebreaker, USS *Staten Island*, in the Amundsen Sea for exploration and surveying along the Eights Coast, an obscure length of the Antarctic coast that was unapproachable due to extensive thick pack ice. It was near there that Captain James Cook made his closest approach to Antarctica in 1774, but the area was largely forgotten until 2011, when the instability of the Thwaites 'Doomsday' Glacier became prominent as an alarming signature of global climate change.

In 1960 a flight from London to Melbourne was a 48-hour test of endurance, with several stops needed for refuelling. On arrival at Melbourne Roberts was able to get a refreshing hot bath, but he had to get his pants on hastily for a press interview. After more flights to Sydney, Auckland, Wellington and Christchurch there were more press interviews, as he had received a personal invitation from Prime Minister Walter Nash to visit New Zealand as a guest of the government. Three days after his arrival at Christchurch he was at last on board *Glacier* for its first voyage to the Ross Sea.

Rough seas, followed by heavy pack ice on crossing the Antarctic Convergence, made for an uncomfortable journey to the Ross Sea. Roberts was initially impressed with *Glacier*'s warmth and comfort,

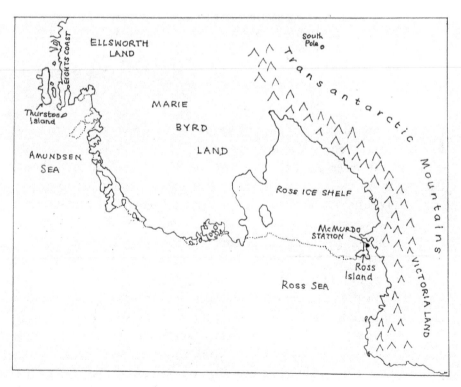

Ross Dependency

but on experiencing the ship's extreme tendency to roll he changed his mind. The impact, noise and juddering crashes on smashing through ice were for Roberts a jarring contrast to his earlier Antarctic voyages on *Penola* and *Norsel*, threading their way along narrow leads of open water, with long static interludes waiting for conditions to improve. There had then been a sense of peace, stillness and timelessness.

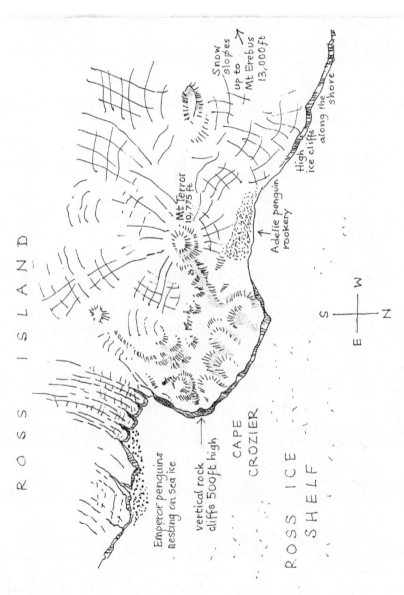

Cape Crozier, after drawing by Edward Wilson

Consolidated pack ice eventually brought *Glacier* to a grinding halt in the Ross Sea. Roberts was landed by helicopter at the US McMurdo base, where he spent three weeks helping Charles Swithinbank with glaciology while awaiting aborted flights to the South Pole station. There was, however, one rare opportunity for some ornithology.

THE EMPEROR PENGUINS OF CAPE CROZIER

The first landing at Cape Crozier had been in 1902, during Scott's first Discovery Expedition. On 7 December 1960 a party of five left McMurdo in two helicopters for Cape Crozier. Three were glaciologists, including Charles Swithinbank and Hugo Neuburg. In fine weather and with memorable views of Mounts Erebus (*Plate 16.1*) and Terror, they landed close to a huge Adélie penguin rookery. The helicopters flew so low over the colony that they caused considerable disturbance to thousands of incubating birds, which scattered, providing skuas with easy pickings from the abandoned eggs. It would take at least a whole day to do a bird count, so Roberts did not attempt it.

From the air the emperor penguin rookery had already been spotted six miles away on the fast ice. Access on foot would be challenging. They would either have to scale formidable 200 ft high rock cliffs or approach from the south across a very rough area of huge crevasses and pressure ridges. One of the helicopter pilots agreed to try and land on the fast ice close to the rookery. The ice being firm, Roberts was dropped safely, along with biologist Donald Wohnschlag plus camping gear, and they went straight over to see the rookery.

After the glaciologists had completed their work along the coast, Neuburg, who had swapped places with Wohnschlag, joined Roberts to camp close under the ice front about half a mile from the rookery. Having set up the tent, they walked over to the rookery. It was by no means Roberts' first sight of an emperor penguin, but the site held a heightened interest owing to its historic importance. Parents were still feeding their young, and many of the well-grown chicks were beginning to moult their down (*Plate 16.2*). As the sun disappeared behind Mount Terror and the temperature plummeted, the birds became inactive and slept. Not so the humans present; having done a bird count that same evening they returned to their tent and cooked a meal at midnight, then got into their sleeping bags and talked for another two hours before snatching a few hours' sleep.

Waking early, they found that the weather was now against them. It was blowing hard and snowing, with drift piling up against the tent. Undeterred they followed the tide crack in poor visibility to find the birds again, no longer huddled together but scattered along the foot of the ice cliffs for about 200 yards. A few hours later the weather cleared and they found it possible to shepherd the birds into small groups to make counting easier. The counts of adults and chicks on two days independently by the two men yielded satisfyingly similar results.[3]

When the anticipated helicopter return flight did not materialize due to strong wind, it was a delight to have another peaceful, calm and sunny evening away from the noise and dirt of McMurdo. They investigated possible access routes to Cape Crozier, concluding that the only one viable was from the south through the pressure ridges and crevasses, and even then only with rope and ice axes and several hours of laborious step cutting. The only other route, around the bottom of the rock cliffs, had become impossible due to the break-up of the fast ice, leaving open water at the foot of the rock cliffs. Early the next morning the two men were collected by helicopter to rejoin the glaciologists and return to McMurdo.

On Christmas Eve *Glacier* left the Ross Dependency for Wellington, rolling more heavily than ever in poor weather and a heavy sea. With the ship listing up to 45°, Roberts was flung out of his bunk several times, leaving him feeling bruised and weary. Up in the mess all the breakfast and crockery was slithering back and forth across the floor. It was impossible to wedge oneself into a comfortable position or to eat a meal. The mission of his student days in the Cambridge Wayfarers' Club "to travel in discomfort to remote places" seemed to have lost its original appeal.

After six days there was general relief on board when New Zealand's South Island came into view. *Glacier* was due for a refit at Wellington, leaving Roberts with a month to kill touring New Zealand until the ship was ready for her second journey to the Antarctic. But despite the natural wonders of the country, the tourist tat and the affluent clientele depressed him, and by the end of January 1961, when *Glacier* was ready for sailing, he was desperate to be back at sea.

ICEBOUND

Once again *Glacier* was rolling heavily, until she reached the Antarctic Convergence. The sea was then transformed into an eerily calm millpond with icebergs and increasingly heavy pack ice. There was almost no wildlife.

Eventually, after 3000 miles of the Pacific Ocean, the Thurston Peninsula came into view. The next day two shore parties were sent out by helicopter. They found that Thurston was not a peninsula but an island: it was to be the sole discovery of the entire six-month expedition.

Roberts was amazed by the Americans' extraordinary mixture of enthusiasm and technical competence in the handling of ships and helicopters, contrasted with a complete absence of rudimentary camping knowhow. Flimsy nylon tents were provided lacking snowflaps but with built-in mosquito nets (there are no mosquitoes in the Antarctic, though there are in Maine in the summer, as the Americans joked). Rations were frequently canned with a high water content; they quickly became frozen and would need prolonged heating on a stove.

By 9 February *Glacier* was completely trapped in fast ice. Another overnight shore party was launched to collect geological specimens and lichens. Setting up camp was still a challenge, and although the stove was kept alight it was cold and draughty inside the tent. Roberts longed for the comfort of a British pyramid tent. Finally the main four-man survey party was launched, with the aim of fixing the position of a nunatak on the Eights Coast some 45 miles south-east of the ship.

THE BLIZZARD

The story of the party's survival over three days and nights in a ferocious blizzard that blew up without warning, by constructing a rock shelter, is described in the Prologue. On their rescue by helicopter they returned to find *Glacier* still icebound. In poor visibility *Glacier* started backing and charging the consolidated 20 ft thick pack ice, but remained stuck fast. By 25 February, with no change in the ice or the weather, rumours were circulating around the crew that they would need to over-winter in the ice. The US press and even the White House were expressing concern over the continued presence of the ship in this treacherous area so late in the season. The Sunday service on board *Glacier* was becoming decidedly popular amongst the crew, attendance going up 300%.

Eventually the ice started to thin out, but it remained at 9/10 cover and severely hummocked. In the thick fog it took four days for *Glacier* to travel six miles north-west, and constant bashing into the heavy ice resulted in the loss of a second propeller blade. There was no trace of a lead or any open water in sight. The only one on board who was not worried in the slightest was Roberts, who knew from experience how rapidly the situation can change. He did not believe for one moment that *Glacier* would end up over-wintering. For him patience was a virtue, but it was not a typical American quality.

GLACIER BLASTS HER WAY OUT

After much backing and charging of the pack ice *Glacier* was eventually able to move and head north. Even with open water present, there was still almost no wildlife. The expedition was now leaving the Eights Coast, having learnt nothing of significance. It was left to Roberts to make some face-saving plans for the remainder of *Glacier*'s voyage up the Antarctic Peninsula and around the South Shetland, South Orkney and South Sandwich Islands.

On 11 March the ice was left behind *as Glacier* passed Peter I Island. Roberts was now on familiar territory as *Glacier* sailed eastwards through Bismarck Strait. Although the weather was dismal and visibility was poor, it was exhilarating for him once more to see Doumer Island where he, Bertram and Fleming had landed in 1935 during the British Graham Land Expedition. *Glacier* sped up Neumayer Channel, crossed Gerlache Strait and received a warm welcome at the Chilean station González Videla at Waterboat Point. It was a unique opportunity for Roberts to visit the site where in 1921-22 Thomas Bagshawe and Maxime Lester had spent a remarkable year living in a beached whale catcher, recording detailed observations of penguins and other wildlife around them.

The ship sped out of Bransfield Strait and past the South Orkney Islands in heavy seas. By now most of *Glacier*'s crew wanted only to go home. With the ship rolling heavily it was impossible to sleep, eat or work, and one night the ship's commander was thrown out of his bunk, cutting his head severely and needing 15 stitches. The next day the expedition's last goal was in sight: Zavodovski Island, a sulphurous volcano in the South Sandwich Islands. But strong wind and swell prevented any helicopter landing.

On the last leg of her journey *Glacier* stopped at Montevideo, where Roberts received an invitation from Admiral Panzarini to visit the Instituto Antártico Argentino in Buenos Aires. Roberts was bemused by his red-carpet welcome, having suspected that his past efforts to protect British-claimed Antarctic territory might make it impossible for him ever again to set foot in Argentina. He flew on to Rio de Janeiro, meeting up with some of *Glacier*'s crew for a midnight bathe on Copacabana beach, a day in the tropical rain forest, and a cable car ride up Pao de Açucar (Sugar Loaf). Mesmerized by the view, Roberts realized only afterwards that he had been robbed of all his money, and he still had several days to survive in Rio awaiting a flight home.

SCOTT BASE, MCMURDO STATION AND THE SOUTH POLE

Ten years later, following an Antarctic Treaty meeting in Wellington, Roberts once again visited the Ross Dependency.[4] He was now 60 and confessed to a certain discomfort at being in a group of 'elderly tourists'. From Christchurch a 7½ hour flight took the party of Antarctic Treaty veterans to 'Willy', the airstrip at Williams Field near Scott Base. Three of them travelled on dog sledges across the fast ice to McMurdo and past Observation Hill to Scott Base. The more geriatric members used motorised transport.

On 14 November the party took off from Willy for a three-hour flight to the South Pole Station. Heavy cloud blocked all the mountain views, but the polar plateau was cloudless with little wind. At the Pole Station the temperature was -45°C and several of the party were suffering from altitude sickness. Entering the station, they descended 30 ft via wooden steps and filed along endless passages to a small recreation room, the walls covered with huge photographs of naked girls. A hurried lunch was taken, with more pictured naked ladies on the tables under their plates. Roberts' neighbour commented: "I am a Frenchman, and I do not like to mix pubic hairs with my noodle soup at lunch time." The plan was to go on to Vostock, but as the temperature there had fallen to -60°C it was cancelled.

After lunch the party was escorted around the station by several bored US naval officers. The visitors felt like unwelcome intruders. They met none of the scientists and were not shown any of the work at the station. To anyone aware of the half-century of human endeavour and sacrifice expended on creating what should have been a work of art, the visit was a dispiriting experience.

Back at Scott Base an uncharacteristic accident befell Roberts when he slipped on a flat hard ice surface and fell heavily, fearing that he had cracked a rib or two. He was furious with himself. Agile, fit and strong in his youth, he had become a fountain of wisdom to others on how to steer clear of trouble in the polar regions, but 15 years of the diplomatic life had taken its toll on his figure and fitness. He was not alone: Soviet delegate Yevgeniy Tolstikov was equally stout, and the two of them agreed to remain in the comfort of Scott Base with a drink rather than participate in a proposed visit to the nearby ice caves, which would involve struggling through narrow gaps on their stomachs.

After a farewell dinner there was one more obligatory visit before returning home: McMurdo Station. It was the largest festering eyesore in Antarctica – a noisy, grimy and ramshackle jumble of prefabricated buildings and dirt tracks, with huge piles of rubbish, discarded equipment and abandoned vehicles. The visitors were escorted by McMurdo's base commander who, without a trace of embarrassment, delivered a speech on the need to "avoid spoiling the Antarctic environment", prompting some muted strong language from the audience; but it was not the occasion to raise controversial issues with their American hosts.

It was a long flight home for Roberts via New Zealand, Los Angeles and New York, punctuated only by relentless meals and refreshments. Roberts was now experienced in adapting to this affluent and mobile 24-hour society, with no meaningful sleeping or eating routine. His solution was to disregard local time, refuse almost all meals offered and work his way through a succession of dry Martinis, even before 'breakfast'. But there would be a price to pay for the continued pressures of such a lifestyle.

17

THE BEGINNINGS OF
ANTARCTIC CONSERVATION

Most of the scientists concerned with Antarctic work merely take a
cynical view that politicians and diplomats are all stupid – as indeed
anyone might well conclude from examining the results of a conference
like this one. Most of them do not make enough effort to understand
the difficulties of achieving international agreement on matters which are
emotional rather than scientific... Their experience of scientific conferences
does not help them to understand the oblique methods of diplomacy, the
necessity for negotiating binding agreements, the succession of drafts
which will express precisely the maximum that can be agreed (but which
often emerge as a compromise that marks no progress).

Brian Roberts[1]

The treaty signed in Washington in December 1959 had committed
the parties to convene annual or biennial Antarctic Treaty
Consultative Meetings to elaborate how the vaguely-worded principles
of the treaty were to be put into practice. The first Treaty Meeting,
convened in Canberra in July 1961,[2] (*Plate 17.1*) had a comprehensive
agenda: procedural arrangements, international scientific cooperation,
rights of inspection, historic sites and – of special concern to the UK
– the secretariat, jurisdiction and telecommunications. These issues
would remain controversial for many years and progress was slow.[3]

Also on the agenda was wildlife conservation. For Roberts it was this that would become his personal agenda. Conservation was deemed to be a relatively non-controversial issue, but it was not going to be an easy ride for him. One problem lay in Article VI of the treaty, which stated that there should be no compromising of states' legal rights to the high seas. It would require painstaking negotiation on Roberts' part to get agreement on legally-binding conservation measures that would inevitably restrict exploitation of the oceans that formed much of the treaty's zone of application.

FIRST EFFORTS TO AGREE MEASURES

In 1960 biologist Martin Holdgate joined the staff of the Scott Polar Institute, to be plunged immediately into a Working Group on Biology set up by the Scientific Committee for Antarctic Research. The remit of SCAR was to provide hard scientific data to the Treaty Meetings. Under Roberts' guidance the working group recommended that south of 60°S all areas of land, fresh water and coastal waters, including fast ice and ice shelves, should be constituted as a protected nature reserve. Species or habitats that were especially valuable or vulnerable were to be protected further by designating selected areas as sanctuaries within which no form of human or motorised vehicle disturbance should be permitted – not even scientific activity. But this created a conflict with Article II of the treaty, which stipulated 'freedom of scientific investigation', and Specially Protected Areas had to be defined and restricted to what was deemed essential for conservation needs.[4]

The 1960 SCAR meeting came up with a number of proposals to protect indigenous animals and plants, avoid the introduction of alien fauna and flora, and prevent harm to wildlife from the activities of field stations and operations. After the meeting Roberts persuaded Holdgate to convert the SCAR proposals into a series of legally enforceable conservation measures that the treaty governments would understand and be willing to adopt, saying: "You write them Martin, and I'll sell them." Despite the apparent general lack of interest in Latin America in conservation,[5] Argentine conservation law was enshrined in a comprehensive document that Holdgate had to translate from the Spanish, a task he found "extremely tedious".[6] But Holdgate and Roberts' work would be the foundation of the most significant recommendation to emerge from the early Treaty Meetings: the Agreed Measures for the Conservation of Antarctic Fauna and Flora (AMCAFF).[7]

The Agreed Measures prohibited the killing, injuring, molesting and removal of native Antarctic birds and mammals without a permit. It was aimed at the protection of seals, penguins, and nesting birds such as petrels, all of which are vulnerable because they concentrate in huge numbers for breeding on a small number of island sites. During the 19th century fur seals had been hunted to near extinction, and diseases and parasites introduced by humans could also have catastrophic consequences.

However a serious limitation of the Agreed Measures was the restriction of protection to animals on dry land, excluding those in the ocean or on ice shelves. Some 80% of Antarctic seals never go ashore. Whales, deemed to be the responsibility of the ineffectual International Whaling Commission, were a particular problem. Unregulated slaughter of whales in commercial competition was driving all species close to the brink of extinction.[8] Regrettably whales had to be excluded from the Agreed Measures, but Roberts had to start somewhere.

On the eve of the Canberra Treaty Meeting Roberts, now raring to go, circulated a draft convention for the protection of wildlife in the Antarctic.[9] But he would soon be confronted with the realities of international diplomacy. Apart from tiresome procedural squabbles – neither the US nor the New Zealanders would approve anything that had not been agreed first in Washington – some national governments were suspicious that SCAR was becoming a supranational authority by stealth. All Roberts could do was to propose deferral of detailed discussion to the next Treaty Meeting. He was having to learn a fundamental lesson in the art of diplomacy: the need for extreme patience.

CANBERRA, JULY 1961

The Antarctic Treaty had been fully ratified only one month before the start of the first Treaty Meeting. There was still an atmosphere of stiff formality hanging over from the Washington conference, with little informal dialogue to oil the wheels of the negotiations, and after a week most delegates were still feeling reserved, tired and irritable.

In formal situations there is often a need for an 'ice breaker'. One arrived fortuitously during a weekend bus excursion arranged by the Australian hosts, intended to impress the delegates with the prestigious Snowy Mountains Hydroelectric Scheme. The engineering works aroused little interest, but on a distant island in the reservoir a troop of hopping kangaroos was spotted, which stimulated much laughter and briefly thawed the diplomatic reserve. However, back in the conference room the frosty atmosphere returned. No agreement was reached on procedures, let alone anything tangible.

The US head of delegation, George Owen, proposed to hold an Interim Group in Washington but was outvoted. Owen's response was to become "uncomfortably truculent, unhelpful and imperious", insisting that no texts of existing drafts should be altered, an impossible demand that failed to take into account the need to coordinate the four conference languages. The UK delegation attempted to push for the creation of a treaty secretariat, only for its location to emerge as an impasse. The US insisted that it had to be located in Washington. Chile and Argentina were not happy for it to be in Canberra. After 48 hours of hard bargaining, a recommendation was approved to provide minimal administrative services, split between Canberra and Buenos Aires; this was to be only an interim measure until the next conference. Phew![10]

There was, however, a little encouragement for Roberts on conservation, and he was able to secure an interim agreement to issue general rules of conduct to field stations. Another welcome – and unexpected – development was the positive attitude of the Soviet delegation. The Soviets and Australians had resumed diplomatic relations, and at a cocktail party given by the Soviet Embassy enormous quantities of caviar and vodka were consumed in the cause of international cooperation and friendship. In contrast to some of the other delegations, the Soviets displayed a constructive approach throughout; they had evidently been instructed to make the Antarctic a showcase for international goodwill, dissociated from the Cold War.

BUENOS AIRES, JULY 1962

The second Treaty Meeting was held one year later in Buenos Aires, shortly after the toppling of the Argentine government. This was not exactly an infrequent occurrence, but the difficulties created for the Latin American Antarctic experts did not bode well for the conference's prospects.[11] In addition there were problems with the New Zealanders, who wanted all interim meetings to be held in Washington. Roberts was alarmed at the prospect of the US becoming a *de facto* secretariat, which would make it difficult to keep Cold War politics out of Antarctic matters.

For the UK team of Robin Edmonds, Gordon Whitehead and Roberts, the outward journey to Buenos Aires was a string of misfortunes. At Geneva their aircraft was prevented from taking off by a bird strike, and after a night spent on hard benches they had to wait several hours more for a replacement engine. Edmonds' proposal to get some sleep on a lakeside park bench was washed out by rain. Whitehead led them on a long walk to visit a 230 ft high fountain, only to find that it was not operating. Finally Roberts took them on an even longer walk to look at an old wooden bridge, but they arrived to find that it had vanished. He then remembered that the bridge was in Lucerne, not in Geneva.

At Rio de Janeiro there was another 13 hours' delay, in stiflingly hot conditions. The three finally arrived 24 hours late at 8:30 am the following day, to be immediately ushered into a reception at the Argentine Foreign Ministry, followed by a meeting with the US delegation which left Roberts needing a stiff drink. Owen was as overbearing and antagonistic as he had been at Canberra. He appeared to have toothache, continually fingering his mouth "just to make sure that it was still painful".

At the opening of the conference the next day, it was soon apparent that the Argentine chairman had little grasp of conference protocol. Senator Mora of Chile opened with an interminable rambling address, urging the need for slow progress. No surprises there. It was reminiscent of his performances at the Washington Conference: "a jungle of noise, like the luxuriant tangled roots, branches and lianas of a mangrove swamp, accompanied by the noise of parrots and chattering monkeys". As he gradually nodded off, Roberts would suddenly wake up with a jerk and wonder what Mora was actually advocating, if anything.

On the issue of jurisdiction the UK delegation encountered unexpected opposition from the Soviets. The Soviet Foreign Ministry had been taken aback by the recent UK announcement of the creation of the British Antarctic Territory as a replacement for the Falkland Islands Dependencies. The choice of name, and the UK enthusiasm for getting jurisdiction inscribed on the conference agenda, were interpreted by the Soviets as reaffirmations of British sovereignty in the Antarctic.

In comparison the conservation of wildlife was non-controversial, but it still got bogged down on procedural aspects. The US even returned to the stale argument over the names 'Antarctica', 'the Antarctic' and 'the Treaty Area', which supposedly had been thrashed out at the Washington Conference. It can take only one obstinate delegate to put the clock back three years. Roberts made many attempts to get through to Owen, getting nowhere. "I doubt whether we can hope to achieve much political co-ordination with the Americans while George continues to hold his present post. It is extraordinarily difficult not to meet his open rudeness with similar behaviour... [but] nothing can be gained from getting angry. I am glad at least to be able to record that I did not lose my temper."[12]

As a result of US interventions and the intransigence of Argentina and Chile over anything that might compromise their sovereignty claims, the final compromise recommendations of the conference were to Roberts a washout. The issue of the secretariat had actually gone backwards: even the hard-won draft recommendation from Canberra was no longer agreed. The final Friday evening plenary session, prolonged by time-wasters and the incompetence of the chairman, left most delegates feeling exhausted and irritable. It had been a most disappointing conference. The UK was no further forward in promoting its internationalist agenda ("putting teeth into the Treaty"). Roberts concluded that the Foreign Office should review UK policy in the south Atlantic and advocate an increase in British activity in the Antarctic to safeguard its legal position. In the context of such a retrograde step, the treaty seemed to have little chance of survival.

At the end of the conference Roberts and Edmonds were taken for a drive round Buenos Aires, an interminable suburban sprawl of poor architecture, vast slum districts and waterlogged potholed roads. The next day they flew to Rio. A pleasant day taking in rain forest and spectacular mountain scenery was followed by inescapable diplomatic functions with the UK ambassador, who took them to visit the Brazilian

Prime Minister at his weekend villa in Petrópolis. Somehow Roberts managed to wriggle out of it and spend the hot sunny afternoon on Copacabana beach. Meanwhile Edmonds never got to meet the Prime Minister and had to endure the whole day with the ambassador and his wife, who made no attempt to conceal their loathing of each other.

BRUSSELS, JUNE 1964

The first two Treaty Meetings had been slow, tedious and unproductive, but by the third Treaty Meeting in Brussels there was a perceptible change in mood, and relations between the UK and the US representatives had improved since the dark days of George Owen. It was now Australia with whom the UK had difficulties. There was however some progress on wildlife conservation, and Roberts was feeling bullish. Sealing had become a hot topic, due to high demand from the European fashion industry and the skyrocketing price of sealskin. The recent voyage of a Norwegian ship *Polarhav* to explore the harvesting of crabeater seals in the Southern Ocean had set conservationist alarm bells ringing. Roberts wanted to push for a convention on wildlife conservation, a concept of his own invention, but it encountered opposition. The Agreed Measures also came unstuck when he tried to include pelagic (open water) sealing. He persisted, even when his UK colleagues attempted to dissuade him from doing so. It was to prove the most contentious issue of the conference, but Roberts' proposals were supported by the Soviets. Following a presentation on the history of sealing and the catastrophic effect of the fashion industry on certain species, session chairman Yevgeniy Tolstikov eyeballed the delegates around the room with the words "Now, who is against seals?" But there was deadlock with the Australians. Roberts blamed the rift squarely on the Australian representative, James Cumes, a lawyer described as an embittered Anglophobe, inflexible and hostile to the point of rudeness.[13] Cumes caused a working group on pelagic sealing to break up when Anatoly Movchan exploded at him in a fit of rage. That evening at the cocktail party Roberts was infuriated even more by Cumes' boasting that he was representing a 'small nation' (Australia) exercising a power of veto against the Soviet Union.

Roberts disliked the cocktail parties, especially when the UK was host and he had to make an effort to be nice to guests. "Only alcohol makes these parties endurable," he wrote. Inviting individual delegates to dinner was often more entertaining. One evening the UK party was joined by two South African delegates, one of whom – oblivious that he was representing a pariah state vilified by almost the entire planet except for Western political conservatives – dominated the conversation with his advocacy of apartheid. His embarrassed colleague offered to pay the exorbitant restaurant bill, causing great amusement to everyone except the white supremacist himself.

Despite differences of opinion between the UK and the US over pelagic sealing, there was for the first time good cooperation between the two delegations: a welcome change from the stiff Anglo-US relations of previous Antarctic conferences. With several nocturnal sessions until 4 am aided by copious quantities of whisky, considerable progress was made on drafting the Agreed Measures. Overall the conference had been productive and amicable, although there was no progress on the sticky issues of jurisdiction and the secretariat. The Agreed Measures had their limitations, but Roberts was greatly buoyed up. They were the first real step forward in international agreement on the Antarctic since the 1959 Washington conference.

Has anyone seen Brian?

18

ISLANDS OF PARADISE
AND DESOLATION

"What would Neptune say if he was deprived of the sea?"
"I haven't a notion!"

Edward Lear

ISLANDS OF PARADISE

On his return from the first Treaty Meeting in Canberra in 1961 Roberts took advantage of a new air service for a much-needed holiday, in Tahiti.[1] His first night was spent at a hotel consisting of thatched huts scattered along the shore in a grove of coconut palms. After the hot sweat of the conference, a walk down to the beach under a full moon, with dark palm trees silhouetted against brilliant stars, and the thunder of surf on the outer reef, was paradise indeed.

Together with Robin Edmonds, his companion from the UK delegation in Canberra, Roberts spent a day in an outrigger canoe, paddling across the lagoon to the inner edge of the barrier reef. Swimming with masks and breathing tubes in the shallows around the corals, they could see clearly for 60 ft or more. Ever since reading about Captain Cook in his childhood Roberts had longed to visit a coral reef, and he was now swimming amongst an exuberance of colour and variety of fish and corals that was intoxicating. At the time, filmmaker and conservationist

Jacques Cousteau's pioneer underwater filming of marine life was only to be seen on black and white television; colour would not arrive in Britain until the end of the decade.

It did not take long for the simplicity of the Tahitian way of life to work its magic on Roberts. Having to kiss almost every girl he met left him cursing his puritan upbringing and struggling to throw off his Western inhibitions, even though Tahitian kissing was traditionally limited to pressing noses together. In the bars of Tahiti's main town, Pape'ete, Roberts found "such throbbing life that I am left wondering whether I shall ever again be able to endure the stuffy boredom of even the gayest English pub".

Roberts learned early on not to sit under a palm tree: a ripe coconut weighs more than 3 lb, and could fall from 30 ft. The fruit and seeds of breadfruit and kapok trees can also fall heavily, while other trees can squirt or spill sticky liquids without warning. One evening Roberts and Didier Raguenet (from the French delegation at Canberra) were invited by an eccentric French artist to a party at his elegant home high up the mountainside with a magnificent view across the coral reefs towards the neighbouring island of Moorea. Seated outside on the veranda under a kapok tree, the guests had constantly to dodge falling 2lb seedpods, until to everyone's relief a sudden rainstorm drove them indoors. This same view of Moorea and its coral reef atoll from high up had also been seen by Charles Darwin on HMS *Beagle* in 1835. Darwin was gathering evidence for his theory that atolls (isolated rings of coral reefs) had originally been formed around extinct volcanoes that had then sunk into the sea.

THE ENCHANTED ISLAND OF MOOREA

Moorea has long been considered by many to be the most beautiful island in the world (*Plates 18.1 to 18.3*). Very early one morning Roberts boarded a boat bound for the island, taking along his rented Vespa scooter. Entering Cook's Bay on Moorea's north coast, they arrived at Pao Pao with a spectacular view of the island's sawtooth peaks. It had a newly-built hotel consisting of small palm-thatched huts in a paradise setting. But paradise always comes at a price, and it was beyond Roberts' means. He had therefore arranged to stay in Afareaitu, a small village about seven miles eastwards around the coastal track.

In the seasonal pouring rain he took shelter in a hut by the jetty. Impromptu hospitality from strangers was never far away, and he found himself invited to an excellent lunch of baked fish with grapefruit, fried bananas and salad, roast pork and sweet potatoes, washed down with red wine. After lunch the party drove west in a truck along the coastal track to Baie de Papetoai. With cascades of descending water and large patches of deep, soft mud, the track was almost impassable in places. Roberts enquired about the state of the track to Afareaitu. Opinions differed, some insisting that it would be madness to attempt the journey until the rains stopped and the land had dried out. He decided to chance his luck, stripping down to bathing shorts and heading eastwards on his scooter. At times the rain felt like a solid wall of water, but the only serious difficulty was the deep mud, and there were always willing helpers around to give the machine a push. The main hazard was from airborne coconuts in the fierce wind.

Roberts had been told to follow the track until it came to a church and a Chinese store opposite a small palm-tufted islet. On arrival at a large house constructed from mambo and plaited palm leaves, he was welcomed by Pauline Teoriki, the sister of a *député* who represented Tahiti in Paris, and who ran the family copra business (drying coconut flesh). During Roberts' stay there was only one other visitor, a Frenchman. The house was situated in a grove of breadfruit trees, bananas and sweet-scented flowers and creepers. Between the guest rooms (small huts) a clear stream flowed, full of fish.

At last the rain stopped. Mme Teoriki provided supper of soup and roast pork with crisp slices of breadfruit fried in coconut oil, followed by papaya and bananas. Afterwards there was beer and singing in the Chinese store, but Roberts was relieved to find that the population of the village turned in at about 8:30 pm, and he fell asleep almost at once.

He did not sleep for long. The bed was damp, and mosquitoes were in abundance. Strange noises kept disturbing him – the rustling of the coconut crests in the wind, thuds of falling coconuts and breadfruit, pigs grunting, dogs barking, and people coming and going through the house. Long before dawn, the cocks began to crow. At sunrise the bird calls increased to such a deafening cacophony that he had to get up to investigate.

Having got up early, he set out under a cloudless sky southwards along the coastal track. Wandering through the villages, he stopped frequently, making friends with children who played at the water's edge. Men were fishing with spears and throwing nets, women fished with rods and lines whilst standing in the sea up to their waists fully clothed. Others were tending crops, collecting coconuts and splitting them open to dry the flesh out in the sun for copra. It all captivated him: bright crimson thickets of hibiscus blooms, the thatched huts amongst the coconut palms and breadfruit trees, swarms of land crabs hurrying into their burrows, and surf pounding heavily on the outer reef. The scent of flowers mixed with the savour of cooking, sudden rich contrasting whiffs of vanilla and pig dung, and the perfume of coconut oil scented with gardenia petals which the women used to anoint themselves after washing. In the heat of the day old men were smoking and gossiping, and girls were chattering and laughing while braiding flower garlands. The enchantment of the island overwhelmed him, and more than once he burst into tears of emotion.

He was invited to join a large family in their hut for a lunch of baked fish and a fruit salad of papaya, grapefruit, bananas and coconut milk. He learnt a great deal about coconuts. During ripening the water inside the coconut changes from bitter to sour to sweet, bitter being the best drink to quench one's thirst. The milk, made by pressing grated coconut meat wrapped in a cloth, is never drunk but is used as a sauce, sometimes mixed with sea water in a bowl to dip your food into. He was shown how to prepare small fish to eat raw, soaked in lemon juice and herbs and then dried in the sun for a couple of hours. After lunch, together with an older boy from the family, he went off to the barrier reef in an outrigger canoe to trap fish. The scene was a myriad contrasts: calm clear lagoon waters with frothing white surf further out; the hot, glaringly white sandy shore below cool deep green coconut palms; all with a backdrop of dark jagged volcanic peaks. Below the water were pale sands with brilliant flaming colours of coral and exotic fish.

Breathing through a snorkel mask, he was guided around the coral reef by the boy, who swam underwater with no breathing equipment. Four older boys joined them for an underwater chasing game, none needing a breathing tube. "It was hard indeed to tear myself away. No one at Afareaitu... seemed in the least surprised when I arrived back in the village at dusk crowned and garlanded with flowers; dried cakes of blood [from the sharp corals] streaming down my bare legs and arms; my mind in a state of exultation. If anyone had met me like this in England, they would certainly have been sure that I was intoxicated."[2]

The next day he had planned to take a Vespa ride right round the island, a 37-mile circuit of narrow, rough and muddy track. But in the morning the scooter was found to have a puncture, and there were no tools available to change the tyre. Almost the whole village of 43 people collaborated in the repair, mostly by offering friendly advice. After some two hours a few industrious Chinese managed to get him out of trouble, and he set off. He had no need to take food. Everywhere he was welcomed with invitations to eat and drink, mostly bananas, fish and coconut water. During the course of the day he stopped to chat with many locals, some repairing fishing nets, others hollowing outrigger canoes from single tree trunks with adzes, building huts, preparing copra, tending crops, spearing fish, plaiting split bamboos or palm-leaves, cooking, or making flower garlands.

Back at Afareaitu, the day concluded with a large Chinese-style supper, most of which, having accepted too much hospitality during the day, he furtively had to feed to the ever-present cats and dogs. Early next morning it was time to board the boat for Pape'ete and bid a sad farewell to Moorea. Amongst the 40 passengers, Roberts was the only European on board. As they left Moorea, he reflected sombrely that he would never again experience anything like it.

OFFER OF A FILM PART

After Moorea, Pape'ete seemed to be rather tatty. Roberts returned to his local bar for a beer. A man studied his English appearance with interest. "Hey buddy, how d'yer fancy a role as a sailor in our movie?"

"What's the film?"

"*Mutiny on the Bounty*. It's being directed by Marlon Brando for MGM."

Roberts recalled his altercation with the captain Red Ryder on *Penola* on New Year's Eve 1936 during the British Graham Land Expedition. Somehow this imitation of life by art seemed apposite. "What's the pay for sailors?"

"Five bucks a day, for starters." More was promised, and Roberts was half tempted. But he was always nervous of any kind of public performance. "What do I have to do?"

"Nothing. Just grow a beard."

Roberts suddenly recalled his singular failure to grow a beard on BGLE. There was also the awkward question of his spectacles, without which he could see nothing. He politely declined the offer, and was relieved to have done so when he spotted some of the movie's sailors who had been recruited in the bars along the waterfront – American, English and French, all of whom had an alternative life-style demeanour: long hair, pigtails, elaborate beards, side whiskers, gold earrings, long sheath knives and bare feet. Most of them knew nothing about the epic story they were supposed to be re-enacting.

After lunch he visited the *Bounty*, moored in a quay across the harbour and being converted into the *Pandora* for filming. Enchanted, he watched a dilapidated schooner, laden with copra, arrive and moor to the quayside. He went aboard, to find that it had been built in France about 50 years ago and was remarkably similar to *Penola*. Every rope seemed almost familiar, and he had a wistful hankering to sail in her. In the evening he drove eastwards along the coast to Point Venus in Matavai Bay, where Cook had landed to observe the 1769 transit of Venus. He had just one day left in Tahiti before heading home.

THE MAN FROM EASTER ISLAND

At breakfast Roberts was surprised to encounter Manuel Bianchi from the Chilean delegation in Canberra. Bianchi, who was now quite transformed from the dour conference delegate, introduced Pedro Chavez, who six years previously had made the voyage from Easter Island to Tuamotu (125 miles from Tahiti) in an outrigger sailing canoe. The distance was some 1900 miles and the journey took 29 days. Chavez knew all about the Kon-Tiki voyage and wondered why so much fuss was being made of it. When Roberts mentioned that he knew Thor Heyerdahl, Chavez spat on the floor in disgust. Heyerdahl's book *Aku-Aku* contained highly disparaging remarks about the Easter Islanders and had offended them deeply.

Over lunch Chavez was asked to describe his methods of navigation, but he was unsuccessful, even with the aid of Tahitian, French and Spanish interpretation and all the knives, forks, salt cellars, pepper pots and glasses of beer spread over the table. No instruments or chart had been used. It was known that by keeping the Southern Cross abeam on the port side they must eventually reach one of the atolls of Tuamotu. Chavez's navigation methods were apparently quite rudimentary, amounting to a very thorough knowledge of the stars and an ability to steer a constant course in daylight hours.

A FORLORN RETURN HOME

It was time for Roberts to leave Tahiti. After farewell drinks Chavez took him to a Chinese restaurant for supper, where the thought of having to leave the islands made the food stick in his throat. At the airport he was given an unforgettable farewell, and on the aircraft many of the passengers were openly crying. He had been in Tahiti for little more than a week. Regretting that he could not have spent longer to find out something genuine about Tahiti, he acknowledged that despite his anthropological training he still had preconceived European ideas of the Polynesian paradise.

During his stopover at Los Angeles he wandered through the streets, feeling lonely and rather lost. "In the evening I went out to explore, but found everything contrary to my mood. This fabulous city, the largest in the world, leaves me quite unmoved. It is a land of make-believe; not something I am at present prepared to absorb with cynical enjoyment. I do not want to go to a fun fair or to sit in an air-conditioned cinema eating popcorn and peanuts. The clamouring advertisements leave me horrified. It is difficult to bear the atmosphere of hurry and worry, the myriad of strained, unattractive faces, the endlessly masticating jaws, the tawdry jewellery. The last is horrible in comparison with fresh flowers. Anywhere would probably be a flop after Polynesia, but this place is perhaps a bigger contrast than most."

His two-day visit was spent sustained only by dry Martinis in the hotel swimming pool, his digestive system having reacted badly to the delicious-looking and tasteless American food. He longed for fresh fish, fruit or coconuts: indeed anything that had not been subjected to freezing and 'hygienic' packaging. During the first afternoon he had the company of a girl from Montreal, but her informed chatter only made him yearn for Moorea, where there had been not much intelligent conversation but endless laughter and a genuine *joie de vivre*. In Los Angeles everything was artificial fun intended to create an escapist world of make-believe, and the canned Hawaiian music jarred in his ears. It was a painful return to Western life. Late that evening he boarded a flight to Washington to attend a committee meeting on Antarctic place names, flying on home to a dull, rainy England.

ISLANDS OF DESOLATION

Three years later, at lunch at the end of the third Treaty Meeting in Brussels in June 1964, Roberts was sitting next to Pierre Rolland, head of the French delegation and of Terres Australes et Antarctiques Françaises (TAAF). Rolland said little about the progress that the conference had made, but had a lot to say about the poor quality of the food and wine. He invited Roberts to be his guest as a zoologist on a forthcoming voyage by TAAF to the French sub-Antarctic islands in the South Indian Ocean. The tour would be made on the relief ship MS *Galliéni*, starting from tropical Réunion and going on to provision bases on the islands of Crozet, Kerguelen and Nouvelle Amsterdam.[3]

Much of the time would inevitably be spent at sea, but the exceptionally rich bird life of the islands, the history of the early sealers and the many shipwrecks were a fascination for Roberts, who had wanted to visit them ever since childhood, even before his interests had turned to the polar regions. The islands boast the world's greatest concentrations of penguins and petrels, as well as fur seals and elephant seals.

RÉUNION

Roberts packed carefully, anticipating a wide range of climatic conditions, and on 1 December flew via Cairo and Nairobi to Madagascar. Arriving on the tropical volcanic island of Réunion, the fierce heat and humidity felt rather like living in a Turkish bath. Sea bathing was ruled out because of the sharp, jagged volcanic rocks, and swimming in the shallow lagoon inside the partial coral reef would result in being flayed alive by the sun. In a small hired car he headed into the mountains where the air was cooler. In places the terrifyingly narrow road was no more than a ledge nicked into vertical cliffs. Stopping for a refreshing lunch of bunches of lychees and bananas, he intended to continue exploring the mountains and keeping cool, but the road was blocked by a long funeral procession. "For nearly 10 km I had to drive at walking speed or stop at intervals in exasperation before moving forward to be blocked once again by this colourful noisy group of laughing mourners." He then took an old mountain route that had recently been replaced by a new coast road. Rounding a corner he came across a bus on its side, wedged against a tree on a steep slope below the roadside. At the roadside was a despondent group of passengers awaiting help. "I offered transport to Saint-Denis (22 km away) and soon had the car loaded with four women and three babies, plus innumerable packages. Their men had to be left behind." At length they reached Saint-Denis, where Roberts had to take each of the women home in turn with their babies and baggage.

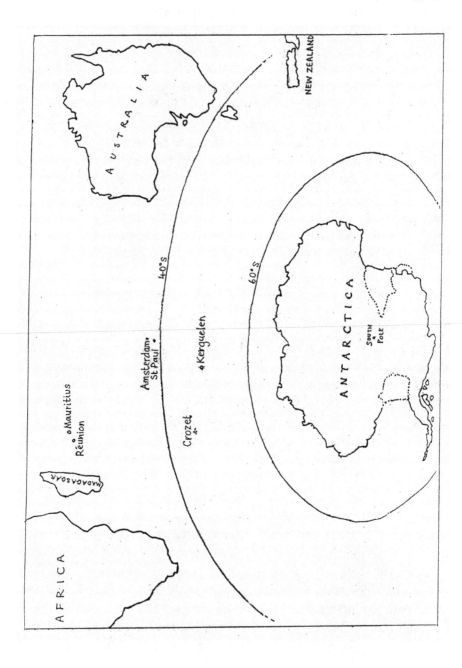

After five days of exploring Réunion, Roberts was collected by taxi to take him to the harbour quayside to board the *Galliéni*. All along the road were overturned smashed cars wedged among the rocks, and his fast and crazy taxi driver seemed hell-bent on joining them. With considerable relief he arrived intact and boarded the ship, to be welcomed by Réné Bost, who was substituting for Pierre Rolland. Roberts then realised that most conversation over the next two months would have to be in French, and he was acutely self-conscious of his limited language skills. Most scientists on board were surveyors, geologists and meteorologists. There was one woman aboard: Geneviève Pillet, a scientist tasked with establishing an ionospheric station at Kerguelen, and one of the few who spoke English.

After supper there was a film show: *Les Grands Secrets*, a documentary about astronomy, evolution and the origin of life introduced by Fred Hoyle. Halfway through the film Roberts discovered that the wine barrel he had been sitting on was covered in a sticky brown mess that had stained his trousers, and he had to hurry back to the cabin for a change and a wash. On his return Hoyle had reappeared as Bottom in *A Midsummer Night's Dream* and in the intervals between the acts was explaining astronomy, stirring cream into coffee to simulate the formation of galaxies. By that time Roberts had lost the thread of the film, as indeed had most of the audience.

At breakfast the following morning Roberts found that it was the convention to shake hands with everyone within easy reach. "I remember this business of hand-shaking as one of our minor social problems on

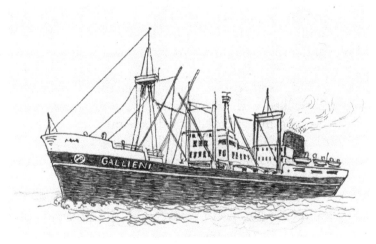

MS Gallieni

Pourquoi Pas? So it has been on *Galliéni*, mainly because one meets so many people during the course of each morning that I cannot always remember which of them I have already greeted!"

The ship headed southward for five days, the temperature progressively dropping and the seas becoming rougher. Fortunately *Galliéni* showed little tendency to roll. The bird life – including albatross – became more abundant. Despite the language difficulties Roberts began to enjoy life on board a French ship, with its excellent food, good films and the congenial, intelligent company of scientists who had an interest in wildlife and conservation, and enjoyed classical music.

CROZET

On 12 December *Galliéni* dropped anchor at Ile de la Possession, one of the six Isles de Crozet lying at 46°S. The one permanent base in the archipelago had been occupied continuously for just one year and there was much unloading of stores to be done. It was cold, wet and windy, with low cloud and squalls of rain obscuring the shore. Roberts could just catch glimpses of the rich bird life: nesting wandering albatross in the distance, three other species of albatross flying around him, innumerable petrels, and several gentoo penguin colonies. Two killer whales appeared close to the ship.

He went ashore. The visibility improved to disclose a vast king penguin colony extending from the beach right up the valley for two miles, larger than any he had seen on South Georgia. Crozet is home to half the world's breeding population of king penguins. King penguins have a 14-month breeding cycle, and as he waded into the colony he was greeted by moulting birds, the previous year's young in their distinctive brown down and, near the sea, incubating birds. In places they were so crowded together that it was difficult to walk through. Moulting birds and unoccupied adults gave way, but the incubating birds jabbed with their beaks or attacked with their flippers. His only route – albeit still crowded – was down the centre of a wide stream a foot deep.

Since 1938 Crozet, like all the French islands in the Indian Ocean, had been designated a nature reserve. Since the relentless slaughter of fur and elephant seals that had brought them close to extinction, elephant seals were starting to increase in numbers, but the fur seal, killed for its pelt, still had a long way to go to recover. On the beach Roberts found the remains of two large iron trypots, used for rendering blubber into oil during the sealing era.

The next morning he went ashore in bright sunshine, observing at close quarters various species of bird, including the wandering albatross *(Plate 18.4)*, sitting on their nests and all fearless of his presence. Full-grown youngsters were being fed by parent birds, and some pairs were performing their extraordinary courtship. On Crozet Roberts observed 20 different bird species, including three penguins and four albatrosses. He was worried about the sheer number of photographs he was taking. "The birds and seals induce photography on a scale that, for me, seems almost reckless. I hope that I have brought enough film." He wistfully complained that he had brought only ten films, half of what he needed. How he would have appreciated today's digital photography.

KERGUELEN

That evening *Galliéni* departed from Crozet in heavy seas. Two days and some 900 miles later the volcanic archipelago of Kerguelen came into view. *Gallieni* dropped anchor in Christmas Harbour, so named from James Cook's landing on Christmas Day 1776. Cook had suggested the name Desolation Islands for Kerguelen, one of the loneliest places on earth. Kerguelen consists of some 300 islands and islets, of which the main island is Grande Terre at 49°S. Cold, windy, rugged and mountainous, it rises to 6,430 ft and is some 93 miles across, its immense coastline heavily indented by long fjords. Whilst unloading was carried out at Port Christmas (Baie de l'Oiseau), Roberts and biologist Benoit Tollu were landed by helicopter high up on Cap Français at the northern entrance to the bay. They made for the colonies of black-browed albatross, each of which was incubating a single egg in a raised cup-shaped nest of mud in the cliffs, completely unafraid of the intruders. For Roberts these islands of desolation were an ornithological paradise. At Port Christmas he recorded a total of 19 species, well over half of which were breeding.

At the evening party he was feeling a little more confident with his French vocabulary, if not with his 'deplorable' grammar. He asked his colleagues whether there were rabbits on the islands, only to be warned not to use the word *lapin* – a French nautical superstition: if one utters the word, there will be strong wind. The French also have the same superstition as the British about not killing wandering albatrosses. The following day *Galliéni*, accompanied by flocks of Wilson's petrels – the first to be seen on this voyage – sailed eastwards around the coast of

Kerguelen to the main base at Port-aux-Français. The ship's arrival was celebrated with a whisky party attended by all on board and ashore, continuing well into the night.

Roberts spent several nights at the station. Next day was Sunday, and thinking he had been invited along to the mess room (*le mess*) for lunch, he found himself attending Roman Catholic mass (*la messe*) instead. The priest, Jean Volot, was also a geophysicist who had built the small chapel himself, dedicated to Notre Dame des Vents. The altar was a big slab of rough-hewn rock, with candlesticks made of whale vertebrae. Despite his aversion to Catholicism, Roberts admitted to finding the experience uplifting.

The large Port-aux-Français station was impressive, with facilities for a wide range of earth sciences, although lacking any for biology. Besides the living quarters, restaurants and kitchens there was a hospital, bar, radio hut, post office, stores, workshops, generators, water pumps, a hydrogen plant, and garages for the many trucks, jeeps and even cars. There were abundant elephant seals, which had come ashore to moult. Nearby was a farm with pigs, ducks and hens, and a flock of sheep was kept on a nearby islet to provide mutton. Game was on hand with recently introduced reindeer, rabbits and a native wild duck, the Kerguelen pintail (now known as Eaton's pintail). Cold frames and a heated greenhouse provided fresh salads and even flowers. A trout fishery had been set up, and locally-caught seafood was regularly on the menu. The French clearly had their priorities in life.

On 21 December helicopter flights were made. Despite rain and fog Roberts was able to view spectacularly large king penguin colonies at Cap Ratmanoff, thousands of immature elephant seals, and nests of wandering albatross. He visited a derelict whaling and sealing station, reminiscent of Deception Island in 1935. While the long programme of discharging 1,400 tons of stores and equipment continued Roberts rambled eastwards along the shore, enjoying the magnificent scenery and wildlife. Returning to a party in the bar on Christmas Eve, he no longer felt a stranger. Almost the entire community attended Midnight Mass.

NOUVELLE AMSTERDAM

Gallieni sailed for three days through the strong winds and heavy swell of the Roaring Forties towards Nouvelle Amsterdam. This isolated island of area 21 square miles has a dormant volcano, and with its slightly milder climate than Crozet or Kerguelen is the only one of the island group to support trees. It once had sizeable areas of *Phylica arborea* forest, which had been much denuded by the sealers. Circling around the ship were numerous yellow-nosed albatrosses, now known to have an important breeding colony on the island. Unusually terns were seen nesting on inaccessible cliff ledges, probably to escape from feral cats. As the wind continued unabated, landing and unloading were impossible. The crew indulged in some fishing for barracuda, a ferocious fish up to 3 ft in length with long, vicious teeth, to be used as bait in langouste (spiny lobster) traps lowered down to the seabed. The next day's fishing produced several more species of fish including trumpeter, each weighing some 12lb. "The excitement when several of these big fish are hauled aboard simultaneously is only exceeded when everyone scatters to escape the snapping jaws of barracuda flapping about the deck," wrote Roberts.

On New Year's Day 1965 the swell subsided and landing operations were started. It was exactly 30 years since Roberts had been on his first Antarctic voyage on the British Graham Land Expedition, experiencing the stomach pains that were eventually diagnosed as appendicitis. This New Year's Day was a happier occasion for him. He arrived in time for a party in the main building of the station to receive a most cordial welcome, and was now feeling confident that his French conversation had made quite a lot of progress. Lunch in the station was all local produce: hot langouste, roast beef and salads.

Like Kerguelen, the station had a flourishing garden with cauliflowers, cabbages, carrots, spring onions and tomatoes, the hardier vegetables that one might expect to find in northern France, and a small farmyard with pigs, ducks, chickens and pigeons. But here there was an additional problem: hundreds of wild cattle close-grazed the hillsides, creating an ecological disaster for the island. Introduced in 1871, they were not eradicated until 2010. Roberts was delighted to find fur seals all along the shore, some with very young pups, but there was otherwise little to enjoy on the island. It rained for three days, and the cliffs of volcanic lava were loose, friable and treacherous. Much of the indigenous flora and fauna had disappeared, and the bird life was impoverished, for which feral cats and rats were largely responsible. Only five species of birds were chalked up.

Gallieni headed back south to Kerguelen, arriving at Port Christmas on 7 January. Once again the bird life was diverse and abundant. Macaroni penguin colonies were at advanced stages of incubation, some with newly-hatched young. At Port-aux-Français Roberts and Tollu spent a day skinning in the biological laboratory, once they had managed to extricate their bird specimens from the freezer, buried under sides of beef, fish and langoustes from Nouvelle Amsterdam.

Galliéni departed for the next four-day leg of the voyage back to Crozet, heading into a westerly gale. As they passed the south-west extremity of Kerguelen, Roberts witnessed a remarkable sight. No prions (a petrel species) had been seen during the day, but "at 1830 there must have been millions of them around the ship, all flying swiftly into the wind, alternately showing their blue-grey backs and white breasts. By 2030, half an hour before sunset, they had all gone".

Reaching Crozet on 13 January, a heavy swell prevented Roberts from going ashore. Stuck on board, he still had the pleasure of watching large numbers of Wilson's petrels feeding close to the ship. In the afternoon *Galliéni* started her five-day voyage back to Nouvelle Amsterdam in rough seas, followed by another five days' sailing on to Mauritius. Many on board were experiencing sea-sickness. Roberts was not one of them, but the long days of shipboard idleness were starting to become wearisome.

Prions

On the north-west coast of Mauritius, *Galliéni* arrived at Port-Louis, where a small party from the ship visited the Royal Botanical Gardens at Pamplemousses, with its exotic flora, giant water-lilies and large endemic tortoises. On 24 January the ship was back at Réunion in an overcast sky that mitigated the searing heat. The next day the death of Winston Churchill was announced, and all flags were at half-mast. Roberts and geologist Gabriel Lucas spent the day exploring corals with masks and breathing tubes, but it was made difficult by rough seas. A second day was spent exploring the island in a hire car, human life teeming wherever they went, in an abundance of weddings and funerals.

Extreme climatic contrast exists between west and east: endless sunshine on the western leeward side, and heavy precipitation on the eastern windward side. As they drove east, passing a metal statue of the Virgin Mary holding aloft a huge metal umbrella, they encountered torrential rain falling on hot streams of molten volcanic lava. Having forgone breakfast in the interests of an early start, and unable to get lunch anywhere, they ended up with a very sticky picnic of a pineapple and some mangoes. But they were rewarded with the beautiful sight of white-tailed tropicbirds.

White-tailed tropic birds

TROMELIN

Administered by TAAF, Tromelin – 280 miles east of Madagascar and 340 miles north-west of Réunion – is a tiny French coral island, an oval-shaped sandbank just over a mile long and only 22 ft in height. With no harbour or means of anchorage, a rough airstrip provides the only access. On 27 January 1964 Roberts and Lucas were given a special opportunity to make a visit, taking the 2-hour flight from Réunion in a four-seater plane. They were greeted by three meteorologists and a dozen labourers from Réunion, living in makeshift shacks, who were building a reinforced concrete meteorological station to replace one destroyed six years earlier in one of the cyclones that constantly batter the island. It was extremely hot.

Tromelin was one of the breeding sites of the green turtle, unrecorded before Roberts' and Lucas' visit.

> "Many turtles had been coming ashore at night to deposit their eggs in shallow excavations in the sand at the back of the beach, about 200-300 ft from the shore. The meteorologists had turned one of them over during the night for us to photograph in daylight. We found it on its back; tears streaming from its eyes. It looked very unhappy, but I understand that, when captured, they survive much longer upside down than the right way up. They tend to suffocate on land in the normal position. The well-known tears are thought to be a physiological adaptation to deal with sand in their eyes. Our specimen was so large (perhaps 400 kg) that we could not turn it over again without the help of several men. While trying to do this I got severely bruised on the legs and thighs by its powerful flippers. Next time I shall know how to do this without getting hurt! The turtle struggled slowly down to the water and swam away with powerful strokes, a remarkable contrast of mobility in two environments."[4]

Young baby turtles were making their hazardous journey down the beach, their half-eaten remains a meal for frigatebirds, rats and hermit crabs. Roberts' chief interest was not so much the turtles as the birds, about which nothing had been recorded. Two breeding species of the gannet family were found: red-footed boobies (an estimated 2000 occupied nests in the low scrub bushes), and a small number of the much larger white boobies. Also present –though not breeding – were a few brown boobies, and large flocks of the magnificent and lesser frigatebirds (*Plate 18.5*).[5] After a two-and-a-half-hour circuit of the island, the two biologists were ready for a cool swim to examine the brilliantly-coloured corals and fish, but this was too dangerous owing to offshore currents, huge breakers, the absence of a boat and the presence of sharks. So they swam close inshore still risking the powerful breakers that could hurl them onto the hard sandstone seabed, but the fish were less interesting and there was no coral.

After lunch they left Tromelin, flying on from Réunion to Madagascar. There was continuous heavy rain. In his hotel room Roberts endured a sweaty night with mosquitoes and an army of bed bugs for company, with constant flashes of lightning and crashes of thunder, which guaranteed a sleepless night. The torrential rain flooded the floor of his room, and his legs still ached from the green turtle incident.

Roberts had been away for two months, compiling a 180-page diary. The one issue which caused him the most frustration was (predictably) place naming. No gazetteers existed, and there was no official ruling

Tromelin island and frigatebirds

on the names for the Isles de Desolation – being variously named as Ile Kerguelen, Iles Kerguelen, Iles de Kerguelen, Archipel Kerguelen and Archipel des Kerguelen – with similar confusion for Crozet and Nouvelle-Amsterdam. None of the three District Chiefs on board *Galliéni* regarded these variations as significant or even noteworthy, and only Roberts could become upset by this. Disappointingly for the authors, his huge photographic collection from the voyage has been either lost or buried in unknown or inaccessible archives.

Plate 16.1 Mount Erebus

Plate 16.2 Emperor penguin chicks at Cape Crozier

Plate 17.1 First Treaty Meeting, Canberra 1961. Roberts is arrowed

Plate 18.1 Coconut palms on Moorea

Plate 18.2 Moorea, Mouaroa from Baie de Papetoa

Plate 18.3 Moorea children in outrigger canoe, with drying fishing nets

Plate 18.4 Wandering Albatross

Plate 18.5 Nesting magnificent frigatebirds, Galapagos

Plate 19.1 Fifth Treaty Meeting, Paris 1968 Roberts centre, John Heap right

Plate 20.1 Roberts at home in Cambridge

Plate 22.1 RRS Bransfield

19

NAVIGATING SEAL CONSERVATION THROUGH POLITICAL ROCKS

Most of the Antarctic fauna exists on what is believed to be a marginal basis of stability, and human influences could easily tip the scale in critical cases. We have discarded the old argument that a species is in no danger because it is still common. The seals, petrels and penguins are especially vulnerable because they concentrate for breeding, sometimes in vast numbers, on relatively few island sites where introduced predators or diseases can have catastrophic results. The scarcity of breeding sites in relation to huge areas of marine feeding grounds presents a special challenge for conservationists. The sudden increase in human activities in places where the fauna has been isolated from outside infection and there is no rapid bacteriological decomposition brings a potential demographic crisis. The Antarctic ecosystem can probably be destroyed even more rapidly than those of temperate regions.

Meanwhile let us do our best to preserve for our successors some of the most interesting and exciting biological spectacles to be found anywhere on earth: the great seal and penguin colonies, the soaring of the wandering albatross, the fantastic evening flight of uncountable millions of prions returning to their nesting islands... a sperm whale leaping clear of the water; a small pink *Colobanthus* flowering in isolated desolation – those who have been fortunate enough to witness these things will never forget the joy they evoked.

Brian Roberts[1]

Flushed with the success of the third Treaty Meeting in Brussels, Roberts was in a bullish mood. Compared with other issues, wildlife conservation had proved to be relatively free from political minefields and there was now broad agreement on the Agreed Measures for the Conservation of Antarctic Fauna and Flora (AMCAFF). The fourth Treaty Meeting would take up Specially Protected Areas (SPAs) and the regulation of pelagic sealing, with recommended guidelines and provisions for protecting the natural ecosystem.[2] This time Roberts would be in the hot seat as leader of the UK delegation, having to make nearly all its speeches.

On 1 September 1966 he, John Heap and David Anderson flew out to Santiago for a preparatory meeting, enjoying a spectacular view of Aconcagua, at 22,800 ft the highest peak of the Andes. In contrast to the trauma of the flight to Buenos Aires in 1962, it was an easy journey and at Santiago they were greeted with a pleasant spring atmosphere of fruit blossoms, humming birds and the scent of fresh lemons.

But at the first morning session Roberts was thrust into his first crisis when the South African Ambassador passed him a note: "Verwoerd stabbed to death in Parliament this morning." Hendrik Verwoerd was the principal architect of South Africa's policy of institutionalized racial segregation. Roberts was no apologist for apartheid, but he had a diplomatic face-saving problem on his hands. Protocol demanded that the loss of any head of state should be acknowledged by a formal expression of condolence by the conference chairman, and it was feared that the Soviet delegation would walk out and create an embarrassing scene. In the end the solution was simple: the Soviets were persuaded to show up late the following morning.

Despite such banana skins, prospects for the main Treaty Meeting were favourable, with advance agreement to discuss Antarctic tourism for the first time. There was even a move to put jurisdiction on the agenda, a sticky topic that until now had been studiously avoided.

SANTIAGO, NOVEMBER 1966

The fourth Treaty Meeting opened amid scenes of some chaos. The venue was the University of Chile where, on getting off a bus from downtown Santiago, the delegates discovered that the meetings were to be held in a lecture theatre. The practical problems of such a venue will be familiar to any university student. Heads of delegation were assigned to front row benches, each of them with a tiny collapsible table which had to be raised by a side hinge to gain access to the seat. Once seated, Roberts, with his large frame, was trapped and unable to get out without a major performance. The delegates had to balance their voluminous papers on their knees, any ill-judged movement resulting in the scattering of documents over the floor. Seated next to Roberts, the French Ambassador expressed his extreme displeasure with the facilities, and resolved to put in an appearance in future only at cocktail parties.

On the topical subject of pelagic sealing, Roberts and Heap had kicked off with an informal and productive all-day session with US delegates Jim Simsarian and Harry Francis. It would take many hours of closely-argued deliberation, but the Americans proved to be good sparring partners and they were eventually won over to the UK position. The conference would be a test of Roberts' inexhaustible patience and good humour, but with many hours of such lobbying in advance he was able to maintain the initiative in formal sessions without arousing opposition or resentment.

At one point a Chilean delegate proposed that measurements of seals should be formally reported.

"Have you ever tried to measure a seal?" Roberts countered.

"No," was the response. Nor had anyone else present.

"Well, I have," replied Roberts. He went on to recount what happened when he did so. Despite his skill in handling birds, when it came to seals there was nothing to grab hold of. His graphic description of himself wrestling with a recalcitrant mass of slippery blubber reduced the conference to tears of laughter and the proposal was promptly dropped.[3]

CRISIS OVER AGREED MEASURES

During the months prior to the conference Roberts had persuaded Launcelot Fleming, now Bishop of Norwich, to introduce into the House of Lords a Private Bill to give UK legal effect to AMCAFF. The Antarctic Treaty Bill had occupied a great deal of Foreign Office time, causing the UK's legal adviser David Anderson to arrive late in Santiago.

The Agreed Measures were proving to be a problem for the Chileans, who wanted to delete any reference to 'the appropriate competent authority' to issue permits. They were panicking because such wording implied the existence of an authority other than the Chilean government for issuing permits for the sector of the Antarctic claimed by Chile. Had this banana skin been raised previously the difficulty could probably have been circumvented, but the UK was now in an impossible situation.

On his arrival, David Anderson tried to explain the problems created by any Chilean amendments to the text. Having been formally adopted as a recommendation at the Brussels conference, AMCAFF was annexed to a UK Antarctic Treaty Bill that had been published and was due shortly to come before Parliament. Any amendment would require a new recommendation by the Santiago conference. But in that event the Bill would have to be withdrawn and reintroduced to the UK Parliament with the amended Schedule. And since it was a Private Member's Bill, the chances of its proposer, Launcelot Fleming, being given a second bite at the cherry would be slim. The UK could not approve AMCAFF until the Bill had become law. Thus the whole conservation agreement – the purpose of which was not in dispute – was in danger of being shipwrecked by a procedural complexity.

Predictably, the labyrinthine procedure for introducing Private Members' Bills to the UK Parliament was baffling to most international delegates. Francisco Oyarzún of the Chilean delegation attempted twice to produce a compromise amendment, only to return each time with acute embarrassment to report President Frei would not accept it.

Since the formal approval of recommendations required unanimity from the participating delegations, it was feasible in principle for the UK delegation to exercise a power of veto over the Chilean amendment. Which they did. But in the diplomatic world vetoing is not a decision to be taken lightly, because it can have unfortunate repercussions for the vetoing party on other issues. It was also an embarrassment because Chile was itself hosting the conference. At an awkward meeting Anderson, in a minority of one in objecting to the Chilean proposal, tackled Enrique Gajardo, who had accepted the original AMCAFF wording at the Brussels conference – to no avail, since Gajardo was no longer head of the Chilean delegation. Anderson did receive some support from Soviet delegate Anatoly Movchan: since the Soviets did not recognise the Chilean territorial claim, to them the concept of a 'non-Chilean competent authority acting within the Chilean Antarctic' was meaningless. In the end Anderson had to exercise the UK veto, but was able to signal that it was only temporary. It was agreed to defer consideration of the Chilean request to the next Antarctic conference two years hence, by which time the UK Bill would have been passed.[4]

The main achievement of the Santiago meeting, apart from surviving the AMCAFF crisis, was the introduction of Specially Protected Areas (SPAs) to protect penguin rookeries. Wildlife conservation was becoming a success story for the Antarctic Treaty System. There were now over 20 recommendations on the conservation of Antarctic wildlife, which would lead to conservation measures more comprehensive than those anywhere else in the world.

Specially Protected Area

On the final evening Roberts retired to bed at 2 am. "One reason why I find these meetings so exhausting," he lamented, "is because I have been unable to learn the art of not listening". At a college dinner in Cambridge astronomer Fred Hoyle had advised him that the technique of many habitual conference people is to exhaust everybody else present with pretentious inconsequential gibberish. "If you listen to everything that is said you become utterly exhausted and unable to take effective part when the really important issues come up," he said. Roberts however did not quite believe that the drivel they had to endure was all malicious filibustering. "Pinto's speeches are intensely soporific, but I feel I must listen intently in case he says something significant.

Fortunately he seldom speaks for more than 5 minutes. We do not now have to endure the hour-long speeches of Senator Mora at the Washington conference."

On the way home Roberts and John Heap took a break in Peru. In Lima the sole tourist attraction was the cathedral tomb of conquistador Francisco Pizzaro, a dilapidated glass-sided sarcophagus containing his shrivelled skin, desiccated flesh, bare skull and exposed skeleton. The next morning they took an uncomfortable flight to Cuzco over high mountain country in a small unpressurized aircraft. Oxygen was provided via a small tube at no extra cost, but was insufficient for breathing purposes. On arrival at Cuzco, at an altitude of 11,150 ft, the passengers were exhausted and needed a two-hour period to recuperate. A day later the two men took an early morning train to Machu Picchu. The narrow-gauge Cuzco-Santa Ana Railway climbs northwards out of the Cuzco valley and then descends 3,200 ft to the grassy plain of Ante to enter the mighty gorge of the River Urubamba, a tributary of the Amazon. Back at Cuzco, a huge produce market displayed potatoes of all varieties – white, yellow, pink, grey, brown, purple, black, spotted and streaked – representing just a small selection of the 3,000 known varieties of Peruvian potato. Roberts, a potato addict throughout life, was in seventh heaven.

TAKING THE AGREED MEASURES THROUGH PARLIAMENT

Despite its limitations, AMCAFF had far-reaching implications. One of its main precepts, prevention of upsets to natural ecosystems, is today relatively well understood, if inadequately complied with. It aimed to prevent the introduction into the Antarctic of all alien species, including predators, parasites and diseases. Dogs had to be inoculated and the importing of any live poultry was prohibited. AMCAFF also laid down protection measures for animals and plants within SPAs, covering for example the avoidance of disruption by motor vehicles.

In June 1966 the Bill aimed at bringing AMCAFF into UK law was presented to the House of Commons. It received all-party support.[5] The Bill also gave full effect to Article VIII of the Antarctic Treaty, enabling jurisdiction that would render UK personnel in the Antarctic liable to prosecution on return to the UK. By 14 April 1967, when the Antarctic Bill was read to the Commons for the third time, Alan Moorehead's

The Fatal Impact had been published, describing for the first time the carnage resulting from visits by hundreds of sealing vessels following Captain Cook's voyages to the Pacific and the southern oceans.[6] But what brought front-page news to the British public was the wreck of the supertanker *Torrey Canyon* which had struck rocks between Cornwall and the Scilly Isles, spilling 30 million tons of thick black crude oil into the sea. It was the beginning of the breeding season and the incident resulted in the deaths of some 10,000 seabirds, including puffins, razorbills, guillemots, shags and cormorants. Seals, shellfish and sea flora also suffered. The AMCAFF Bill was welcomed by bodies such as the Nature Conservancy, which pointedly regretted the absence in Britain of measures for the protection of fauna and flora that were being proposed for the Antarctic.[7]

On 1 May Fleming proposed the second reading of the Bill in the House of Lords. It received wholehearted support from the president of the Fauna Preservation Society, quoting from Roberts' own words at the head of this chapter. The Bill was read for the third time to the Lords on 24 July, thereby passing into UK law.

EDWARD WILSON'S BEST MEDICINE

Roberts' political work was steadily gaining increasing recognition, but at the same time there was an unwelcome development in his state of health: for nearly four months in the spring of 1967 he was laid up in bed with hepatitis and jaundice. He was however able to use this time effectively to achieve a long-held ambition. Amongst the gems in SPRI's collections are the drawings and watercolour paintings of Edward Wilson, who, as doctor, biologist and artist, accompanied Scott on his two Antarctic expeditions (the *Discovery* 1901-04 and the *Terra Nova* 1910-12). Largely unpublished at the time, the sheer number of paintings and sketches of birds reflect Wilson's devotion to ornithology. Since many of the Antarctic species were recorded for the first time by Wilson, they remained unidentified until Roberts selected the illustrations for his *Edward Wilson's Birds of the Antarctic*.[8] Published in large format by the Blandford Press, its generous-sized reproductions of Wilson's work were described as "almost unbelievably excellent" by the *Geographical Journal*. In the accompanying text Roberts provides comprehensive biographical details and uses Wilson's own words from his diaries and letters to convey his methods, ideas and the difficult conditions under which he laboured.

PARIS, NOVEMBER 1968

The fifth Treaty Meeting took place in Paris against a background of political turbulence. Difficulties were also encountered within the conference with the Australians on meteorology and telecommunications. Despite extensive late-night lubrication with the aid of whisky and gin and tonic in Roberts' hotel room, they were unable to agree on anything much, except Australian sovereignty, appeasement of Australian public opinion and their objections to the 'creeping internationalisation' promoted by the UK.

On Monday 18 November 1968 the conference opened at the Quai d'Orsay (the French Foreign Ministry). The UK delegation included Roberts as its head, together with John Heap and Leslie Fielding (*Plate 19.1*). The opening plenary session was more than usually tedious, but there was some encouragement for Roberts, who was given the opportunity to introduce plenary sessions on Antarctic tourism and historic monuments. At the time of the previous conference in Santiago some 50 tourists had visited the Antarctic. During the coming season a thousand visitors were expected and there were increased concerns over souvenir hunting. The Argentines agreed that some control would be necessary on tourism, but acrimony prevailed and the Chileans were sensitive to accusations of looting refuge huts.

PUSHING FORWARD ON PELAGIC SEALING

Shortly before the Paris conference, the Scientific Committee on Antarctic Research hosted a working group of seal biologists in Cambridge. It was a sobering experience for Roberts, who reflected that "there could have been no clearer demonstration that SCAR must never be allowed to exercise uncontrolled administrative authority – otherwise they will create situations far more stupid than anything governments have yet achieved".[9] Biologists had proposed the total banning of southern sealing until sufficient data had been collected on the numbers of each species, their distribution, their breeding biology and the age structure of the populations. But such information could be obtained only from the activities of a sealing industry in the first place. Roberts and legal advisor Anderson were eventually able to convert the SCAR proposals into a workable draft Convention that Roberts was able to present to the Treaty Meeting. Because it was impossible to define an 'optimum sustainable yield', he proposed that quotas should be referred to as 'permissible catch', namely the best estimate based on existing knowledge but with no claims to accuracy. They were intended essentially as a rough guide to governments on whether too many seals were being killed. The initial response was quite favourable and seven countries were prepared to negotiate a Convention immediately. But trouble was in store for Roberts. Japan and the US were dragging their feet, other parties wanted to await full ratification of the Agreed Measures, and there was also the awkward 'Chilean amendment' left hanging over from the Santiago conference.

The penultimate day of the Paris conference had an inauspicious start. The Working Group on Seals was held in the lobby of a hotel which had no private meeting room available.[10] No chairs were provided, the attendees having to sprawl around a large marble-topped table supporting an ugly centrepiece of metal flowers. What started as a small group at one end of the table became progressively larger as others gradually joined in to listen. The latecomers could join in only by wriggling across the table, which was greatly amusing to onlookers but not at all to the conference delegates, who were becoming quite ill-tempered. Norwegian Torger Øritsand, provoked beyond endurance by the Russian Yevgeniy Tolstikov, got up in a rage and walked out. Roberts followed and persuaded him to return, only for Tolstikov, provoked in turn by Jim Simsarian, to lose his temper five minutes later and leave equally abruptly. Tolstikov said that he was exhausted: the Soviet instructions were to accept the SCAR proposals and nothing else. Roberts protested that no government could be expected to accept a SCAR paper that had not been properly drafted with the aid of a legal adviser.

At the final plenary session the working group produced its latest compromise proposals on pelagic sealing. Roberts thought that he had been able to get the Soviets and the Americans to agree. He hadn't. The US delegate Jim Simsarian was now proposing to reopen the whole debate in plenary. Roberts was thoroughly alarmed and asked the chairman to allow a pause for private discussion. He begged Simsarian to desist from further debate, which could result only in fruitless argument and a Soviet veto. Returning to the rostrum, he proposed that the text of the draft recommendation should now be agreeable in two versions, Russian and English (the French and Spanish versions being direct translations from the English). To his huge relief the recommendation went through unopposed, with no further interventions – either from Simsarian or from Tolstikov.

The outcome was that agreement had been reached to refer the draft Convention on pelagic sealing to the next Antarctic conference, and in the meantime voluntarily to take note of its principles. This shift from Agreed Measures to a Convention on wildlife conservation – seemingly just a tortuous piece of semantics – turned out to be a sea change in the operation of the treaty that would lead ultimately to the Convention on the Conservation of Antarctic Seals (CCAS) and the hugely significant Commission for the Conservation of Antarctic Marine Living Resources (CCAMLR). That night Roberts sipped his after-dinner cognac with a feeling of satisfaction on surviving a diplomatic tightrope walk.

HONOURS AND CARPETS

In May 1969 Roberts was awarded the Companionship of the Order of St Michael and St George (CMG) "in recognition of the valuable services you have rendered". Such awards were astutely interpreted by him as "carefully graded insults" and a source more of amusement than of personal pride. The main tangible outcome was an improvement in his carpets and office furniture at the Foreign Office, which created a major upheaval due to the simultaneous arrival of new map presses and the need to replace the carpets before the presses could be installed. Moreover different contractors had to be employed for disconnecting the telephones, removing telephone wires from under the carpet, removing the old carpet, laying the new carpet, boring holes for the wires in the new carpet, and reconnecting the telephones.[11] In the end a conference of all parties was convened so that they could quarrel with each other. John Heap decided to deal with it himself, advising Roberts to keep away and to go and feed the ducks in St James' Park. Roberts spent the day contentedly in the British Museum.

To Roberts the most significant honour was actually not the CMG but the Polar Medal, and he was particularly upset by the numerous instances of delays or failures to award it to those whom he strongly felt deserved it. He was nonetheless delighted to receive the many letters of congratulation on the CMG from his friends and colleagues. Perhaps the most apposite comment was from Launcelot Fleming: "I hear that honours and awards don't interest you very much, but so long as they happen there is a merit in these going to the right people. But I do hope Brian that you are keeping fitter."

20

THE ROAD TO CAMALAR

'Camalar' is a colloquial verbal name for the unpronounceable acronym CCAMLR, the Commission for the Conservation of Antarctic Marine Living Resources, a cumbersome title that conceals some of the most far-sighted conservation measures ever achieved. It evolved from the Agreed Measures for the Conservation of Antarctic Fauna and Flora and the Convention for Conservation of Antarctic Seals that Roberts had done so much to promote, but CCAMLR would not appear until 1982, after his death.

The Antarctic Treaty System was becoming an increasingly complex affair. Roberts' personal diary of the sixth Treaty Meeting in Tokyo reveals a severe case of appendicitis, containing 91 annexes.[1] With the endless correspondence, telegrams and long-distance telephone calls – one of the consequences of the continued absence of a secretariat – planning for the event took many months and included seven preparatory meetings. Mineral prospecting and unresolved issues over pelagic sealing were to occupy more time than anything else. The UK proposals had met with opposition from the Japanese government, and only by deferring signature of a separate Convention on sealing could the conference hosts avoid the appearance of sponsoring a restrictive fisheries agreement to which Japanese public opinion would be sensitive. And so was born the Convention for the Conservation of Antarctic Seals (CCAS).

TOKYO, OCTOBER 1970

The UK delegation to the sixth Treaty Meeting consisted of Roberts, John Heap and legal advisor David Edwards. Heap had been appointed a temporary Queen's Messenger and under the prevailing UK economy drive had had to travel from the Foreign and Commonwealth Office to London's Heathrow airport by bus, carrying a diplomatic bag containing classified papers. This caused some consternation at the air terminal: Queen's Messengers had traditionally been driven straight to the airport in an official car, so as not to risk the loss of sensitive documents on public transport.

In Tokyo the delegation was greeted by oppressive heat, humidity and photochemical smog. Roberts was horrified by "the worst example I have yet experienced of human desecration of the environment, ugly development, air so polluted that one could not breathe without nausea, and once beautiful waterways now stinking with garbage and domestic sewage, and devoid of fish". Traffic police were wearing oxygen masks.

On the first Saturday evening the UK team met the Australians, who – true to form – seemed to be an ill-assorted delegation, none of them having much apparent respect for the others. But progress was made, aided by Roberts' customary bottle of whisky. On the Monday morning the conference was officially opened with speeches, as usual completely anodyne, until E I 'Robbie' Robertson of New Zealand proposed discussion of Antarctic mineral exploitation. There was a stunned silence. Robertson was promptly slapped down by Yevgeniy Tolstikov, who said that the Soviet delegation was not prepared to discuss the subject at all. Nor, it seemed, was anyone else.

Eventually the UK's proposed Convention on Antarctic Sealing got to the top of the agenda. Roberts still faced an uphill task: the Australians saw no need for the Convention. Roberts persisted relentlessly, explaining and defending his ideas about seal conservation, continuing into the evenings at cocktail parties that he detested but which he was able to exploit effectively to lobby "the few people who really mattered". But he was irritated by Robertson, who was quite open and cynical about the personal power of veto that he had acquired. As a result Roberts had to indulge in horse-trading. Robbie said that he would support UK proposals on conservation if Roberts would support Robbie on radio-isotopes. Even with all his experience

Roberts was appalled that scientists could behave like gamesters every bit as unscrupulous as politicians.

At the time relations between the UK, Argentina and Chile were difficult, with much dispute over Specially Protected Areas. SPAs and historic monuments were both proving to be unexpectedly contentious issues. But there was considerable encouragement for Roberts when it was agreed to proceed with the Sealing Convention. For him it had been an immense personal challenge to find some agreed solution, with sustained lobbying on his part at several Treaty Meetings to promote what he thought was a relatively simple idea and to secure the agreement of 12 governments in the face of scepticism and indifference. Now, at last, it was all going to happen.

THE SEALING CONFERENCE, LONDON 1972

On 3 February 1972 the moment had arrived for the Convention for the Conservation of Antarctic Seals, an opportunity to provide protection for seals on floating ice which the Agreed Measures had been unable to.[2] Since the Convention was not restricted to signatories to the Antarctic Treaty, the Foreign and Commonwealth Office, which hosted the conference, was confronted with the prospect of many observers from non-government conservation and wildlife organisations that were either invited or insisted on attending. As acting head of the UK delegation, Roberts' skill and experience in international coffee-break diplomacy would be exercised to the full.

For Roberts at least, the motive for the Convention was not restricted to seals. Since the slaughter of the early 19th century the populations of most seal species had recovered, and they were no longer considered to be endangered. Roberts admitted in his opening address that conservation had not always been the top priority in his personal life:

> "During my first visit to the Antarctic, in 1934-37, the expedition of which I was a member possessed only very small financial resources. We had to live by hunting the local animals. So we had to eat seal meat every day for 3 years. I think I can assert with confidence that I have had to eat more Antarctic seals than anyone else in this room. At the time – now nearly 40 years ago – we did not think about this as a problem related to conservation. We were young and hungry. We were actively engaged in exploring new lands and we scarcely gave a thought to the possible consequences of our discoveries or to the ever-increasing pressures on natural resources which might lead to commercial exploitation."[3]

Underlying the convention was an idea going much further than the conservation of Antarctic seals. Roberts was aiming at an international protocol for managing Southern Ocean resources in general, in particular krill.

There was indeed confusion in some quarters over the aims of the conference. Public opinion, particularly in North America, was interpreting the agenda as an encouragement of the exploitation of seals, not conserving them. Representatives from Canada had been invited to attend, but had declined to do so for that reason. The organisers were bombarded with enquiries and protests from people who wanted to ban sealing operations entirely. Roberts had to explain with his customary patience that it was the absence of an international agreement that was a licence to the wholesale slaughter of Antarctic seals. Conservation could be achieved only by regulating and limiting catches to a sustainable level and it had to be done before any sealing industry got going.

Most of the countries represented fielded the usual number of delegates, between two and six. The US fielded nine, to which were added ten more representatives from various conservationist bodies, making a total of 19. Something rather strange was going on. The US delegation was led by State Department fisheries expert Donald McKernan, described as "a particularly arrogant, boorish and bullying roving ambassador".[4] But whatever were the shortcomings in McKernan's personal charisma, he was caught between a rock and a hard place, being persuaded by his delegation to push for means of enforcement that were too draconian for the Antarctic Treaty parties. Inspection had long been a bone of contention. The idea of setting up a 'police state', apart from being unworkable, was not favoured by any of the other delegations, including the Soviets. A supranational Scientific Advisory Committee proposed by the US was dismissed on the grounds that governments would refuse to ratify it. In his address halfway through the conference Roberts, who himself had similar concerns over the Scientific Committee on Antarctic Research (SCAR), explained that the creation of a committee with such powers would result in uncontrollable political pressures within it.[5] The US delegation, despite its inflated size, found itself to be in a minority of one. In the end it grudgingly agreed to sign the conference's Final Act, on the grounds that some progress on conservation was better than none. But it had taken a week of head banging to get to that point and there were times when a successful outcome hung on a cliff-edge. The meeting had to be extended by an extra day to enable the Final Act to be signed, at midnight on 11 February 1972. In the end the Convention was able to set permissible catch levels for crabeater, Weddell and leopard seals, a prohibition on killing the more endangered Ross, elephant and fur seals, and a system of inspection to be introduced once permissible catch levels were approached. Probably for the first time ever in human history, agreement had been reached on control measures prior to any hunting and exploitation of a wildlife resource. As Roberts emphasized in his report on the conference:

"There is at present no industry exploiting Antarctic seals, which now represent by far the world's largest unexploited mammal stock... Although there is no immediate need to conserve Antarctic seals, there is a growing need to start on the process of conserving the Southern Ocean creatures generally. Krill could provide a potential harvest conservatively estimated to be equal to or greater than the present total world annual catch of fish from the sea. Because krill form the base of the food chain upon which all Antarctic animals depend, it is important that a regime for controlling an industry based on this resource should be developed before exploitation gets out of hand... The Conference marked the first step towards this goal and may be expected to set a precedent for the international regulation of a krill industry. In both cases the basic need is international agreement on adequate regulatory measures before much capital has been invested and to avoid repetition of the disastrous story of whaling."[6]

At the end of the conference Roberts and three members of the UK Delegation were invited by the Russian delegates to lunch at the Soviet Embassy.[7] At the time Anglo-Soviet relations were in a parlous state, Prime Minister Edward Heath having expelled 105 Soviet diplomatic staff from the UK in late 1971.

The party of four gingerly approached the massive oak door of the embassy and rang the bell. Eyed suspiciously by several heavyweight bouncers wearing ill-fitting suits, they were escorted into the large panelled hall, up the staircase past Soviet paintings of heroic workers and a portrait of Lenin, and into an elegant dining room to be plied with aperitifs served by waitresses dressed in colourful Georgian national costume. There was a lengthy menu: caviar, fish, a large meat course, desserts and cheese, several excellent Crimean wines, Georgian brandy and cigars. The hospitality was reminiscent of Roberts' and Terence Armstrong's experience in Leningrad 15 years previously and the meal continued for several hours, with toasts of friendship being exchanged repeatedly. Eventually the inebriated guests staggered off home along the streets of London. It had been a memorable occasion for Anglo-Soviet diplomacy.

WELLINGTON, OCTOBER 1972

In July 1972 Roberts flew out to New Zealand for a preliminary to the seventh Treaty Meeting. London to Wellington was the longest and most exhausting flight that the UK diplomatic service had to endure. Due to engine trouble, arrival at Sydney was six hours late and Roberts missed his connecting flight, adding a further 24 hours to the already weary three days of travel. All this for a meeting lasting just three days. Roberts spent the interminable delays writing a long list of complaints about his working life, not only at Antarctic Treaty meetings but also in Cambridge. At the age of 61 (*Plate 20.1*) his energy levels were declining and he was starting to resent the burdens of self-imposed treaty management due to other people's incompetence and indifference. The dominance of the UK delegation at Antarctic conferences was not what he had wanted: he complained that nearly every significant advance had to be cajoled and coaxed out of the other participants.[8] The criticism was directed chiefly at the US. Although likeable as individuals, as a delegation they seemed to Roberts to have no coherence, no agreed policy, no real appreciation of the problems, no understanding of other nations' views and no realistic forward-looking ideas. "Why can they not appoint someone with guts and authority to speak for the US at these meetings?" he wrote. "I feel frustrated by the obvious lack of coordination between the National Science Foundation and the State Department." Roberts was still more critical of SCAR. "The necessary links with SCAR have had to be engineered almost exclusively by us [the UK delegation]... we have a special responsibility and opportunity because the SCAR Secretariat is in Cambridge, but John Heap and I cannot expect to go on redrafting SCAR proposals which are so often appallingly vague or contradictory, but this seems unavoidable with such a diverse group of international scientists who rightly want to demonstrate their independence from political influences."

On 24 October Roberts, John Heap and David Anderson flew out for the main Treaty Meeting, arriving in Wellington six hours late. Roberts was decidedly gloomy. Although a SCAR report indicated that the Agreed Measures seemed to be having some effect, exploitation of marine life and minerals continued to be intractable issues. At the time governments had been able either to refuse applications for licences, or to fob off enquirers with political excuses, since any issue of a licence by an Antarctic Treaty government would meet with strong objection from some or all of the others. But a UN intervention on Antarctic resources for its Economic and Social Council Standing Committee on Natural Resources (ECOSOC) looked like being the writing on the wall. To Roberts it was essential to get the treaty parties to agree on the matter, but the need to achieve unanimity – required by the treaty – was to prove unattainable. The US refused to consider any kind of moratorium. The exploitation issue would test the resilience of the Antarctic Treaty to breaking point.

OSLO, JUNE 1975

Things were no easier at the eighth Treaty Meeting, the last one that Roberts attended. Although no longer the UK head of delegation, he still ended up as usual having to make the running. The agenda was heavy and contentious, including items on human impact on the environment, tourism, review of SPAs and Sites of Special Scientific Interest, cooperation in transport, activities of non-parties to the treaty, and exploitation of minerals and marine living resources.[9]

Roberts was profoundly disturbed. With the increasing complexity of the Antarctic Treaty System and the potential complications from the ongoing Geneva conference on the Law of the Sea (UNCLOS III)[10] there was a shift in mood amongst some delegates who, in his view, were burying their heads in the sand by calling for a 'common heritage' approach to the Antarctic and the sweeping away of the treaty.[11] New Zealand's Labour government wanted to make the Antarctic a 'world park', a proposal also advocated by some environmental groups. Simultaneously, one of the Antarctic states was demanding recognition of its territorial claim before it would allow any serious discussion on minerals exploitation. Addressing the conference, Roberts dished out a salutary warning that if this sort of confusion, procrastination and time-wasting continued, the Antarctic Treaty's authority would become paralysed. The only outcome would be that the treaty would end up in the hands of more than a hundred nations of the UN, most of them with no experience whatever of Antarctic affairs: in other words, chaos. Until then the parties had got away with deferring the problems of exploitation that they could not solve. They could do so no longer. If they abdicated their position of authority over the Antarctic, events would simply overtake them. This was the last address that Roberts would make to a Treaty Meeting, and the message was a sombre one.[12]

Tore Gjelsvik, Roberts' Norwegian colleague, observed the toll that the Treaty Meetings were taking on him. "The Treaty meetings could be very long and tedious, disagreements were common, and the needed consensus was often far away. In some cases nothing of importance had been agreed, even as the last day was approaching. Brian was most unhappy; his kind eyes sad, face red from exhaustion and dissatisfaction. But he never gave up."[13]

Later that day, on Gjelsvik's initiative, Roberts was interviewed by Norway's wide-circulation daily newspaper *Aftenposten*,[14] which published a photograph of a contented Roberts puffing at his pipe and surrounded by clouds of tobacco smoke (shown on the cover). It is hard to relate this image to his evident anxiety at the Oslo meeting. His fears for the future of the treaty seem to have been pessimistic. At the time of writing this book, more than 40 years on, there is no obvious sign that the Antarctic Treaty is falling apart.

Addressing the key issues identified by Roberts in Oslo, the agenda of the ninth Treaty Meeting in London in September 1977 focused on Antarctic minerals and on CCAMLR, the latter now perceived as urgent owing to the threat of a krill fishing industry. The London conference passed a recommendation on overfishing, with a broader ecosystem standard to protect not only krill stocks but also the predator species that depend on them. The zone of application was stretched out to the Antarctic Convergence, the natural oceanic boundary of the krill population. CCAMLR would turn out to be a breakthrough in marine conservation law, representing the boldest and most effective effort made by the treaty powers to regulate Antarctic fishing. But for Roberts himself CCAMLR came too late. By 1977 he had retired from the Foreign and Commonwealth Office and he did not attend the London Treaty Meeting. His 1977 paper on Antarctic conservation[15] makes no mention of CCAMLR, then in its infancy, and he would not live to see it come to fruition.

21

THE ARCTIC PROBLEM

"Where are we going to on this Expotition?" asked Pooh.

"We're going to discover the North Pole."

"What is the North Pole?" asked Pooh.

"It's just a thing you discover," said Christopher Robin carelessly, not being quite sure himself.

A A Milne, *Winnie the Pooh*

Ditchley Park, a country house in Chipping Norton, Oxfordshire, hosts regular conferences aimed at promoting international understanding, especially Anglo-American relations. Under the Chatham House Rule discussions are private and non-attributable, aimed at airing controversial issues and enabling the expression of personal opinions that might otherwise result in official dismissal. Over the weekend of 14-17 May 1971 a Ditchley conference was held to discuss the Arctic Ocean.

The conference was timely. In early 1971 a huge ice-strengthened oil tanker USS *Manhattan* had ventured successfully through the North West Passage in the Canadian Arctic. The voyage was controversial and relations between the US and Canada were at a low ebb. Canada had unilaterally passed its Arctic Waters Pollution Prevention Act, allowing the seizure of any suspect ship within 100 miles of its Arctic shores.

The brief of the conference was to examine the ramifications of opening up Arctic sea passages, with special reference to exploitation of oil, minerals and fisheries, claims of the coastal nations, jurisdiction over maritime and air traffic, and questions of safety, pollution and conservation.[1]

A LUKEWARM INVITATION

The Foreign and Commonwealth Office was uneasy about the proposed conference and thought the UK should keep out of it. But by March 1971 several invitees had agreed to attend, including Henry Hankey, Terence Armstrong, Sir Solly Zuckerman, Frank Fraser Darling, Graham Rowley of the Canadian department of Indian affairs and northern development, and Tore Gjelsvik, director of the Norwegian polar institute.

On 13 April 1971, just one month before the conference, Harry Hodson, self-titled Provost of the Ditchley Foundation, wrote to Roberts: "This brings you a very warm invitation to take part in a conference on the Arctic Ocean… I believe you must have heard about this in the FCO, whose official representatives have been most anxious for you to be included in the membership. With so many interests to be represented, this has only now become possible through the regrettable defection of another expected member of the British team."[2]

An inauspicious invitation: Roberts' inclination was to say thanks but no thanks. But he would be disappointed to miss Graham Rowley. He also smelt an opportunity: perhaps the conference could provide the stimulus for a future Arctic Treaty? Roberts accordingly accepted.

Hodson replied to Roberts, requesting a discussion paper for advance circulation and asking him to serve as *rapporteur* (minute taker). Roberts complained to Rowley that this was adding injury to insult: "I must confess I had rather hoped to enjoy meeting people and listening without such a chore." With his ten years' in-depth experience of the Antarctic Treaty, Roberts was the one person who would have been most suited to provoking and engaging in discussion, rather than having to report it without any expression of his own views. Hodson, an Oxford economist, was out of his depth in the subject. Out of the 35 invitees 32 were from the UK, US and Canada. No attempt had been made to invite a representative from the USSR, a glaring omission considering the Russians' half century of experience in ice navigation of the North East Passage.

In the event Roberts carried out his task of rapporteur diligently, and by all accounts with fairness and objectivity. It was however difficult for him to avoid writing what he thought ought to have been said, but wasn't.[3] The setting down of principles for a future multinational Arctic Treaty would have been quite within the meeting's terms of reference. But this vision never got off the starting blocks. As Hankey reported: "In my opinion Dr Roberts succeeds in reproducing the substance of the Conference and the tone of its discussions admirably... [but is he] over-stepping his role as Rapporteur in the way in which he plugs his own (admirable) views about the need for international agreement and cooperation in the conclusions of the Report?"[4] On many topics – energy policy, mineral resources, rights of indigenous people, pollution risk, extent of jurisdiction, legal questions concerning floating ice, fluctuations in ice cover due to climate change – Roberts' account could do little more than express a statement of the problem. He was at least able to make the salient point that international collaboration on essential scientific research was working well in the Antarctic and not at all in the Arctic. But there was no enthusiasm amongst any of the delegates for the concept of an Arctic Treaty, and in the absence of significant territorial sovereignty disputes between nations active in the Arctic there was – in contrast to the Antarctic situation – little incentive to create one.

After the initial plenary session, the conference split according to Ditchley's convention into three working groups, each of which produced their own reports. Group C considered measures for dealing with safety, pollution and conservation. There was considerable disagreement over the damage to Arctic marine ecology from oil spills and whether international agreement should be a precondition for undertaking development projects which might have irreversible effects. Group B discussed questions of jurisdiction over maritime and air traffic, defence and police cases, revealing a disagreement between Canada and other Arctic states on what was meant by 'international waters'.

Group A, attempting to grapple with the exploitation of natural Arctic resources, produced fireworks. Hodson had appointed as Group A chairman Russell Curtis, the general manager of the Humble Oil Refining Company's Marine Department. The company had been granted a concession by the US government to exploit the Prudhoe Bay oil reserves off Alaska, but it had no permission to build a pipeline, which had long been delayed by the State Department over concerns with pollution. Curtis complained bitterly about the inconvenience caused to the oil company by the delay. Backed up by a representative of BP, he guaranteed that no significant pollution could result either from the pipeline or from modern powerful icebreaker oil tankers, which had containment several feet thick and which could smash their way through ice of any thickness, as demonstrated by the *Manhattan*. The rest of his audience was sceptical, and history has justified their scepticism with the environmental disasters from the *Torrey Canyon* and subsequent *Exxon Valdez* and *Deepwater Horizon* incidents.

The Group A final report was described as abrasive, and the Canadian representatives did not wish to be associated with it. Agreement to publish the Group A report was achieved only in the early hours of the final morning of the conference. By this time Hodson and Fraser Darling were exhausted; never before had a Ditchley conference turned out to be so fractious. A couple of days later Hodson resigned as Provost. For Roberts it was a challenge to produce an impartial account of the proceedings. The Canadians were pleased with his efforts. There was no response from the US.

AN ARCTIC TREATY?

Some time after the conference Roberts commented to Richard Laws, director of the British Antarctic Survey: "This [was] supposedly about the Arctic Ocean, but in reality about quite a lot of other issues. I do not think I have previously had to report for publication anything so controversial at this level of representation. The occasion was for me an attempt to launch for the Arctic something equivalent to the Antarctic Treaty... it almost certainly foreshadows some of our mutual problems in the Antarctic and will perhaps set precedents..."[5] But was this anything more than a Roberts pipe-dream? There had never been any serious attempt to formulate an Arctic Treaty. In the southern hemisphere Argentina, Australia and Chile had always been the parties most sceptical and suspicious over the Antarctic Treaty's intentions. Why were the northern hemisphere states so keen on pushing for a treaty for the Antarctic, while showing no interest in creating one for the Arctic?

The UK government's position over the Arctic is now changing, primarily in response to environmental changes with potential geopolitical implications. Since 1999 the FCO Polar Regions section has become active in Arctic as well as Antarctic affairs, representing the UK on the Arctic Council on which it has observer status.[6] It remains unclear whether a more proactive UK policy would be welcome to the Arctic states,[7] which is a similar situation to the Antarctic in 1956, except that today there is no Brian Roberts to make it happen.

22

THE BRITISH ANTARCTIC
SURVEY COMES OF AGE

The coming into effect of the Antarctic Treaty in 1961 had caused some head-scratching in Whitehall. Even with its scientific programme the *raison d'être* of the UK 'sovereign presence' in the Antarctic was now being questioned, particularly by the Treasury. The Falkland Islands Dependencies were to be confined to the Falkland Islands and South Georgia, while the area claimed by the UK within the treaty zone (south of latitude 60°S) became the British Antarctic Territory. On 1 January 1962 the Falkland Islands Dependencies Survey became the British Antarctic Survey. Subsequently several UK environmental and conservation research institutes were merged into a new National Environment Research Council, into which BAS was incorporated in 1967.[1]

Incorporation within NERC was a convenient means for BAS to airbrush out its Colonial Office past, but the window dressing created another problem. Some managers of NERC were not particularly keen on BAS and from time to time consulted the Foreign and Commonwealth Office to ask if there were some way that they could "dump it". The issue came to a head during the 1974-76 Labour government in which James Callaghan was Foreign Secretary. Roberts' visceral loathing of Callaghan (which was not unique amongst Callaghan's civil service advisers) is revealed in a letter to his brother Denis' family on failing to show up one evening for supper:

"All three of you must be furious with me, and I deserve this odium. I am so desperately sorry about tonight. I have no excuse for not letting you know that I could not come for supper – only some explanation. I am writing this at 2 am after returning from the Argentine Embassy – absolutely exhausted and sustained only by a quite a lot of whisky. Tonight I had a particular job of placation to perform. It was so urgent and important that I forgot everything else.

"I was struggling into my bitterly hated dinner jacket for the <u>third</u> time this week to attend yet another hateful function. Tonight it has been just a sordid grind to obey my new Master in the F.C.O. Since the election my life has sometimes seemed to be almost entirely without common sense or reason. Callaghan has deeply eroded all my hopes and faith in international human co-operation. He seems bent on quarrelling with Latin American countries for reasons I cannot accept. I have only met him once personally, but I don't ever want to meet him again. He has been treating even his most senior advisors like naughty schoolboys."[2]

The incident that triggered this reaction is obscure, but Roberts' antipathy to the new Foreign Secretary was not unexpected. The continual worries over retrenchment of the UK's position in the Antarctic had not gone away.[3] It was a frequent topic of conversation when Charles Swithinbank visited Roberts at his Cambridge flat.[4] Once late at night during a more than usually voluminous consumption of gin and tonic, the normally circumspect Roberts let slip details from confidential minutes of a Cabinet meeting on the Antarctic, at which Callaghan had expostulated: "Why don't we dump the whole lot, this is costing us lots of money."

Despite – or perhaps because of – its enhanced status and funding following the 1982 Falkland Islands war,[5] the British Antarctic Survey has often needed to defend its position. One of the most serious situations arose in 2012. NERC, faced with a large cut in its annual and capital expenditure allowance, proposed to subsume BAS within the National Oceanographic Centre based in Southampton and Liverpool to create a new institution to be called the NERC Centre for Marine and Polar Science. This scheme to circumscribe BAS' earmarked funding status resulted in an outcry from scientists and politicians and board resignations within BAS. But once it was realised that the disappearance of BAS would be interpreted globally as a weakening of British interest in the Antarctic, the proposed merger was abandoned.

In 1973 Vivian Fuchs retired from the directorship of BAS and was replaced by Richard Laws. Laws' first task was to create a headquarters for the organisation. Until then BAS had been a collection of isolated units scattered around the UK and radio communications between the London office, the scientific units and the Antarctic stations and ships were restricted, particularly in winter due to fluctuations in the ionosphere. Several UK universities had expressed interest in having BAS on their campus. But the dice were loaded: both Laws and Fuchs were Cambridge men. Ironically the main opposition to locating BAS headquarters there came from within Cambridge itself. The Scott Polar Institute's director Gordon Robin was unhappy about having such a large and well-funded government organisation competing in his own backyard. Laws lamented that relations between the two organisations had never been cordial.[6]

During his directorship Laws would meet Roberts every Saturday morning for a wide-ranging chinwag, covering management issues, logistics of operations and the history and politics of the British presence in the Antarctic. At the end of 1975, while the new BAS headquarters was being built in Cambridge, Laws presented Roberts with a retirement gift: an invitation to be his guest on the relief ship RRS *Bransfield* (*Plate 22.1*). They would be observing BAS at the sharp end of its operations, out in the Antarctic.

A LAST RETURN TO THE ANTARCTIC

Bransfield's tour would take in the Falkland Islands, South Georgia, Signy Island, Halley Bay, the South Shetland Islands, the Argentine Islands and Rothera station on Adelaide Island.[7] For Roberts this polar swan song was an emotional voyage, his first sight of the Argentine Islands, Marguerite Bay and South Georgia since his formative years there four decades earlier on the British Graham Land Expedition. Roberts and Laws flew to Punta Arenas to spend the New Year at their old haunt the Hotel Cabo de Hornos (Cape Horn). Visiting the Puerto Bulnes reconstructed fortress and other monuments to Chilean history, Laws was intrigued but Roberts was unimpressed, making jaundiced comments on the museum's "major distortions of Antarctic history from Bernardo O'Higgins onwards".

On 3 January 1976 the party boarded the BAS vessel *John Biscoe* to head for the Falkland Islands. It was a period of turbulence in the South Atlantic, both meteorologically and politically. At Port Stanley harbour they encountered *Bransfield* and HMS *Endurance*. *Endurance* had recently arrived with Eddie Shackleton on board, intending to carry out an economic survey of the Falkland Islands. Relations between the UK and Argentina were extremely tense. On *Biscoe*'s arrival Roberts and Laws were promptly summoned to Government House by Falkland Islands Governor Neville French, who was evidently in urgent need of someone to talk to. They had to change into black tie for dinner, the conversation consisting of small talk until the ladies retired and the men talked about fish.

Bransfield then headed for South Georgia, encountering heavy seas during the night. The ship was noisy and rolled badly, but in his opulent cabin Roberts was demob happy, having just relinquished his burdensome responsibilities at the FCO. Around Bird Island off South Georgia's western tip, it was cold, windy and snowing, but the rich wildlife was a source of joy. After a two-day stop at Grytviken, *Bransfield* departed for the South Orkneys. Roberts spent a day ashore on Signy Island visiting seabird colonies, gratified to know that since his original PhD work on Wilson's storm petrels others had followed.[8]

On 19 January *Bransfield* sailed for the Brunt Ice Shelf, the site of the BAS Halley station. The Weddell Sea was strangely ice-free. Heavy ice had been reported off the west coast of the Antarctic Peninsula, but at that time of year ice conditions can change rapidly. Roberts was impressed by the flexibility shown by BAS in adapting the programme to ice and weather conditions. Any competent polar expedition leader does this today as a matter of course, but it was one of the key failings of earlier Antarctic ventures, such as Roberts' experience of the rigidly imposed schedules on the US Operation Deep Freeze.

Bransfield approached the ice front to find that it was clearly unstable, constantly breaking off. Cargo had to be unloaded farther north, some 40 miles and a six-hour journey by Sno-Cat tractor to the Halley III station. The base hut was 25 ft below the ice surface and covered in snowdrift. Despite poor weather conditions, a painfully slow relief operation, and second-rate 1960s movies for entertainment, there were few complaints by the base staff: a far cry from the early days of the Falkland Islands Dependencies Survey.

The relief operation took three weeks in the difficult conditions, with a 40 mph wind, blowing and drifting snow, continuous calving of the 'quayside' and zero visibility. *Bransfield* shuttled back to Signy Island and South Georgia, taking six hours to punch its way into a 70 mph head wind and swell to reach Grytviken. By the end of the week the wind was approaching hurricane strength.

THE GOVERNOR'S WOBBLER

After four days of waiting at Grytviken for conditions to improve, *Bransfield* returned to Port Stanley, arriving on 29 February. Disquieting news was in store. An Argentine destroyer had attempted to arrest RRS *Shackleton* south of the Falkland Islands, firing shots across her bows. Calling at Government House Roberts was mistaken by Governor French for the eccentric ionosphere physicist Roy Piggott. Attempting to explain who he was, Roberts gave up in the face of French's unstoppable verbal onslaught addressed to anyone within earshot. The next day Roberts was summoned back for more political discussion. Once again French delivered a rambling monologue, pacing around the room animatedly, frantically searching for lost documents and haphazardly ranting on unrelated topics: the Argentine government, the new Falkland Islands constitution, the administration of BAS, the problem of finding a successor for his aged gardener and the affair between his butler and one of the maids in Government House. Roberts had the impression that the Governor was heading for a nervous breakdown. It was a relief to have only one more day in Stanley before *Bransfield* sailed for Punta Arenas.

The next day, on board *Bransfield* heading for Punta Arenas in a heavy sea, Roberts was summoned to the radio telephone. On learning that the Governor wished to speak to him, he approached the instrument with some trepidation. What on earth did the Governor want now?

To Roberts' surprise and delight the call was to relay an FCO message that the Royal Geographical Society had awarded him its prestigious Founder's Medal for 1976.

A NOSTALGIC VOYAGE DOWN THE ANTARCTIC PENINSULA

After several days spent by the BAS team in the bar of the Hotel Cabo de Hornos in Punta Arenas, *Bransfield* sailed for the South Shetland Islands across an unusually placid Drake Passage. On 12 March the voyage continued south through Gerlache Strait, past Port Lockroy, along

Lemaire Channel, past the Argentine Islands and out to sea through French Passage with its multitude of islands and reefs, including Lumus Rock (named after Lummo, the BGLE cat[9]). Three days later *Bransfield* had rounded Adelaide Island to call at the new BAS station at Rothera. Just four people were overwintering there; today it has grown into a large complex accommodating up to 130. The following day, news was broadcast that Harold Wilson had unexpectedly resigned as UK Prime Minister. Eric Heathorn, *Bransfield*'s steward, described by Roberts as a "rabid Conservative", produced champagne to celebrate. The party rapidly degenerated into a political and personal verbal slanging match, fuelled by alcohol.

On 19 March *Bransfield* crossed Marguerite Bay to anchor off the Debenham Islands. Roberts went ashore with the two Spanish speakers Steve Wormald and Kenn Back to the nearby Argentine base San Martín,

Portrait of Brian Roberts by David Smith

close to the site of the original BGLE southern base hut. The BAS team invited the Argentines on board *Bransfield* for a convivial party, an antidote to the prevailing political unpleasantness and embarrassment.

During a return stop at Rothera, Roberts had his portrait drawn by the expedition's artist David Smith. This was something that Roberts had encouraged for other members of the party, but he was not so keen on when he was himself the subject.

On leaving Rothera *Bransfield* headed up the inside of Adelaide Island and chanced her arm through the narrow icebound passageway of the Gullet. In glorious Antarctic weather, she continued serenely towards the Argentine Islands. Roberts paid a nostalgic visit to his moss bank near the site of the original BGLE northern base, the site of his Wilson's petrel study of 40 years earlier. Today, another 40 years on, the moss bank is still there with the burrows marked out with red-painted pegs. But nearby the ice cover had receded tremendously, exposing large areas of bare rock and causing the original ice cave of 1935 to collapse. In 2016 there was a wholesale collapse of the ice cliff and the cave has now disappeared beneath it.

MORE POLITICAL RUMBLINGS

That day a new Argentine government was installed, only for a military junta to seize power and displace it within 24 hours. There was a nationwide general strike. *Bransfield* headed up Gerlache Strait, visiting the Argentine station Almirante Brown in Paradise Bay. The weather was foul and Paradise Bay is a miserable place in such conditions, but they had a cordial reception from the base party who were enjoying the peace of the Antarctic far from the turbulence at home.

Bransfield headed back to the Falklands, where Roberts had to endure more formalities at Government House but was also able to have useful discussions with bird man Ian Strange. With his visionary conservation ideas Strange was in a difficult position, completely at odds with the sheep farming community.[10] On his last day in the Falklands, returning to board *Bransfield* at Port Stanley's jetty in cold and stormy conditions Roberts came upon the crew of Shackleton's ship *Endurance*, most of whom were inebriated to the point of requiring paramedical assistance in boarding their ship.

Bransfield sailed on 3 April for Punta Arenas. Two evenings later the BBC announced that Harold Wilson had been replaced by James

Callaghan as Prime Minister. Nobody, least of all Roberts, was in the mood for celebrating. The flight back home from Punta Arenas was miserable, several of the party suffering from Montezuma's revenge. Following his return to Cambridge late on 8 April, Roberts spent a week in bed recovering from an infection that he had picked up in Punta Arenas. It was a melancholy finale, but the voyage had been memorable and BAS had put on a good performance. They could look forward to the official opening of the new headquarters in Cambridge, opening up a new era for BAS. Roberts, now semi-retired, was living full-time in Cambridge and looking forward to a quiet life. But he was not to get one.

23

A SURFEIT OF POLAR INFORMATION

The Senior Tutor had made an intellectual decision founded on his conviction that if a little knowledge was a dangerous thing, a lot of it was lethal.

Tom Sharpe, *Porterhouse Blue*

A WEIGHTY PROBLEM

During the 1970s Roberts' reputation in Antarctic Treaty circles would continue to carry more and more weight. Unfortunately, so would he. No matter what he tried his body weight kept on increasing, and he was booked into a Cambridge nursing home for an investigation into what was euphemistically referred to as 'metabolism'. During his first stay in January 1973 he was fed on tomato and orange juice, tea or Bovril without milk, and a large quantity of pills. He was instructed to remain in bed except for one 20-minute walk around the garden each day. After a month of this routine he was discharged with the comment that there was no explanation for his condition and that the 'treatment' was not working. Two years later, in the spring of 1975, he was again admitted to the nursing home and subjected to a similar routine. He was utterly miserable, complaining that the treatment was useless and that he could have done better himself by swimming in the Mediterranean, as he had always done on holiday in Mallorca.[1]

Later on that year his brother Denis visited the Causewayside flat, to be greeted by a smiling Brian, rubbing his hands with glee. "My doctor has put me on a potato diet," he exclaimed, "I can eat as many potatoes as I like." This treatment at least improved his psychological – if not necessarily his physical – health.

AN UNWELCOME TRANS-ANTARCTIC EXPEDITION?

One day in 1973, seated at his desk at the Foreign and Commonwealth Office, Roberts was startled to discover that Sir Ranulph Twistleton-Wykeham-Fiennes was not a fictional creation of novelist P G Wodehouse but a real person, and that he was planning a Trans-Globe Expedition circumnavigating the Earth in a north-south direction along the Greenwich meridian via both poles. Fiennes was aged 35 and had minimal polar experience. He had been warned that without logistical support from Antarctic bases he was on a hiding to nothing, and such help would be available only with the approval of the UK Government.

Fiennes accordingly made an appointment to visit the FCO Polar Regions section, but his prospects were not good. The seventh Treaty Meeting in Wellington in 1972 had recommended that private expeditions should be thoroughly scrutinized in regard to their feasibility and logistic support required. Partly due to Fiennes' poor reputation acquired in the Canadian Arctic,[2] the Trans-Globe proposal was criticized by many in the UK polar community, including the British explorer Wally Herbert,[3] and Vivian Fuchs felt the need to dissociate himself from it.[4] Nor was any support forthcoming from the Scott Polar Institute, British Antarctic Survey, Royal Geographical Society or the Ministry of Defence.[5]

Nevertheless Fiennes, not one to be easily dissuaded, made an effort to meet the officials on their own terms (suit and tie) and turned up at the FCO to present his proposal. "Over my dead body," was Roberts' immediate response.[6] But Fiennes persisted, and eventually got past all the bureaucratic obstacles that were put in front of him. By 1979 the Transglobe expedition was underway and Roberts was dead. So, in a sense, both men got what they wanted. John Heap, Roberts' successor as head of Polar Regions, judged that Fiennes would not give up easily, and since that time the FCO policy has been not to bar individuals from the Antarctic but to allow them to go whilst imposing strict conditions.[7]

RETIREMENT FROM THE FOREIGN OFFICE

Shortly after the eighth Treaty Meeting in Oslo, Roberts announced his intention to retire. A handover date of 1 January 1976 had been agreed for Heap to become his successor as head of the FCO Polar Regions section. Unlike government and diplomatic posts in which individuals are moved on and replaced every two years, the Polar Regions section has always retained a period of overlap to allow the incoming head enough time to gain experience of the highly-specialised post.[8] This is intended to discourage Whitehall from appointing a non-specialist who might damage the UK's solid reputation in the Antarctic.

On 15 December 1975 Robin Edmonds held a retirement party for Roberts at the Turf Club. In his valedictory speech Roberts acknowledged his debt to his former boss Arnold Toynbee for enabling him to "penetrate the fortress of the Foreign Office through the back door. I knew quite well that my formal qualifications could never possibly qualify me for proper admission to the Foreign Office through the front door – more especially if it should become known that my chief paper qualification lay in a PhD thesis on the sexual physiology of penguins".[9]

Six months later Roberts was awarded the Founders' Gold Medal by the Royal Geographical Society.[10] In his introductory resume of Roberts' career the RGS president mentioned the "wartime work for the War Office and for Naval Intelligence". Ironically in the audience was Roberts' nemesis from 33 years previously, Clifford Darby, who had engineered Roberts' dismissal from the Admiralty NID5 division in 1943. It is not known whether Roberts and Darby conversed at the meeting.

The following year Roberts was invited to address a Symposium on Development of the Antarctic, held in Punta Arenas, Chile. He repeated the warnings expressed at the Oslo Treaty Meeting, emphasizing the urgent need to establish a joint licensing authority and a regime for protecting the Antarctic environment.[11]

Two months later, personal tragedy struck when his brother Denis was suddenly taken ill with pancreatic cancer. Three days after being presented by Brian with a volume of his newly published UDC catalogue for polar libraries, Denis died at the age of 67. The family was devastated by Denis' sudden death, and Brian never recovered from the loss.

DISILLUSIONMENT WITH CAMBRIDGE

Confronted with numerous delays on his flight to the Punta Arenas Symposium, Roberts had too much time to reflect on his personal problems, which largely concerned the Scott Polar Research Institute. Relations between SPRI, BAS and the FCO had become strained. "We have now almost reached the stage when FCO and BAS can both get on quite well together without the SPRI help and cooperation which used to be essential," he wrote. "I cannot grumble about this because it is something for which I have worked over many years, but I am sad that Gordon's personal antipathies can make so many difficulties... there is no reason why we should not receive further help from the FCO if only Gordon could bring himself to go about it in the right way."[12] But to SPRI director Gordon Robin, direct UK government support for the institute was anathema.

Tension between Roberts and Robin had been simmering ever since the appointment of Robin as SPRI director in 1957.[13] Roberts' main complaint was that Robin never put his cards on the table. He had been invited repeatedly to join the regular Saturday morning discussions between the FCO, BAS, SPRI and SCAR but had never done so, retaining an "immense distrust and chronic resentment of government and civil servants". Roberts was particularly disturbed by Robin's management of SCAR: "Gordon still does not seem to recognise that SCAR can operate successfully only under the umbrella of the Antarctic Treaty. He holds some desperately unrealistic ideas that it only needs a few intelligent scientists to get together to solve all these problems of international cooperation and side-track government obstruction." In private, Roberts fumed that Robin's longevity as SPRI director was part of the problem.[14] Such observations reveal as much about Roberts as they do about Robin, and in the end Roberts answers his own question: "This is Cambridge, not Whitehall. I now know that I will never really get used to the switch between the ways of the FCO and the casual administrative procedures in Cambridge."

THE SPRI LIBRARY

By the 1960s the Universal Decimal Classification scheme that Roberts had promulgated for polar libraries had become well advanced at SPRI.[15] But librarians Harry King and Ann Savours were not alone in finding the UDC system confusing and difficult. As Charles Swithinbank said: "Brian had no formal position in the SPRI library, but he had strong opinions about how the library classification system should work. There were times when he brought Harry King near to tears and Harry's assistants really in tears."[16] The publication in 1976 of the SPRI library catalogue – a comprehensive 19-volume author/subject/regional card index classified by UDC – should have been a moment of triumph for Roberts, the fulfilment of his endeavours ever since 1932.[17] But it was tarnished when Robin signed the contract with the publishers without consulting Roberts, whose guide to the catalogue then had to be extensively reworked by the overwrought SPRI library staff. Swithinbank commented further that "Brian was very, very thorough in training up cataloguers not to write the catalogue card from the title, but to read enough to say what it was really about... he was very, very fussy about that and he virtually ruled the successive librarians in the Institute with an iron fist... He could not legally overrule the librarian, but the librarian was submerged, drowned by Roberts' arguments".[18]

Roberts saw himself as "officially appointed by the University with overall responsibility for SPRI information services", but these were not quite the terms of reference of his appointment to the post of Research Associate: "Dr Roberts will be responsible to the Director of the Institute for the general coordination of the Information Services of the Institute."[19] To Roberts this was just one more example of administrative sloppiness in academia.

With the coming of the information technology revolution, the UDC would in any case be superseded. In September 1972 Roberts, addressing a meeting of polar librarians at SPRI, quoted a National Science Foundation report: "It is quite likely that by about the year 2000 librarians will have been phased out in favour of information scientists, computer programmers and systems analysts. The traditional library of books on shelves may have been replaced by an on-line terminal connected to a central data bank and the only readers will be the ghostly forms of microform readers under their polythene covers."[20] While welcoming the potential for automated searching, Roberts protested against the sheer volume of new publications. "No one has the time to wade through the welter of paper disguising some trivial discovery under a multiplicity of different titles. Original results should be published in full once and once only." He also expressed what was already becoming a common fear of the future: "I hope that we shall not forget the joys to be derived from well-written and beautifully-produced books. It will be a sad day when all we can do is to plug into some far-distant data bank and sit back to watch a television screen... I do not really want to live in such a brave new world." Perhaps fortunately for Roberts, he died before he had to.

THE LAST YEAR: UNFINISHED BUSINESS

By early 1977 Roberts realised that owing to his age and infirmity his unfinished projects would have to be passed on to others. He had been able to hand over the baton on the Antarctic Treaty System to John Heap and the work on place naming to Geoffrey Hattersley-Smith. Another project successfully delegated was the *Chronology of Antarctic Exploration*. This had been published in 1958 in *Polar Record*,[21] but needed continual revision and updating, a task which was left to the Cambridge polar scholar Robert Headland and would take Headland several years. It appeared in 1989 as a 700-page 'doorstop' that included details of 5,000 expeditions.[22]

Later on that year Roberts took his old school and university colleague Peter Falk to lunch at the Travellers' Club. It was a time for reflection. Roberts lamented that despite his slow start in life and later pre-eminence he had "made almost no progress in the art of human relationships".[23] There was no implied bitterness: it was simply an admission that he put people's backs up and he did not understand why. He had failed in his greatest ambition, which was to become director of SPRI. Falk commiserated with Roberts over the immense effort he had dedicated over the years to building up the institute. But academia has never rewarded loyalty, and Falk pointed out to Roberts that had he secured the directorship he could never have nurtured the momentous Antarctic Treaty and ensured its survival during its formative and critical first years.

In May 1978, during a two-week holiday in Dubrovnik, Brian suddenly became extremely unwell. Back in Cambridge he was rushed into hospital, diagnosed with bowel cancer, operated on and kept in intensive care at the nursing home for three months. On being discharged he remained bedridden in his Causewayside flat, to be nursed alternately by his sister Joy and sister-in-law Lilian. They fed him one of his childhood favourites: cucumber sandwiches with the crusts removed.

On the morning of Saturday 7 October 1978, Toni Martorell visited the Causewayside flat. Finding its occupier asleep, Martorell decided to let him rest. Later that day he called in again, only to receive a grumpy complaint from Brian for not waking him up. On the Monday morning back in London Martorell was shocked to receive a telephone call from Brian's housekeeper: "Brian won't wake up; I think he is dead". This was confirmed later that day by Terence Armstrong. Over the weekend Brian had died from a deep-vein thrombosis, probably brought on by prolonged bedridden inactivity. He was 66.

Following the funeral at Churchill College, Cambridge on 19 October, a Service of Thanksgiving for Brian Roberts was held in London at St Paul's Cathedral on 11 December. It was attended by over a hundred people, with representatives from his family, friends and colleagues (two from overseas), SPRI, Churchill College, the FCO, BAS, Royal Geographical Society, National Maritime Museum, International Glaciological Society, Royal Society, SCAR, the Directorate of Overseas Surveys, the Admiralty – and the Arctic and Antarctic Clubs, of whom six had been Brian's colleagues on BGLE. The list of attendees was a testament to the sheer number and variety of people and institutions whose lives Brian had touched. In the opening statement of his address Terence Armstrong acknowledged that Brian would have been his most severe critic: "No waffling, Terence: stick to the facts."

Whether the authors of this biography have likewise succeeded in meeting Brian's demands can only be left for the reader to judge. Armstrong's closing words to the congregation are however indisputable: "Most of all, his [Brian's] monument is in the hearts and minds of us, his friends and relations, who recall a very human person, of dedication, generosity, modesty, sensitivity and courage. All of us are richer for this, and we will not forget him."

The sole aim of this book is to ensure that Brian Roberts is not forgotten, by those who never knew him as well as those who did.

EPILOGUE

Archie Norman was one of those acquaintances of Roberts at Emmanuel College, Cambridge who, though they had few common interests, remained a lifelong friend. Norman read Medicine and Psychology and went on to become a Great Ormond Street paediatrician specializing in disorders such as cystic fibrosis. He died in December 2016, aged 104, outliving Roberts by nearly 40 years.

During our interviews and correspondence with people who knew Brian Roberts, the inevitable question kept cropping up: What would Roberts be thinking if he were still alive? It is of course a hypothetical question. Owing to his declining state of health Roberts had no chance of reaching Norman's great age. But any assessment of Roberts' legacy warrants an attempt at an answer.

Roberts would probably have been elated that the Antarctic Treaty, on which he expended so much energy yet which towards the end of his life seemed to be in a precarious state, is not only still in operation, but growing in strength and continuing to dictate the rules of all activity in the Antarctic, with a proven effectiveness in avoiding international conflict and in promoting environmental protection measures far in advance of anywhere else on Earth. The treaty has kept going for 60 years and its future is guaranteed at least until the year 2048. On every previous occasion when it has been up for review, there has been no inclination to wind it up. Much of the development of the treaty from Roberts' time onwards lay in the hands of John Heap, his successor as Head of the Foreign Office Polar Regions section. involving negotiations that were every bit as challenging as those faced by Roberts.

Even more significantly, public awareness of the polar regions and their critical role in global environmental and climate issues has snowballed. This has been exploited to the full by the British Antarctic Survey; Roberts would be amazed that the chaotic Falkland Islands Dependencies Survey of the 1940s and 1950s, unable even to obtain an icebreaker, has matured and grown in stature to such an extent that whenever attempts are made by bureaucrats to clip its wings – or even to send it into oblivion by losing its name – there is an outcry, as there was in 2012.

Roberts' passions were however directed far more at the Scott Polar Research Institute and the journal *Polar Record* than at his diplomatic and political work. In addition to building up the institute into one of the most comprehensive polar archives in the world, he left in his will a vast collection of books and papers, as well as a large cash sum to the 'B B Roberts Fund' for polar research. *Polar Record* is now an independent electronic-only journal, still published by Cambridge University Press, but with an international editorship. The days when SPRI staff were obliged to attend sessions to stuff paper copies of the journal into envelopes and lick postage stamps are long gone.

What Roberts would think of SPRI today can only be guessed at. He was never in favour of it becoming a sub-department of Cambridge University's Department of Geography. When *Polar Pundit* was published in 1995 there was already a feeling that SPRI's international reputation had declined since the 1960s, but the ever-growing interest in polar matters has helped the scientific research and teaching sides to flourish. The institute's arcane system of privileges of access to its vast quantity of polar historical material wins it few friends amongst historians. In contrast the excellent museum, completely refurbished with a large award from the Heritage Lottery Fund, provides a valuable resource for its many visitors.

Probably above all else there is the question of wildlife conservation. Some political historians of the Antarctic Treaty have argued that in focusing on this issue during the early Treaty Meetings Roberts was using it purely as a test case that would be easily accepted, and that the motive underlying it was an aim at gaining acceptance of far trickier issues such as jurisdiction. Roberts did himself mention such ideas in his conference diaries and his focus on seals might lead one to interpret his approach accordingly. But despite being the ultimate pragmatist when it came to diplomatic manoeuvring, he was at heart a passionate conservationist. Had be not been so, he would not have striven as hard as he did. It was no pushover to get the proposed conservation measures accepted by the Treaty Meetings, and today CCAMLR is running into difficulties in achieving unanimity on marine protected areas amongst its 25 parties. It takes individuals with exceptional vision and drive to achieve what Brian Roberts did.

ANNEX I: THE ROBERTS AND THE BIRLEYS

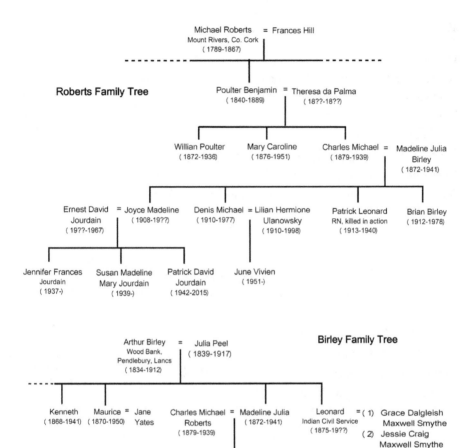

Family portraits are shown in Plates 1.1 to 1.6.

ANNEX II: THE BGLE PARTY

Shore Party

W E Hampton ('Ham'), first pilot and engineer

Surgeon Cdr Ted Bingham, RN ('Doc'), medical officer and dog handler

Alfred Stephenson ('Steve'), surveyor and meteorologist

Quintin Riley, meteorologist

Jim Moore, second engineer

Lt I F Meiklejohn_('Michael'). wireless officer

Launcelot Fleming, chaplain and geologist

Brian Roberts, biologist (later swapping with Bertram and transferred to the Ship's Party)

Ship's Party

Lt R E D Ryder RN ('Red'), ship's master and hydrographer

Lt H M Millett RN ('Chief'), chief engineer

J H Martin, first mate

Captain Lisle Ryder, second mate

G C L Bertram ('Colin'), biologist

Norman Gurney, deckhand

V D Carse ('Duncan'), deckhand (joined BGLE at Port Stanley)

ANNEX III: PRINCIPLES OF PLACE NAMING

The essential function of a place name is that it should be clear, unique and unambiguous. In the Antarctic it had generally been assumed that priority of discovery and naming was the most important criterion in the attribution of a name to a feature, but the problem was that both priority and discovery were frequently disputed. Roberts was striving to establish and maintain a consistent treatment of the names that had either been proposed by explorers and surveyors or that had somehow come into use. The decisions on acceptance or rejection of any name had to be guided by a set of principles, a brief outline of which is provided below.

1. The purpose of a name is to supply a means of identifying the feature beyond doubt.
2. Permanence in naming can be ensured only by correct identification of features and by avoidance of duplication or ambiguity in the use of names.
3. An existing name, once it has been accepted, should not be altered without good reason.
4. As a general rule, a name should be rejected if the accurately determined position is found to differ greatly from its earlier reported position(s).

Existing names may be altered for the following reasons:

1. When no English form of a name has previously been used.
2. When confusion has been caused by the use of one and the same name for two different features in the Antarctic.
3. When a name has already been shortened by local usage or its original form is inconveniently long.
4. When more accurate survey has shown that the generic part of a name is inappropriate.
5. When a name has been corrupted or has been mis-spelt.
6. When account has been taken of correct diacritical marks.

In the case of completely new names proposed for the first time, one should be guided by common sense and suitability. No name is accepted unless adequate information is available on its origin and on the position and location of the feature. Names should be concise,[1] euphonious and in good taste, avoiding unnatural and incongruous combinations of words (including combinations of words in different languages), corrupted names, names of obscure origin, and names with a connotation of obscenity or blasphemy. Naming of features after well-known place-names elsewhere is not favoured, nor use of the names of sledge dogs or pets (although such names have been adopted in the past).[2]

One of the biggest problems encountered by Roberts was the sheer number of new features being discovered that required new names. The provision of new names proved to be as much as a headache as unscrambling the plethora and confusion of existing names. His solution was the concept of group naming, i.e. naming groups of geographically related features after corresponding associated groups of persons or ideas – political, scientific or artistic, for example. The system had the advantage of promoting international acceptability but has not always been popular with critics. Geoffrey Hattersley-Smith, who took over from Roberts on his retirement, provides fuller details concerning the principles of place naming and discusses the complex issues that can be encountered.[3]

ANNEX IV: PUBLICATIONS OF BRIAN ROBERTS

"Manx shearwaters' departure flight from land", *British Birds* 23(8), (1930), 223-4

"The Cambridge Expedition to Vatnajökull, Iceland 1932", *Geographical Journal* 81(4), (1933) 289-313

"Vatnajökull, Iceland: the history of its exploration", *Scot Geog Mag* 50 (1934), 65-76

"The gannet colonies of Iceland", *British Birds* 28(4), (1934), 100-5

"Notes on the birds of central and SE Iceland, *Ibis* (1934), 239-64

"Notes on Icelandic birds, including a visit to Grimsey", *Ibis* (1934), 799-807 (with D L Lack)

"Notes on East Greenland birds, with a discussion of the periodic non-breeding among Arctic birds", *Ibis* (1934), 816-31 (with G C L Bertram and D L Lack)

« Rapport préliminaire sur les observations dans le Hurry Inlet », *Annales Hydtrographiques* 14, (1934), 69-73 (with G C L Bertram and D L Lack)

"The Cambridge expedition to Scoresby Sound, East Greenland in 1933", *Geog J* 85(3), (1935), 234-51

"Notes on the scientific work of the BGLE 1934-37", *Geog J* 91(6), (1938), 508-32 (with WLS Fleming, A Stephenson and G C L Bertram)

"Whale oil and other products of the whaling industry", *Polar Record* 3(17), (1939), 80-86

"Design for a sledge wheel", *Polar Record* 3(18), (1939), 103-4

"Antarctic ornithological observations made during Bellinghausen's voyage of circumnavigation in 1919-1821", *Ibis* (1939), 699-711

"Notes on the selection and care of polar footwear", *Polar Record* 3(19), (1940), 235-67 and 309-26 (with NAC Croft)

"Notes on the Barrow collection of Arctic equipment", *Geog J* 95(5), (1940), 368-80

"The life cycle of Wilson's Petrel, *Oceanistes oceanitus*", *British Museum Sci Repts* 1(2), (1940), 141-94

"The breeding behaviour of penguins, with special reference to *Pygoscelis papua*", *British Museum Sci Repts* 1(3), (1940), 195-254

"Tidal observations in Graham Land", *British Museum Sci Repts* 1(8), (1941), 327-35 (with R H Corkan)

"A bibliography of Antarctic ornithology", *British Museum Sci Repts* 1(9), (1941), 337-67

"Three Antarctic years", *Canad Geog J* 22(1), (1941), 3-39 (with G C L Bertram and W L S Fleming)

"Game conservation in Arctic Canada", *Polar Record* 3(23), (1942), 499-509

"The reindeer industry in Alaska", *Polar Record* 3(24), (1942), 568-72

"Anti-frostbite ointments", *Polar Record* 4(25), (1943), 30-31

"The study of man's reaction to a polar climate", *Polar Record* 4(26), (1943), 63-9

"The scientific results of the Shackleton Antarctic expeditions", *Polar Record* 4(26), (1943), 72-6 (with J M Wordie)

"Sound effects in polar conditions", *Polar Record* 4(27), (1944), 123-5

"Sea ice: terminology, formation and movement", *Polar Record* 4(27), (1944), 126-33 (with J M Wordie)

"The North Pechora railway and the development of the Pechora coalfields", *Polar Record* 4(29), (1945), 236-8

"The protection of fur seals in the North Pacific Ocean", *Polar Record* 4(39), (1945), 264-71

"Administrative divisions of the Soviet Arctic and sub-Arctic", *Polar Record* 4(31), (1946), 320-3

"The Kurtl Islands (Chishima)", *Polar Record* 4(31), (1946), 332-5

"The exploration of Antarctica", *Nature* 159, (1947), 388-99

"The place-names of Svalbard", *Polar Record* 5(35/36), (1948), 172-84

"International organisations for polar exploration", *Polar Record* 5(37/38), (1949), 332-4

"Norwegian-British-Swedish Antarctic expedition 1949-52", *Nature* 165(4184), (1950), 8-9, 20 and *Polar Record* 5(39), (1950), 463-6

"John Miers' account of the discovery of the South Shetland Islands", *Polar Record* 5(40), (1950), 565-75

"Historical notes on Heard and McDonald Islands", *Polar Record* 5(40), (1950), 580-4

"Shelf ice – a note on terminology", *J Glaciology* 1(8), (1950), 413-5

"Richard Sherratt's chart of the South Shetland Islands 1821", *Polar Record* 6(43), (1952), 362-5

"Preliminary note on bird ringing by the FIDS 1945-51", *Ibis* 94, (1952), 538-40 (with W J L Sladen)

"Argentine and Chilean Antarctic expeditions 1942, 1943, 1947 and 1947-48", *Polar Record* 6(45), (1953), 656-67 (with J E Thomas)

"Adjustments of coastal place-names in the Antarctic 1951", *Polar Record* 6(45), (1953), 693-7

"Ice shelf terminology", *Polar Record* 6(46), (1953), 838

"Stations and depot/refuge huts in the FID 1953, 1956 and 1961", *Polar Record* 7(48), (1954), 227-30; 8(52), (1956), 57-62; 10(69), (1961), 618-29 (with J E Thomas)

"Suggested terms for ice features", *Polar Record* 7(49), (1955), 331-2 (with E F Roots and C W M Swithinbank)

"Illustrated ice glossary", *Polar Record* 8(52), (1956), 4-12; 9(59), (1958), 90-96 (with T E Armstrong)

"The British title to sovereignty in the Falkland Islands Dependencies", *Polar Record* 8(53), (1956), 125-51

"The Arctic Institute, Leningrad", *Polar Record* 8(55), (1957), 306-16 (with T E Armstrong)

"Iceports", *Polar Record* 9(59), (1958), 150

"Chronological list of Antarctic expeditions", *Polar Record* 9(59), (1958), 97-134; 9(60), (1958), 191-239

"The names East Antarctica and West Antarctica", *Polar Record* 9(61), (1959),358-9

"The British contribution to Antarctic ornithology", *Ibis* 101 (1), (1959), 107-14

"The organisation of polar information", *SPRI Occasional paper* 1 (1960)

"Iceberg tongues", *Polar Record* 10(67), (1961), 409

"Terminology of Antarctic ice features", *J Glaciology* 3(30), (1961), 1167-8 (with T E Armstrong)

"Glaciologists and Antarctic place-names", *Ice* 9, (1962), 10-18.

"Universal Decimal Classification for use in polar libraries, 2nd edition", *SPRI Occasional paper* 2 (1963)

"Antarctic gazetteers", *Polar Record* 12(76), (1964), 83-6

"Proposed new terms and definitions of sea ice for the use of submariners", *Polar Record* 12(77), (1964), 197-210 (with T E Armstrong)

"Antarctic" in A L Thomson (ed.), *A new dictionary of birds* (London: Nelson, 1964), 51-5

"British naval hydrographic surveys in the Antarctic 1948-64", *BAS Bulletin* 5, (1965), 43-6

"Wildlife conservation in the Antarctic", *Oryx* 8(4), (1966), 237-43

"Illustrated glossary of snow and ice", *SPRI Special publication* No. 4 (1966) (with T E Armstrong and CWM Swithinbank)

"Note on the identification of Wilson's bird records", in Edward Wilson, *Diary of the Discovery Expedition to the Antarctic regions 1901-1904* (London: Blandford, 1966), 406-7

"Les recherches scientifiques britannique dans l'Antarctique", *TAAF* 35 (1966), 3-23

Edward Wilson's birds of the Antarctic (London: Blandford Press, 1967)

"Unauthorised names of glaciers", *J Glaciology* 10(60), (1971), 409

The Arctic Ocean: report of a conference at Ditchley Park, 14-17 May 1971

"Conservation in the Antarctic", *Phil Trans Roy Soc B Biol Sci* 279 (963), (1977),97-104

"Proposed new terms and definitions for snow and ice features", *Polar Record* 18(116), (1977), 501-2 (with T E Armstrong and C W M Swithinbank)

"International cooperation for Antarctic development: the test for the Antarctic Treaty", *Polar Record* 19(119), (1978), 107-20

"The place-names 'Greater Antarctica' and 'Lesser Antarctica' versus 'East Antarctica' and 'West Antarctica'", *BAS Bulletin* 53 (1981), 257-60.

Roberts' publications also include 20 obituaries in Polar Record, several gazetteers and a number of Whitehall reports including the 1941 War Office *Handbook on clothing and equipment*, 1942 NID5 *Geographical Handbook* on Iceland, 1945 Handbook *Territorial claims in the Antarctic* and the 1948 *Antarctic Pilot*.

ACKNOWLEDGEMENTS

This book is dedicated to the memory of Charles Swithinbank, one of Brian Roberts' longest-standing friends and colleagues. Charles was a great stimulus to us and pressurized us to "get on with it, otherwise it will be too late [for him to read]". Sadly it was too late. Charles died long before the task could be completed. He and six other former colleagues of Brian Roberts who provided us with much anecdotal information have to be thanked posthumously: Dr Charles Swithinbank, Sir John Freeland and Dr Bernard Stonehouse died in 2014. Sir Richard Parsons, Dame Margaret Anstee, Dr Stan Evans and Dr Fred Roots died in 2016.

We are immensely grateful to Peggy Heap for her magnificent hospitality over the years during our many visits to the archives in Cambridge and for introducing us to some of the polar fraternity. Throughout the entire project Peter Rymill has been a constant source of information, lively discussion, encouragement and support. Ann Savours Shirley also played a crucial role in publishing *Polar Pundit*, without which this project would have been very difficult to get off the ground. Others we would like to thank for their generous help include Lisle and Ralston Ryder, John Dudeney (BAS), John Sheail, John Glen (IGS), David Anderson, Jane Rumble (FCO), Heather Lane, Toni Martorell, Hallgeir Elvehøy (senior engineer/glaciologist, NVE), Sir Martin Holdgate, Mark Bertram, Bryan Lintott, Jane and Allen Clayton, Diana Rowley, John Croxall, Nigel Milius and Wendy Hare, Ian Hendry, Petra Searle, John Killingbeck, Sir Christopher Audland, George Hemmen, Colin Clements, and friends Vic Hansen, Mellie and Dave Lewis and Jonathan Wood.

We also had stalwart support from June's daughters Katherine Ring and Sarah Emmerson, son-in-law Rich Thomas, and other family members Jennifer Rushworth, Susan Jourdain and Lesley Roberts, who contributed family background material.

Naomi Boneham of SPRI provided us with an outstanding archival service. We are also grateful to archivists Lucy Martin (SPRI), Ieuan Hopkins and Joanna Rae (BAS), Louise Buckingham (IGS), Amanda Goode (Emmanuel College), Jacqui Cox and staff of the Churchill College Archives Centre, Cambridge University Library and the National Archives in London.

The author and publisher have made every effort to contact holders of copyright relating to material reproduced in this book. If it appears that any item has been reproduced without permission, please contact us so that the omission can be rectified. Photographs, artwork and text have been reproduced by kind permission of the following: Line drawing of Brian Roberts (BAS Archives Ref. WA/D1), courtesy of the estate of David Smith. Photograph of Wilson's Petrel chick from the PhD thesis by B B Roberts, courtesy of the Syndics of Cambridge University Library (MS-PHD-01108-000-00001.tif and MS-PHD-01108-000-00002.tif (PhD.1108). Portrait of Brian Roberts in the Journal of Glaciology, courtesy of the International Glaciology Society. Photographs from the 1938 original edition of *Southern Lights* by John R Rymill, courtesy of Peter Rymill. Photograph of RRS Bransfield, C A Clayton (photographer), 1971, reproduced by courtesy of the British Antarctic Survey, BAS Archives Service ref. AD6/19/3/B91 (original photograph copyright BAS/UKRI). Photograph of the UK delegation at the 5th Antarctic Treaty Consultative Meeting, Paris 1968, reproduced by permission of the Ministère des Affaires Étrangères, France and the Chancellor, Masters and Scholars of the University of Cambridge acting through SPRI. Photograph of the first meeting of Antarctic Treaty countries after treaty signing CAYP 25870 W5944 24/AMZPCO123.28, reproduced by permission of Archives New Zealand, The Department of Internal Affairs Te Tari Taiwhenua. Original bird paintings by Lisle Ryder, courtesy of Ralston Ryder. Photograph of Mount Rivers, courtesy of Lesley Roberts. Photographs from the 2019 re-enactment of the 1932 Iceland expedition, courtesy of Oliver Vince. All other photographs are from the authors' private collection. Material in Chapter 14 taken from an article by Steve Heavens in *Polar Record* is reproduced by permission of Cambridge University Press. Material from the UK National Archives, Kew, London is crown copyright and reproduced under the terms of the Open Government Licence (www.nationalarchives.gov.uk/doc/open-government-licence/version/3/).

ILLUSTRATIONS
AND SOURCES

Except where otherwise stated, all photographs are from the authors' collection, taken by themselves, Brian, his father Charles, or by Ena Thomas. All line drawings are by June Roberts, except for the portrait of Brian Roberts by David Smith (BAS Archives), reproduced by permission of Elizabeth Smith.

Back cover: Brian Roberts at Oslo conference, 1975 (SPRI archive P74/7)

9.2   Wilson's petrel chick (B B Roberts, PhD thesis). Reproduced by permission of Cambridge University Library

9.3   String vest, made in 1943

9.4   Bomb damage, Fulham Road: view from Denis' flat

9.5   Bomb damage, Pelham Court

10.1   Roberts climbing with friends on Theodul Pass, with Matterhorn

10.2   Large wave over Rockall, March 1943 (James Fisher, *Rockall*, London: Country Book Club 1956). Crown Copyright (expired)

10.3   Eyrie with two golden eagle chicks and dead rabbit

10.4   Roberts at the wheel of *Heather*, Shiant Islands

10.5   Maudheim base buried by snowdrift

11.1   Ena Thomas on Macquarie Island

11.2   Nesting rockhopper penguin, Macquarie Island

11.3   Nesting black-browed albatross, Macquarie Island

11.4   Nesting sooty albatross, Macquarie Island

11.5   Nesting sooty albatross, Macquarie Island

16.1   Mount Erebus. Reproduced by permission of Charles Swithinbank

16.2   Emperor penguin chicks at Cape Crozier

17.1   First Treaty Meeting, Canberra 1961. CAYP 25870 W5944 24/ AMZPCO123.28. Reproduced by permission of Archives New Zealand The Department of Internal Affairs Te Tari Taiwhenua.

18.1   Coconut palms on Moorea

18.2   Moorea: Mouaroa from Baie de Papetoa

18.3   Moorea children in outrigger canoe, with drying fishing nets

18.4   Wandering albatross

18.5   Nesting magnificent frigatebirds, Galapagos

19.1   Fifth Treaty Meeting, Paris 1968. Roberts centre, John Heap right (B B Roberts, Personal Diary, SPRI MS1308/17, reproduced by permission of SPRI)

20.1   Roberts at home in Cambridge (J Glaciology Vol 25(92) (1980), 353). Reproduced by permission of the International Glaciology Society

22.1   RRS *Bransfield*, photograph by C A Clayton 1971, reproduced by permission of the BAS (Archives Service, ref. AD6/19/3/B91, original copyright BAS/ UKRI).

ACRONYMS AND ABBREVIATIONS

AA   Automobile Association
ACAN   Advisory Committee on Antarctic Names
AINA   Arctic Institute of North America
AMCAFF   Agreed Measures on Conservation of Antarctic Fauna and Flora
ANARE   Australian National Antarctic Research Expedition
APNC   Antarctic Place Names Committee
ATCM   Antarctic Treaty Consultative Meeting
BAS   British Antarctic Survey
BBC   British Broadcasting Corporation
BGLE   British Graham Land Expedition
CCAS   Convention for the Conservation of Antarctic Seals
CCAMLR   Commission for the Conservation of Antarctic Marine Living Resources
Cdr   Commander
CMG   Companion of St Michael and St George
CTAE   Commonwealth Trans Antarctic Expedition
CUL   Cambridge University Library
CUP   Cambridge University Press
DNI   Director of Naval Intelligence
FCO   Foreign and Commonwealth Office
FID   Falkland Islands Dependencies
FIDASE   Falkland Islands Dependencies Aerial SurveyExpedition
FIDS   Falkland Islands Dependencies Survey
FORD   Foreign Office Research Department
FRGS   Fellow of the Royal Geographical Society

FRUS	Foreign Relations of the United States
GWR	Great Western Railway
HMG	His/Her Majesty's Government
HMS	His/Her Majesty's Ship
ICI	Imperial Chemical Industries
IGY	International Geophysical Year
Lt	Lieutenant
MA	Master of Arts
mph	miles per hour
NASA	National Aeronautics and Space Administration
NBSX	Norwegian-British-Swedish Expedition
NBSE	Norwegian-British-Swedish Expedition
NERC	National Environment Research Council
NID	Naval Intelligence Department
NVE	Norges Vassdrags- og Energidirektorat
OBE	Order of the British Empire
PI	Photographic Interpretation
RAC	Royal Automobile Club
RAF	Royal Air Force
Rev	Reverend
RGS	Royal Geographical Society
RIIA	Royal Institute of International Affairs
RMS	Royal Mail Ship
RMV	Royal Mail Vessel
RN	Royal Navy
RRS	Royal Research Ship
SCAR	Scientific Committee on Antarctic Research
SOE	Special Operations Executive
SPA	Specially Protected Area
SPRI	Scott Polar Research Institute
TAAF	Terres Australes et Antarctiques Françaises
TNA	The National Archives, London
UDC	Universal Decimal Classification
UGC	University Grants Committee
UK	United Kingdom of Great Britain and Northern Ireland
UN	United Nations
UNCLOS	United Nations Conference on the Law of the Sea

US	United States of America
USBGN	United States Board of Geographical Names
USSR	Soviet Union
VAD	Voluntary Aid Detachment
WVS	Women's Voluntary Service

GLOSSARY

Crevasse	A deep open crack in a thick ice field or glacier
Fast ice	Ice fastened to the coastline or sea shore
Fid	Colloquial name for a recruit to FIDS
Hummock	A hump or ridge in an ice field
x/10	Estimate from a ship of the proportion in tenths ice cover of sea surface that is iced over
Knot	Nautical speed measurement. 1 knot = 1 nautical mile/hour = 1.15 mph Historically a nautical mile corresponded to 1° latitude
MI5	Domestic counter-intelligence and security agency of the UK government
MI6	Foreign intelligence service of the UK government
MI9	War Office department supporting Resistance networks and assisting escape from capture in Europe
Outrigger	A long narrow canoe hollowed out from a tree trunk
Pack ice	Sea ice formed by freezing of seawater
Raised beach	An emergent coastal landform raised above the shoreline by a relative fall in the sea level
Shilling	A historic unit of British currency prior to decimalisation. £1 = 20 shillings. 1 shilling = 12 pence
Tussock	A grass that grows in dense clumps, typically 6 ft in height, in wet coastal lands. The variety that is otherwise spelt 'tussac' is native to South America and islands in the South Atlantic.
Tussock cutter	Someone who collects tussock grass for feeding ponies
Whitehall	The British government Civil Service in London

ICELANDIC PRONUNCIATION

á	ow as in 'cow'
ó	ow as in 'glow'
ú	oo as in 'boot'
ö	as in German
ae	as in 'mile'
ð	soft th as in 'bathe'
Þ and þ	hard th as in 'think'
j	y as in 'year'

NOTES AND REFERENCES

CHAPTER 1: FAMILY BACKGROUND AND EARLY CHILDHOOD

1. Princess Louise was later destined to become the Queen of Sweden, and received several medals in recognition of her WW1 work. Later she devoted her life to charity work in England and Sweden and to improving the quality of life and pay for nurses in Sweden.

2. Simon Moody and Alan Wakefield, *Under the devil's eye: the British military experience in Macedonia 1915-1918* (Barnsley: Pen & Sword, 2011)

3. Ibid., 187.

CHAPTER 2: ADVENTUROUS ALPINE MOTORING

1. Charles L Freeston FRGS, *The high-roads of the Alps: a motoring guide to one hundred mountain passes*, 2nd ed. (London: Kegan Paul, Trench, Trubner & Co Ltd, 1911), 52.

2. The drive-on ferry was not introduced until 1953.

3. Salmons were coach builders and became famous for their coaches, dog-carts and ralli-carts, which sold around the world.

4. Charles Roberts to Joy, 19 July 1926, authors' collection.

5. Ibid.

6. Freeston, op. cit., 233.

7. During the 1960s Denis went there with his wife Lilian and their teenage daughter June, whose recollections of the hotel staff seemed not quite in keeping with the spirit of the place. Upon their arrival on a Saturday evening

they were met by a stern woman with a large bunch of keys jangling from her belt, who informed them that they were required to attend the 10 am Sunday service at the church next door(this instruction was disobeyed). It was the height of the tourist season but the huge hotel was almost empty, the only other guests being a single Frenchman and a German couple. June joined them for a memorable day's hiking – on what turned out to be the same high mountain trail taken by Brian, Denis and Charles some 40 years earlier.

CHAPTER 3: SEABIRDS AND SMALL ISLANDS AROUND THE BRITISH ISLES

1. The Birley family home was later turned into the site museum and research centre housing the excavation finds. Eric Birley's sons Robin and Anthony continued excavations at Vindolanda, pioneering the reconstruction of sections of wall, ramparts and ditch. Today the Vindolanda Trust continues with Eric's grandson Andrew. In 1973 the oldest surviving handwritten documents in Britain were discovered in a waterlogged part of the site. The hundreds of ink-written writing tablets provide a unique insight into everyday life on the Northern Frontier of the Roman Empire.

2. Three generations later the boat trips continue today as a thriving family business.

3. John Sheail, *Nature in trust* (Glasgow: Blackie & Son, 1976), 54.

4. Grace Watt, *The Farne Islands, their history and wildlife* (London: Country Life Limited, 1951), 171.

5. Ibid., 174-176.

6. G E Mitton (ed.), *Black's Guide to Scotland* (London: Adam and Charles Black, 1907), 163.

7. Ibid., 182-3.

8. Like others, the ferry would soon be replaced by one with greater capacity for cars and a turntable, and finally in 1984 by a bridge.

9. Charles Roberts to Brian 22 October 1929, SPRI MS 1308/43/32.

10. Brian Roberts, Introduction to "River Wye canoe trip 16-21April 1929". All quotations from this journey are from *Diary: River Wye*, SPRI MS 1308/43/17.

11. Ibid.

12. Ibid., entry 17 April.

13. 'Tubenose' refers to the distinctive pair of extra tubes on their beaks, a means of expelling excessive salt from the seawater they are constantly absorbing.

14. Another ringing scheme was begun at the same time at Aberdeen University by Arthur Lansborough Thomson and the two schemes were eventually merged and handed over to the British Trust for Ornithology in 1937.

15. Brian Roberts, "Manx shearwaters' departure flight from land", *British Birds* 23(8), (1930): 223-4.

16. Quotations from the Ireland journey are from 3 sources: Brian Roberts, *Diary: Ireland* (1930), 22-28 August, SPRI MS 1308/43/18; ibid., School Essay: The Holidays, Life in a Lighthouse, 23–29 August 1930; *The Wayfarer* (Cambridge, 1934): 26-29.

17. Brian Roberts, *Diaries: Mullion Island and Oslo* (1931), entry 12 April, SPRI MS 1308/43/19.

CHAPTER 4: A NORDIC INTRODUCTION TO THE ARCTIC

1. Charles Roberts to Denis, 1 June 1931, authors' collection.

2. Hallgeir Elvehøy, personal communication 30 January 2018. A Norwegian report describes the glacial outlet collapse on 28 August 1931, close to the time of the Roberts family visit.

3. Hallgeir Elvehøy, personal communication 7 February 2018.

4. Anon, "British Jostedals Expedition, 1970", *Polar Record* 15(98) (1971): 724.

5. Brian Roberts, photographs: Norway 1931, authors' collection.

6. *Baedeker's Norway, Sweden and Denmark* (Leipzig: Karl Baedeker, 1909), 68.

7. Brian Roberts, op. cit.

8. John L Stoddard, *John L Stoddard's lectures: Norway* (1901), Dodo Press reprint, 37.

9. For the motorist today who wants only to get from A to B regardless of scenery there is another option: a road connecting Oslo to Bergen via a tunnel 15 miles long, making the drive less hazardous in the winter.

CHAPTER 5: NECESSARY EVILS: SCHOOL AND UNIVERSITY

1. The fagging rule applied to all new boys at Uppingham for the first two years. From year 3 they were relieved from fagging duties and the trouser pockets could be unstitched.

2. J Sands, *Out of this world, or life in St Kilda*, (Edinburgh: Maclachlan & Stuart, 1878). Personal copy owned by Roberts, from which he gave his first talk.

3. Peter Falk in H G R King & Ann Savours (ed.), *Polar pundit: reminiscences about Brian Birley Roberts* (Cambridge: Polar Publications, SPRI 1995), 51.

4. H G Ponting to B B Roberts, 18 September 1930, *SPRI Correspondence and papers 1930-1964*, SPRI MS1308/37

5. Phillip Law, "Obituary: Brian Birley Roberts", *Polar Record* 19(121) (1979): 399

6. R H Owen to Charles Roberts, 31 December 1930, *Uppingham School*, SPRI MS 1308/43/5.

7. Brian Roberts, "Obituary: David Lambert Lack FRS" *Cambridge Bird Club Report* 46 (1972): 5

8. David Lack, *Darwin's Finches* (Cambridge: CUP, 1947).

9. John Heap to Launcelot Fleming 7 June 1967, private collection of Peggy Heap.

CHAPTER 6: THROUGH SLUSH AND LAVA DESERT

1. Such rations were used in 1929 and 1930 by Gino Watkins on BAARE.

2. Giles Hunt, *Launcelot Fleming, a portrait* (Norwich: Canterbury Press, 2003), 21.

3. Brian Roberts, *Journal: Cambridge expedition to Vatnajökull, Iceland June-August 1932*, entry 25 June, SPRI MS 1308/1.

4. J Angus Beckett, *Iceland adventure: the double traverse of Vatnajökull by the Cambridge expedition* (London: H F & G Witherby, 1934), 41.

5. Hunt, op. cit., 20.

6. Peter Falk, "The Journey to Hvannalindir", chapter VII in Beckett, op. cit., 110.

7. Beckett, op. cit., 79.

8. Brian Roberts, "The Cambridge expedition to Vatnajökull 1932", *Geog J* 81(4), 1933: 296-7.

9. Brian Roberts, *Journal: Cambridge expedition to Vatnajökull, Iceland June-August 1932*, entry 21 July. SPRI MS 1308/1

10. Ibid., entry 22 July

11. Ibid., entry 1 August

12. Beckett, op. cit., 156

13. Many years later one of the authors had similar delight at being taught an Icelandic round about whimbrel coming to the southern plains in springtime.

14. Beckett, op. cit., 159.

15. Brian Roberts, *Journal: Cambridge expedition to Vatnajökull, Iceland June-August 1932*, entry 14 August, SPRI MS 1308/1.

16. Hunt, op. cit., 22.

17. Almost 40 years later in 1973, Helgafell suddenly erupted. In seven weeks it engulfed half the town and threatened to destroy the port, which would have resulted in the loss of Iceland's most important centre for the cod fishing industry. Following an evacuation of the 3,000 inhabitants, millions of gallons of seawater were pumped onto the lava to cool and slow down its advance towards the port and harbour, a remarkably successful operation.

18. Oliver Vince, Glen Gowers and John-Henry Charles, "Return to Vatnajökull 1932-2019" https://www.sledgereport.com.

19. The Cambridge expedition took place near the beginning of a sharp rise in Iceland's temperature between 1930 and 1960, causing even greater summer melt than could have been anticipated. Helgi Björnsson, *The Glaciers of Iceland*, Advances in Quaternary Science, Vol 2 (Atlantis Press, 2017), 92-93.

CHAPTER 7: WITH DR CHARCOT TO MUSK-OX LAND

1,   Brian Roberts, *Journal: Cambridge East Greenland expedition 1933*, entry 9 July. SPRI MS 1308/2.

2.   Ibid., entry 11 July.

3.   Ibid., entry 12 July.

4.   Rorke Bryan, *Ordeal by Ice: Ships of the Antarctic* (Cork: Collins Press, 2011), 248-56.

5.   Roberts, op. cit., entry 20 July.

6.   Ibid., entry 26 July.

7.   Greenlandic term for an isolated mountain peak protruding through glacial ice.

8.   Roberts, op. cit., entry 9 August.

CHAPTER 8: THREE YEARS IN THE ANTARCTIC: THE BRITISH GRAHAM LAND EXPEDITION

1.   R E D Ryder, unpublished lecture: *A voyage to the Antarctic*, private collection of Lisle Ryder.

2.   William McC Meek & Co Ltd, naval architect drawing *Penola: TS Auxiliary Topsail Schooner*, private collection of Lisle Ryder. Reproduced in Rorke Bryan, *Ordeal by Ice: Ships of the Antarctic* (Cork: Collins Press, 2011), 349.

3.   Kenneth Birley to Brian Roberts, 19 August 1934 in BGLE 1934-1937: Expedition file IV *Original plans, financial papers and agreements*, SPRI MS 400/4. His generosity was commemorated by Birley Glacier on the Graham Land coast.

4.   Brian Roberts, *BGLE 1934-1937 Letters to parents* 2 (12 November 1934). SPRI MS1447/2.

5.   Brian Roberts, *Personal Journal British Graham Land Expedition: Vol. I, December 1934 to 9 December 1935*, retrospective introduction 9 August 1937, SPRI MS1308/3/1.

6.   Penguin studies had been made by G Murray Levick on the 1910 *Terra Nova* Expedition, Louis Gain on Charcot's 2nd French Antarctic Expedition 1908-1910, and by Thomas Bagshawe on the 1920-21 Graham Land Expedition (published 1938). See also Robert Cushman Murphy, *The penguins of South Georgia* (New York: Museum of the Brooklyn Institute of Arts and Sciences, 1915) and *Oceanic birds of South America* (New York: Macmillan, 1936).

7.   Brian Roberts, *BGLE 1934-1937 Letters to parents* 4 (29 November 1934), SPRI MS1447/4.

8.   John Rymill, *Southern Lights: the story of the British Graham Land Expedition* (London: Chatto & Windus, 1938), 48.

9. Brian Roberts, *Personal Journal, BGLE Vol 1, December 1934 to 9 December 1935*, entry 20 January 1935, SPRI MS1308/3/1.

10. In Cambridge this choice of expedition base site caused some dissatisfaction. Debenham wanted the base to be set up much farther south at 67°S. Frank Debenham to B B Roberts, 1 June/2 July 1936, *SPRI Correspondence and papers 1930-1964*, SPRI MS 1308/37.

11. Brian Roberts, *Personal Journal, BGLE Vol I, December 1934 to 9 December 1935*, entry 9 February 1935, SPRI MS1308/3/1.

12. Ibid., entry 10 February 1935.

13. R C Murphy, *Oceanic birds of South America* (New York: Macmillan, 1936), 420.

14. Brian Roberts, "Notes from Kidney Island 28.11.36-4.12.36", *Ornithological Notebook Vol 5 Sphenisciformes: observations made during the BGLE1934-37*, SPRI MS 1308/20/5.

15. Having probably the most luxuriant area of vegetation on the western side of the Antarctic Peninsula, as well as a large blue-eyed shag colony, Green Island was subsequently designated a Specially Protected Area under the Antarctic Treaty System.

16. W L S Fleming, G C L Bertram and B B Roberts, "Three Antarctic Years: the British Graham Land expedition of 1934-1937", *Canad Geog Journal* 22(1) (1941): 13.

17. Until 1900 the death rate from appendectomy was 40%. After King Edward VII was successfully operated on, awareness of the symptoms increased and patients were then treated before rupture and sepsis occurred. Until the mid 1930s there were no antibiotics and the commonest treatment was laxatives. The incidence of appendicitis in young men in the Antarctic is still unusually high.

18. Peter Rymill, personal communication 10 October 2016. This account by his father was probably elaborated on every re-telling.

19. E W Bingham, *BGLE Diary*, entries 6-9 July 1935, SPRI MS 1509/31.

20. Alfred Stephenson, *BGLE Journal, 31 December 1934 to 17 April 1937*, entry 6-9 July 1935, SPRI MS432/4/1.

21. Brian Roberts, *Personal Journal, BGLE Vol. I, December 1934 to 9 December 1935*, entry 6 August 1935, SPRI MS1308/3/1.

22. Fleming et al, op. cit., 16.

23. Murphy, op. cit., 407.

24. Brian Roberts, *Personal Journal, British Graham Land Expedition Vol. II, 10 December 1935 to 17 May 1937*, entry 29 March 1936, SPRI MS1308/3/2.

25. Brian Roberts, *BGLE 1934-1937 Letters to parents* 7 (18 June 1936), SPRI MS1447/7.

26. Betty Creswick to B B Roberts, 25 May 1936, *SPRI Correspondence and papers 1930-1964*, SPRI MS1308/37.

27. Brian Roberts, *Personal Journal, BGLE Vol. II, 10 December 1935 to 17 May 1937*, entry 30 June 1936, SPRI MS1308/3/2.

28. Robert Headland, *The island of South Georgia* (Cambridge: CUP, 1984), 114-31 gives a detailed account of the whaling and sealing industries.

29. Creswick, op. cit., 2 July 1936.

30. Debenham to Roberts, op. cit.

31. Debenham to Roberts, ibid. 12 November 1936.

32. Brian Roberts, *Personal Journal, BGLE Vol. II, 10 December 1935 to 17 May 1937*, entry 3 September 1936, SPRI MS1308/3/2.

33. Ibid., entry 6 September 1936.

34. Ibid., entry 18 September 1936.

35. Ibid.

36. Ibid., entry 25 September 1936.

37. Ibid., entry 9 October 1936.

38. M J Anstee, Minute 1 June 1951, op. cit.

39. Pablo Garcia Borboroglu and P Dee Boersma, "Penguins: Natural History and Conservation" (University of Washington Press, 2013), 10.

40. Roberts and Strong counted 1195 adults, and 942 chicks which were segregated under the care of 123 of the adults.

41. Chris Furse, *Elephant Island: An Antarctic expedition* (Shrewsbury: Anthony Nelson, 1979), 131-43. Furse, a member of the Joint Services Expedition to Elephant Island in 1970-1971, was an ornithologist who made the first ascent of Mount Irving and returned in 1976-1977. Subsequently a number of censuses have been made of the huge southern fulmar colony and chinstrap penguin rookeries on Clarence Island, although they were carried out from the safety of a ship.

42. Brian Roberts, *Personal Journal, BGLE Vol. II, 10 December 1935 to 17 May 1937*, entry 21 November 1936, SPRI MS1308/3/2.

43. Ibid., entry 28 November 1936.

44. Ibid., entry 31 December 1936.

45. Ibid., entry 8 January 1937. Today Beauchene Island is a protected site with restricted access by permit only.

46. Ibid., entry 9 May 1937.

CHAPTER 9: WARTIME

1. Brian Roberts, "The breeding behaviour of penguins, with special reference to *Pygoscelis papua* (Forster)," *British Graham Land Expedition 1934-37 Scientific Reports* 1(3) (London: British Museum Natural History, 1940), 195-254; "The life cycle of Wilson's Petrel, *Oceanites Oceanicus*", ibid. 1(2), 141-94; "Tidal observations in Graham Land", ibid. 1(8), 327-35; "A bibliography of Antarctic ornithology", ibid. 1(9), 337-67.

2. B B Roberts, "Notes on the scientific work of the British Graham Land Expedition 1934-37: Birds", *Geog J* 91(6), (1938): 526-8.

3. Thomas Wyatt Bagshawe, *Two men in the Antarctic: an expedition to Graham Land 1920-1922* (Cambridge: CUP, 1939).

4. T W Bagshawe, "Notes on the habits of the Gentoo and Ringed or Antarctic Penguins", *Trans Zoological Soc London* 24(3) (1938): 185-306

5. B B Roberts, Note "F H A Marshall", December 1956, *Roberts: Cambridge and BGLE 1934-56*, SPRI MS 1308/43/13.

6. Brian Roberts, "Wilsons Petrel", op. cit. 176-87; A Lansborough Thomson, *Bird migration*, 2nd ed. (London: H F & G Witherby, 1942), 34.

7. Brian Roberts, *Scott Polar Research Institute, war-time activities 1939-46*, Annex II: "Notes on the SPRI during the War" (compiled 1967): 74-85. SPRI MS 188.

8. Ibid.

9. Michael Smith, *Polar crusader: A life of Sir James Wordie* (Edinburgh: Birlinn, 2007), 212.

10. Andrew Croft in H G R King and Ann Savours (ed.), *Polar pundit: reminiscences about Brian Birley Roberts* (Cambridge: Polar Publishing, SPRI 1995): 49.

11. B B Roberts, "Cold climate warfare equipment, clothing and techniques" in *Cold Climate Warfare Papers 1939-46*, SPRI MS 1308/52.

12. Dorothy Fetherstonhaugh to Roberts 5 July 1939, *SPRI Correspondence & papers 1930-1964*, SPRI MS 1308/37.

13. An explanatory note pencilled in by Roberts.

14. Dorothy Wright to Roberts, 8 January 1940, *SPRI Correspondence & papers 1930-1964*. SPRI MS 1308/37.

15. Andrew Croft and Brian Roberts, "Notes on the selection of polar footwear", *Polar Record* 3 (19) (1940): 235-67 and 3(20) (1940): 309-26

16. Madeline Roberts to Brian 12 September 1940, authors' collection.

17. Peter Pirker, *Subversion deutscher Herrshaft: Der britische Kriegsgeheimdienst SOE und Österreich*, (Göttingen: V&R unipress, Vienna University Press, 2012), 279-305, 321-33. Peter Ulanowsky's code name was Peter Brand.

18. Lilian Roberts to Denis, 6 August 1945, authors' collection.

19. H C Darby, "Outline history of the work of the Geographical Handbooks Section (N.I.D.5) Cambridge 1940-45", CUL GB 12 MS Add .8701; Peter Speak, *Deb: geographer, scientist, Antarctic explorer* (Guildford: Polar Publishing, 2008), 94.

20. Minutes of the SPRI Committee of Management, 28 March 1942, *SPRI Correspondence and papers 1930-1964*, SPRI MS1308/37.

21. *Geographical Handbook Series: Iceland* (Naval Intelligence Division, BR504. July 1942. Restricted).

22. Wright to Roberts, op. cit., 17 May 1942.

23. B B Roberts, "Notes on the Polar Record", ibid., 27 September 1942.

24. Frank Debenham, "Notes on the Polar Record by B B Roberts", ibid., 15 October 1942.

25. Debenham to J M Wordie, ibid.,16 October 1942.

26. Speak, op. cit., 96 quotes a few examples. SPRI possesses a collection of letters from Debenham to Elizabeth Rought, to which access was denied.

27. Allen Evans to B B Roberts, 22 February 1943, *Visit to the United States and Canada August-November 1943*, SPRI MS 1308/52/11.

28. B B Roberts, *Journal: Visit to United States and Canada* 1943, entry 7 October 1943, SPRI MS 1308/5.

29. J M Wordie, telegram to Message Center, OSS Washington, 12 October 1943, *Visit to the US and Canada Aug-Nov 1943*, SPRI MS 1308/52/11.

30. E G N Rushbrooke to B B Roberts, 10 November 1943, *Admiralty Naval Intelligence Division, Geographical Handbooks*, SPRI MS 1308/52/4.

31. W L Cadman, Admiralty to DNI 20 July 1943, *Visit to the United States and Canada*, SPRI MS 1308/52/11.

32. B A D NID18 to Admiralty, ibid., 16 September 1943.

33. Smith, op. cit., 213.

34. H C Darby, op. cit., confirms that Wordie resigned in November 1943 and that Darby was "in charge" thereafter, but says nothing about the circumstances. This account by Darby was presented to CUL in 1987. A further unpublished account written retrospectively in 1988 describes the reorganisation of NID5 (naturally reflecting Darby's side of the story) and includes a letter dated 10 January 1946 from DNI Rushbrooke congratulating Darby on taking control and "dealing with the staffing problems". See Hugh Clout and Cyril Gosme, "The Naval Intelligence Handbooks: a monument in geographical writing", *Progress in Human Geography* 27(2) (2003): 153-73. Reference 14 dated 1988: "Comments by H C Darby on the paper by B B Roberts entitled Scott Polar Research Unit war-time activities (manuscript)", contains no clues to the whereabouts of this manuscript.

35. R N Rudmose Brown to B B Roberts, 3 February 1944, *Admiralty Naval Intelligence Division, Geographical Handbooks, Handbook on Svalbard*, SPRI MS 1308/52/4/6.

36. John R Dudeney and David W H Walton, "From Scotia to Operation Tabarin: developing British policy for Antarctica", *Polar Record* 48 (04) (2012): 342-60; Adrian J Howkins, *Frozen empires: A history of the Antarctic sovereignty dispute between Britain, Argentina and Chile 1939-1959* (Thesis, University of Texas, Austin 2008), 79-94. https://repositories.lib.utexas.edu/handle/2152/3860.

37. Sir Allan Cardinall to C F G Stanley (Colonial Secretary), 23 March 1943, TNA CO 78/215/8.

38. J L Hayward to Sir W Battershill, ibid., 30 April 1943.

39.   A B Acheson to R A Gallup, ibid., 27 May 1943.

40.   B B Roberts, "Obituary: Dr James William Slessor Marr", *Polar Record* 13(82), (1966): 94-7.

41.   N A Mackintosh, "Memorandum on the South Orkney Islands, the South Shetland Islands and Graham Land", 28 June 1943, TNA CO 78/215/8.

42.   B B Roberts, note written over telegram, Sir Allan Cardinall to Colonial Secretary, 13 November 1943, *FIDS Correspondence and committee papers 1943-45*. SPRI MS 1308/22/1.

43.   Oliver Stanley (Downing Street) to Sir Allan Cardinall, 3 November 1943, TNA CO 78/215/9.

44.   J V Perowne, Minute A8239 9 September 1943, TNA FO 371/33528.

45.   W E Beckett, Minute A8984, ibid., 27 October 1943.

46.   J V Perowne, Minute A8984/25/2, ibid., 15 November 1943.

47.   J M Wordie to J V Perowne A10810/25/2 "Proposal that Mr B B Roberts should assist the FORD in the compilation of a booklet on the Arctic [*sic*] regions", 29 November 1943, TNA FO 371/33528.

48.   Robert A Longmire and Kenneth C Walker "Herald of a noisy world – interpreting the news of all nations. The Research and Analysis Department of the Foreign and Commonwealth Office: a history", *Foreign Policy Document Series* (Special Issue) No. 263, Foreign & Commonwealth Office (1995), 18-25. https://www.gov.uk/government/ uploads/ system/uploads/attachment_data/file/361922/Herald_of_a_Noisy_World.pdf

49.   B B Roberts, Foreign Office Handbook *Territorial claims in the Antarctic*, 1 May 1945. Redacted version released in 2007 as an annex to "Application by HMG to the International Court of Justice", TNA FO 371/119821. Unredacted versions can be found in Australian National Archives A4311 #365/8, https://recordsearch.naa.gov.au/ SearchNRetrieve/Interface/ViewImage. aspx?B=3435898 and in "Foreign Office handbook on territorial claims in the Antarctic with Dominium Office comments", TNA DO 35/1414.

50.   B B Roberts "Notes on the future activities of the SPRI", November 1944, *SPRI Correspondence & papers 1930-1964*. SPRI MS 1308/37.

51   W L S Fleming to Roberts, ibid., 24 and 30 November 1944.

52.   J M Wordie to H R Mill, ibid., 31 January 1945.

53.   Speak, op. cit., 96.

54.   J M Wordie to H R Mill, 17 June, 24 June and 27 July 1945, *SPRI Correspondence & papers 1930-1964*, SPRI MS 1308/37.

55.   Stan Evans, personal communication 26 February 2014, recalled that it was common knowledge at SPRI that Debenham had threatened to resign if Roberts were ever offered a post.

CHAPTER 10: EARLY YEARS OF THE BRITISH ANTARCTIC SURVEY

1.   W Ellery Anderson, *Expedition south* (London: Travel Book Club 1957), 18.

2.   Vivian Fuchs, *Of ice and men* (Oswestry: Anthony Nelson, 1982), 23.

3.   E W Bingham to B B Roberts 10 January 1946, *FIDS Correspondence and committee papers 1946.* SPRI MS 1308/22/2.

4.   Michael Roberts to Brian Roberts, 11 January 1946 [*actually 1947*], *FIDS Correspondence and committee papers 1947*, SPRI MS 1308/22/3.

5.   Vivian Fuchs, op. cit., 134.

6.   "FIDS Meteorological Work: Notes on a Conversation between Dr B B Roberts (FORD) and Mr Howkins", 13 September 1946, Falkland Islands Association 255/46, cited in Adrian J Howkins, *Frozen empires: a history of the Antarctic sovereignty dispute between Britain, Argentina and Chile, 1939–1959* (Thesis: University of Texas, Austin, 2008): 125. https://repositories.lib.utexas.edu/handle/2152/ 3860

7.   Stephen Haddelsey, *Operation Tabarin* (Stroud: The History Press, 2014), 114.

8.   Minutes of meeting of FID Scientific Committee at the RGS, 13 November 1952, *FIDS, Correspondence & papers related to topographical mapping 1953-55*, SPRI MS 1277/3.

9.   Howkins, op. cit., 197-208.

10.   B B Roberts, "Note on reasons for recommending high priority for air survey in the FID", 12 August 1954, *FIDS Correspondence & papers related to topographical mapping 1953-55*. SPRI MS 1277/3.

11.   Peter Mott, *Wings over ice* (Exeter: A Wheaton & Co, 1986), 72.

12.   Ibid., 85.

13.   Haddesley, op. cit., 213-4.

14.   Andrew Taylor, interviewed by Joanna Rae 14 October 1987, *Oral history project BAS AD6/24/1/6.*

15.   B B Roberts to Major Madeley, 12 January, 4 April and 10 April 1946, *Cambridge and BGLE 1934-56*, SPRI MS 1308/43/13.

16.   Madeley to Roberts, ibid., 17 and 30 April 1946.

17.   Minutes of FIDS Committee meeting, 12 November 1946, *FIDS Correspondence and committee papers 1946*, SPRI MS 1308/22/2.

18.   Brian Roberts to E W Bingham, ibid., 6 December 1946; also in BAS AD1/D1/0/13.

19.   J M Wordie to B B Roberts. 11 January 1947, *FIDS Correspondence and committee papers 1947*, SPRI MS 1308/22/3.

20.   Michael Smith, *Polar crusader: a life of Sir James Wordie* (Oswestry: Birlinn, 2007), 221.

21.   John Huckle, *Trepassey* ship's report 2-21 January 1947, *FIDS Correspondence and committee papers 1947*. SPRI MS 1308/22/3.

22. B B Roberts to C J J T Barton, ibid., 7 March 1947.

23. Kevin Walton, *Two years in the Antarctic* (Malvern: Knell Press, 1982), 188-90.

24. B B Roberts to C A E Shuckburgh, Minute Sheet 30 October 1947, TNA FO 371/61300; Roberts to G A Howkins 14 January 1948, *FIDS Correspondence and committee papers 1948*, SPRI MS 1308/22/4.

25. C A E Shuckburgh, Notes A8594 to Private Secretary, 29 September and 8 November 1947, TNA FO 371/63100.

26. Roger Makins to Shuckburgh, "Antarctica", ibid., 17 October 1947.

27. Shuckburgh, ibid., 9 December 1947.

28. J E Thomas to V E Fuchs, 21 February 1948, *FIDS Correspondence and committee papers 1948*, SPRI MS 1308/22/4.

29. Richard M Laws, *Autobiography: Large animals and wide horizons: adventures of a biologist. Part I Seals' teeth and whales' ears*: 146-68 www.spri.cam.ac.uk/ resources/autobiographies/richardlaws/richardlaws1.pdf

30. Bernard Stonehouse, interviewed by the authors 14 October 2013. In his opinion the ships, equipment and clothing provided by FIDS were useless, the FIDS administration was incompetent and Roberts was a power-hungry bully. Stonehouse was however nursing a lifelong grudge over Roberts' refusal to help publish his emperor penguin studies.

31. B B Roberts, Memorandum 28 February 1956, *FIDS Correspondence and committee papers 1955-56*, SPRI MS 1308/22/9.

32. Many UK research scientists of that period were head-hunted by a US university or company and chose to take up the offer, never to return.

33. B B Roberts to N A Mackintosh, 28 November 1946, *Ronne Antarctic Expedition 1947-48 Correspondence & papers*. SPRI MS 1278; Roberts to J V Perowne, ibid., 31 December 1946

34. Brian Roberts to Graham and Diana Rowley, 7 February 1950, *Operation Lyon Correspondence & papers 1949-1951*, SPRI MS 1280; A Stephenson, "United States Exploration in the Antarctic: Review of 'Antarctic Conquest' by Finn Ronne", *Geog J* 115 (4/6) (1950): 233-5.

35. FIDS report, entry 9 January 1947, BAS AD8/1/13(2) CSS-2/4/2.

36. Walton, op. cit., 102.

37. B B Roberts, *Journal: British Antarctic Survey 1975-1976*, entry 23 March 1976, SPRI MS 1308/47.

38. Joan N Boothe, *The storied ice* (California: Regent Press, 2011), 256; Fuchs, op. cit., 71-2.

39. Peter Rymill, personal communication 24 November 2019. The idea of a local tidal wave was suggested by Steve Cuthbertson, a member of BAS who was at Vernadsky station during 1993-96.

40. B B Roberts, *Diaries: Rockall flight, seal flight 1947*, SPRI MS1308/43/20.

41. Hansard, House of Lords, Isle of Rockall Bill, 13 December 1971 Vol 228 c199.

42. James Fisher, *Rockall* (London: Geoffrey Bles, 1956), 88-93 gives an English translation of Charcot's account of these landings.

43. James Fisher, *The fulmar* (London: Collins New Naturalist Series, 1952).

44. James Fisher, "Rockall and seal flights 1947", *Notes and Records of the Royal Soc of London* 6(1), (1948): 12-17.

45. B B Roberts, *Diaries: Outer Hebrides 1949-1962*, SPRI MS1308/43/21.

46. Neil E Elliott to H M Taylor, 17 December 1951, CUL MS UA FB 202 Box 212.

47. Michael Russell, *A poem of remote lives: images of Eriskay – the enigma of Werner Kissling 1895-1988*, (Neil Wilson, 1997); Michael Russell, *A different country: the photographs of Werner Kissling* (Edinburgh: Birlinn, 2002).

48. B B Roberts to W L S Fleming, 8 January, 19 February and 4 March 1947, *NBSX Papers 1946-50*, SPRI MS1275/1.

49. B B Roberts to Joint Polar sub-Committee, 20 May 1952, *NBSX Papers 1951-57*, SPRI MS 1275/2. We have used the acronym NBSE to replace NBSX.

50. This was subsequently accepted by Sverdrup (H U Sverdrup, "Die Norwegische-Britisch-Schwedische Expedition in die Antarktis," Polarforschung, Bremerhaven, Alfred Wegener Institute for Polar and Marine Research & German Society of Polar Research, 21(1), 70-71. https://epic.awi.de/id/eprint/27703/.

51. B B Roberts, *Journal: NBSX 1949-52*, entry 26 January 1951, SPRI MS1308/7.

52. Harald Sverdrup, Maudheim diary 20 February 1951, quoted in Peder Roberts, *The European Antarctic* (New York: Palgrave Macmillan, 2011), 117.

53. Stan Evans, personal communication 2 March 2014.

54. Fred Roots, personal communication 28 October 2013. One of the authors recalls the words of Dr Hugh Plommer, classicist and first praelector of Wolfson College, Cambridge (and, like Roberts, a lifelong bachelor) on being related a story about a student who spent his entire time inside CUL and ending up by marrying a staff member. "Well, it bears Confucius out, I suppose", he ruminated, "if all you can get out of a library is a librarian".

CHAPTER 11: ANTARCTIC MAPS AND WHITEHALL RUMBLINGS

1. Margaret Anstee, *Never learn to type* (Chichester: John Wiley, 2003), 75; David Anderson, personal communication 3 January 2014.

2. Brian Roberts, "Autobiographical note on early Foreign Office days", January 1963, SPRI MS 1308/43/24.

3. Dame Margaret Anstee, interviewed by the authors 4 June 2014.

4.   Francis Spufford, *I may be some time* (London: Faber & Faber 1997), 150-8.

5.   B B Roberts, *Journal: Antarctic Conference, Washington* 1959, entry 19 November, SPRI MS1308/9.

6.   Peter Clarkson in H G R King and Ann Savours (ed.), *Polar pundit: reminiscences about Brian Birley Roberts* (Cambridge: Polar Publications, SPRI 1995), 42-3.

7.   Jane Clayton, personal communication 25 July 2016.

8.   Peter Rymill, personal communication 6 May 2016.

9.   Peter Rymill, personal communication 21 December 2019.

10.   Lincoln Ellsworth, *Beyond horizons* (New York: Heinemann, 1938), 212.

11.   Geoffrey Hattersley-Smith, "The History of Place-Names in the British Antarctic Territory", BAS Scientific Reports 113 (1991): 42.

12.   D A Scott, memorandum to T Garner, *Antarctic Place Names Committee Correspondence 1950*, SPRI MS 1274/2.

13.   B B Roberts, Foreign Office Handbook *Territorial Claims in the Antarctic* 1 May 1945, TNA FO 371/119821; Australian National Archives A4311 #365/8. https://recordsearch.naa.gov.au/SearchNRetrieve/Interface/ViewImage. aspx?B=3435898.

14.   Steve Heavens, "Brian Roberts and the origins of the 1959 Antarctic Treaty", *Polar Record* 52(6), (2016): 717-28

15.   Taylor Downing, *Spies in the sky* (London: Abacus, 2011), 44.

16.   Christine Halsall, *Women of intelligence* (Stroud: The History Press, 2012), 152-66.

17.   P A Carter to B B Roberts, 11 January 1950, *Antarctic Place Names Committee Correspondence 1950*, SPRI MS 1274/2.

18.   B B Roberts to J H Mankin, 24 February 1950, *FIDS Correspondence and papers relating to topographical mapping 1950-52*, SPRI MS 1277/2.

19.   Ronald Hyam, *Understanding the British empire* (Cambridge: CUP, 2010), 268-95.

20.   J S Bennett to A S Fordham, 12 April 1950, *FIDS Correspondence and papers relating to topographical mapping 1950-52*, SPRI MS 1277/2.

21.   J S Bennett to B B Roberts, 13 April 1950, *APNC Correspondence 1950*, SPRI MS 1274/2.

22.   B B Roberts, Minute A15219/2, 28 April 1950, *FIDS Correspondence and papers relating to topographical mapping 1950-52*, SPRI MS 1277/2.

23   Bennett to Roberts, op. cit., 10 August 1950.

24.   Roberts to Bennett, ibid., 26 August 1950.

25.   R Cecil to Bennett, ibid., 12 September 1950.

26.   M J Anstee, Minute A1524/2 8 January 1951, TNA FO 371/90436.

27.   D A Scott to T Garner, 6 December 1950, *APNC Correspondence 1950,* SPRI MS 1274/2.

28.   Roberts to Cecil, ibid., 27 October 1950.

29.   Cecil to G G Fitzmaurice, ibid., 7 December 1950.

30.   Margaret Anstee, op. cit., 77-83; Roland Philipps, *A Spy named Orphan: the enigma of Donald Maclean* (London: The Bodley Head, 2018).

31.   Philipps, op. cit., 268

32.   M J Anstee, Minute 1 June 1951, *APNC Correspondence 1951*, SPRI MS 1274/3.

33.   D D Maclean, ibid., Note 21 May 1951.

34.   F E Evans, ibid., Note A1524/10, 29 May 1951.

35.   Philipps, op. cit., 319.

36.   Philipps, op. cit., 381.

37.   R T Reed, B4B Briefing Sheet, 11 May 1951, TNA KV 2/4140.

38.   M J Anstee, op. cit.

39.   E J Passant, ibid., 2 June 1951.

40.   R Cecil, ibid. Minute A1524/1, 9 June 1951.

41.   J S Bennett to B B Roberts, 13 May 1952, *APNC Correspondence 1952*, SPRI MS 1274/4.

42.   G G Fitzmaurice to Bennett, ibid., 15 May 1952.

43.   Bennett to N Pritchard, ibid., 9 June 1952.

44.   R Cecil, ibid., Note 13 June 1952.

45.   B B Roberts, ibid., 17 July 1952.

46.   B B Roberts to H Saunders, 18 October 1951, *APNC Correspondence 1951*. SPRI MS 1274/3

47.   B B Roberts to H Saunders, 18 February 1953, *APNC Correspondence 1953-56*, SPRI MS 1274/5.

48.   Saunders to Roberts, ibid., 16 March 1953.

49.   Roberts to Saunders, ibid., 8 April 1953.

50.   B B Roberts to H Saunders, 3 March 1952, *APNC Correspondence 1952*. SPRI MS 1274/4.

51.   B B Roberts, Minute A 15213/1 to G G Fitzmaurice, 6 February 1953, *APNC Correspondence 1953-56*, SPRI MS 1274/5.

52.   J E Thomas to H Saunders, ibid., 16 February 1953.

53.   Three of the Staff, *The voyage of the Scotia* (Edinburgh: William Blackwood, 1906), 236.

54.   D J H Searle, "The evolution of the map of Alexander and Charcot Islands", *Geog J* 129(2), (1963): 156-66. Original copies of maps in authors' collection.

55.   B B Roberts, *Diary Notes: Polar Record*, 25 March 1975, SPRI MS1308/43/23.

56. The front cover of *Polar Record* 17(108), (September 1974) states: "Place-names used in *Polar Record* are those authorised by the administrative authority of each area as recognised by the British Government. Names not yet so authorised are avoided, where possible, or placed in quotation marks."

57. Brian Roberts "The place-names 'Greater Antarctica' and 'Lesser Antarctica' versus 'East Antarctica' and 'West Antarctica'", *BAS Bulletin* 53 (1981): 257-60.

CHAPTER 12: THE BATTLE OF THE ICE SHELF

1. J M Wordie to Cdr Alun Jones, 2 April 1948, *Antarctic Place Names Committee Correspondence 1944-49*. SPRI MS 1274/1.

2. B B Roberts, Minute A1524/18 "Antarctic Place Names Committee", 6 November 1951, *APNC Correspondence 1951*. SPRI MS1274/3.

3. Terence Armstrong, Brian Roberts and Charles Swithinbank, *Illustrated glossary of snow and ice* (Cambridge: Scott Polar Research Institute, 1966).

4. Brian Roberts, Introductory note (January 1974), *APNC Correspondence 1944-49*. SPRI MS 1274/1.

5. B B Roberts, "Shelf Ice – a note on terminology", *J Glaciology* 1(8) (1950): 413-5; J M Wordie, ibid., "Barrier versus Shelf", 416-20.

6. Wordie to Jones, op. cit.

7. B B Roberts to Wordie, ibid., 12 July 1948.

8. Wordie to Roberts, ibid., 14 July 1948.

9. J M Wordie to B B Roberts, 27 April 1950, *APNC Correspondence 1950*. SPRI MS 1274/2.

10. Hans Ahlmann to Roberts, ibid.,16 May 1950; long correspondence between Harold Saunders and Roberts, ibid., May-June 1950; Scott to J E Thomas 19 February 1951, *APNC Correspondence 1951*, SPRI MS 1274/3.

11. B B Roberts to J M Wordie, 20 June, 3 August and 16 August 1951, *APNC Correspondence 1951*, SPRI MS 1274/3; Wordie to Roberts, ibid., 14 August 1951.

12. Roberts to Wordie, ibid., "Antarctic Place Names Committee", 24 October 1951.

13. Wordie to Roberts, ibid., 30 October 1951.

14. Roberts to Wordie, ibid., 2 November 1951.

15. Roberts, Minute A1524/18 "Antarctic Place Names Committee", ibid., 6 November 1951.

16. Roberts, Minute "Shelf ice terminology", ibid., 25 November 1951.

17. B B Roberts to J M Wordie, ibid., 30 November 1951.

18. B B Roberts to L Kirwan, 31 January 1952, *APNC Correspondence 1952*. SPRI MS 1274/4.

19. Roberts to G Seligman, ibid., 8 March 1952.

20. Seligman to Roberts, ibid., 11 March 1952.

21. Roberts to Seligman, ibid., 7 April, 20 April and 2 May 1952.

22. Roberts, Minute A1528/9 to G G Fitzmaurice, ibid., 29 March 1952.

23. Wordie, Note "Dr Roberts and the RGS decision", ibid., undated.

24. D Cleary to G C L Bertram, ibid., 8 August 1952.

25. Saunders to Roberts, ibid., 29 August 1952.

26. Minutes of the Advisory Committee on Antarctic Names, ibid., 3 October 1952.

27 Wordie to Saunders, ibid., 28 October 1952.

28. Phillip Law to Roberts, ibid., 17 November 1952.

29. Roberts, Minute on A1528/32, ibid., 11 December 1952.

.30. B B Roberts to H Saunders, 3 January 1953, *APNC Correspondence 1953-56*, SPRI MS 1274/5.

31. Roberts to Saunders, ibid., 3 February 1953.

32. Roberts to Saunders, ibid., 21 May 1953.

33. Roberts, Minute A15213/6 to G G Fitzmaurice, ibid., 22 May 1953.

CHAPTER 13: CRISIS AT THE POLAR INSTITUTE

1. Graham Rowley in H G R King and Ann Savours (ed.), *Polar pundit: reminiscences about Brian Birley Roberts* (Cambridge: Polar Publications, SPRI 1995), 109.

2. Giles Hunt, *Launcelot Fleming – a portrait* (Norwich: Canterbury Press, 2003), 41.

3. Brian Roberts to Launcelot Fleming, 6 April 1949, *SPRI Correspondence and papers 1930-1964*, SPRI MS 1308/37.

4. Named after Cape Dorset on south-west Baffin Island, where the first discoveries were made.

5. Graham W Rowley, *Cold comfort: my love affair with the Arctic*, 2nd ed. (Montreal: McGill-Queen's University Press, 2007), 270-2; B B Roberts, *Journal: Operation Lyon 1949*, entries 21-26 August, SPRI MS 1308/6.

6. B B Roberts to J M Wordie, 30 September 1949, *SPRI Correspondence and papers 1930-1964*, SPRI MS 1308/37.

7. Brian Roberts to Graham and Diana Rowley, 7 February 1950, *Operation Lyon Correspondence and papers 1949-1951*, SPRI MS 1280.

8. B B Roberts to W L S Fleming, 13 January 1954, *SPRI Correspondence and papers 1930-1964*, SPRI MS 1308/37.

9. Fred Roots, personal communications 5 and 9 November 2013, was sceptical of the offer of a post from AINA, but Roberts recorded that he had mentioned it to Roots.

10. B B Roberts to G C L Bertram, 26 January 1954, *SPRI Correspondence and papers 1930-1964*, SPRI MS 1308/37.

11. T Garvey, Note A1523/23 "Proposed trans-polar expedition", 17 August 1953, TNA FO 371/103140.

12. B B Roberts, Minute A1524/11 to Young and Garvey, 3 December 1953, *CTAE Papers Vol 1 1953-1956*, SPRI MS 1281/1.

13. Stephen Hicks, Bryan Storey and Phillippa Mein Smith, "Against all odds: the birth of the CTAE 1955-1958", *Polar Record* 48(1), (2013): 50-61.

14. G C L Bertram to Sir John Slessor, 1 March 1955, *CTAE Papers Vol 1 1953-1956*, SPRI MS 1281/1.

15. G C L Bertram to Sir John Slessor, 18 August 1955, BAS MS AD3/1 AS177 Part 1.

16. Rear Adm C R L Parry to Bertram, ibid., 25 August 1955.

17. John Glen, interviewed by the authors 13 January 2014.

18 B B Roberts to V Fuchs, 3 September, 16 September and 7 October 1955, *CTAE Papers 1955-1956*, SPRI MS 1281/1.

19. G E Fogg, *A history of Antarctic science* (Cambridge: CUP, 1992), 168-9; Deborah Shapley, *The seventh continent* (Washington: Resources for the Future, 1985), 82-4.

20. B B Roberts, "Russian interest in the Antarctic", A1522/4 March 1955, TNA FO 371/113959; Roberts, "The United States contribution to the IGY", ibid., 1 April 1955.

21. B B Roberts, Memorandum to Cahill, 17 December 1954, *IGY Foreign Office papers: Great Britain 1946-1958*, SPRI MS1308/51/7.

22. Roberts, Memorandum A1522/6, ibid., 6 April 1954.

23. Roberts, Minute "Proposed IGY station and Vahsel Bay", ibid., 6 March 1955.

24. G C L Bertram, "Visit by Sir David Brunt", ibid., 1 May 1955.

25. C C C Tickell, Minute A1522/9, ibid., 1 June 1955.

26. "Progress Report to Cabinet on Antarctica" A1527/98/G, ibid., 20 July 1955.

27. B B Roberts, Confidential note to G C L Bertram, "SPRI liaison with and advice to government departments", 12 August 1955, *SPRI Correspondence and papers 1930-1964*, SPRI MS 1308/37.

28. G C L Bertram to J M Wordie, 25 October 1955, BAS MS AD3/1/AS/177/A(2) Part 1.

29. Bertram to George Binney, ibid., 6 November 1955.

30. Binney to V E Fuchs, ibid., 7 November 1955.

31. Fuchs to Binney, ibid., 12 November 1955.

32. Sir Francis Evans, "Telegram from Naval Attaché Buenos Aires" A1525/2, 4 January 1956, *CTAE Papers 1953-56*, SPRI MS 1281/1.

33. Sir Vivian Fuchs and Sir Edmund Hillary, *The crossing of Antarctica* (London: Cassell, 1958), 12. The main CTAE party appeared to repeat the error on the *Magga Dan* the following year, the erratic course possibly due to inadvertent switching off of the gyrocompass (Stan Evans, personal communication 29 August 2013).

34. I F S Vincent, Minute A1529/2 16 January 1956, *IGY Foreign Office papers: Great Britain 1946-1958*, SPRI MS1308/51/7.

35. Stan Evans, personal communication 18 November 2013, recalled being on board *Tottan* at the time, but was unsure who had sent the press release.

36. John Tuck Jr, to Walter S Rogers 15 March 1959, quoting from the *Report of the General Board on the constitution of SPRI as a sub-Department within the Department of Geography*, November 1956, Churchill College MS CCAC110/21.

37. B B Roberts to Hilda Richardson, January 1970, "Roberts and SPRI in the post-war period", SPRI MS 1308/43/27.

38. F Debenham to Benny Farmer, 7 May 1957, BAS MS AD3/1/AS/177/A(2) Part 2.

39. Peter Speak, *Deb: geographer, scientist, Antarctic explorer* (Cambridge: Polar Publishing, 2008), 96.

40. L P Kirwan to B H Farmer, 8 May 1957. BAS MS AD3/1/AS/177/A(2), Part 2.

41. Launcelot Portsmouth [Fleming] to Farmer, ibid., 17 May 1957.

42. Launcelot [Fleming] to Alfred Steers, ibid., 29 June 1957.

43. J M Wordie to J A Steers, ibid., 31 May 1957.

44. Wordie to Steers, ibid. See also Smith, op. cit., 248. Wordie claimed that Roberts was deliberately sabotaging the work of the British IGY Committee, but it is not obvious how he could have done so: Roberts' name is absent from the British committees in Annals of the IGY, Volume 9. Bill Sloman of the Colonial Office was the sole Whitehall contact for the British national committee for IGY (George Hemmen, personal communication 3 July 2013).

45. Ann Savours, personal communication 9 February 2020.

46. L P Kirwan to B B Roberts, 31 July 1957, *SPRI Correspondence and papers 1930-1964*, SPRI MS 1308/37; Bertram to Roberts, ibid., 8 August 1957; Fleming to Roberts, ibid., 15 October 1957.

47. Roberts to Terence Armstrong, ibid., 22 August 1957.

48. Roberts, Terence Armstrong and H G R King, "Note on SPRI policy", ibid., 29 September 1957.

49. Roberts, Minute "Scott Polar Research Institute", ibid., 16 October 1957.

50. H A A Hankey, Minute A15223/1 "The SPRI and the position of Dr B B Roberts," ibid., November 1957

51. Despite the university takeover and Robin's manifestly successful long reign at SPRI, Cambridge never quite saw him as 'one of us'. On the SPRI letterhead he was not allowed to include his degrees, which were awarded by an Australian university (Ann Savours, personal communication 9 February 2020).

CHAPTER 14: THE FOREIGN OFFICE AND THE BIRTH OF THE ANTARCTIC TREATY

1. B B Roberts, "Autobiographical note on early Foreign Office days", January 1963, SPRI MS 1308/43/24.

2. Steve Heavens, "Brian Roberts and the origins of the 1959 Antarctic Treaty", *Polar Record* 52(6), (2016): 717-28, from which much of this chapter is reproduced.

3. R Bulkeley, "Polar internationalism, diplomacy and the IGY" in Lüdecke, C (ed.), "National and trans-national agendas in Antarctic research from the 1950s and beyond", *Proc 3rd workshop of the SCAR history group on the history of Antarctic research*. BPRC Technical Report 2011-01, Columbus, Ohio 26-27 October 2007: 24–32. https://kb.osu.edu/dspace/bitstream/handle/1811/53605/BPRC _Tech_Rept_2011-01.pdf?sequence=1

4. R L Speaight, "1948 Proposals for UN Trusteeship or a Condominium in the Antarctic", 29 February 1956, TNA FO 371/119835.

5. Gerald Maude to C A E Shuckburgh 148/219/48, 2 September 1948, TNA FO 371/68254.

6. B B Roberts to Shuckburgh, "Note on French attitude to the Antarctic," ibid., 9 September 1948. Also in TNA CO 537/3527.

7. A F Liotard to B B Roberts, 30 September 1948, TNA CO 537/3527; Roberts to P J Sterling, ibid., 9 October 1948.

8. Ronald B St John, "The Bolivia-Chile-Peru dispute in the Atacama desert", *Boundary and territory briefings* 1(6) (Durham University, 1994). https://www.cur.ac.uk/ibru/ publications/download/?id=205.

9. John Dudeney and John Sheail, *Claiming the ice: Britain and the Antarctic 1900-1950* (Cambridge: Cambridge Scholars Publishing, 2019), 342.

10. Colonial Office, "Scale of operations of the Falkland Islands Dependencies Survey", 17 January 1950, TNA FO 371/81131.

11. B B Roberts, Minutes, ibid. 26 January and 5 May 1950.

12. J Berguño, "The search for an organisational framework for Antarctic research (1948–1985)", in: Lüdecke op. cit.: 47-9.

13. Adrian J Howkins, *Frozen empires: a history of the Antarctic sovereignty dispute between Britain, Argentina and Chile, 1939–1959* (Thesis, University of Texas, Austin, 2008): 197-220. https://repositories.lib.utexas.edu/handle/2152/3860

14. B B Roberts, Minute A1527/9 and Memorandum A1527/4G "British policy in the Antarctic",13 January 1955, TNA FO 371/113971.

15. B B Roberts, Note A1522/4 "Russian interest in the Antarctic", March 1955, TNA FO 371/113959; Roberts, "The United States contribution to the IGY," ibid., 1 April 1955.

16. Dudeney and Sheail, op. cit., 328.

17. M C G Man to R L Speaight "Antarctica", 26 January 1955, TNA FO 371/113971.

18. B B Roberts to M C G Man and R L Speaight, A15228/1 12 March 1955, TNA FO 371/114000.

19. Man, Note appended with 3 drafts by Roberts, ibid., 14 March 1955.

20. G G Fitzmaurice, "Our Antarctica claims", 21 March 1956, TNA FO 371/119835; International Court of Justice, *Pleadings, oral arguments, documents. Antarctica Cases (UK v. Argentina, UK v. Chile,* Orders of March 16th 1956: Removal from the list (The Hague: Oxford reports on international law. Case numbers ICJ Rep 12 ICGJ 178 (Argentina), ICJ Rep 15 ICGJ 177 (Chile)). https://www.icj-cij.org/files/case-related/27/027-19550504-APP-1-00-BI.pdf

21. Marquis of Salisbury to Prime Minister, 27 April 1955, TNA FO 371/113972.

22. Viscount Hood, Notes A15214/12G "Antarctica", 22 January and 12 February 1957. TNA FO 371/126125.

23. R L Speaight, "Antarctica", A1527/126 26 August 1955, TNA FO 371/113976.

24. H M (Secretary of State), Response to minute A1527/126, ibid., 29 August 1955.

25. W Ellery Anderson, *Expedition south* (London: Travel Book Club, 1957), 152-3.

26. Hansard, House of Commons 7 November 1955, Vol 545 c1451-2, c1481-1611.

27. B B Roberts, Memorandum A1527/132 "UK policy in the Antarctic", 28 October 1955, TNA FO 371/113976.

28. M C G Man, ibid.,10 November 1955.

29. R L Speaight, "Antarctica", ibid., 1 November 1955.

30. D F Muirhead to I F S Vincent, Despatch A1523/33, 20 April 1956, TNA FO 371/119819.

31. Brian Roberts, *Journal of a visit to the USSR 28 May to 9 June 1956,* SPRI MS1308/8. In every daily entry the lavish meals are described.

32. Peter Rutter to Department of State, Despatch No. 3165 "Soviet Arctic and Antarctic activities", 20 June 1956, US Naval Academy 703.022/6-2056.

33. I F S Vincent, 22 February 1956, TNA FO 371/119835 is one of many documents in this folder expressing hostility to the Indian initiative.

34. A J Howkins, "Defending polar empire: opposition to India's proposal to raise the 'Antarctic Question' at the United Nations", *Polar Record* 44(1) (2008): 35-44.

35. M R D Foot and J M Langley, *MI9: escape and evasion 1939-1945* (London: Book Club Associates, 1979), 77.

36. C Empson to H A A Hankey, A1523/53 24 September 1956, TNA FO 371/119820.

37. H A A Hankey, Note AU1057/3 "Restoration of confidence in US/UK relations", 15 November 1956, TNA FO 371/1120342.

38. Sir John Freeland, personal communication 18 February 2014; Sir Richard Parsons, interviewed by the authors 23 February 2014.

39. R E C F Parsons, interviewed by Malcolm McBain, 20 June 2005. Oral History programme, Churchill Archives Centre, Cambridge. https://www.chu.cam.ac.uk/ media/uploads/files/Parsons_Richard.pdf

40. Hansard, op. cit.

41. Parsons, op. cit.

42. H M Carless, interviewed by Malcolm McBain, 23 February 2002, Oral History programme, Churchill Archives Centre, Cambridge. https://www.chu. cam.ac.uk/ media/uploads/files/Carless.pdf

43. Brian Roberts, *Personal Journal: British Antarctic Survey 1975-76*. Annex I: "Origin and history of the Polar Regions Section". SPRI MS 1308/47.

44. H G R King and Ann Savours (ed.), *Polar pundit: reminiscences about Brian Birley Roberts* (Cambridge: Polar Publications, SPRI 1995), 130.

45. B B Roberts, "Historical note", *Journal: Antarctic conference, Washington 1959*. SPRI MS 1308/9.

46. B B Roberts to K McQuillen, 31 July 1965, Churchill College MS CCAC/110/31.

47. G C L Bertram, "Antarctic Prospect", *International affairs* 33(2) (1957): 143–53.

48. Royal Institute of International Affairs, Chatham House "Antarctica: Summary of a private discussion meeting on 13 December 1956", 22 January 1957, TNA FO 371/126121; RIIA "Private discussion meeting on 'the problems of Antarctica', Thursday 13 December 1956" A15238/4 [Attendees list], FO 371/119847.

49. I F S Vincent, Note A15238/4 to RIIA, ibid., 20 December 1956.

50. B B Roberts to G C L Bertram, 24 June 1957, private collection of Mark Bertram.

51. Charles Empson to Harold Beeley A15214/22, 4 April 1957, TNA FO 371/126125.

52. Viscount Hood to Empson, Note A15214/22, ibid., 12 April 1957.

53. Foreign Office, "Report of the Cadogan committee", Appendices G–I, October 1953, TNA FCO 158/177.

54. D C Hopson to H.A Hankey, 28 December 1956, TNA FO 371/126118.

55. H A A Hankey, Memorandum A15214/17G 31 January 1957, TNA FO 371/126125.

56. P Roberts, "What has all this to do with science? The rhetoric of scientific devotion in British government plans for the IGY" in Lüdecke, op. cit., 16-17.

57. Sir Vivian Fuchs, *Of Ice and Men* (Oswestry: Anthony Nelson, 1982), 166; Rodolfo N Panzarini in King and Savours, op. cit., 106.

58. H A A Hankey to Sir F Hoyar Millar, 2 August 1957, TNA FO 371/126127.

59. Minutes of a meeting held at the CRO 15 August 1957, TNA DO 35/6986.

60. Sir John Freeland, personal communication 18 February 2014.

61. M A Willis to H A Hankey, A15214/49G with appended CO minute (P Rogers to Sir John Macpherson), 29 April 1957, TNA FO 371/126126.

62. H A A Hankey, Minute A1526/5 "Sovereignty in the Antarctic", 5 September 1957, TNA FO 371/126118; Dominions Office "Antarctica: a working paper for discussions between representatives of UK, Australia, New Zealand and South Africa in London on 12–13 September 1957", TNA DO 35/6986.

63. Minutes of meetings held in the CRO on 12th and 13th September 1957, A15214/79G, TNA FO 371/126127.

64. H A A Hankey to I Pink, "Antarctica", A15214/89 26 September 1957, TNA FO 371/126128.

65. Viscount Hood, address to quadripartite talks, Department of State 7-8 October 1957, Annex A "An international regime for the Antarctic", Foreign Office 3 October 1957. TNA FCO 7/3248.

66. J R Freeland to G G Fitzmaurice, "Draft convention setting up an international regime for Antarctica", 29 November 1957, TNA FO 371/126129.

67. Paul C Daniels to Secretary of State, Memorandum: "Antarctica", 9 December 1957, FRUS 1955-1957 XI: 716-8.

68. H G R Bass, "Fourth meeting of SEATO Council". 6 March 1958, TNA FO 371/131906.

69. Viscount Hood to C D W O'Neill, A15214/2 14 January 1958, TNA FO 371/131905.

70. P J Beck, "Preparatory meetings for the Antarctic Treaty 1958-1959", *Polar Record* 22(141) (1985): 653–64; B B Roberts, "Historical note," *Journal: Antarctic Conference, Washington*: 5-7. SPRI MS 1308/9.

71. H Caccia to Foreign Office, Despatch A15214/30, 6 February 1959, TNA FO 371/138958.

CHAPTER 15: THE HISTORIC ANTARCTIC CONFERENCE IN WASHINGTON

1. Toni Martorell in H G R King and Ann Savours (ed.), *Polar Pundit: reminiscences about Brian Birley Roberts* (Cambridge: Polar Publications, SPRI 1995), 98-101.

2. Peter J Beck, "Preparatory meetings for the Antarctic Treaty 1958-1959", *Polar Record* 22(141) (1985): 653–64; B B Roberts, "Historical note," *Journal: Antarctic Conference, Washington*: 5-7. SPRI MS 1308/9.

3. Sir Richard Parsons, interviewed by the authors 23 February 2014.

4. Sir John Freeland, personal communication 18 February 2014.

5 B B Roberts, *Journal: Antarctic Conference, Washington* 1959, entry 6 November, SPRI MS1308/9.

6. Roberts, ibid., passim.

7. Roberts, ibid., "Introduction".

8. A de la Mare, Despatch A15214/83 to H A A Hankey, 20 September 1957, TNA FO 371/126127; Freeland, op. cit.

9. Roberts, op. cit., entry 15 October.

10. Ibid., entry 16 October.

11. Ibid., entry 4 November.

12, Only if a change in UK law takes place is there a constitutional requirement for Parliament to debate an international treaty to which the UK proposes to be a party.

13. Hansard, House of Lords 18 February 1960, Vol 221 cc 158-191.

CHAPTER 16: ROLLING ROUND ANTARCTICA WITH UNCLE SAM

1. B B Roberts, *Journal: United States Operation Deep Freeze 61 Nov 1960 to April 1961*, entry 21 December 1960, SPRI MS1308/10.

2. Rorke Bryan, *Ordeal by Ice: Ships of the Antarctic* (Barnsley: Seaforth Publishing, 2011), 427-30.

3. B B Roberts, op. cit., entry 8 December 1960.

4. B B Roberts, *Journal: Seventh Antarctic Treaty Consultative Meeting, Wellington 1972*, entries 11-19 November, SPRI MS1308/44.

CHAPTER 17: THE BEGINNINGS OF ANTARCTIC CONSERVATION

1. B B Roberts, *Journal: Second Antarctic Treaty Consultative Meeting, Buenos Aires 1962*, entry 18 July, SPRI MS1308/12.

2. B B Roberts, *Journal: First Antarctic Treaty Consultative Meeting, Canberra 1961*, SPRI MS1308/11.

3. Pope, Philip N D, "British influence on the Antarctic treaty system 1959-64", M Phil thesis, SPRI (1997): 7. https://doi.org/10.17863/CAM.27515

4. Martin Holdgate "The Antarctic protected areas system in the new millennium", keynote address in Birgit Njåstad (ed.), "Antarctic Protected Areas Workshop", Tromsø (23 May 1998): 8-23. Norsk Polarinstitutt Rapport No 110. https://documents.ats.aq/OTHER1998/fr/OTHER1998_fr001_e.pdf

5. Ian Strange, *The Bird Man* (London: Gordon & Cremonesi, 1976), 75

6. Sir Martin Holdgate, interviewed by the authors 26 June 2013.

7. David Anderson, "The conservation of wildlife under the Antarctic Treaty", *Polar Record* 14(88), (1968): 25-32; Martin Holdgate, *Penguins and Mandarins* (Durham: The Memoir Club, 2003), 123-4.

8. In 1986 the International Whaling Commission agreed a ban on whaling to enable stocks to recover. As a result there has been an extremely slow recovery.

9. Pope, op. cit., Appendix I.

10. The issue over the secretariat remained controversial for another 40 years. Roberts and the UK delegation were in favour of siting it in Argentina, as was MP Jeremy Corbyn (Hansard, House of Commons 21 July 1994 Vol 247 c586-95); but the UK government continued to veto it until 2003, despite the secretariat being purely an administrative function with no legal status.

11. B B Roberts, *Journal: Second Antarctic Treaty Consultative Meeting, Buenos Aires* 1962: 3, SPRI MS1308/12.

12. Roberts, ibid., entry 24 July.

13. The recent European Common Market negotiations in Brussels had apparently left a sour taste in Cumes' mouth. He was later appointed Australian Ambassador to several European Union countries and ended up becoming deeply embittered by the experience of diplomatic life.

CHAPTER 18: ISLANDS OF PARADISE AND DESOLATION

1. B B Roberts, *Journal: First Antarctic Treaty Consultative Meeting, Canberra* 1961, entries 26 July - 3 August, SPRI MS 1308/11.

2. Ibid., entry 31 July.

3. Brian Roberts, *Journal of a visit to French Islands in the Indian Ocean,* entry 30 November 1964, SPRI MS1308/14.

4. Ibid, entry 27 January 1965.

5. A hundred years previously rats had arrived on Tromelin, but today they have been successfully eradicated and most bird species are breeding once more.

CHAPTER 19: NAVIGATING SEAL CONSERVATION THROUGH POLITICAL ROCKS

1. Brian Roberts "Wildlife conservation in the Antarctic", *Oryx* 8(4), (1966): 237-43.

2. B B Roberts, *Journal: Fourth Antarctic Treaty Consultative Meeting, Santiago* 1966, entry 15 September, SPRI MS1308/15.

3. F E Mason, Confidential Ambassadorial report on the 4th ATCM, Santiago 1966, quoted in John Heap to Launcelot Fleming, 7 June 1967, private collection of Peggy Heap.

4. David Anderson, personal communications 3 January 2014 and 7 August 2017.

5.	Hansard, House of Commons 15 June 1966 Vol 729 c1464.

6.	Alan Moorehead, *The fatal impact: an account of the invasion of the South Pacific 1767-1840* (London: The Reprint Society, 1986), 191-206, 217-9.

7.	Hansard, House of Commons 14 April 1967, vol 744 c 1591.

8.	Brian Roberts (ed.), *Edward Wilson's birds of the Antarctic* (London: Blandford Press, 1967)

9.	B B Roberts, *Journal: Fifth Antarctic Treaty Consultative Meeting, Paris 1968*, entry 19 November 1968, SPRI MS1308/17.

10.	David Anderson, personal communication 3 November 2017.

11.	Brian Roberts to Ena Thomas, 21 November 1969, authors' collection.

CHAPTER 20: THE ROAD TO CAMALAR

1.	B B Roberts, *Journal: Sixth Antarctic Treaty Consultative Meeting, Tokyo 1970*, SPRI MS1308/18.

2.	ibid.

3.	Brian Roberts, Speech as Deputy Leader of the UK Delegation, *Report of the Conference on the Conservation of Antarctic Seals*, London, 3-11 February 1972 (London: FCO, 1972).

4.	Richard M Laws, *Autobiography: Large animals and wide horizons: adventures of a Biologist. Part III: Antarctica and Academe*: 48. https://www.spri.cam.ac.uk/ resources/autobiographies/richardlaws/richardlaws3.pdf

5.	Advisory Committee Scientific Working Group "Statement by Brian Roberts to Ad Hoc Committee, 7 February 1972", TNA FCO 7/2350.

6.	John Heap, "Has CCAMLR worked? Management policies and ecological needs", in A Jorgensen-Dahl & W Ostrey (ed.), *The Antarctic Treaty System in World Politics* (London: Palgrave-Macmillan, 1991), 45-6.

7	Laws, op. cit., 48-9.

8.	B B Roberts, *Journal: Seventh Antarctic Treaty Consultative Meeting, Wellington 1972*: Introduction, SPRI MS1308/44.

9.	B B Roberts, *Journal: Eighth ATCM, Oslo 1975*, entry 8 August, SPRI MS1308/45.

10.	Stuart B Kaye, "Territorial sea baselines along ice covered coasts: international practice and limits of the Law of the Sea", Ocean Dev & Internat Law 35 (2004): 75-102. In the event the Treaty partners succeeded in preventing any consideration of the Antarctic in UNCLOS, which was in any case concerned primarily with deep-sea mining of minerals such as manganese on the ocean seabed remote from the polar regions (David Anderson, personal communication 10 November 2017).

11.	B B Roberts, *Journal: Eighth ATCM, Oslo 1975*, entry 13 June, SPRI MS1308/45.

12. Brian Roberts "International cooperation for Antarctic development: the test for the Antarctic Treaty", *Polar Record* 19(119) (1978): 107-19.

13. Tore Gjelsvik in H G R King and Ann Savours (ed.), *Polar pundit: reminiscences about Brian Birley Roberts* (Cambridge: Polar Publications, SPRI 1995): 65.

14. Huw Lewis-Jones, *Face to Face: Polar Portraits* (Cambridge: Polar World, 2008), 165; *Aftenposten*, 18 May 1974.

15. B B Roberts "Conservation in the Antarctic", Phil Trans Roy Soc London B279 (1977), 97-104.

CHAPTER 21: THE ARCTIC PROBLEM

1. Draft terms of reference, *Ditchley Park Conference papers, May 1971*, entry 15 July 1970, SPRI MS 1279.

2. H V Hodson to B B Roberts, ibid., 13 April 1971.

3. Brian Roberts, *The Arctic Ocean: Report of a Conference at Ditchley Park 14-17 May 1971* (Oxford: The Ditchley Foundation, 1971), 7-23.

4. H A A Hankey to Gallagher, 12 July 1971, *Ditchley Park Conference papers, May 1971*, SPRI MS 1279.

5. B B Roberts to R M Laws, ibid., 19 November 1971.

6. Jane Rumble, interviewed by the authors 23 February 2016.

7. Duncan Depledge, "The United Kingdom and the Arctic in the 21st century", *Arctic Yearbook* (2012): 130-8. https://arcticyearbook.com/images/yearbook/2012/ Scholarly_Papers/7.Depledge.pdf

CHAPTER 22: THE BRITISH ANTARCTIC SURVEY COMES OF AGE

1. Martin Holdgate, *Penguins and Mandarins* (Durham: The Memoir Club, 2003), 150.

2. Brian Roberts to Lilian Roberts, 9 May 1974, authors' collection.

3. John Heap in H G R King and Ann Savours (ed.), *Polar pundit: reminiscences about Brian Birley Roberts* (Cambridge: Polar Publications, SPRI 1995), 5.

4. Charles Swithinbank, interviewed by Paul Merchant (2010). British Library: *An oral history of British science*: 213.

   https://sounds.bl.uk/related-content/TRANSCRIPTS/ 021T-C1379X0003XX-0000A0.pdf

5. John Croxall, Ian Boyd, Ian Parker and Geoffrey Cook, *Richard Maitland Laws CBE, 23 April 1926 – 7 October 2014*. Biogr Mems Fellows Roy Soc. https:// royalsocietypublishing.org/doi/pdf/10.1098/rsbm.2015.0006.

6.   Richard M Laws, *Autobiography: Large animals and wide horizons: adventures of a Biologist. Part III: Antarctica and Academe*: 53. www.spri.cam.ac.uk/resources/ autobiographies/richardlaws/richardlaws3.pdf

7.   B B Roberts, *Personal Journal: British Antarctic Survey, 1975-76*, entries 10 January – 24 March 1976, SPRI MS1308/47.

8.   J R Beck and D W Brown, "The Biology of Wilson's Storm Petrel at Signy Island, South Orkney Islands", *BAS Scientific Report* 69 (London, 1972).

9,   The name Lumus Reef was originally a temporary survey marker. It acquired immortality when the Argentines appropriated it from a photocopy of BGLE's original manuscript chart. The published Argentine chart was in turn copied by the UK Admiralty Hydrographic Department.

10.   Ian Strange, *The Bird Man* (London: Gordon & Cremonesi, 1976), 32

CHAPTER 23: A SURFEIT OF POLAR INFORMATION

1.   Diana Rowley, personal communication 28 May 2014.

2   J U Taylor to J A Heap, "Proposed expedition by Sir Ranulph Fiennes", 29 May 1974, TNA FCO 7/2725.

3.   Wally Herbert to J A Heap, "Proposed Antarctic Expedition – Sir Ranulph Fiennes", 22 January 1976, TNA FCO 7/3251.

4.   V E Fuchs to B B Roberts, ibid., 13 May 1974

5.   B B Roberts, "Capt Fiennes: Transglobe expedition – political aspects", ibid., 29 May 1974; J A Heap, "Captain Sir R T-W Fiennes: New Zealand attitude", ALZ 22/3, ibid., 13 December 1974.

6,   Ranulph Fiennes, *To the Ends of the Earth: Transglobal Expedition 1979-82* (London: Mandarin, 1983), 21.

7.   Jane Rumble, interviewed by the authors 23 February 2016.

8.   Ibid.

9.   B B Roberts, "Notes for a speech at dinner given by Robin Edmonds", 15 December 1975, *Miscellaneous Papers 1970-78*, SPRI MS 1308/43/16

10.   AGM 7 June 1976, Meetings: Session 1975-76, *Geog J* 142(3) (1976): 569-76.

11.   Brian Roberts, "International cooperation for Antarctic development: the test for the Antarctic Treaty", *Polar Record* 19(119), (1978): 107-20 reproduces the text of Roberts' address to the Punta Arenas conference.

12.   B B Roberts, *Journal: Symposium on the development of the Antarctic, Punta Arenas 1977*, "Draft: Chile Diary" below entry 18 April, SPRI MS 1308/48.

13.   Stan Evans, personal communication 20 July 2014.

14.   June Roberts, recollection of a dinner with Brian Roberts in 1976.

15.   Brian Roberts, "The Organisation of Polar Information", Cambridge Occasional Paper No. 1 (1960); M Gilbert and H Lane, "Forty-five numbers for snow: a brief introduction to the UDC for Polar libraries", www.ukrbook.net/UDC_n/st_13.pdf

16. Charles Swithinbank, personal communication 27 May 2013.

17. B B Roberts, *Journal: Symposium on the development of the Antarctic, Punta Arenas* 1977, entry 9 April 1977, SPRI MS 1308/48.

18 Charles Swithinbank, interviewed by Paul Merchant (2010). The British Library, *An Oral History of British Science*. https://sounds.bl.uk/related-content/TRANSCRIPTS/ 021T-C1379X0003XX-0000A0.pdf

19. *Cambridge University Reporter*, 9 December 1959: 441.

20. B B Roberts, "Meeting of Polar Librarians, SPRI 11-12 September 1972", *Miscellaneous papers 1970-78*, SPRI MS1308/43/16.

21. Brian Roberts, "Chronological list of Antarctic expeditions", *Polar Record* 9(59), (1958): 97-134; ibid. (continued) 9(60), (1958): 191-239.

22. R K Headland, *Chronological List of Antarctic Exploration and Related Historical Events*, (Cambridge: CUP, 1989); R K Headland, *A Chronology of Antarctic Exploration. A Synopsis of Events and Activities from the Earliest Times until the International Polar Years, 2007-9* (London: Bernard Quaritch, 2009) is a revised edition containing a further 1,500 entries.

23. Peter Falk in H G R King and Ann Savours (ed.), *Polar pundit: reminiscences about Brian Birley Roberts* (Cambridge: Polar Publications, SPRI 1995), 53.

ANNEX II

1. For example, double and triple names are invariably shortened in the field. Long names take up too much space on maps and charts, obscuring topographical detail.

2. Notably Lumus Rock. (Chapter 22 reference 9)

3. G Hattersley-Smith, "The History of Place-Names in the British Antarctic Territory", BAS Scientific Reports No. 113 (1991).

INDEX

ACAN (US Advisory Committee on Antarctic Names) 213, 223

Adelaide Island 119, 159, 333, 336-7

Admiralty 167, 174-5, 180, 182-4, 190, 219, 225, 244, 341, 345; Blue Books, *see* Geographical Handbooks; Naval Intelligence Divisions NID5 174, 177, 341; NID18 178

albatross 29, 40, 195: black-browed 158, 297; sooty 154; wandering 296-8, 305; yellow-nosed 299

AMCAFF (Agreed Measures) 279-80, 284-5, 306-11, 313-4, 316, 318, 323

Ahlmann, Hans 197

Akureyri 106-8, 111

Alexander Land (Island) 144, 160, 213-4

Amundsen, Roald 56, 66-7

Amundsen Sea 269

ANARE (Australian National Antarctic Research Expedition) 207

Anderson, David 306-8, 313, 323

Anderson, F W 80, 83, 92, 97, 100

Angelica archangelica (plant) 85, 87

Anstee, Margaret 203, 210-1

Antarctic: conservation 278-85, 296, 305-24, 337, 347-8; Convergence 198, 256, 270, 274, 324; East and West Antarctica 215-6; historic monuments 192, 312, 318; ice shelves 217-24, 232, 256, 261-2, 279-80; international governance xi, 240-2, 246, 248, 250-3, 255, 260, 265; jurisdiction 260-1, 263, 265, 278, 283, 285, 306, 310, 347; Place Names Committee, *see* APNC; Peninsula, *see* Graham Land; secretariat 278, 281-3, 285, 316; South Pole station 272, 276; territorial claims 179, 181, 205, 255, 308, 324; tourism 306, 312, 323

Antarctic Treaty: conference, Washington xi, 180-1, 240, 246, 249-65; Consultative Meetings: Buenos Aires 1962 282-3; Brussels 1964 284-5, 293, 306, 308; Canberra 1961 265, 278, 280-3, 286-7, 291; London 1977 324-5; Oslo 1975 323-4; Paris 1968 312-4; Santiago 1966 306-9, 312-3; Tokyo 1970 316-8; Wellington 1972 322-3

APNC (Antarctic Place Names Committee)   205-6, 209, 211-3, 215-6, 218, 220, 222, 224

appendicitis 137-8, 299, 316

Arctic fox 89, 113, 115

Arctic Institute of North America (AINA) 225, 229-30

Arctic politics: conference 326-30; Council 330; Treaty 327-9; wartime 168, 183

Arctic poppy 68-9, 112

Argentina: Antarctic programme 178-9, 186, 192-3, 231-5, 240, 243, 245, 248, 336-7; attitudes to Antarctic Treaty 242, 249, 251-2, 257-61, 263, 265, 281, 283, 312, 329; conservation 279; internal politics 244-5, 251, 282, 337; place names 212-3, 256; relations with UK and Chile 179-80, 186, 228, 243-6, 248-51, 276, 318, 332, 334-5

Argentine Islands 130-1, 135, 140, 143, 156, 159, 166, 192, 333, 336-7: Galindez Island 131-2, 193; Stella Creek 131, 136; Winter Island 131

Armstrong, Terence 214-5, 228, 239, 247-8, 322, 327, 345

arrest of Roberts on *Penola* 157

Atacama Desert 242

Atkinson, Robert 194-7, 211

Australia: Antarctic programme 207, 244; attitudes to Antarctic Treaty 252-3, 261, 265, 280-1, 284, 312, 317, 329; claims to Antarctica 240; Melbourne 238; place names 206, 215, 222-3

Baffin Island 76

Bagshawe, Arthur 122

Bagshawe, Thomas 166, 275

Barlas, William 147, 152

Barton, Juxon 189-90

Bass Rock 29, 46

Battenberg, Louise 7

Bear Island 99, 104

Beascochea Bay 139

Beauchene Island 158

Beckett, Angus 80, 85, 91, 95-6, 100-2

Benest, Kathleen 175

Benest, Derek 255

Bennett, John   190, 208-12

Bentley (car) 11, 19, 20

Berthelot Islands 135

Bertram, Colin: member of Greenland party   104, 112-4, 116; BGLE member 121, 125, 135-6, 139, 141, 144, 155, 160, 275; Chatham House 250; directorship of SPRI 202, 227-9, 231-4, 236, 238; wartime work 165, 167-8, 175

BGLE (British Graham Land Expedition) 118-61, 165-7, 169, 192-3, 204, 213, 290, 336-7, 345, 350

Bingham, E W (Ted) 121-2, 124-5, 128-9, 137, 137-8, 185, 189

bird ringing 40-2

Birley, Eric 25

Birley, Kenneth 122

Birley, Madeline 4-5, 8, 11, 14, 25, 55, 60-1, 170-1

Birley, Maurice 4, 8, 11, 20, 70

Bishopgarth 4-5, 70, 138, 171

Blomfield, June 202

Blosseville, Jules de 116

Blue Books, *see* Geographical Handbooks

Bounty (ship) 290-1

Boy's Own Paper 68

Brain, Norman   255

Bramuglia, Jan Artilio 242

Brierly, James 240-1

British Antarctic Survey (BAS) 184, 204, 215, 248, 329, 331-8, 340, 347

British Antarctic Territory 283, 331

British Glaciology Society 222

British Graham Land Expedition, *see* BGLE

Brun, Henrik 168

Brunt, David 232-3

Brunt Ice Shelf 231-2, 334

BTO (British Trust for Ornithology) 195

Burgess, Guy   211, 245, 249, 251

Burrival, North Uist 196

Byrd, Richard 118, 191

Callaghan, James 331-2, 338

Cambridge Bird Club 75-6

Cambridge University 72-6: Air Squadron 76; Churchill College 249-50, 345; Department of Chemistry 226; Department of Earth Sciences 73; Department of Geography 167, 235, 238, 347; Department of Mineralogy and Petrology 202; Emmanuel College 74-5, 165, 175, 346; Museum of Archaeology and Anthropology 197; St Johns College 179; Trinity Hall 225-6

Canadian Arctic 135, 202, 227, 326-8

Canary Islands   161

Crozet 293, 296-7, 300, 304

CTAE (Commonwealth Trans-Antarctic Expedition) 224, 230-2, 234-5, 245

Cuba (missile crisis), 248

Cumes, James 284

Curtis, Russell 328-9

Cuzco 310

Daniels, Paul 252-3, 257-60

Daring (ship) 170

Darling, Frank Fraser 195, 327, 329

Darby, Clifford 174, 177-8, 183, 341

Darwin, Charles 76, 287

DCS (Directorate of Colonial Services) 187, 208

Deacon, George 155

Debenham, Frank: BGLE 119, 121, 145, 150; Iceland 78, 80; recruitment of Roberts 56. 73-4; SPRI in wartime 167-70, 174-6, 182-3; views on Roberts 182, 236

Debenham Islands 144, 159, 336

Deception Island: BGLE 118, 131, 139-43, 156, 158-9, 298; strategic importance 179, 231-2, 243, 246

Dening, Esler 255, 258-9, 263

Denmark 106, 122

Discovery II (ship) 125, 131, 138-40, 153-5

Discovery Committee 125, 174, 178-9

Ditchley Park 326-9

Dolomites 21-3

Dorset culture, *see* Inuit

Dulles, John Foster 252-3

Easter Island 291

Eastern Front 7, 170

ECOSOC (UN Economic and Social Council Standing Committee on Natural Resources) 323

Edmonds, Robin 282-4, 286, 341

Edward VIII abdication 156

Edwards, David 317

egg collecting (robbing) 26-7, 29-30, 87, 107-8, 133-5, 142, 153-4

France: Antarctic 109, 206, 240, 244, 293-301, Arctic 106, 109; attitudes to Antarctic Treaty 242, 255-6, 260, 263, 299, 307, 312; motoring 13-6, 19-20; wartime 6-7, 170, 172

Francis, Harry 307

Freeland, John 249, 251-3, 255-6, 264

Freeston, Charles 12-13, 21

French, Neville 334-5

frigatebird 302-3

Fuchs, Vivian 'Bunny' 185, 230-2, 234-5, 333, 340

fulmar 40, 47, 72, 108, 155, 194-5

Furka Pass 19

Gajardo, Enrique 258, 308

Galindez Island, *see* Argentine Islands

gannet 29, 45-6, 51, 101, 108, 194-5, 303

General San Martin (ship) 234-5, 243

Geographical Handbooks ('Blue Books') 174-5, 177-8

George VI 160-1

Gerlache Strait 129, 275, 335

Germany 7, 20, 22, 154, 168, 170, 172, 196-7, 200, 232

Giaever, John 199, 201

Gislason, Skarphjedinn 81, 92, 94-7, 102

Gjelsvik, Tore 324, 327

Glacier (ship) xii, 269-76

Glacier: Aletsch 193; Brenndals 62; Briksdal 60-62; Casey 204; Emmanuel 114, 117; Kjenndals 61; Madatsch 21, 23; Melkevolls 60-61; Rhone 19; Styggebreen 64; Thwaites 270; Tjota 61

glaciology 139, 222, 272

Glen, Alexander 169, 177

Godfrey, John (DNI) 174, 177

golden eagle 32, 196

Graham Land: Bagshawe 166; BAS 333; BGLE 118-20, 128-30, 139, 150, 165, 275; FIDS 178, 220; maps, place names and survey 105, 120, 126-7, 130-1, 155, 160, 165, 204, 212, 220

Greenland 66, 76, 78-80, 104-19, 122-3, 135, 151, 174

Grimsey 107-8, 117

Manhattan (ship) 326, 329

Marguerite Bay 119, 140, 143-4, 159, 191, 333, 336

Marshall, F H A 166

Martin, J H 121, 123-4, 133, 135, 150-1, 157

Martorell, Toni 254, 345

Matha Bay 138

Maudheim base 198-201

Mauritius 300-1

Mawson, Douglas 121, 223

Mayr, Ernst 176

Meikeljohn, I F 121, 132, 143

Mikkelsen, Ejnar 105, 111

Mill, Hugh Robert 182

Millett, H F 121, 135, 147, 151, 156

Ministerial Committee on Antarctica 243-4, 251

Monte Rosa 193

Montevideo 123, 276

Moore, Jim 121, 135

Moorea 287-90, 292

Moorehead, Alan 310

Mora, Marcial 258, 261-2, 282, 310

Morrison, Herbert 210

Mossop, John 179-80

Mott, Peter 186-7

Movchan, Anatoly 284, 308

Mullion Island 52

Murphy, Robert Cushman 142-3, 166

musk ox 104, 112-3, 115

Nansen, Fritjov 56, 66-7

Nansen sledge 80, 122

Nash, Walter 257, 261, 270

National Science Foundation 322, 343

NBSE (Norwegian-British-Swedish Expedition) 197-202, 209

NERC (National Environment Research Council) 331-2

Netherlands 21-22

Neuburg, Hugo 272

Neumayer Channel 129, 275

Nevers (town) 6-7

New Zealand: 240, 270, 273, 277, 322; Antarctic claims 240; attitudes to Antarctic Treaty 242, 252, 257. 261, 280, 282, 317, 323; place naming 206, 215

Nicholson, Max 195

Nordenskjöld, Otto 155

Norman, Archie 346

Norsel (ship) 198-201

Norway: 54-67, 99, 324; Antarctic claims 197, 201, 206, 240; Antarctic expeditions 155, 191, 197-201, 209, 244; wartime 168, 170; whaling and sealing 147-8, 152, 154, 284, 313

Norwegian-British-Swedish-Expedition, *see* NBSE

Nototheniid fish 152

Nouvelle Amsterdam 293, 298-300, 304

nunatak 114 , 274

Odadahraun 85, 87, 107

Ommanney, Francis 155

Operation Deep Freeze xii, 269-76, 334

Operation Greenleaves 172

Operation Tabarin 178-81 , 184, 186-7

ornithology 24-5, 106, 112, 146, 150, 153-4, 194-5, 272, 311

OSS (Office of Strategic Services) 176

Oslo 55-6, 64-7, 155, 197, 323-4, 341

Owen, George 281-4

Panzarini, Rodolfo 251, 276

Paradise Bay 166, 337

Parsons, Richard 249, 255-7, 264

Peeler, Jim xiv

Pelham Court 171-3, 179, 188

pemmican 80-1, 85, 87-91, 94-6, 113, 115, 135

penguin: Adelie 143, 272; chinstrap (ringed) 141-3, 155; emperor xv, 198, 214, 272; fossil 155; gentoo 133, 142-3, 153-4, 166, 275, 296; king 153-4, 296, 298; macaroni 298; Magellanic 125, 156; rockhopper 125, 133, 142

Penola (ship) 122-5, 128-9, 131-3, 139-41, 143-52, 155-61, 271, 290-1

Peron, Juan 244

petrel: 293, 296, 305; cape 128, 155-6; European storm 40, 42-3, 196; fulmar (grey) 108, 128, 155-6; prion, *see* Prions; Wilson's storm 132, 136, 141, 159, 165-6, 198, 300, 334, 337

Petrov, Vladimir 253

Phleger, Herman 257, 260

pink-footed goose 87

Plymouth Brethren 3

Polar Committee 205, 208, 224, 230

Polar Medal 147, 167, 314

Polar Pundit (book) x, 347

Polar Record (journal) 61, 169-70, 175-6, 182, 214-5, 239, 344, 347

Ponting, Herbert 73

Port Lockroy 128-31, 186, 193, 335

Port Stanley 124-5, 128, 140, 144, 146, 149, 155-8, 169, 185, 187, 191, 334-5, 337

POTUS (President of the United States): Eisenhower 257

Pourquoi Pas? (ship) 104-9, 111, 115-7, 119, 124, 151, 296

prion 300, 305

ptarmigan 88-9

puffin 26, 47, 72, 108, 311

Punta Arenas (Magallanes) 146, 333, 335, 337-8, 341-2

Quai d'Orsay 255, 312

RAF Medmenham 206

RAMC (Royal Army Medical Corps) 6, 170

razorbill 27, 52, 311

Réunion 293-5, 301, 303

Reykjavik 99, 106, 117

RGS (Royal Geographical Society): funding 80, 104, 120, 150; committee on ice terminology 207, 220-4; Founder's Medal 335, 341; Roberts' membership 74, 76

Riley, Quintin 120, 131, 140

Roberts, Charles: death 170; family life 4-7, 9-33, 41-5, 49-52; medical work 4-8; motoring 8-32, 41, 51, 54-65

Roberts Cove 50

Roberts, Denis: childhood 4, 19, 23, 33, 41-3, 51-2; death 341-2; education 69, 74-5; letters 173, 260, 331; Norway 54, 58, 61-2, 64-5; UDC ix-x, 173, 341; wartime 170-4, 179

Roberts, Hodder 50

Roberts Ice Piedmont 213

Roberts, Patrick 4, 33-9, 41-3, 51, 68, 170

Roberts, Poulter Benjamin 3, 49

Robertson, E I 'Robbie' 317

Robin, Gordon 214-5, 238-9, 333, 342-3

Rocamadour 17-8

rock shelter xiii, xv, 274

Rogers, Philip 251-2

Rolland, Pierre 293, 295

Rolls Royce (car) 20-21, 29, 54-5

Romsdal Valley 55, 57-8

Ronne, Finne 191-2

Roots, Fred 202, 229

rope bridge 136

Rosenvinge Bay 111, 116

Ross Ice Shelf 218-9, 223

Ross Sea 218, 269-72

Rothera station 333, 336-7

Rowley, Graham 225, 227-9, 327

Royal Geographical Society, *see* RGS

Rudmose Brown, Robert Neal 177-8

Ryder, Lisle 121, 123, 128, 132, 136, 143, 146, 151, 165

Ryder, Robert 'Red' 121, 128, 130, 138, 148, 150-1, 156-8, 290

Rymill, John 77, 118-22, 124, 128-9, 133, 135, 137-40, 204

Salonika 7, 170

Saltee Islands 51-2

Salvesens 147, 149

Såmi 62-3

Saunders, Harold 207, 212-3, 223-4

Savours, Ann 343

SCAR (Scientific Committee on Antarctic Research) 279-80, 312-3, 320, 322-3, 342

Schwabenland expedition 200

Scott, Robert Falcon 4, 73, 79, 176, 214, 217, 236, 272, 311

Scott Base 276-7

Scott Polar Research Institute, *see* SPRI

Sealing xi, 128, 136, 147-8, 152-4, 176, 227, 284-5, 296, 298, 306-7, 311-4, 316-8; London conference 318-21

Seals: Antarctic 131, 133, 135-6, 179, 280, 305, 319-20; crabeater 284, 320; elephant 147, 151, 153, 293, 296, 298; fur 158, 280, 293, 296, 299, 320; grey (Atlantic) 28, 51, 195-6, 311; hooded 110; leopard 320; Ross 320; Weddell 153

seasickness 81, 100, 123, 198, 300

Scilingo, Adolfo 257-9, 263

Scilly Isles 40-41

Scoresbysund 105-7, 109, 111, 116

Scotland 24, 29-33, 170, 195, 197

Searle, Derek 214

seismic sounding 80-1, 83

Seligman, Gerald 222

Seymour Island 155

Shackleton (ship) 335

Shackleton, Eddie 265, 334, 337

Shackleton, Ernest 118, 189, 192, 230

Shearwater: Manx 40-43, 47; sooty 156

Shirley Institute 168

Shuckburgh, Evelyn 190, 243

Signy Island 179, 190, 333-5

Simsarian, Jim 307, 313-4

Sir David Attenborough (ship) 248

Skelligs 44-50

sledging 84, 119, 135, 138-40, 144, 160, 192, 217, 227, 230, 276

Slessor, John 231

Slingsby, William 61

Smith, David 336-7

SOE (Special Operations Executive) 172

South Africa 260, 285, 306

South Georgia 145-8, 150, 152-5, 160, 166, 178, 230, 296, 331, 333-5

South Orkney Islands 153, 155, 178-9, 208, 275, 334

South Sandwich Islands 275

CPSIA information can be obtained
at www.ICGtesting.com
Printed in the USA
LVHW021555170820
663413LV00031B/2400